The New Edinburgh History of Scotland

VOLUME 6

Scotland Re-formed

The New Edinburgh History of Scotland

General editor: Roger Mason, *University of St Andrews*

Advisory editors: Dauvit Broun, *University of Glasgow*; Iain Hutchison, *University of Stirling*; Norman Macdougall, *University of St Andrews*; Nicholas Phillipson, *University of Edinburgh*

Scotland Re-formed 1488–1587

Jane E. A. Dawson

Edinburgh University Press

For Marian Dawson

© Jane E. A. Dawson, 2007

Edinburgh University Press Ltd
22 George Square, Edinburgh

Typeset in 11/13 Ehrhardt
by Servis Filmsetting Ltd, Manchester

A CIP record for this book is available from the British Library

ISBN 978 0 7486 1454 7 (hardback)
ISBN 978 0 7486 1455 4 (paperback)

The right of Jane E. A. Dawson
to be identified as author of this work
has been asserted in accordance with
the Copyright, Designs and Patents Act 1988.

Publisher's acknowledgement
Edinburgh University Press thanks Mercat Press, publishers of
the *Edinburgh History of Scotland*, for permission to use *The New
Edinburgh History of Scotland* as the title for this ten-volume series.

Contents

Analytical Table of Contents

Maps, Tables and Illustrations

Preface

I have been able to write this book only because I have been standing on the shoulders of that amiable and generous giant, the community of all those interested in Scotland's history, to whom I owe more than can easily be expressed. I have a specific debt to Frances Dow, Elizabeth Ewan, Ken Emond, Norman Macdougall and Roger Mason, who commented on the draft of this volume and whose insights and coloured pens have greatly improved it: all remaining mistakes are my own. Roger has been an ideal series editor and a tower of strength throughout the book's long gestation. Following the revisions, Nancy Bailey worked her accustomed miracle by producing the final version of the text under immense time pressure. It is not possible to acknowledge everyone whose conversation, correspondence and unpublished papers have contributed over many years so greatly to my understanding. My warmest thanks go to them all, though they must forgive me for not mentioning them by name; the list would be very long indeed.

Since the 'tyranny of the lower margin' has been deliberately avoided in this volume, notes within chapters have been inserted only to reference direct quotations. The Further Reading points readers to the next step in their search for additional information and the select bibliography contains fuller bibliographical details. The constraints of space led to the pruning of a range of specialised sources and articles and, if anything essential has unintentionally been omitted, I apologise and hope this general acknowledgement of my debt to the scholarship of others will serve in its place.

Like many others, I have been admirably supported by the National Library of Scotland, in all its departments, and also by the holders of Scotland's other national collections, the National Archives of Scotland, the National Museum of Scotland, the National Galleries of Scotland,

Historic Scotland and the Royal Commission on the Ancient and Historical Monuments of Scotland, who have also given permission for most of the illustrations (full acknowledgements in the List of Illustrations). Once more I have benefited from the generosity of the Duke of Argyll and the Earl of Moray in permitting me to consult their archives and Charles McKean has kindly allowed me to reproduce his reconstruction of Balvenie Castle. The university libraries at Edinburgh and St Andrews have been of great assistance. Grateful acknowledgement is made to the Arts and Humanities Research Council and Edinburgh University for granting me leave to write this book. My colleagues in the University of Edinburgh have provided support in a myriad of ways, especially my fellow ecclesiastical historians, past and present, and all those in New College, who collectively make it such a pleasant place to work. All my family and friends, especially Linda Frost, have given much greater support than most of them realise, and the book is dedicated with love and gratitude to my mother.

Epiphany, 2007

General Editor's Preface

The purpose of the New Edinburgh History of Scotland is to provide up-to-date and accessible narrative accounts of the Scottish past. Its authors will make full use of the explosion of scholarly research that has taken place over the last three decades, and do so in a way that is sensitive to Scotland's regional diversity as well as to the British, European and transoceanic worlds of which Scotland has always been an integral part.

Chronology is fundamental to understanding change over time and Scotland's political development will provide the backbone of the narrative and the focus of analysis and explanation. The New Edinburgh History will tell the story of Scotland as a political entity, but will be sensitive to broader social, cultural and religious change and informed by a richly textured understanding of the totality and diversity of the Scots' historical experience. Yet to talk of the Scots – or the Scottish nation – is often misleading. Local loyalty and regional diversity have more frequently characterised Scotland than any perceived sense of 'national' solidarity. Scottish identity has seldom been focused primarily, let alone exclusively, on the 'nation'. The modern discourse of nationhood offers what is often an inadequate and inappropriate vocabulary in which to couch Scotland's history. The authors in this series will show that there are other and more revealing ways of capturing the distinctiveness of Scottish experience.

The century between 1488 and 1587 was one of profound change for the people of Scotland. It witnessed the emergence of a self-confident Stewart monarchy, proud of its independent status on the European diplomatic stage, and the kingdom's subsequent transformation into a satellite of the English crown; the overthrow of the Roman Catholic church and the establishment of a new Protestant kirk; and the reconfiguration of the kingdom's regional politics in the face of more intrusive royal government and the gradual evolution of a new class of local landowners. Yet, as Jane Dawson shows in this admirably lucid volume, while Scotland was quite literally 're-formed' during the period, continuities with the past remain as striking as the breaks with traditional practice. The revolutionary events of the reign of Mary, Queen of Scots – the great religious, diplomatic and constitutional crisis of the Stewart dynasty – mask underlying continuities in the way of life of the majority of Scottish men and women. It is this nuanced approach to Scotland's changing place in Britain and Europe, to the roots and implications of the Protestant Reformation, and to the transformation of local society, that characterises Professor Dawson's richly detailed study of the period. The result is a compelling account of one of the most dramatic centuries in Scotland history.

Introduction
The Kingdom of the Scots

The kingdom of Scotland was held together between 1488 and 1587 by a strong sense of place and an even stronger sense of people and kinship and its story can best be told by interweaving the lives and experiences of individual Scots into the narrative and seeing the regions in which they lived and worked through their eyes. The identity of early modern Scots had two strong roots: the first was their family and kindred who provided support in good and bad times alike; the second, their locality and their region, the places they regarded as home. Since they looked at the wider kingdom through this local lens, a regional perspective is an essential ingredient when seeking to understand the world of sixteenth-century Scotland. In his *Description of the Western Isles*, Monro offers a unique chance to view a region through contemporaries' eyes.

THE REGIONS AND THE KINGDOM

Donald Monro was born in the parish of Kiltearn on the Cromarty Firth around the start of the century and in 1526 moved west to become vicar of Snizort on Skye and the neighbouring island of Raasay. After more than twenty years of experience, he wrote his description in 1549, possibly as a briefing memo for an incoming bishop. His friend, Buchanan, explained Monro, 'travelled all these Iles upon his feete, and saw them perfitly with his eyes'.[1] The good archdeacon, though not managing the miracle of walking on water, knew all about boats and travelling by sea, having personally visited many of the 251 islands he listed. His description moved

---

[1] *Monro's Western Isles of Scotland and Genealogies of the Clans*, ed. R. W. Munro (Edinburgh, 1961), 27.

from the Isle of Man in the south, the seat of the original diocese of the Isles, up to the northern Hebrides with North Rona and the rocky outcrop of Sula Skeir more than forty miles north of Lewis (see Map I.1). The diocese was split along national lines in the fifteenth century with Man kept within English jurisdiction and the Scottish section placing its headquarters and cathedral on Lismore. Though for completeness, Monro opened his description with Man, the rest of the islands lay in Scottish territory, with the Western Isles being treated as one of the diverse regions within the kingdom of Scotland. As 'High Dean' or Archdeacon of the Isles, Monro had the responsibility of visiting the parishes of the diocese, sailing his galley in the sea lanes uniting the Hebrides and the western coast of the mainland. Amongst the things Monro's eyes witnessed on his travels, only certain aspects were deemed worth recording. He described the islands' physical characteristics, including practical advice on where a boat could be landed. He identified the civil and ecclesiastical power centres, noting for each island the chief nobleman and any castle or fortification, sometimes adding sidelights, such as MacLeod of Lewis's habit of retreating to the church on Pabay, 'quhen he wald be quiet or feirit'.[2]

Being a cog in the ecclesiastical organisation, Monro took for granted the administrative structure of his diocese, contenting himself with a list of the churches, chapels and religious houses. This underlying ecclesiastical framework was precisely what gave the Western Isles their firmest territorial definition. The political power of the MacDonalds, the Lords of the Isles, supplemented the regional identity since their unifying Gaelic authority encouraged a distinctive culture, most visible in the surviving monumental sculpture with its magnificent standing crosses and massive carved graveslabs (see Figures 4.1 and 5.2).

The ecclesiastical definition of the Western Isles was precisely restricted to islands, while the region's political and cultural boundaries stretched over a wider area and included the western littoral of the Scottish mainland. The precise points at which the region merged into other parts of the Highlands were unclear. When Dean Monro finally left the Western Isles in 1560, their distinctive regional status was being undermined. The dissolution of political unity following the 1493 forfeiture of the Lordship of the Isles was compounded at the Reformation by the removal of the solid diocesan structure of the medieval church. Losing some of their separate identity, the Western Isles drew closer to the adjacent mainland and became more firmly associated with the Highlands. This re-alignment formed part of a perceptual shift whereby

---

[2] Ibid., 2, 82.

two 'super regions' of Highlands and Lowlands were superimposed upon the regional diversity of the kingdom.

A blurring of the edges was common in early modern Scotland where all regions overlapped. Regions were essentially political entities and did not necessarily correspond to ecclesiastical and civil administrative units, such as dioceses and shires. A region's core was its active political community, a fluid body subject to change. In areas such as the Borders, the region and its constituent parts altered according to one's standpoint. The different agricultural and social patterns and their local political allegiances made those living within the eastern Borders conscious of being quite distinct from their western neighbours. However, the crown would often deal with Borderers as if they comprised a single unit and sometimes as if they constituted a separate and 'lawless' category within the kingdom: perception and perspective made all the difference.

During the early modern period, Scotland's regional complexion underwent a series of changes. By the reign of James VI it was axiomatic the boundaries of the kingdom were settled and the Northern and Western Isles lay inside them: something by no means certain at the end of the fifteenth century. The emergence of the 'super regions' of Lowlands and Highlands overrode the former nuanced distinctions between the Scottish regions. A heightened awareness of the unity and integrity of the kingdom developed, leading to the assumption it should act as a single political entity.

COMMUNICATIONS WITHIN SCOTLAND

Scotland's regions were both joined together and kept distinct by their system of communications in its three different manifestations: travel by sea and land; oral transmission of ideas; and reading written and printed documentation.

Archdeacon Monro's experience of using a boat for work or travel was a relatively common one, since Scotland possesses a coastline longer than that of the eastern United States. With its ragged shore, abundant sea lochs and shallow inlets, the northern and western coastal waters were ideally suited to the galleys providing the main method of transport in these regions. Using oars and sails, these multipurpose descendants of the Viking long-ships carried men, goods and the more intangible cargo of news between the mainland and the Isles, and across the North Channel to Ireland (see Map 1.1). The sea lanes also linked the western seaboard of Scotland to Wales and western England and to the Atlantic coasts of France and Spain.

Among the Scottish regions only Orkney and Shetland shared with the Western Isles the centrality of the sea to their region's existence and identity. For those moving up and down the east of Scotland, sea travel was an alternative, rather than the sole option as in the west. Instead of hugging the shoreline, being larger and more substantial than the galleys, North Sea vessels stood a little further out to sea: east-coast shipping was more expensive and tied more closely to trading or fishing. Many Scottish land routes still relied upon small boats and ferries to carry people across lochs, rivers and firths, especially the great long rivers on the east of the country, running from the uplands into the North Sea. Unlike the river network in continental Europe, Scotland's fast-flowing rivers rarely offered a highway for bulk transportation. Because of the Tay's immense volume of water, the bridge at Perth was permanently vulnerable and when in spate ferry points as high up river as Moulin (modern Pitlochry) could not be used. Freshwater lochs were more convenient: the length of Loch Awe allowed easy access by boat from one part of Argyll to the other, though being a wind funnel, Loch Ness offered more difficult waters. Normally plain sailing, the firths of Forth and Clyde carried the heaviest traffic with long crossings, such as North Berwick to Earlsferry, or Ayrshire across to Argyll, becoming dangerous in stormy conditions. The most politically significant small boat ride took place in 1568 when Mary, Queen of Scots commandeered a fishing smack to cross the Solway Firth, thereby leaving Scotland for good. Two years later, high on aroma if low on dashing military style, the Clyde herring boats provided troop transports for the Queen's Men. Scots used their water communications well with the sea or fresh water uniting localities on opposite shores rather than being a barrier separating them.

Land travel remained the norm in most regions, and for magnates, near-constant travel was a political necessity to keep in touch with the court, their regional powerbases and fellow nobles. Their physical stamina and their horsemanship were impressive, for they thought little of riding relays of horses day and night, should the situation demand it and their itineraries kept the salve for saddle sores high on every noblewoman's recipe list. By contrast, the majority of Scots regarded travel as an expensive and complicated distraction from the hard business of survival and they focused upon the transport infrastructure of their immediate locality and region.

Being no-one's direct responsibility most roads were badly maintained. Pilgrim routes were the best-kept roads since they attracted pious donations and were under the watchful eye of pilgrimage centres aware a direct correlation existed between their income and ease of access to the shrine.

Map I.1 The regions of Scotland

- Below 250m, about 800ft
- 250–450m, about 800–1500ft
- Above 450m, about 1500ft

0 10 20 30 40 50 Kilometres

0 10 20 30 40 50 Miles

ORKNEY
Kirkwall

Pentland Firth

Butt of Lewis

CAITHNESS

SHETLAND

OUTER HEBRIDES

LEWIS

SUTHERLAND

HARRIS

ROSS

Moray Firth

SKYE

Inverness   MORAY

BUCHAN

GARIOCH

INNER HEBRIDES

Great Glen

BADENOCH   River Spey

River Don   MAR   Aberdeen

MOIDART

Cairngorms   River Dee

Rum

LOCHABER   The Mounth

MEARNS

Ardnamurchan   △ Drumochter

Ben Nevis   ATHOLL   ANGUS

Coll

APPIN   BREADALBANE   STRATHMORE

Tiree

Lismore   River Tay   GOWRIE   Dundee

Iona   MULL   LORN   STRATHEARN   Perth   Firth of Tay

St Andrews

ARGYLL   MENTEITH   Stirling   FIFE

LENNOX   Dumbarton   Firth of Forth

Glasgow   Queensferry   Leith

STRATHCLYDE   River Clyde   Edinburgh   LOTHIAN

ISLAY   BUTE   Pentlands   Lammermuirs

MERSE

KINTYRE   ARRAN   KYLE   River Tweed

Ayr   River Teviot

Mull of Kintyre

North Channel   CARRICK

Nithsdale   Annandale

IRELAND   GALLOWAY

Solway Firth

The attraction of the relics of St Andrew, the national saint, ensured routes to the Fife burgh received special attention. The queen's ferry crossing the Forth provided one of the principal access points between Lothian and Fife, and the fine bridge spanning the Eden at Guardbridge improved the route from the north. Even where a road formed part of this privileged network, it could be in bad repair, as at the marshy 'Gullets' at the west end of Loch Leven: ideal for ambush, it was probably the spot for the abortive attempt to kidnap Lord Darnley in 1565. The bad state of road repair encouraged travel by horseback rather than by coach, first introduced into Scotland by Mary of Guise. In the Highlands, 'shank's pony' and the occasional real horse ruled supreme: the wheel was a positive nuisance on narrow paths, steep contours or boggy moorland. In the Lowlands wheeled vehicles, such as farm wains, transported bulky goods short distances and the carriage service owed by tenants remained an important resource much utilised by feudal superiors.

Some of the most experienced travellers within Scotland were the royal messengers, expected to know the routes within their designated regions. Their duties involved them in the other strands of communication across the kingdom, bearing oral messages and written documents to their destinations. Charles Murray was a messenger charged with deliveries within Perthshire, Fife and Clackmannanshire, carrying the white wand signifying his important office. He made royal proclamations standing at the mercat cross of the principal burgh of the shire or declared an outlaw by blowing his horn three times: this ritualised gesture gave its name to the entire process of 'horning' or 'being put to the horn'.

Royal messengers' duties symbolised how much of the governance of Scotland was conducted by word of mouth with decisions frequently having to be spoken and heard in addition to being made and written. The mixture of spoken and written and the constant translation between them also characterised the language mix in Scotland. Gaelic was spoken by nearly half the population (see Map I.1) and Norn was the first language of Shetlanders and many Orcadians, with Scots being the vernacular for the remainder of the kingdom. These languages also had regional and local dialects and variations. By the end of the fifteenth century, Latin was beginning to lose its monopoly as the language of the written word. In both its ecclesiastical and scholastic and its humanist forms, Latin was also a vibrant spoken language, and French was well known among the Scottish elite. Such linguistic diversity was unremarkable and there was no perceived barrier to moving between languages. For example, the Gaelic learned orders were trilingual and were constantly transmitting information between Latin, Scots and Gaelic and translating for their respective constituencies. Such cultural bridges were common, crossing linguistic divides and providing connections between the literary and oral worlds. The advent of printing followed by the use of the vernacular in government and, crucially, in the Protestant kirk, transformed attitudes towards language in Scotland.

Oral and aural transmission retained its central place in society and was especially valued within Gaelic literary culture. In the Highlands and Islands, poetry was composed to be declaimed or spoken, and was memorised and preserved within a vibrant oral tradition, with writing treated as a low-grade adjunct. Throughout Scotland, relationships between spoken and written words were multifaceted with communications rarely confined to one format. Business of all types was transacted by letter, with the transmission of sensitive or confidential matters or personal details about the family's health and welfare entrusted to the letter-bearer to be spoken directly to the recipient. Sixteenth-century Scots felt short-changed if all they received were the words on the page.

Literacy was a prized skill and as its value increased the ability to read became more widespread, particularly in the burghs. The less crucial skill of writing was normally acquired subsequently, leaving a large pool of those who could read, without being able to write, who fail to appear in modern statistics for literacy levels. The common experience of having a notary lead one's hand at the pen to form one's signature became a mark of lower social status by the end of the sixteenth century. Such a stigma reflected the way literary skills had become desirable and normal for most male members of the noble and urban elites. An increasing number of women were also literate, though few could emulate the stunning calligraphy of Esther Inglis, who made her living at the end of the sixteenth century through this skill. Once formal schooling in such attributes became a higher priority, education provision changed, creating a larger pool of educated laymen and women, such as the literary family of the Maitlands of Lethington, with consequences for recruitment into crown service, the emerging professions of law and medicine, and many cultural pursuits. The existence of a literate laity also increased demand for religious reform, especially with Christian humanist ideals as a model. After the Reformation, the adoption of Protestantism placed a further premium upon literacy for many Scots, because it enabled them to read the Bible.

Written documentation and formal legal processes had traditionally gone hand in hand and an increasing emphasis upon a legal approach to social and political problems was accompanied by a higher valuation and use of documents and the written record. The arrival of printing, the major technological innovation of this period, transformed the place of written documentation and brought profound consequences for literacy. The increased availability of printed material created a sharper divide between the literate and non-literate in Scotland and between oral and literary culture. At the end of the fifteenth century, the diversity of the Scottish regions was regarded as a normal facet of political life and the distinct identities of the peoples who inhabited the realm were held together by their common allegiance to the king of Scots. When needed, travel, particularly by water, helped connect the different parts of Scotland, and despite a mixture of languages, spoken and written words moved easily across the geographical distances and between the differing linguistic constituencies. Scotland's communications system provided a sufficient basis for a sharing of culture and identity. Additional integration and uniformity were not yet seen as desirable goals for the kingdom.

REGIONAL CLIMATES AND LAND QUALITY

The kingdom's resources were predominantly drawn from the land and its rhythms provided the beat of everyday life. With less than 5 per cent of the approximately 800,000 Scots living in burghs, the lives of the great majority were dominated by the agricultural round. The quality of the soil they worked and the altitude determined their farming prospects and settlement patterns (see Map I.2). Altitude was crucial, as can be seen in the extreme case of the central Grampian plateau which possesses a genuinely arctic climate with only a short ice-free period each year. The fortunate grew crops on the fertile machairs in the Hebridean islands, the rich loams of Angus or the sandy soils of the Ayrshire coast, protected from excessive rain by the shadow of Arran's Goat Fell. However, pastoral farming was the only option for those living with the poor soils and harsh climate found in much of Scotland. Livestock were kept on the upland pastures within the Southern Uplands, the Grampians or Wester Ross and the short days and rainfall in the northern islands of Yell and Unst similarly restricted their farming. The Highland fault line running from Dumbarton to Stonehaven divided the country geologically and determined the soil type and productivity of the land. Although small pockets of fertile land existed within the Highlands, the general quality was low and the vast majority of highly-productive land was located in the Lowlands.

Regional settlement patterns, social structures and wealth were directly related to land quality and climate. Cattle rearing encouraged

Map 1.2 The land quality and growing seasons in Scotland

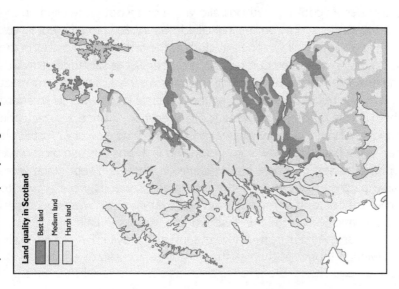

Land quality in Scotland

- Best land
- Medium land
- Harsh land

Growing seasons in Scotland
Months with mean temperature above 6°C

- 7–8 months
- 5–6 months
- 4 months or less

scattered settlements and the move to higher pastures during the summer remained common in the Southern Uplands as well as in the Highlands. By contrast, the more intensively cultivated areas, such as the Merse in the eastern Borders or the north-eastern corner of Aberdeenshire and Banffshire, boasted denser and more nucleated settlements. For richer areas, producing a surplus in a good year, maintaining subsistence still constituted an achievement and a run of bad harvests brought famine knocking at the door: in the marginal areas, privation was a near-constant companion. The immense importance attached to hospitality and feasting in Gaelic bardic eulogies to Highland chiefs throws a cultural veil over the stark economic reality: the need to re-distribute food among the kin and clan groups simply to keep them alive.

Diet

During the period there was a gradual shift in Lowlanders' diet towards a greater dependence upon cereals, particularly oatmeal. The Highlands retained the former pattern of reliance upon meat and animal products, such as cheese or butter. Scots were fortunate fish was plentiful and sheep, goats, pigs and chickens helped enliven their diet. They consumed much of their carbohydrate intake through drinking ale made from barley while eating the rest as bread, usually flat baked since only towns and large establishments had dedicated bread ovens. Scots calculated social level by the bread being consumed: the whiter the flour and the bread, the higher the social cachet. For all levels of society, one of the preferred cooking methods, allowing a single pot to be used on the hearth, was long, slow boiling in a cauldron packed with different layers, such as a ham shank wrapped in cloth at the bottom with pulses in the surrounding water and quick-cooking cabbages, like kail, added towards the end. With salting down being the main method of preserving meat and fish, spices were used to disguise the taste by all who could afford them. Those who had a sweet tooth used honey, since a sugar cone imported from the east was an almost unimaginable luxury. Most Scots had enough land to grow some food and in towns burgage plots were a prized possession where pigs, chickens or goats were kept. In the vegetable patches many plants now dismissed as weeds were grown to provide extra food or medicines. Whilst every woman was expected to have a basic herbal lore, the 'wise' women, like Alison Balfour in Orkney or Margaret Aitken from Balwearie, usually provided more specialist knowledge, though at the risk they might be accused of witchcraft.

With the onset of the Little Ice Age, sixteenth-century weather was worse than today's, especially in the winter, with 1564 experiencing thirty-three days of continual frost and rivers and lochs freezing. The worsening climate produced more regular subsistence crises, particularly following the bad harvests in twenty-six years within the half-century after 1550 and leading to the severe famine of the mid-1580s. Although the price of grain rose sharply, there were no peasant uprisings or grain riots, as happened on the European continent. The burghs pursued a policy of rigid price control over essential commodities, thereby reducing the number of townspeople starving to death, while hitting hard tradesmen such as baxters (bakers).

Though by modern standards farming offered a hard and insecure livelihood, the main ambition for many Scots was being able to work their land and pass it or the tenancy to their heirs. The uptake of feus during the sixteenth-century feuing boom was testimony to Scots' desire to gain heritable possession of their land. By buying estates as soon as they could afford them, merchants acknowledged the centrality of land to Scottish status and identity. The sense of place in Scotland was deeply grounded in the soil in which most Scots worked.

THE GOVERNANCE OF SCOTLAND

The farthest outpost of Scotland was the island of St Kilda though unlike today, the island was inhabited. However loosely, it formed part of the kingdom of the Scots and was governed in the same way. For the island's community, governing authority wore two faces, civil and ecclesiastical. Each midsummer the steward of MacLeod of Harris, the island's owner and clan chief, and the chaplain of their parish of Kilbride in Harris sailed over to collect the rents and baptise the babies. Stripped down to the minimum, this experience of governance in St Kilda by church and noble lord was shared by the rest of the kingdom. These remote islanders had one advantage over their fellow Scots: external authority arrived in their locality accompanied by ale-making equipment. During the great annual brew, the entire island population, 'baith men, women and bairnis were deid drunkin, so that thai could not stand on thair feet': probably leaving the memory of being governed as something of a rosy-tinted blur.[3] A prolonged midsummer party would probably not have been the way fellow Scots described their own more frequent, and sometimes abrasive, encounters with civil and ecclesiastical authority.

[3] Ibid., 78.

In Scotland authority was exercised in a highly visible manner with identifiable features. Being enacted in their locality, onlookers watched and heard formal or legal decisions that directly affected their lives. In the ceremony of sasine, they witnessed a land transfer as a divot was cut and handed to the new superior; or they saw the parish clerk inducted by receiving the church key, gospel and Mass book. In the burgh marketplaces at the public Tron, the great chalder cauldron was filled with bere barley or oatmeal, ensuring accurate measure was bought and sold, or a length of cloth was measured against the marker, such as the Dornoch stone, still lying in the ground next to the cathedral. In Scotland's daily business, the symbol or ritual action was so closely identified with the decision it represented, that seeing literally became believing.

THE FAMILIAR FACE OF THE POLITICAL PROCESS

When thinking about the way they were governed, Scots would be at one with the islanders of St Kilda and think first of the familiar faces of the actual people who ruled them. The normal method of getting anything done was to approach the people one knew rather than the institution that dealt with that issue. Throughout this period, people and place lay at the centre of Scottish politics and the network of a Scot's contacts started with his kindred and his own locality or region. Though ordinary Scots rarely participated directly in political affairs and the pursuit of power, the structure of politics affected everyone. Political life moved within three interlocking territorial layers, from local to regional and national. While retaining its own perspective, each layer interacted with the others. The peers were engaged within the national political arena and were also active at regional and sometimes local levels. The lairds and burgh hierarchies were involved in regional and local politics and occasionally at the national level. The lower echelons of society were usually restricted to the local level and rarely found themselves in the regional or national arenas or making their voices directly heard. Despite being passive participants for much of the time, ordinary Scots were members of vertical social groups cutting through the horizontal layers and bringing all levels of society into some contact with Scottish political life. The nobility provided the axis around which the vertical and horizontal lines pivoted, and kinship, lordship and locality were the vital, vertical connectors, proving as strong, if not stronger, than the horizontal divisions of political society.

The family and the extended kindred were the first and most important port of call when trouble arrived and they were expected to stand by when all other help departed. A blood relationship continued to matter over the generations and, however remotely, to be 'of the House' or 'of the blood' of a nobleman was an entitlement to his support. This solidarity extended to those whose kinship might be more fiction than fact. The Highland clans were theoretically united by their common descent from an eponymous ancestor, such as the early fourteenth-century Gregor from whom the MacGregors descended, or Farquhar, son of Shaw of Rothiemurchus, progenitor of the Farquharsons, a clan which only solidified in the mid-sixteenth century. The surname held a similar position in the Lowlands, with the Johnstones of Annandale, one of the most notorious Border 'names', able to mobilise hundreds of kinsmen for their raiding parties. Loyalty to the chief ran deep, as Hume of Wedderburn commented: 'if his Chiefe should turn him out at the foredoore, he would come againe at the back-doore'.[4] Since such allegiance was presumed, the prime measure of noble power was the size of a noble's kindred and in Hay's 1579 *Estimate of the Scottish Nobility* the earls of Glencairn were noted 'of greate power of their own surname' (Cunningham) whilst Sinclair of Caithness was weak, having 'few landed men by that Erldome of his surname'.[5] As late as 1585 the Privy Council accepted that some of Maxwell's tenants could not be expected to follow him, being assigned instead to the chief of their name, Grierson of Lag.

Kinship produced reciprocal relationships, with a chief protecting his clan or kinsmen in return for their service. The language of kinship was carried over lock, stock and barrel into bonds of manrent between a lord and his man and was extended to other relationships such as fostering children or becoming their godparents or 'gossips'. Kinship was supplemented by ties flowing from land and lordship. Within feudal society land had originally been held in return for direct military service and, despite the evolution of alternative military arrangements, a firm link remained between land holding and manpower. More generally, holding land was the key to political power in locality and region. Possession and occupation of particular tracts of land made the first nine points of the law with the point of the sword not infrequently adding the tenth and clinching argument. Clan Chattan's military muscle kept their possession of the rich lands along the River Spey, rather than charter right. Similarly, in the Lowland south-west the Kennedys remained 'kings of Carrick' as much

---

[4] Cited and discussed in K. Brown, *Bloodfeud in Scotland 1573–1625* (Edinburgh, 1986), 36, n. 59.
[5] Alexander Hay, *Estimate of the Scottish Nobility*, ed. C. Rogers (Grampian Club, 6, London, 1873), 10, 15.

by raw power as by feudal law. A lord's protection of his tenants was part of their reciprocal agreement: for example, the men of Teviotdale told the abbot of Jedburgh they were not paying their 'mails' or dues because he 'was not worthy therof be ressoun he wald not defend thaim'.[6]

Reinforcing kinship and lordship were region and locality as the feudal holding of land merged into a general lordship over the surrounding countryside. Magnates regarded localities or even a region as their 'country', and hence their responsibility. The different types of ties had become virtually indistinguishable by the end of the fifteenth century: a magnate's affinity drew together all those who served or 'looked' to him and whom he would defend or say, 'I maun do' for him, known generically as 'keeping kindness'. A well-established affinity could survive the temporary setbacks of a minority or political eclipse: despite his fall Morton could boast his Douglas affinity remained intact: 'I thank God, they that I aught to cair for, ar nocht destitute of freinds, bot ar als able to do a guid turne for another to thair neighbouris.'[7]

At the local level, neighbours tended to become enemies as often as friends. Disputes among those living close by each other in burghs were common and frequently led to violence. An altercation in a Dundee tavern in 1553 led to Jonet Cragy's complaint to the burgh court 'that Richard Corbeis man dang her because she asked her money again of a pint of mixed wine which she brought again to him of before'.[8] With a strong code of hospitality to the stranger, those branded as different, such as the gypsies, or 'Egyptians', did not arouse suspicion on sight. By the close of the period, however, the fear of external threats was increasing, helping stimulate the witch panics of the 1590s and the following century. The antagonism towards a witch was normally based upon local knowledge and local reputation in addition to the fear of diabolical intervention; the perceived threat came from the human enemy within the community as much as from the supernatural enemy outside it. As the pattern of witch prosecutions demonstrates, the links between locality, region and nation travelled both ways. A local matter could be forced up to national level and equally a national concern could be inflicted upon a locality from above. The interconnections within Scottish society, of kin, lordship and locality, ensured politics could never be confined or contained within the royal

---

[6] Cited and discussed in M. H. B. Sanderson, *A kindly place?: living in sixteenth-century Scotland* (East Linton, 2002), 178.

[7] *Memorials of transactions in Scotland 1569–72 by Richard Bannatyne*, ed. R. Pitcairn (Bannatyne Club, 51, Edinburgh, 1836), 344.

[8] 24 July 1553, Dundee Burgh Court Book 2, f. 240. My thanks to Elizabeth Ewan for this reference.

court. Rulers and ruled were linked to each other in far more complex ways than a simplistic chain of command from the top to the bottom of society.

KINGSHIP

During the period royal authority was clothed with a distinctive personality and wore a recognised face. Through their coins, the king's or queen's features were known to their subjects and even that ponderous medium showed Scots James V had grown older and now sported a beard. The personal touch and the royal presence remained at the heart of ruling. There was the chance, rather higher with that restless monarch James IV, of seeing the ruler in person whilst they travelled on progress where ceremonial was minimal, and receiving a word, a coin or a royal wave was a common experience for those on the route. Whilst the theory of the king's two bodies, his physical one and the formal embodiment of royal authority, had developed to offer safeguards against the abuse of power, the monarch still ruled in person, making the key decisions of government him or herself. Governmental institutions, such as Parliament, the Conventions of Estates or Burghs, or the Councils, were categorised during this period as ways of giving 'counsel' to the ruler. As the fifteenth century had shown, when united and forceful, the 'counsel' given by the unicameral parliament or a well-attended General Council was difficult for a monarch to ignore. However, the consultative institutions did not take part in the day-to-day running of affairs, only being summoned when needed. From the middle of the sixteenth century the emergence of the Secret or Privy Council for the first time gave the executive arm of government a formal and institutionalised existence. Even with the Council's rapidly-increasing power, there was no sharp line between its deliberations and the informal 'counsel' the monarch received from those in the royal household or attending court. Consequently, gaining the royal ear was more important politically than membership of the Council or attendance at parliament. During the minorities of James V and James VI possession of the king's person was essential for ruling the country. Throughout the period the right of access to the monarch was the most prized of political assets and one worth fighting with intrigue or sword to retain.

Since there were clear parameters for legitimate behaviour and decision-making, personal rule by the monarch did not automatically result in arbitrary government. The crown and its agents were expected to act within the boundaries of law, custom and reason, as well as the accepted norms of Christian morality and the European-wide honour code binding aristocratic society. The major limitations to the exercise of royal authority lay in fundamental assumptions about the purpose of rule. Maintaining society's stability and preserving the common weal were conceived as the prime aim of governance with the provision of justice as one of its central attributes. Such a static and reactive view of governing offered little conceptual room for rulers to implement policy programmes. This strong ethical framework, rather than institutional constraints, was believed to prevent or cure bad governance; good governance depended upon the monarch possessing the right personality and exercising the correct kingly skills. Within such a context, kingship provided the main focus for political thinking and the monarch's performance was discussed at all levels of the community. Debate ranged from the systems presented by political philosophers such as Mair or Buchanan, to the 'mirror of princes' literature written for individual monarchs by Ireland or Lindsay, to the general moralising or specific criticisms found in popular ballads, satires or proverbs and daily comments passed in markets and alehouses. Without worrying overmuch about precision, Scots assumed the king's authority was as broad as it needed to be. In trying to describe the Scottish governmental system for their French allies, even the high-powered legal authors of the *Discours* in 1560 resorted to a basic definition of 'imperial rule': rather than possessing an empire, Scotland's king had 'as much pre-eminence and royal authority as other Christian kings have or could have over their subjects, not recognising any superiors other than God, the king of kings'.[9]

THE STRUCTURE OF THE SCOTTISH CHURCH

Among the monarchies of late medieval Christendom it was common to regard the Church and the crown as the twin pillars upon which Christian society rested and this metaphor offered a reassuringly solid and static image for a system that functioned more like two circles with a large overlapping segment. The church presented the most sophisticated and complex institutional structure Scots encountered during their lives. Through baptism, the rite of passage into church and society, all were incorporated into Christendom and came under the church's jurisdiction,

---

[9] P. McNeill, ed., *Discours Particulier D'Escosse 1559/60*, in *Miscellany II*, ed. D. Sellar (Stair Society, 35, Edinburgh, 1984), 101.

giving every Scot some experience of governance by ecclesiastical authority. In its comprehensive territorial organisation, powers of taxation and formal and professional legal system, the church possessed many more of the attributes of a modern state than did the civil kingdom of Scotland. Thanks to the church's territorial framework, everyone lived within a parish, the lowest unit of an ascending hierarchy of ecclesiastical authority. The territorial principle also operated at diocesan level, the areas over which a bishop had jurisdiction, with the archdioceses and provinces under archbishops and the pope forming the apex of the hierarchy.

The awareness of being part of a single organisation stretching across Christendom and under papal authority existed alongside the equally powerful sense of a Scottish church with its national identity. The country was strengthened once the boundaries of the Scottish church became coterminus with those of the political kingdom, though Scotland only gained its first archbishop in 1476. By the end of the fifteenth century, the jurisdictional claims over parts of Scotland by the English archbishop of York and the Norwegian archbishop of Trondheim had been successfully repelled and all Scottish dioceses were within the provinces of St Andrews or Glasgow. However, the intense rivalry between the two archbishops prevented the Scottish church from acting as a single body or speaking with one voice. The lack of a clear line of command at the top disguised the immense potential of the ecclesiastical organisation as a vehicle for greater cohesion and integration within Scotland.

To sustain its organisation and authority, the church possessed a system of regular taxation securely embedded in its parish structure. The teind or tithe, a 10 per cent levy on all products of a person's labour and wealth, was originally devised to provide support for the clergy who ministered to the parish. However, in nearly 90 per cent of Scottish parishes these revenues were being diverted to other parts of the ecclesiastical machine. Resources were being sucked upwards and as a result, parishes were starved of finances, whilst monasteries, cathedrals, collegiate churches and universities dined well. This system of 'appropriation' also affected the clergy serving in the parish: legally the appropriating body took the place of the rector, and since it could not fulfil his parish duties, it appointed a vicar to serve the cure of souls. In many instances the vicar copied the process and appointed a poorly-paid substitute, with 'Sir John Latinless' becoming one nickname for the clerical proletariat of curates and chaplains who actually ministered to the religious needs of most Scottish parishioners.

Every Scottish parish was enmeshed in this exploitation of the benefice system and the nameless chaplain who sailed to St Kilda was probably paid a pittance by Kilbride's rector, Finlay Tormotson, holding the benefice because he was related to MacLeod of Harris. By the close of the fifteenth century these arrangements had ossified: ecclesiastical benefices were treated as blocks of property rights generating an income and were completely divorced from the parishioners who paid the teinds. All the power and policy-making and most resources were controlled by the clerical elite: the ecclesiastical tail was wagging the dog.

As befitted a state-like organisation, in addition to its comprehensive coverage and taxation regime, the church possessed its own legal system. The spiritual jurisdiction of the church covered all Christians and extended exclusively over its clergy and institutions. One of the sinews holding Christendom together was its hierarchical network of courts spiritual, enforcing canon law. Based on a written Latin code interpreted by experts and with set procedures, church courts served as a working model of a professional system of law. Courts spiritual took cognisance of areas of ordinary life with little apparent connection to religion. Thanks to their sacramental association, matters linked to birth, marriage or death came before the courts spiritual, such as legitimacy, impotency or adultery as well as wills and testaments. Economic affairs, such as money loans or contracts agreed with an oath, also fell within their remit. Over its own personnel, the church asserted exclusive jurisdiction, in the so-called 'benefit of clergy', whereby a cleric could be repledged or transferred from a civil to an ecclesiastical court.

This sophisticated and hierarchically-controlled machine was far from the monolithic organisation it appeared from the outside. The church contained an extremely diverse group of institutions pulling different ways. Amongst the clergy a sense of common purpose was normally conspicuous by its absence with clerics paying as much attention to rank and status as the rest of Scottish society. Dress helped differentiate ecclesiastical personnel: the lordly bishop in his purple, the lowly chaplain in his threadbare gown, the friar with his habit and sandals, or the prioress in her wimple and her lapdog were instantly recognisable to Scottish audiences. Ostentatious markers of clerical status were often on display, such as the fur maniple trailing over the left forearm that proclaimed Dean Brown's rank in the portrait in his Prayerbook.[10]

A fundamental division existed within the church between the regular and secular clergy: the former following a Rule and the latter in sacramental orders. By the fifteenth century the orders of monks, nuns, friars

[10] Miniature from Dean Brown's Prayerbook, Flanders, c. 1498, National Library of Scotland MS 10270 f. 17v.

and canons came in a bewildering range of shapes and sizes. To distinguish between the Dominican, Franciscan, Carmelite and Trinitarian orders contemporaries resorted to colour-coding, speaking of the black, grey, white or red friars. Such a medley resulted from the medieval tendency to create a new order as the chief method of reforming or revitalising an existing one. This was still happening in the late fifteenth and early sixteenth centuries when the 'Observance' of the Rule introduced among the Dominicans and Franciscans produced two different sets of friaries within each order. New and old orders learned to co-exist, resulting in parallel and overlapping organisations and intense rivalries. Efforts to consolidate the regular orders were rare and usually doomed to failure.

The monasteries were by far the wealthiest corporations in Scotland, holding much of the best agricultural land and nearly a third of the total. For many Scots monasteries were their feudal superiors, governing them as their secular lord. The regular orders in particular and the church in general had the added advantage that, once donated, land remained in their 'dead hand' as part of their patrimony for ever. The abbey of Arbroath topped the league table of rental income, enjoying gross annual revenues of at least £13,000, and the receipts for at least another seven foundations exceeded £5,000 a year. Collectively monastic income alone dwarfed royal income and by 1560 the total annual revenues of the church were approximately £400,000, at least ten times those of the crown.[11] Unsurprisingly, the king and the nobility devised methods in the sixteenth century to 'recover' the wealth and land donated by their ancestors to the church. Paradoxically, their efforts brought the crown and the church even closer together, forming an institutional hybrid with entwining ecclesiastical and civil personnel to govern the kingdom.

Over many centuries the close relationship between royal administrations and the higher reaches of the ecclesiastical hierarchy had generated a significant overlap of personnel. In Scotland during the reigns of James IV and James V that relationship grew closer as crown influence over top church appointments reached a peak. The crown enjoyed a pre-paid administration since many royal officials drew salaries from ecclesiastical benefices. Control over the benefice system also supplied the king with a substantial pool of patronage and gifts constantly renewing itself, since benefices could not be directly inherited. The spoils of the benefice system were permanently available to smooth the rubs of power politics as well as to keep the administrative wheels turning, and king's men or

---

[11] Figures from *The Books of Assumption of the Thirds of Benefices*, ed. J. Kirk (Records of Social and Economic History, NS 21, British Academy, Oxford, 1995), lvi.

members of the royal family were rewarded with senior ecclesiastical positions. The spiritual lords, bishops and abbots, held the rank of peers, forming the First Estate in parliament and frequently acted as royal councillors. Commanding independent power and resources in the regions, they provided the crown with a counter-balance to the regional and national influence of the hereditary magnates. The crown gained substantial political and administrative advantages from this intermeshing of royal and ecclesiastical personnel and it seemed almost inconceivable the realm could be governed successfully without such arrangements.

The Scottish crown became totally dependent upon ecclesiastical resources when James V raised an unprecedented level of taxation from the church, permitting him to live and govern in style, considerably beyond his normal means. At the levels of personnel, finance and executive rule, the monarchy rested upon ecclesiastical resources and by the middle of the sixteenth century the upper levels of governance were sustained by a new hybrid grown from the intermingling of church and crown. Although the 1560 doctrinal break from Rome with its subsequent creation of a new kirk was clean and decisive, the institutional structure of the pre-Reformation church remained intact. Once its central religious function had been removed and the chance of restoration receded, that institutional structure slowly withered. The death of its main root in turn killed the church–crown hybrid, with far-reaching consequences for the governance of Scotland. By 1587 the hybrid that had governed the realm earlier in the century was a fading memory.

JURISDICTIONS

During this period government did not have today's all-encompassing embrace and communities were expected to run themselves without the assistance of a police force, health service or tax inspectorate. Scots viewed the process of being ruled in terms of jurisdictions, the legal authorities that administered justice, and those wielding authority in church or kingdom were acutely sensitive to their jurisdictional boundaries and the preservation of their rights and privileges.

However small the barony, holding a jurisdiction was an essential attribute of noble status and was one of the defining characteristics of nobility: its possession operated as a visible dividing line between a noble, who had the right to hold a court, and a commoner, who did not. Noble families jealously guarded their heritable right to hold courts which legalised the coercive power they employed to uphold the law. Over forty lordships of regality existed where baronies were consolidated into a single jurisdictional entity with the privilege of hearing pleas of the crown and excluding royal officers. Whilst royal and noble justice were supposed to be separate systems, in many regions there was confusion over which was the appropriate court for a particular case and the presiding noble was sitting sometimes in his own right, sometimes as a royal official. Throughout the period the cry for justice sounded a constant refrain, demanding two types of 'right': either having a 'wrong' made 'right' or having an existing 'right' or privilege recognised and upheld.

Whilst jurisdictions gave rights, power politics determined whether they could be exercised effectively and in early modern Scotland 'might' would sometimes overturn 'right'. Clashing jurisdictions were the source of many feuds between kin groups, involving noble honour and prestige as much as legal boundaries. Such tussles over jurisdictions were frequently the main external symptoms of a regional or local power struggle and always had the damaging potential of spreading upwards and outwards. Defending a jurisdiction could threaten the legal order it was designed to uphold.

The law courts were the public and visible aspect of these jurisdictions. For the majority of Scots, the lowest level of secular courts, the barony courts or, for urban dwellers, the burgh courts, impinged most frequently upon their lives and dealt with the legal consequences of daily living. The lands of the barony, a matter of consuming interest for a landward community, would be set at the Whitsun court for the following year. The court policed the running of the barony, dealing with offences such as fence breaking, payment of dues or regulation, as in the decree at Killin ordering husbands to accompany wives on visits to the local alehouse, probably causing a change of venue for local hen parties. Breaches of 'good neighbourliness' were part of the court's remit: two women summoned to Carnwath court explained, though blood had been spilled during an argument, 'it vas in play & nocht in ernyst'.[12] From the community's perspective what mattered was that the women had patched up their quarrel before the case came to court and they escaped with a fine for spilling blood, thereby defiling the lord's land. The restoration of peace among neighbours was the prime objective, and the assumption by the hot-tempered women of Carnwath that private and public justice offered alternative and complementary methods of dealing with disputes and feuds was common to all levels of Scottish society. During the latter

[12] *Court Book of Barony of Carnwath*, ed. W. Croft Dickinson (Scottish Historical Society, 3rd ser. XXIX, 1937), 108.

part of the period the central place of private justice within Scottish society was being undermined by an emphasis upon the 'rule of law' as administered through a more centralised legal system.

URBAN LIFE

Burgh courts were more intrusive than barony courts, meeting more frequently and regulating in much greater detail the commercial activities of the burgh such as the brewing of ale. One area of perennial concern was the price of items on sale in the burgh's market and the supervision of weights and measures at the Tron, with the weighing machine giving its name to the location. Further regulation came from the merchant and craft guilds within the burgh who oversaw the training and accreditation of their members, as well as providing a portfolio of religious and social welfare services.

Women and ale

Brewing ale was a female occupation during this period and in the 1509 list compiled for Aberdeen Burgh Council all of those named as 'broustaris' were female, though the maltman was male; similar lists of women brewers were made for Edinburgh's council at later dates. Since brewing ale was a domestic occupation and an extension of the normal business of housekeeping, it had not yet come under a male-dominated craft guild. This contrasted with the bakers or fleshers which were crafts run by a comparatively small number of free male burgesses, ever mindful of their manufacturing monopoly. Burgh councils regulated brewing, hence the list carefully organised by burgh quarter compiled by its own serjeant with a distinction being made between free (those with burgess rights) and unfree brewers, since only the former were permitted to brew the best and strongest ale and charge the higher prices. On the list the majority of the women were recorded in their husband's name; those given their own names were spinsters or widows; comprising 16 per cent of the total, and throwing light on the many women who headed urban households, forming approximately a fifth of the total.[13]

---

[13] E. P. Dennison, D. Ditchburn and M. Lynch, eds, *Aberdeen before 1800, A New History* (East Linton, 2002), 146–7; N. Mayhew, 'The Brewsters of Aberdeen', *Northern Studies* 32 (1997), 71–81.

A useful service, valued by Scots doing all manner of business, was the registration of agreements in the court books, providing a written record binding in law: in Peebles the burgh court book was even used to register a bet. The desire for formal legal records was sufficiently strong to turn this period into the golden age of the notary. Providing most of the legal advice and clerking services needed by Scots, notaries with their protocol books were vital to the smooth running of ordinary life, especially within the burghs. Becoming a notary was a standard career path for priests trained in law who had not attained a benefice. The clerical and lay personnel comprising this professional group were a prime example of the intermingling of the law, the church, royal and local government whose presence increased the social diversification of urban life.

Each burgh had a charter, granted by the crown, an ecclesiastical lord or baron, containing a collection of rights and privileges exercised within its boundaries, marked by its ports or gates, ditches and sometimes walls. The burgh was a privileged corporation proudly using its own seal, such as Perth or St Johnstone, whose seal portrayed its name saint. The most significant rights the burgesses received were those to manufacture and to trade, to which they were usually able to add the privilege of self-government. Overseas trade was the assertively-protected right of royal and greater burghs who joined together in the Convention of Burghs to give themselves a formal political voice. Life in the smaller burghs was less stratified and their urban experience resembled more closely their rural neighbours with most trade conducted within their own hinterland. Contemporaries were acutely conscious of the difference in status and privilege between a burgh and its rural environs. The number of burghs of barony mushroomed during the period with the rush to achieve urban status driven neither by economic expansion nor the demands of trade or manufacture, but by the nobility's social expectations. Every medium-level baron sought to add to his collection of status symbols the prestigious accessory of a burgh within his barony.

By the end of the fifteenth century the pattern of burgh government was established with the same faces in authority in the burgh council, courts and merchant guild, like the Menzies family at Aberdeen who monopolised the provostship for a hundred years. Small self-perpetuating groups of the wealthiest merchants formed the urban, political and social elite. For the increasing number of town dwellers who were not free burgesses, authority was imposed upon them by these urban oligarchies who became obsessed with the maintenance of order and social control. The medieval rhetoric of a single political and social body persisted, with the burgh's treasury still called the 'common good', but much of the reality had drained way. As social divisions sharpened, the privileges of urban life were accessible to fewer inhabitants and there emerged an underclass of the excluded poor. The feast of Corpus Christi was intended to celebrate a single urban community united through the body of Christ, exemplified by the eucharistic wafer carried in procession around the burgh. However, the community's harmony and unity were likely to be marred by squabbles over precedence within the procession organised along strictly hierarchical lines: the 'unfree' were pushed to the sidelines and among the free burgesses some were clearly more equal than their fellows.

The solidification of oligarchical rule and the emergence of an impoverished underclass reflected the relatively depressed economic position of the burghs. They were still struggling to regain the levels of overseas trade achieved prior to the Wars of Independence and apart from a surge in the 1530s only managed to sustain a full recovery in the last quarter of the sixteenth century. The staple port of Veere on the Scheldt estuary handled much of the raw materials Scotland exported, particularly wool, woolfells, hides and skins, with cloth providing an exportable manufacture. At the end of the 1470s more than half the crown's customs revenues came from wool exports, a proportion dropping to less than a quarter a century later, hitting hard burghs like Haddington. West-coast ports, like Ayr or Dumbarton, experienced a drop in hides' exports, forcing them to rely more on the fishing industry. Economic diversification became a harsh fact of urban life, causing a slow and often painful process of change upon Scottish burghs, even major ones such as Perth, as the Tay silted up. The major winner was Edinburgh, whose 65 per cent share of the realm's cloth exports in the 1470s, climbing to 80 per cent by the 1530s, signalled its rise to dominate Scottish overseas trade, turning its port of Leith into the main gateway between Scotland and Europe.

SCOTLAND AND EUROPE

For a people on the edge of Christendom, the self-confident Scots had no hesitation in participating as fully as they could in European diplomacy, culture and trade. Since the Wars of Independence, diplomatic strategy had revolved around the triangular politics of Scotland, France and England. The 'auld alliance' with France acted like a sheet anchor holding the realm firmly within the mainstream of European life. Anti-English feeling formed one of the bedrocks of Scottish national sentiment and was the default setting for the kingdom's foreign policy, though this did not preclude trading links between Scotland and England.

Denmark, the birthplace of Queen Margaret, James IV's mother, was Scotland's North Sea neighbour and a natural ally. Major trade links with Flanders made friendly relations with its Burgundian and later Habsburg rulers a high priority. Much Scottish trade passed to and through France or Spain or, presaging future developments, found its way east through the Sound into the Baltic. Scots were enthusiastic importers of manufactured and luxury goods, especially from Flanders and France, with Highland chiefs and Lowland merchants alike anxiously awaiting the arrival of the next consignment of French wine. The country readily embraced most European fashions and cultural trends usually after they had acquired a French flavour by travelling via the auld ally. Far from being an inward-facing community with little mobility or contact with the outside world, Scotland resolutely faced outwards to continental Europe and to Ireland. This guaranteed the realm would be deeply affected by European events: although a very late import – the arrival of the Protestant Reformation – was to have the greatest impact upon the religious lives and beliefs of Scots.

RELIGIOUS BELIEFS

Scots assumed it was part of the created order that supernatural powers operated routinely on earth, with God, his saints and the Devil bringing good and evil into their daily lives. Though relegated to the penumbra of official recognition, their world was also populated by fairies, spirits and ghosts. From bitter experience everyone understood the power of the forces of nature; how a storm could ruin crops in hours or the plague could sweep through a community, killing indiscriminately.

With death a constant companion, Scots measured their existence within an eternal perspective, seeking the answers as to how they should live and die within the shared framework of belief operating throughout late medieval Christendom. The image of life as a pilgrimage through this world to the next was frequently used to make sense of living with continual awareness of death and the afterlife. William Dunbar was reflecting a common experience when he borrowed for his poem the opening phrase from the Office of the Dead, 'Timor mortis conturbat me' (The fear of death distresses me).

To cope with such supernatural fears, Scots turned instinctively for help to people and places, mirroring what they did when in earthly trouble. They envisaged the heavenly realm ruled by God the Father as operating like a royal household and looked to those who had access to the

Disease

In 1516 Lord Somerville lost his wife and two younger sons to smallpox; it was a common experience since disease was no respecter of social status. Scots also faced periodic and recurrent visitations of the 'pest': bubonic and pneumonic plague. Although none rivalled the mortality rates of the Black Death in the mid-fourteenth century, the plague remained a serious killer, especially in burghs, and during the 1498 outbreak in Dunfermline it possibly killed the poet Robert Henryson. The first medical treatise written in Scots, Gilbert Skene's 1568 *Ane Breve Descriptioun of the Pest*, offered advice about the plague along classic humoral lines, with bloodletting from the right arm in addition to treatment by herbal concoctions. In traditional manner he also reminded his readers 'the principal preservative cure of the pest is to returne to God'.[14] Cholera and typhoid were also common, especially among armies, with the former probably being responsible for the death of James V. Syphilis came to Scotland in the last years of the fifteenth century arriving via the ports as most epidemics did. Called the 'grand-gore', this sexually-transmitted disease rapidly spread through Scotland. Leprosy was endemic, with most burghs having a leper house situated outside the walls and granting licences for lepers to beg, provided they carried the clappers warning healthy citizens of their approach. Burghs, with their close and unsanitary living conditions, were especially vulnerable to the spread of infection, and they introduced strict regulations, such as Provost Otterburn's attempt to quarantine Edinburgh during the 1530 plague, and in 1578 the capital created a post equivalent to a medical officer of health. Scotland was relatively well provided with hospitals, usually run by religious orders and as concerned with spiritual as with physical health. Archaeological discoveries at Paisley Abbey and Soutra Hospital suggest a high level of expertise and the use of a wide range of medicinal plants. The incorporation of the barbers and surgeons in Edinburgh in 1505–6 marked an important stage in the development of a medical profession, independent of the church, though their services were expensive and ordinary Scots relied upon folk practitioners. Many of these were midwives employing herbal remedies, practical experience and charms to heal ailments. By the second half of the century they had come under suspicion and female healers, such as Agnes Sampson of North Berwick fame, found they faced charges of witchcraft.

[14] Cited and discussed in H. Dingwall, *A History of Scottish Medicine* (Edinburgh, 2003), 56.

divine presence. Topping the list of intercessors were family members, the mother and son of God, the Virgin Mary and Christ, but there was a veritable host of those able to assist a supplicant place their plea before the divine throne. Each saint had a known specialism making them sympathetic to a particular plight, such as St Triduana for eye troubles, whose shrine was at Restalrig. A special devotion, following a saint as one would a local lord, tied a supplicant to their name saint, or to the guild, local or national saint. In contemporary religious paintings, such as the Trinity College altarpiece, the patron saint was placed close to their devotee as if about to perform the necessary introductions in the heavenly palace. Late medieval Christians assumed that knowledge of the transcendent God could be visually mediated and their five senses were channels for divine grace.

Access to the holy was made easier by a profound awareness of sacred ground and space, which recognised particular places as holy because they contained a sacred relic, had enjoyed a saint's presence during life or had been blessed by a priest for sacred use. Throughout Scotland a sacred place was never far away; in addition to all the ecclesiastical buildings, standing crosses (see Figure 4.1) were found by the wayside and there was a plethora of holy wells and trees. Even in a Highland parish where the church might be a dozen miles away, there were holy sites within easy reach of every settlement. The direct connection between physical objects and sacred power brought supernatural assistance into Scots' houses, such as the blessed candles taken home after Candlemas or the personal protection of an amulet worn around the neck. Late medieval Scots combined their sense of the sacred in localised and physical settings with the recognition of the universal and all-pervasive nature of divine power. Because the sacred was both here and everywhere, there was no compartmentalisation of religion. It formed an integral part of daily living, from the instinctive blessing of a person who sneezed to the anchorite's total dedication to the contemplative life.

The Reformation provided a dramatic challenge to some of these beliefs and in the long run brought a fundamental shift in religious culture. It modified views about life after death by denying the existence of purgatory, and so limiting the afterlife to two possibilities, either heaven or hell. However, the arrival of Protestantism did not undermine the fundamental assumption that supernatural forces were at work in the world. These remained to provide the underpinning for the witch trials that developed into a craze at the end of the sixteenth and into the seventeenth centuries.

SCOTLAND RE-FORMED

Covering almost 100 years, this volume examines the period from 1488 to 1587, beginning with the death of James III and ending with the execution of Mary, Queen of Scots. It deliberately avoids the century breaks of 1500 and 1600 and chooses a regnal date to open but not close the book. During James IV's entire reign, rather than on the day he became king, Scotland experienced a period of transition; a slow move without a sharp break from late medieval to Renaissance monarchy. Designating 1587 as the terminal date emphasises two key aspects of the chronology of early modern Scotland. First, the death of Mary, Queen of Scots marked a significant stage within the long reign of James VI, signalling the conclusive end to his extended royal apprenticeship: within the New Edinburgh History of Scotland series, the adult reign of James VI should be examined in one volume and not artificially broken in 1603 by his accession to the throne of England. Second, telling the story of the kingdom demands more than regnal dates because broader changes and developments affecting the lives of ordinary Scots rarely attach themselves neatly to a single year. The decade of the 1580s offers the best vantage point from which to assess the gradual disappearance of the world known to those alive in the 1480s.

In the following chapters specific threads, carrying the political, religious, cultural, economic, social and international developments, will be seen running through the narrative, giving colour and form to Scotland's story. Between 1488 and 1587, Scotland was re-formed within four broad areas: the nature of its governance and political structure; its ecclesiastical and religious lives; the integration of the kingdom; and its place in the world. These transformations in turn brought changes to the culture, society and economy of the kingdom.

In 1587 the re-forming of Scotland was incomplete, since many of the changes described in the following chapters were happening at the pace of a glacier, grinding its path across a hundred years. The realm was not made anew, only re-formed, and the continuities with the fifteenth-century kingdom were strong and of deep significance. Scotland was a kingdom based upon working the land and little altered in its agricultural rhythm. In 1587, as in 1488, what held Scots together was their deep-rooted sense of people and of place.

PART ONE

'Glore of all Princely Governing'

CHAPTER I

The Princely King: James IV (1488–94)

THE FIELD OF STIRLING, 1488

As befitted a warrior king, the reign of James IV started and ended on the battlefield. Unfortunately, the enemy on that first field was James' own father, James III, who was killed at the end of the battle, thus automatically inaugurating the reign of his son and heir. Although bringing a myriad of problems, there was no constitutional crisis, since the succession of the Stewart dynasty had passed from father to eldest son with no serious challenge to James IV's right to rule. Such an outcome was not what Queen Margaret of Denmark had had in mind when she counselled, 'James, my eldest boy, I am speeding towards death, I pray you, through your obedience as my son, to love and fear God, always doing good, because nothing achieved by violence, be certain, can endure'.[1]

James III's aggressive and vindictive policies, especially against the Humes, a prominent family based in the Merse in Berwickshire, had provoked considerable opposition by 1488. Through the appointment of their kinsman John as prior, the Humes had secured control over Coldingham Priory, a lucrative and influential monastery lying inside their territory and part of the defences against England. Riding roughshod over the Humes and their local position and prestige, James III intended to reduce the priory to a collegiate church and pocket the revenues. It was the manner more than the matter of royal actions which made the Scottish nobility afraid and wonder who might be the king's next victim.

---

[1] Cited and discussed in N. Macdougall, *James IV* (Edinburgh, 1989), 1.

The rebellion of 1488 had the considerable advantage of including the heir to the throne. Whether or not the fifteen-year-old prince believed his father threatened his position, young James, duke of Rothesay, was a willing adherent and deliberately employed the title 'Prince of Scotland'. The campaign combined complex manoeuvrings around Scotland, fruitless negotiations and a smidgeon of armed confrontation. The prince had to flee from a skirmish at Stirling Bridge in early June 1488, but returned with all the rebel forces to Scotland's most fought-over tract of land to take part in the decisive battle on 11 June on the Field of Stirling, or Sauchieburn. Much of James III's support came not from peers but loyal lairds such as Sempill of Elliston, who died in the fighting, or the twenty-four Roxburgh men accompanying their sheriff, Douglas of Cavers. Regional and local feuds determined allegiances as much as approval or fear of James III. Lord Maxwell joined the rebels because his Dumfriesshire rival, Murray of Cockpool, was with the king, as was Crawford, the newly-made duke of Montrose, ensuring Angus would be a rebel. There was confusion over the most important event, the death of the king, who was possibly leaving the battlefield when he was killed close to the Bannockburn mill. Contemporary accounts speak of him being slain, not murdered, by 'vile' persons, meaning those of low rank. The colourful descriptions populated with witches, prophecies and details such as a grey horse or counterfeit priest only emerged in the later versions of Lindsay of Pitscottie and Buchanan.

Defeating the king was one thing, killing him quite another: although he raised the royal standard in direct defiance, the prince had given explicit orders no-one should lay violent hands upon his father. For the rest of his life, James IV carried a sense of his moral responsibility for two of the deadliest of sins, parricide and regicide, and in a private act of penance wore an iron belt around his waist, adding a further weight each year. More surprisingly, it took him until 1496 to make the conventional public demonstration of grief by endowing Masses for King James' soul, possibly delaying until he had reached a genuine sorrow to accompany his contrition for the sin.

The Augustinian canons of Cambuskenneth Priory, whose lands had been ravaged a few days earlier, were aware of the battle raging close to their precincts. Their church became a temporary morgue and, when James III's body arrived, they sang the funeral offices with due ceremony, as pictured in James IV's Book of Hours. The late king was buried next to his queen and in sight of the royal castle of Stirling: avoiding deliberate humiliation, this was a low-key closing to a turbulent reign.

Prayers for the dead

Praying for the dead was central to late medieval life, placing a considerable burden upon the living. In medieval Christendom beliefs about
the afterlife focused upon an individual judgement which all faced
immediately following death, as well as the great collective Last
Judgement. Most Scots assumed their lives had been neither so bad
they would go to Hell, nor sufficiently saintly to attain Heaven; they
would be sent to Purgatory for the time needed to purge their sins.
Once dead, they had to rely upon the living to speed their journey
through Purgatory by means of intercessory prayer and Masses said for
their souls. The immense demand for Masses distorted the balance of
worship and the structure and organisation of the church, creating an
army of priests whose main or sole function was to celebrate that
sacrament, normally in batches of trentals (thirty Masses). The upper
nobility switched from endowing monasteries to establishing collegiate
churches to pray for them, such as Lord Drummond's foundation in
1508 at Innerpeffray or St Mary's, Biggar, established by Lord Fleming
in 1546. Those with more limited means funded a chapel or a priest for
a specified number of Masses. Multiple chantry altars were common in
parish churches, with St John's, Perth, having thirty-seven, two more
than its Dundee neighbour, St Mary's. One of the prime functions of
religious and craft guilds was to pay for their members' funerals and
requiem Masses and a small weekly payment made this accessible to
most levels of society. In addition to its main liturgical function, the
Office of the Dead became a framework for private daily devotion,
forming a major section within the Books of Hours used by the laity,
thus demonstrating the strong link forged between praying for the
dead and one's own salvation (see Figure 1.1). Acutely conscious that
kinship was not restricted to the living, embracing ancestors and successors, most Scots spent much of their time, money and effort in the
service of the dead. Society gained from the side effects of these bene-
factions, being provided with extra parish clergy, education, hospitals,
almshouses, music, artistic commissions and doles for the poor and
needy.

THE CORONATION OF A PRINCELY KING

Amidst the uncertainty following the battle, at least the next step was
obvious: following a monarch's death, the heir should be crowned. The

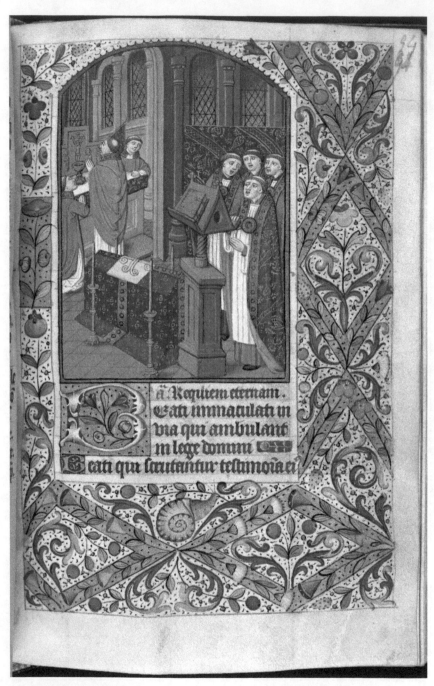

Figure 1.1 'Service of the Dead', from a late-fifteenth-century Book of Hours made for a Scottish owner. [EUL MS 43 f. 94r]

victors at Stirling Field quickly proclaimed the new reign and issued a Great Seal charter the next day. On 24 June, the anniversary of Bannockburn, James was crowned at Scone by Bishop Blackadder of Glasgow who had supported the rebels. This was a snub to the loyalist archbishop of St Andrews whose recently established primacy over the Scottish church was hotly disputed by Glasgow. Additional blessing was sought from the presence at the coronation of St Fillan's Bell, possibly accompanied by his crozier or 'Quigrich', carried from Glendochart by its custodial family, the Dewars. Ten years later, mindful of the saint's aid, James IV eloquently expressed his devotion to St Fillan and confirmed the Dewars' privileges as relic keepers. The presence of the Scottish nobility was harder to obtain, with the notable absence of Errol, the hereditary Constable, and the Earl Marischal who had ceremonial roles to play during a coronation.

Though now crowned, James remained in a quasi-princely role through an undeclared and self-imposed minority while the victorious faction created their regime. For the next six years the princely king carefully learned the craft of kingship and like James VI, his great-grandson, he benefited from observing the mistakes of others and made good use of his vicarious experience later in the reign. During these opening years, James' ebullient personality was channelled into warrior pursuits as he acquired a more rounded military apprenticeship in the campaigns against the rebels and indulged his passion for working with artillery. Being an active, outdoor person, James took his time to master the skills practised more sedately inside, such as making difficult political judgements and dealing with the tasks of daily government. This long, slow beginning made James IV a more successful adult ruler, but it provided a bumpy few years for his subjects.

To observers in the Scottish regions, whilst the battle had changed the king, one faction had simply replaced another and the previous reign's disastrous course seemed set to continue. Those allies from the eastern Borders, the Hepburn and Hume families, moved with speed to establish their regime by seizing the spoils of victory, including around £24,000 of James III's treasure, some found in a coffer resting in the battlefield's mire. The Master [or heir] of Hume became Chamberlain, whilst Patrick Hepburn, Lord Hailes, became Master of the Household and his uncle, John, prior of St Andrews, took the all-important Privy Seal controlling royal patronage, one of the most contentious issues of the previous reign. The two earls who had attended the coronation, Angus and Argyll, were included in the new administration, with Argyll taking the chancellorship from William Elphinstone, bishop of Aberdeen. Since they had been

James III's last victims, this faction sought redress, looking to gain 'justice' by getting their own 'wrongs' righted and re-establishing their own 'rights'. In so doing, they victimised others and undermined their previous rallying cry of seeking justice.

THREE CRISES: 1488, 1489, 1492

For the next three years the new regime lurched from one crisis to the next as feuds created or exacerbated by the untimely ending of the previous reign raged within the regions. The structure of Scottish politics ensured a regime based upon a faction found it very difficult to rule with an even hand or step outside regional feuds because each faction member stood at the head of their own vertical-interest group of kin and locality. Great pressure was generated through these vertical links to secure patronage and power and, once achieved, to use that patronage and power to serve the interests of the faction rather than the common weal. As a result, national political life nearly collapsed in the three years following Sauchieburn and it took a series of semi-successful rebellions to broaden the regime's base of support beyond the narrow faction of Humes and Hepburns who had overthrown James III. Without, as yet, a strong royal hand to bring equilibrium, a sufficiently large part of the political nation needed to be involved in the regime to restore some form of balance; this took several years to achieve.

The air of uncertainty immediately after the battle was not helped by the delay until October in summoning a parliament. During fifteenth-century crises, parliament had given credence to settlements ending violent upheavals in Scottish political life and had provided the legislative authority for forfeitures for treason. The potential danger of gathering the estates, thereby allowing an airing of grievances, had encouraged the regime to procrastinate. The pomp of 'belting' a new earl, as Hailes became earl of Bothwell, tried to set the tone of settled authority. The main business was to offer an explanation for James III's death which removed any taint of regicide: one of the more memorable phrases excusing a death in suspicious circumstances was invented when parliament declared James III 'happinnit to be slane' on the battlefield.[2]

During the debate about James III's alleged breach of an agreement reached in April 1488, the new administration was fortunate Glamis,

[2] Cited and discussed in N. Macdougall, *James III: A Political Study* (Edinburgh, 1982), 259.

whose awareness of documentary niceties might have arisen from his being a graduate, unlike most of his fellow peers, produced a copy of the agreement with the flourish of a lawyer revealing damning evidence. The adoption of the well-tried medieval formula for rebellion – that the king had been misled by evil counsellors – left the unsettling possibility that in the future any loyalist might be pursued as an 'evil counsellor'. By contrast, the provost of Lincluden, who had held the Privy Seal until March 1488, gave a forthright explanation when seeking a papal dispensation for shedding blood in the battle of Stirling Field; a serious problem for one in priestly orders. His startling assertion that the rebel cause was just because the kingdom had been 'badly and confusedly governed' by the king and his counsellors was as straightforward a statement of the right of resistance as one would find for the next 100 years.[3]

At regional and local levels the fall-out from Sauchieburn was considerable, intensifying existing feuds. The deaths of Lords Kilmaurs and Ruthven allowed their respective rivals Lords Montgomery and Oliphant to gain advantages in Ayrshire and Perth. The Ayrshire district of Cunningham faced disruption because of the long-standing feud between the Montgomery and the Cunningham kindreds over the office of bailie. Montgomery received the office after Sauchieburn and, in his attempts to force his authority upon the Cunninghams and crush their power in north Ayrshire, he killed Kilmaurs' heir. In 1492 a neutral third party with sufficient power to contain the warring kin groups was inserted when Angus received the lordship of Kilmarnock as part of a swap of lands and offices with the Hepburns. However, Angus' neutrality was more apparent than real and his intervention revived the Boyds, his wife's family, and their allies, the Cunninghams, the victims of Montgomery's homicidal ways. In central Scotland Drummond took control of the stewardship of Strathearn from his rival, William Murray of Tullibardine, who had held it for over fifty years. The Drummonds evicted the Murrays and hampered George Murray, abbot of Inchaffray. During 1490 an affray between the two kindreds spiralled out of control when the Master of Drummond and his brother-in-law, Campbell of Dunstaffnage, cornered twenty Murray men (not the women and children of later legend) in Monzievaird church, burning the building whilst a piper allegedly played a march. With bloodfeuds creating a breakdown of political life in some regions, it was essential to demonstrate that

---

[3] Discussed in N. Macdougall, 'The Estates in Eclipse?: Politics and Parliament in the reign of James IV', in *The History of the Scottish Parliament* Vol. 1, eds K. M. Brown and R. J. Tanner (Edinburgh, 2004), 152–3.

certain actions would not be tolerated, and the Strathearn massacre led to the execution of the two main perpetrators, with the bloodfeud waiting a further ten years to be settled. Though under a temporary cloud, Drummond remained in royal favour, and had the disputed Strathearn offices confirmed in October 1495. His position at court was strengthened by his marriage alliances with the powerful earls of Angus and Argyll and the king taking his daughter as a mistress in 1496.

During its first six months, the new regime had failed to reassure the political nation that crown patronage would be evenly distributed and justice equitably imposed: the perennial issues uniting the opposition to James III. Unlike his father, the young king was personally present at justice ayres, though this had not prevented judgements penalising past loyalists and favouring unduly erstwhile rebels. At the Dumfries session MacLellan of Bombie, a supporter of the late king, found remissions being granted to those who had burnt his house and even to the man accused of rape. More damaging was the alienation of Stewart of Darnley, who had finally been recognised as earl of Lennox, and his son Matthew and Lord Lyle. These western lords felt insufficiently rewarded for their support in 1488 and unappreciated by the inner clique of Humes and Hepburns, including Lord Drummond who had received the judicial office in Renfrewshire Lyle felt should have been his own. Holding their castles of Crookston and Duchal and the royal fortress of Dumbarton against the crown, the lords raided the Sempills, their Renfrewshire rivals. Sempill, whose father had been killed at Sauchieburn fighting for James III, demonstrated his loyalty in September 1489 when he received the office of sheriff of Renfrew and was sent the artillery to bombard Duchal; the castle gave its name to one of the victorious cannon. Dumbarton was a harder nut to crack, for a sally from the castle had driven Argyll's besieging troops from the town.

Rebellion had also broken out in the north-east where the loyalists, the Earl Marischal, Master of Huntly and Lord Forbes had rallied round the banner of the 'bloody sark' of the dead king and formulated an impressive list of grievances. On their march to join the northern rebels, Lennox and his 2,000 men, drawn from his Stewart kin and regional allies, the Lindsays, Colquhouns, Galbraiths and MacFarlanes, camped at Gartloaning. Fortunately for the nearby royal forces, Drummond's vassal, Macalpine, told his master their whereabouts and a surprise night attack forced the rebel leaders back to Dumbarton Castle. James, who had been with his troops, gave a thank offering at Kippen church before heading to the Clyde to renew the siege on Dumbarton. Its cost, running to £537 14s in its final week, helped concentrate minds, and another parliament was called, thereby acceding to one of the rebels' demands and signalling compromise was possible. Parliament annulled the forfeitures of Lennox, his son and Lyle and, in a unique gesture, the composition of the king's Secret or Privy Council was chosen by the estates. Even without military success, the rebellion had achieved its purpose, forcing a change of personnel at the centre, bringing Lennox, Marischal and Lyle and even stalwarts of James III's final years, such as Ross of Balnagowan and the duke of Montrose, to join the Hepburn and Hume faction which had struggled to maintain themselves since Sauchieburn. The crucial return in the summer of 1490 was that of Elphinstone, bishop of Aberdeen, whose personal integrity and government experience gave the ballast and credibility which the unstable regime so badly needed.

Problems remained, particularly resulting from Hepburn pressure upon 'Bell-the-Cat' Douglas, the earl of Angus, who had been forced to give up his three wardenships of the Border marches, the sheriffdom of Lanark, some Berwickshire lands and even his castle at Broughty Ferry. This determined attempt to lever Angus out of his power base in the eastern and middle Borders benefited Bothwell and his Hume allies as they tightened their grip on those areas. It also contained an exaggerated reaction to the ghost of 'Douglas past', which had previously haunted the Scottish political community. It was raised again when Angus sought to be recognised as heir to the Black Douglas patrimony in 1491 after the earl of Douglas died in his peaceful confinement at the abbey of Lindores. By October the king was back on campaign with his beloved cannons besieging Angus in his imposing castle at Tantallon. A negotiated compromise, rather than a military victory, ensued. Angus swapped his Borders lordship of Liddesdale and Hermitage castle for the lordship of Kilmarnock. The earl's secret agreement with King Henry VII the following month justified the Council's suspicion though it did not prevent James from continuing his friendship with Angus and losing yet more money to him at cards. Though not easy to work alongside, Angus was an accepted face at court whether at the council board or at the card table, enabling a smoother transition following the virtual coup placing him and his supporters at the centre of government in 1492. One element of its success was the awkward realisation that it was easier to have Angus on the inside of the political charmed circle than on the outside fomenting trouble.

The changing European diplomatic situation, with the Anglo-French peace of Etaples at the end of 1492, left the pro-French policy championed by Bothwell in expensive tatters. Having little else in common, Elphinstone and Angus did share an Anglophile foreign policy and the most significant administrative change was the replacement of the prior of St Andrews as Keeper of the Privy Seal. The bishop of Aberdeen held that office with its control of royal patronage for the remainder of the reign. The abbot of Cambuskenneth, another safe pair of administrative hands, took the Treasurer's post and, following the death of Argyll, Angus became chancellor. By the beginning of 1493 Angus and his allies had achieved political control.

THE LEGACIES OF SAUCHIEBURN

The crises of 1488, 1489 and 1492 had distracted attention from four fundamental issues facing the minority regime. As it had throughout the fifteenth century, the call for justice played a prominent part in each crisis, and the relationship of the crown and central administration to the regions, especially the Lordship of the Isles and Orkney and Shetland, had also not been settled. Although the church in Scotland provided a unifying thread, it was split at the top by the rivalry between St Andrews and Glasgow and in the Council there was a division of opinion about the best course in foreign policy, whether to ally with France or England.

Within the regions the need for justice was the most pressing concern. By travelling in person with the justice ayres, James IV gave the immediacy and personal touch craved by his subjects in the provision of 'good lordship'. However, for royal lordship to be 'good' it had to be perceived as fair and not weighted in favour of one faction. In the dispute between the burghs of Renfrew and Paisley, Abbot Schaw, a Sauchieburn rebel, had received a new charter for the abbey's burgh of Paisley, granting it the same privileges as a royal burgh. Objecting to such competition, the men of Renfrew had smashed the stones of the new market cross. Behind the struggle over trade and its urban setting lay the regional power struggle between Sempill and Lennox. Although Paisley's position was upheld by James at the justice ayre, Sempill received a Lordship of Parliament and on 16 March 1492, he and Lennox renounced their feud.

The legacies of Sauchieburn were very hard to overcome, even in the church. The political alignments already visible at James IV's coronation were made worse when the bishop of Glasgow had his claim for an archdiocese championed at Rome. On 9 January 1492, the pope elevated Glasgow, a 'special daughter' of the Holy See, into an archbishopric, placing Scottish dioceses under its jurisdiction. Although technically retaining his primacy over the Scottish church, the archbishop of St Andrews was left with little national authority. The imposing Renaissance-style, bronze medallion struck the previous year mocked Scheves' powerlessness as he was frozen out of the political community. The building of a chapel in Culross, the presumed place of Kentigern's education, and Blackadder's renovation of the saint's shrine in his cathedral reinforced Glasgow's status. The archbishop also flexed his jurisdictional muscles by placing on trial for heresy in his cathedral city a group of Lollards based in Kyle, Ayrshire. The king's personal presence and his alleged support for some of the accused ensured there were no executions. The only surviving record of the trial was a list of accusations from the Official of Glasgow's court used half a century later by John Knox in his *History of the Reformation*. His description revealed a network of inter-related kindred and friends in the Kyle and Cunningham areas whose heretical ideas were spread by personal contacts. Assessing the extent of Lollardy within Scotland or distinguishing it from general criticisms of the church's practices is not easy. The activities of the Kyle Lollards were driven underground and formed a continuous line of dissent down to the Reformation. Abjuration of heresy did not harm the social standing of lairds such as Reid of Barskimming, or prevent Campbell of Cessnock from becoming sheriff depute of Ayr in 1500 and 1505.

Orkney and Shetland had been pawned in 1468 and 1469 by the Danish king as part of the dowry of Queen Margaret, and in 1472 James III had agreed with William Sinclair to take into royal hands the earldom of Orkney and lordship of Shetland in return for substantial compensation. This left the precise sovereign status of the Northern Isles unresolved, creating an underlying tension in Scottish–Danish relations for the next century. However, in Scotland there was a clear determination to retain the Isles as an integral part of the kingdom, though there was no systematic attempt to impose Scottish language, law and custom and, whether conscious or not, a policy of gradual assimilation was pursued. Orkney had experienced extensive migration from Scotland throughout the fifteenth century and the Scots language was already widely used and understood. Shetland, with relatively few Scots settling, was different, speaking Norn and retaining its legal and social customs. Here the Scots and royal servants among the clergy of Shetland were an important vehicle for extending Scottish influence.

What mattered to the crown was the exercise of political control, and it was content to continue traditional offices, such as the *foud*, with powers similar to a sheriff, so long as it appointed the officer. Holding comital rights in the Isles, the king had the secure feeling he was in charge of the islands. The only exception to a generally light touch was when the crown's authority was not acknowledged, as Magnus Herwood found in January 1502. He had obtained the office of archdeacon of Shetland from the king of Denmark but was threatened with treason when James IV presented his own candidate, Henry Phantouch, the illegitimate son of the bishop of Orkney, who secured the benefice and built a fine teind barn near Lerwick on the proceeds.

The greatest civil authority in the Northern Isles was held by Sinclair of Sumburgh, an illegitimate son of the previous earl. He was in royal service on both sides of the North Sea, receiving the prestigious post of keeper of Bergen Castle in Norway and then, possibly after supporting the Swedish rebels against King Hans, becoming keeper of the Scottish castles of Dingwall and Redcastle in Ross. Since the Danish empire and Scotland were allies and Sir David could travel in his ships between the two kingdoms, straddling two political arenas remained possible. The sea-lanes preserved the bonds between Scandinavia and the Northern Isles and at the end of the fifteenth century, a shared North Atlantic community still existed, as Sinclair's testamentary gifts to the cathedrals of Kirkwall and Roskilde witnessed.

The Sinclair family, with their landed interests in Lothian, Fife and Caithness in addition to the Northern Isles, had played a significant role

---

Fishing

Contemporaries believed Orkney's abundance of fish had an effect upon the Kirkwall women, who were 'given to excess in carnal pleasures' because of their fish consumption.[4] In fact sea and freshwater fish formed an important part of the general Scottish diet, replacing grain when it grew scarce, and being the main item on religious fasting days, every Wednesday and Friday, the eve of major feasts and the forty days of Lent. A wide variety of fish found their way to Scottish plates, such as the ever-popular herring, the 'mudfish', cod and ling, the exotic oysters and lamprey, and salmon, trout, eel and pike. Fish were often used to pay rent or sent as a gift, with salmon making a popular present. In February 1562 a royal charter re-granted the assize of herring in the West Sea which gave rights over the fishing from the Pentland Firth in the north to the Mull of Galloway in the south and as far as sea water flowed up the Clyde. The herring trade was an extremely lucrative business throughout Scottish coastal waters. All the east-coast burghs were heavily involved in fishing, which formed a substantial part of their trade. In all the North Sea fisheries the well-organised Dutch fleets were a dominant factor,

---

[4] *MacFarlane's Geographical Collections*, ed. A. Mitchell, 3 vols (Scottish History Society, 1st ser. 51–3, Edinburgh, 1906–8), III, 319.

moving into the Northern Isles whose original trading patterns had run through Norway, the Hanse merchants and the Baltic. On the Clyde alone several hundred inshore herring boats were working, taking fish into ports for export, such as the consignments noted by the Clerk of Ayr in 1582 bound for La Rochelle and Bordeaux. Even the Solway ports were involved with a Wigtown burgess in 1538 obtaining an Exchequer licence to fish in the Outer Isles with a French or Breton ship, indicating the long-distance geographical connections the trade brought. For export, inland travel and for preservation, fish were salted, dried or smoked and large numbers of barrels were required, keeping the coopers busy. Scottish exports went to France, England and the Baltic. The Dutch, who caught their own fish in Scottish waters, were severely hit by the six-year war, 1544–50, with Scotland. By the 1570s and 1580s the Scottish exports of herring and, to a lesser extent, cod and salmon were a significant factor aiding the recovery of overseas trade and thereby boosting the Scottish economy.[5] During that period, exporting fish to the Baltic and returning with timber (see the box on backpacking in Poland, p. 287) was part of the business empire of 'Danzig Willie' Forbes whose profits built the splendid Craigievar Castle in Aberdeenshire.

in Scottish Lowland politics throughout the fifteenth century. Their graceful, if not entirely willing, relinquishment of Orkney and Shetland left them with the title of earl of Caithness, a power base at Rosslyn outside Edinburgh and continued power and influence. Sinclair cadet branches remained firmly embedded in the Isles and the northern mainland since a shift of power at the top level did not automatically disrupt the rhythms of life beneath. Having some legal basis, the royal seizure of the Isles from Denmark and the Sinclairs did not create a focus for rebellion at either aristocratic or local levels. Consequently, the Northern Isles avoided being labelled a problem region and, whether by luck or judgement, a successful *laissez-faire* policy was pursued there.

'DAUNTING' THE ISLES

From the government's perspective, the Western Highlands and Islands were regarded as a problem area and a threat to the rest of the kingdom,

[5] See graphics in *Atlas of Scottish History to 1707*, eds P. McNeill and H. L. MacQueen (Scottish Medievalists, Edinburgh, 1996), 241; and discussed in D. Ditchburn, *Scotland and Europe* (East Linton, 2001), 142–9.

best countered by *daunting*. During the fifteenth century, the Lords of the Isles had expanded their territories, and sought to maintain a hold over the earldom of Ross. This eastward movement broke the homogenous unity of their western power base which was held together by the sea; from southern Kintyre to the Butt of Lewis the castles and communication routes all focused upon the western sea lanes (see Map 1.1). By the century's closing decades the lordship was fracturing under its own weight as rival kindreds and antagonisms across Clan Donald's generations disrupted a unified authority under one ruler. John MacDonald, the last Lord of the Isles, was a weak leader whose authority had been fatally damaged in 1476 when he submitted to parliament accepting the loss of Ross, Knapdale and Kintyre as the price for holding his other lands under a new royal charter. Any chance this settlement, much harsher than that for the Northern Isles, would provide the basis of a long-term solution was dashed by the opposition of John's illegitimate son Angus Og, who defeated his father in the sea battle of Bloody Bay off the north-east of Mull in around 1481.

It was a tribute to the lordship's strength that far beyond its natural mainland 'border' it had maintained an eastward drive into Easter Ross; across the Aird into Moray; the Great Glen into Badenoch and Lochaber into Perthshire. Clan Donald's involvement in this broad swathe of the central and northern Highlands and their adjoining lowland areas awakened the suspicion of the crown and brought conflict with a range of new enemies.

By stepping on the toes of the crown and the three most powerful earls – Huntly, Angus and Argyll – the MacDonalds once more put themselves on the political agenda with the label 'trouble' attached. In 1488 Angus Og captured Inverness and raided the surrounding countryside, and in 1491 his cousin, MacDonald of Lochalsh, stormed the burgh's castle, plundering the Sheriff of Cromarty's lands, before being defeated by the Mackenzies at the Battle of the Park (*Blàr na Parc*) in Strathconon. With his own ambitions in Inverness and its environs, Huntly quickly became involved. To the south, Angus perceived a threat in Ayrshire from the MacDonald settlement at Greenan, three miles south of Ayr. The Ayrshire coast and royal Stewart lands in Bute were put at risk from the raids of the Islesmen in the Firth of Clyde. This also affected the Campbell heartland and the earls of Argyll were always concerned about an eastward push from the MacDonalds.

The well-known forfeiture of the Isles in 1493 was very similar to the forfeiture of 1476 and was not planned as total and irrevocable, as it has subsequently been portrayed. It attempted to enforce the concept that all

Map 1.1 The Western Isles

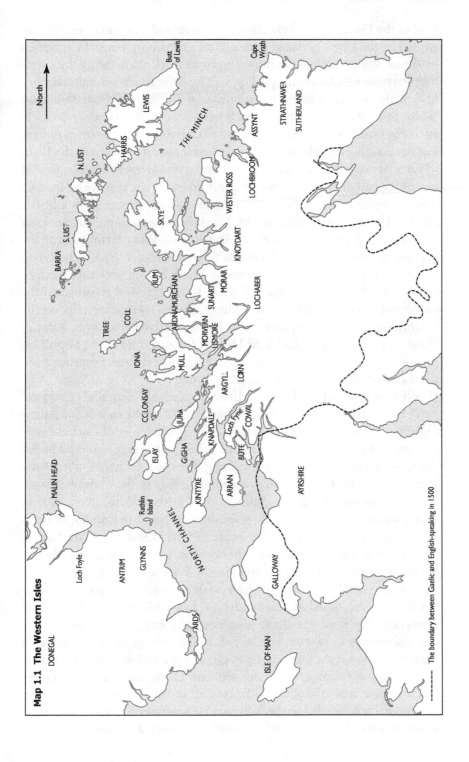

North

DONEGAL

Loch Foyle

MALIN HEAD

ANTRIM

GLYNNS

Rathlin Island

NORTH CHANNEL

ARDS

ISLE OF MAN

KINTYRE

GALLOWAY

ARRAN

BUTE

AYRSHIRE

COWAL

Loch Fyne

KNAPDALE

G.GHA

ISLAY

JURA

ARGYLL

LORN

C.CLONSAY

IONA

MULL

TIREE

COLL

ARDNAMURCHAN

MORVERN

LISMORE

SUNART

RUM

MORAR

LOCHABER

BARRA

S. UIST

SKYE

KNOYDART

N. UIST

HARRIS

THE MINCH

WESTER ROSS

LOCHBROOM

ASSYNT

LEWIS

Butt of Lewis

Cape Wrath

STRATHNAVER

SUTHERLAND

------- The boundary between Gaelic and English-speaking in 1500

land in the kingdom was held from the crown and this was to be demonstrated by the king's personal presence on expedition. James IV travelled
by sea in August 1493 to the imposing royal castle dominating the excellent harbour of Dunstaffnage, Lorn. The impressive ceremonial, including the formal offering of submission by the chiefs of the Isles,
sidestepped the underlying issue of whether these chiefs really wanted to
enter the world of Scottish politics and what it might offer them in return.
For royal authority to be more than a pleasant summer jaunt to the Firth
of Lorn, it needed a regional presence, and in the Western Highlands that
meant the earl of Argyll. The extremely conspicuous absence of the earl
from an event in the heart of his domain gave the proceedings a brittle
quality. The deliberate exclusion of Argyll from national politics between
1493 and 1495 furnished his rival, Angus, with short-term gains at the
expense of the long-term objectives for the Western Isles. The much
vaunted 'daunting' of the Isles was shadow-boxing and the Western
chiefs sensed it. In 1494 James IV came to Kintyre and refurbished the
castle at Tarbert, Loch Fyne, and Dunaverty on its southern tip, on the
assumption they would protect the Firth of Clyde. However, John of
Dunyvaig whose family had held Dunaverty was in no mood to pull his
punches. He retook the castle and allegedly hung its new governor from
the walls in full view of the departing royal fleet.

John, last Lord of the Isles, might have accepted his annual pension of
£133 6s 8d and his fate, but his kin had not. After the murder of Angus
Og in his bed in Inverness by his Irish harper, Alexander of Lochalsh was
recognised by the Council of the Isles as his uncle's successor and he led
the 1491 raid on Inverness. John's young grandson, Donald Dubh, being
kept by his mother's family in protective custody in the Campbell castle
of Innischonnell, also had a claim to the lordship. With other septs of
Clan Donald challenging for the position, the regime in Edinburgh had a
golden opportunity to play the game of divide and rule. MacIain of
Ardnamurchan decided the best chance of enhancing his own authority
lay in co-operation with the government. With a stark ruthlessness, he
became the hatchet man who dealt with the two most powerful contenders for the lordship, Alexander of Lochalsh and MacDonald of
Dunyvaig, which increased the instability of the region and encouraged
the disintegration of the fragile political bonds holding the lordship
together. Without the political foresight and the will to produce a coherent strategy for dealing with the separate chiefs and clans, the crown
failed to gain from the internal fracturing of the lordship. Royal intervention helped destabilise the Western Isles politically, making it harder
to develop the slow process of integration through assimilation.

In contrast to the Northern Isles, the region's clergy were completely embedded within local society, and whilst they acted as cultural bridges between the Scots- and Gaelic-speaking worlds, they were not agents of integration. The majority of serving clerics within the Highlands and Islands came from the Gaelic learned orders, hereditary families who formed a separate section of Gaelic society preserving cultural and artistic skills and crafts. The succession in ecclesiastical benefices from father to son, regarded as a virtue rather than a breach of clerical celibacy, did not prevent these clerics being as active as their Lowland counterparts in taking cases to Rome where they could obtain the necessary dispensations for sons of priests to hold benefices. Two surviving monuments at Ardchattan Priory, a fine family tomb chest and a cross, carved in 1500 by the Iona sculptor John Ó Brolchán, record that Dugall MacDougall succeeded his brother Duncan as Prior of Ardchattan and was followed by Eugenius, a relation, who fathered three sons. The Gaelic clergy, rigorously trained in Gaelic literary culture in addition to the Latin learning of Christendom, were as comfortable in European capitals as they were in the Western Isles; such ecclesiastics were less well acquainted with the Scottish court or Lowlands.

A TRUCE WITH ENGLAND

The minority regime had more than the Western Isles on its mind. They also worried about Scotland's relations with its neighbours. The Estates had granted taxes for expensive diplomatic initiatives to find the young king a bride, though without success. The alliance with France had been renewed in March 1492, facilitated by the strong undercurrent of anti-English sentiment in Scotland, illustrated by the careful manuscript copies made by Prior Ramsay in 1488 and 1489 of Blind Harry's poetical celebration of William Wallace and Barbour's stirring epic of Robert Bruce (see Figure 1.2). Wood of Largo, a poacher turned gamekeeper, captured some English pirate ships which had ventured into the Forth, an exploit widely acclaimed by his contemporaries and handed down in Fife as a swashbuckling yarn for Pitscottie to include in his later history. However, the Scots were fortunate Henry VII of England was anxious to maintain peace and a seven-year truce was concluded in 1493 reflecting the Anglophile influence of Angus and Bishop Elphinstone. It offered a basic, if unglamorous, stability undermined the following year by the European diplomatic revolution caused by the French invasion of Italy.

In 1494 James IV reached his twenty-first birthday and celebrated the

Harping

Harpers and their music were found all over Scotland with the most-prized performers coming from Gaelic society. Harps were played by male professionals and by amateurs of both sexes using two types of harp, the brass wire-strung *clarsach*, preferred in the Highlands, and the gut-strung harp, and a quill or the nails on the left hand to pluck the instrument. The three surviving instruments, the 'Queen Mary' and Lamont harps in the National Museum and the third in Dublin, were all constructed in the Argyll–Perthshire area, showing similarities with the clarsach and other decoration carved on stones at Keills in Knapdale. The use of hornbeam, imported from England, and the elaborate decoration on Queen Mary's harp indicated the instrument's high value, reflected in the 20s compensation awarded Agnes MacDonald when her harp was taken from her in 1490. Within Gaelic society, as well as providing its own musical entertainment, harping accompanied the recitation of bardic verse. A professional harping family, such as the MacEwans, were able to serve the earls of Argyll as poets and *sennachies* (clan historians) as well as harpists. James IV appreciated a good harpist, sending 14s in reward after he had been entertained during a visit to Tain. From the middle of the sixteenth century, 'ports', or distinctive harping tunes, were developed to provide instrumental music, with the earliest datable tune, 'Port Robart', composed in the 1570s for the musical patron, Robert Stewart, commendator of St Andrews and bishop of Caithness. These tunes were taken up by lutanists and reflect the rise of the lute – Mary, Queen of Scots' preferred instrument. In the Highlands, the *clarsach* remained an important part of the culture of a chief's household, though on the battlefield it was superseded by the bagpipes (see the box on bagpipes, p. 169). As the sixteenth century progressed, Scotland's common heritage of harping gradually disappeared as the lute replaced the harp at the royal court and in country houses.

birth of his first child, an illegitimate daughter born to his current mistress, Marion Boyd. Displaying a maturity beyond his years, James did not grab the first opportunity to take personal control of the kingdom but waited patiently for the political dust to settle. By changing the composition of his Council and bringing Argyll and Drummond back from the political wilderness, James signalled to the political community he was

Figure 1.2 Prior John Ramsay's manuscript copy of Barbour's *Bruce*, 1489. [NLS Adv MS 19.2.2]

making the decisions. Unlike the drastic methods of other Stewart kings on emerging from their minorities, he did not feel the necessity of excluding Bothwell and the Hepburns from all political power.

James IV's succession had been irregular but, unlike Henry VII of England, he was not a usurper, and Scots accepted without question his right to rule. Sauchieburn had left a legacy of feud and instability which time slowly diminished. The three crises of 1488, 1489 and 1492 had rocked the minority regime, though they had brought a broadening of the faction in control and more balance in the distribution of royal favour and justice. The emergence of rival archdioceses created a division that hampered the Scottish church until the Reformation. The differing treatment accorded the Northern and Western Isles was significant and boded ill for future assumptions about their place within the kingdom, though the irrevocable nature of the 1493 forfeiture of the lordship only became plain with hindsight. By 1495 the rocky years of rebellion were over, leaving the opprobrium of unpopular policies to fall upon the minority regime and not the young king; he could enjoy a fresh start.

CHAPTER 2

The Thistle and the Rose:
James IV (1495–1504)

The country was ready to make a fresh start in 1495 for it now possessed that asset so prized among kingdoms of the day, an adult male monarch in the prime of his life, a 'lusty' king in every sense. James displayed all the physical self-confidence of a healthy, well-muscled young man who was good at sports and enjoyed demonstrating his prowess on the tournament or hunting fields and in his lovemaking. He was an immensely active ruler who delighted to leave the paperwork to others, whilst he energetically travelled the country. Though the king was perpetually on the move wearing out his household and sometimes driving his administration to distraction, he put his itchy feet to good use by personally dispensing justice throughout his kingdom. Even if thinking about the next day's hunting, James was prepared to sit on the bench and be seen to give judgement in his traditional role as law-giver and enforcer of justice. He was a master of the art of the personal appearance, popping up all over his kingdom, chatting to his subjects about mending shoes, pulling out a tooth or healing a 'sair' leg, and delighting in bestowing a deliberately excessive reward, such as the gift of nine shillings to the child bringing him apples at Dumbarton. By conforming so well to the popular stereotype of liberality in a ruler and most of all by simply being there, James built up a store of good will which functioned as a protective blanket insulating him from the unpopularity of particular policies.

THE WARRIOR LEADER

His real enthusiasm lay in being a warrior leader, a key attribute of medieval kingship. James had a straightforward view of his role: he led his subjects into battle, fighting in the front ranks, using his weapon skills and sharing the dangers. As the Spanish ambassador, Pedro Ayala, recorded in 1497 the king, 'said to me that his subjects serve him with their persons and goods, in just and unjust quarrels, exactly as he likes, and that, therefore, he does not think it right to begin any warlike undertaking without being himself the first in danger'.[1]

James' visit to the Isles in the early summer of 1495 enabled him to learn about mounting a military expedition and over the previous winter he involved himself in the elaborate naval preparations. In May the king sailed to Kintyre, accompanied by most of his Council, including Argyll whose regional power was essential for the implementation of royal policy. In a gesture of support for MacIain, James sailed to the Sound of Mull, staying in Mingary Castle in Ardnamurchan where, as local tradition recounts, he hunted boar. This armed royal progress brought the king's presence and favour to those loyal to the crown. Its success gave the progress the feel of military manoeuvres instead of warfare and going to the Isles furnished a good demonstration for domestic consumption of firm rule. However, in the military stakes, winning a provincial match was not the same as competing in the international championship; that involved fighting against England. The young king sought to prove to himself, his fellow monarchs and his subjects that he was a fully-fledged war leader who could manage a proper campaign as well as win personal honour on the battlefield.

PERKIN WARBECK AND WAR WITH ENGLAND

The start of James' personal rule was marked by a shift in foreign policy, especially in relation to England since the emergence of Perkin Warbeck, the pretender to the English throne, was too good an opportunity to miss. Warbeck arrived in Scotland following a failed rising in Ireland and the previous July James had entertained O'Donnell of Tyrconnell (modern Donegal), in Glasgow, making an alliance and discussing Warbeck. While the Scottish king was well aware of using Ireland as a means of exerting pressure upon a weak spot in the Tudor state, his interest in the English pretender was essentially as a pawn in the European diplomatic game. The French invasion of Italy in 1494 had ushered in a new diplomatic era and created two unstable alliance blocks. In this febrile atmosphere James had to manoeuvre very carefully to be taken seriously by the monarchs of the Empire and Spain as well as his traditional ally of France and old

[1] Cited and discussed in N. Macdougall, *James IV* (Edinburgh, 1989), 286.

enemy England. Supporting Warbeck was a significant diplomatic move, though an expensive one with the merchants of the burghs north of the Forth paying most of the pretender's annual pension of £1,344. Catherine Gordon, Huntly's daughter, was expected to think of Scotland when she performed her duty by marrying Warbeck; she had the consolation of an expensive court wedding in January 1496 at Edinburgh Castle with tournament included. Military support for the pretender provided an excellent diplomatic cover for war with England, but was not its cause as the September timing of James' campaign revealed. By the time the following year's campaign was underway Warbeck, no longer a useful asset, had been packed off to Ireland. A relieved Andrew Forman, having performed the thankless task of escorting the pretender, was rewarded with the commendatorship of Pittenweem.

The military campaigns against England of September 1496 and July 1497 allowed James to shine as a leader of men. His flamboyant challenge to fight in single combat for Berwick signalled to his countrymen that recovering the burgh had not been forgotten. The immediate strategy was more pragmatic, combining large-scale raids across the Border with attacks upon fortifications in the English East March. James wanted to employ a full artillery train in war and to test his bronze cannon, the 'must-have' military hardware of his age. A vast quantity of oxen and an army of labourers were required to move the guns to the Tweed, including the mighty Mons Meg, trundled out of Edinburgh to the sound of music. Although it took a pounding that damaged the West Gate, Norham Castle did not fall; the experience gained did help in the successful assault during the Flodden campaign. The fighting produced no spectacular Scottish success and the planned English retaliation was disrupted by the Western rebellion and that all-purpose excuse, the weather. James' military gambles had luck on their side and, as legend related, divine help. 'Our Lady of the Steil [salmon pool]' miraculously saved the king from drowning after he had fallen into the Tweed. In thanks James vowed a church to the Virgin Mary which could not be destroyed by fire, and the distinctive stone-vaulted and tiled roof of Ladykirk with its stone interior furnishings and impressive watch-tower was built. This fortified church, located on the bank opposite Norham Castle, protected the preferred fording-point on the Tweed. If James rode his luck in 1496–7 he made the most of the lessons he learned. As well as being popular in Scotland, the war against the English established James' credibility among his fellow rulers, generating sufficient diplomatic capital for him to operate successfully in European power politics.

STRENGTHENING DOMESTIC CONTROL

In 1497 James made two crucial moves in domestic politics: appointing his brother as archbishop of St Andrews and removing Angus from political power. Swiftly following his loss of the chancellorship to Huntly, Angus found himself warded first in Dumbarton and then for seven years on the island of Bute. This sustained level of royal suspicion was fed by Bothwell, Angus' inveterate enemy and Borders rival. Being a Douglas, the earl's name evoked mistrust, making his fellow peers less than sympathetic to his fate, especially following the renewed agreement with his relative Hugh, dean of Brechin, to pursue the claims to the carldom of Douglas. The shadow of past history fell across the filling of the vacancy created by the death of Archbishop Scheves on 28 January 1497. By moving James, duke of Ross, into the church and out of dynastic reckoning, the king shrewdly disarmed the potential threat a legitimate royal brother might pose. Alongside its dynastic advantages, the appointment demonstrated James IV's intention to bring the highest office of the Scottish church within the royal family and treat the most lucrative ecclesiastical benefices as a supplement to the family's income. Controlling the church directly and drawing extensively upon its revenues marked an important stage on the path of convergence between church and crown. This scandalous appointment was meekly accepted by the Scottish hierarchy after Elphinstone's protest, based on the canon law principles enunciated by Tudeschis, fell on deaf royal and papal ears. James IV further sweetened the deal with his brother in subsequent years by adding the lucrative monastic commendatorships of Holyrood, Dunfermline and Arbroath. The addition of the chancellorship in 1501 gave the archbishop the highest status, after the crown, though Bishop Elphinstone actually administered the Great Seal as well as the Privy Seal, properly in his keeping. As a member of the daily Council, the archbishop took his turn sitting on the session on civil causes and might have developed his own political presence at court if he had not died unexpectedly in 1504.

ECCLESIASTICAL AND EDUCATIONAL REFORM

If he could not prevent inappropriate church appointments, the bishop of Aberdeen could institute some ecclesiastical reform, beginning at home. According to Hector Boece, his admiring biographer, he set a personal example of piety, and frequently spoke of the Passion of Christ, collecting sermons and meditations on the subject and praying all night on

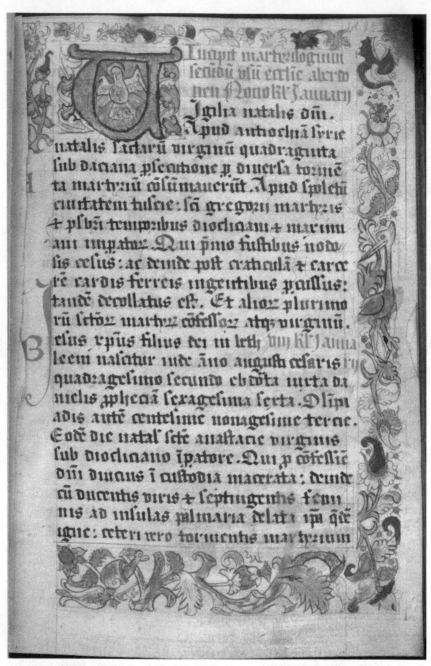

Figure 2.1 Martyrology of the Use of Aberdeen produced for Elgin Cathedral, c. 1550s. [EUL MS 50 f. 25r]

the eve of Good Friday. Elphinstone carefully performed his pastoral duties, and by fighting to retain control over diocesan appointments improved clerical standards. His liturgical innovations (see p. 70) and the development of the Use of Aberdeen spread into the neighbouring diocese of Moray, as seen in the later Martyrology (see Figure 2.1) whose amateurish illustration shows Scottish illumination was some way behind the standard of the Low Countries.

More ambitious ecclesiastical reforms needed royal and papal approval and in 1495 he secured both when he obtained a papal bull founding a university in Aberdeen. King's College, originally called St Mary's, was formally erected in 1505 and refounded in 1514 and, being well acquainted with financial matters, Elphinstone ensured it was properly endowed. The college offered a balance of subjects, with theology, canon and civil law and medicine in addition to the basic arts curriculum. One of Elphinstone's chief aims was inculcating clergy with the spirit of Christian humanism and King's first doctor of theology was John Adamson, later Provincial of the Scottish Dominicans. Laymen were explicitly included and the college improved legal training in Scotland, having both a civilist and a canonist on its foundation. A similar concern lay behind the 1496 Act of Parliament calling for a school in each parish to ensure the sons of nobility were literate and able to discharge their legal duties. During the next century, a demand for legal expertise in all law courts increased and influenced government thinking and procedure.

Portraiture

Bishop Elphinstone in his episcopal vestments and mitre is portrayed in a fine painting on wood that has remained in his university foundation of Aberdeen. It is one of the earliest and finest portraits of a Scottish subject to survive and was probably painted by a Scots artist using Flemish techniques. In religious art the earliest likenesses can be found with clerics, such as Deans Bonkill (Trinity Altar) and Brown and Archbishop Blackadder (prayerbooks), and the royal family (Trinity Altar and the prayerbooks of James IV and Margaret Tudor). James IV and James V did have their portraits painted in a courtly setting, but there was a surprising gap in Mary's personal reign. Given her upbringing in the Valois court, where as a princess she was drawn and painted by top European artists, such as the beautiful Clouet sketches, Mary did not commission adult portraits, with the exception of the joint portrait with Darnley (now at Hardwick Hall). The queen reflected a Scottish pattern, where displaying heraldic identities, leaving an architectural

Portraiture (continued)

memorial or an elaborate tomb seemed more important than a portrait. Most of the surviving noble portraits were directly connected to the Low Countries where Mark Ker and Helen Leslie were painted at the end of the 1550s, their half-length figures showing the Newbattle Commendator in a civilian, though sober, outfit and Helen, holding a piece of music in her hand, wearing a dark dress with rose-coloured sleeves. Hans Eworth's sensitively painted 1561 wedding portraits (see Figure 11.1) were as beautifully executed as the expressive miniatures commemorating the brief marriage of the earl of Bothwell and Jane Gordon, showing her looking self-possessed in her fashionable dress and her husband in his buttoned-up gold doublet, 'with the uncomfortable look of hyper-active people when they are asked to sit still'.[2] Seton commissioned two portraits in the Netherlands in the 1570s, the first showing his elaborate red garments and distinctive wand of Mary's Master of the Royal Household and a family portrait (see Figure 13.1). Portraits were completed of the Regents, Moray, Mar and Morton, with Van Bronckhorst painting Morton sporting a tall black hat as part of his work as court painter to James VI. Making the young king sit for his picture might have contributed to his extreme dislike of the practice later in life. During their English childhood portraits were painted of Darnley and his younger brother, with marriage prospects in mind and after Darnley's murder the countess of Lennox commissioned the 'revenge' portrait. Scots had been slow to show their faces to the world, though by the end of the century the fashion had spread down the social ladder with lairds such as Campbell of Glenorchy or Napier of Merchiston spending money on large portraits.

EXPLOITING CROWN LANDS

Whilst the financial resources of the church were the long-term solution to balancing the royal budget, other measures were also required. Customs revenues could not easily be raised thanks to sluggish trade and the use of middlemen or 'farmers' to collect the rates upon taxed goods, giving the crown a flat sum and taking a profit for themselves. However, income from the crown's lands and rights as feudal superior could be

[2] M. Sanderson, *Mary Stewart's People* (Edinburgh, 1987), 38.

increased. One blanket method was to use an Act of Revocation, annulling all royal grants made during a king's minority. The nobility were prepared to tolerate this blunt instrument because it imposed a time limit on the rewards taken by minority regimes. Having reached his twenty-fifth birthday on 17 March 1498, James issued a revocation, though most lands were reissued after payment for a new charter. The chiefs of the Western Isles, with their recently-bestowed charters, found they had to repeat the process, making it hard for them to recognise any benefit from holding their land directly from the crown.

From the mid-1490s the crown's tenants-in-chief faced a permanent campaign to increase revenue through the exploitation of royal rights as their feudal superior. A more efficient method of keeping records created a land register, allowing royal officials to track land transactions and identify breaches of crown rights. Administrators searched for vassals who had alienated more than half their lands or had failed to be 'served heir'. The crown could then 'recognosce' the alienated lands to establish who held them and charge an heir for 'non-entry'. Once found to have breached these undeniable feudal rights, individuals had little option but to negotiate the size of the payment. Those who could not, or would not, pay faced losing their lands through legal action. Persistent criticism from chroniclers and poets of these oppressive practices emphasised the way confiscation or payments were passed down the tenurial chain to those who actually worked the land. Struggling royal officials investigated the leasing of crown lands, ensuring rents were properly collected and, where possible, increased, hitting landholders enjoying low or token payments, granted in return for past service. This straw in the wind signalled the gradual shift over the next century to treating land as a cash-creating resource rather than a provider of service and men.

In 1502 to maximise revenue, the £20 crown lands of Rannoch were taken from Stewart of Fortingall who had held them rent-free for past service, and feued to his neighbour, Menzies of Weem, who was prepared to pay £60 a year and risk pledging all his other lands. Despite having the relevant documents with a royal seal, this did not automatically change occupation on the ground. Menzies had been granted the bailiery of the Appin of Dull, but he lacked the local support and the military muscle to enforce his authority when Stewart of Fortingall fought for his hereditary lands, raiding the Appin of Dull, burning Weem and imprisoning Menzies in Garth Castle. In his campaign Stewart had the active or tacit support of his powerful neighbours, the Campbells of Glenorchy and the MacGregors, neither of whom wanted a dominant

Menzies presence in their area. The king came riding up to Perth, obtained Menzies' release, punished Stewart and commissioned Huntly to serve as royal 'enforcer' in the area. In the long term, although Stewart was dispossessed, Menzies failed to establish himself in Rannoch and struggled to pay his dues to the crown. Royal fiscal demands had dislocated landholding, brought disruption and raiding, and created a power vacuum. Since Huntly could not establish a permanent influence this far south the major beneficiaries were the MacGregors, who occupied Rannoch in the following two decades by 'sword right', helped by their current allies and protectors, the Glenorchy Campbells. The blind implementation of James IV's financial policy with scant regard for the immediate local consequences or the long-term political balance of the region produced a serious problem that remained until the seventeenth century. The crown was capable of dispossessing a tenant-in-chief, but the replacement had to be strong enough to establish his own control. Rannoch provided a smaller-scale example of similar disruptive effects caused by royal policies within the larger region of the Lordship of the Isles.

THE DANISH AND ENGLISH ALLIANCES

In 1501 King Hans of Denmark faced a rebellion from his Swedish subjects and under the terms of his 1492 alliance sought military aid from his Scottish nephew. James saw the opportunity for military glory and obtained a massive war tax of £12,000. The expedition was commanded by Arran, aided by Sinclair, the former Danish royal servant, and assisted by Hume's military experience. Service abroad was unpopular and levies from the sheriffdoms of Fife and Forfar had to be augmented by offering enlistment as an alternative to prison. To supplement the royal vessels, ships were required to transport the army and Seton promised his ship, the *Eagle*, and was paid £400 to re-equip it. After endless delays the exasperated king went to Inverkeithing to speed up the refitting and though the music-loving Seton dispatched his minstrel to play soothing music to pacify James, he still faced a swingeing fine of £1853 13s 4d. The Scottish force eventually sailed from Leith with about 2,000 troops on board, arriving too late to help Queen Christina hold Stockholm. The expedition was a costly mess and more an embarrassment than a help to Denmark. The 1502 fiasco made James determined to prepare better in the future and within a couple of years he had begun in earnest to construct a royal navy.

Andrew Halyburton and the Scottish staple

Andrew Halyburton was an Edinburgh merchant based in Flanders whose business ledger has survived, revealing the patterns of trade in the final years of the fifteenth century. He handled on his own and others' behalf the primary products that comprised the bulk of Scottish exports, particularly wool, and in return imported luxury goods, especially wine and spices, such as pepper and ginger, clothes, featherbeds and cushions. Halyburton's wife, Cornelia, the daughter of the painter Sander Bening, connected him to the Flemish artistic community, helping him supply works of art for his Scottish customers or arrange for Piers the painter (Peeken Bovelant) to come to James IV's court. Ecclesiastics relied upon him to procure church vestments, plate and liturgical books, such as Dean Brown of Aberdeen's beautifully-illustrated Prayer Book, and the St Andrews Archbishops Scheves and Stewart commissioned their elaborate tombstones while their archdeacon purchased 1,000 floor tiles, and Elphinstone of Aberdeen added gunpowder to his long shopping list. Since he already dealt in many European currencies, Halyburton offered a basic banking service for clerics and laymen needing money to be sent to Rome for business in the courts. Holding the position of Conservator of Scottish privileges in the Low Countries during the 1490s made him Scotland's economic negotiator, diplomatic representative and cultural linkman. Trading partners agreed to sell their products through specific ports, or staples, where their merchants were granted special privileges. Situated in the busy Scheldt estuary, Halyburton and the Scottish Staple traded from the Zeeland ports of Middleburg, Veere and Bergen-op-Zoom. Scottish overseas trade was still recovering from the long slump that began with the Wars of Independence and continued until the last quarter of the sixteenth century, as it struggled to find additional exports to compensate for the decline in the trade in raw wool.

Meanwhile, negotiations for peace with England were going well, led by that wily ecclesiastic and consummate diplomat, Andrew Forman. Since Henry VII was anxious to avoid war with Scotland, he was prepared to offer his daughter's hand as part of a new alliance. On 17 December 1502 James sealed his formal ratification of the grandiloquent-sounding Treaty of Perpetual Peace, beautifully illustrated by the court painter, Sir Thomas Galbraith, with the illuminated initial capital 'J' of the marriage contract displaying delicate, white marguerites and bright-red, flat Tudor roses entwined around pinky-purple Scottish thistles. Inevitably, the 'thrissill and the rois' became the catchphrase of the alliance and the ubiquitous logo for the wedding. The thistle, having been James III's personal badge, became one of the kingdom's heraldic emblems, utilised by the poet William Dunbar to symbolise the king's duty to protect and defend his realm.

WEDDING CELEBRATIONS

In Scotland a royal wedding and the prospect of a legitimate heir were most welcome, though James had already proved his fertility. Such a positive response did not necessarily extend to his bride; anti-English feeling remained high in the kingdom which had disliked James III's Anglophile foreign policy and approved his son's war against the English in 1496–7. Although the English alliance made good sense given the European diplomatic situation, James needed to present it in the best possible light and a wedding allowed him to use spectacle to convey the positive benefits of the alliance. The self-confident Scottish king was able to display his sophistication and culture on the international stage and the master of informal kingship could demonstrate he was equally proficient on a formal stage.

Like most royal brides, Margaret had to leave home and travel to a foreign country to marry a man she had not seen. The thirteen-year-old was initially accompanied by her father Henry VII, who had recently lost both his elder son and his wife. His gift of a Book of Hours personally inscribed 'Remembre your kynde and lovyng fader in your good prayers. Henry R' suggested the parting was not easy.[3] The leisurely progress north gave Margaret time to become familiar with the separation and to practise acting as a queen. Riding on her white horse surrounded by her 500-strong entourage, Margaret arrived in Dalkeith, ten miles south of Edinburgh. James paid an unscheduled visit, putting Margaret at her ease with the sure touch of a ladies' man by chatting, having a game of cards and playing some music on his lute for her. On the last stage of her journey he sent a tame hart as a stylised declaration of courtly love, though with more concern for poetic symbolism than the dinner table, the hart was allowed to elude the hounds.

The couple came together for the first set-piece celebration at the formal entry into Edinburgh when Margaret was presented with the

---

[3] Cited in L. Bowdith, *The Thistle and the Rose Exhibition Catalogue* (Stirling Castle, 2002), 13.

Table 2.1 The royal line with the Hamiltons and the Lennox Stewarts

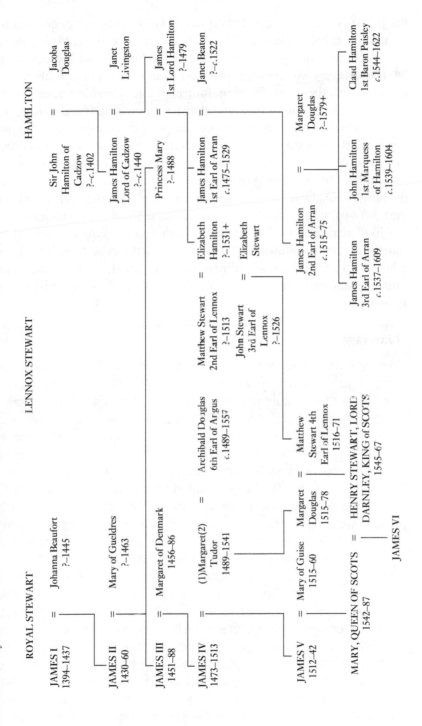

burgh's keys. The first sight the capital had of their future queen was her riding pillion behind James. The studied gesture of the lad bringing his lass home gave way to the ritual of pageants, bursting with classical and biblical imagery concerning love and marriage. Seeing four women standing with their feet placed on four men's necks made a great spectacle: such an inversion of the natural order was acceptable, providing the women represented the four Virtues trampling their respective vices, and portrayed the benefits flowing from beneficent royal rule. It did not reflect the power balance within the royal marriage nor challenge the gender roles upheld by sixteenth-century society. As well as enjoying the show, the burgh's inhabitants drank the wine flowing from the fountain next to the newly-painted town cross and witnessed with pride the reliquary with St Giles' arm processed from their burgh church. James extended the courtly gesture of allowing Margaret to kiss the relic first. The Entry achieved an effective combination of religious ritual, elaborate pageantry and the vital ingredient of making the mystery of royalty visible and accessible.

Marriage

Marriage was an extremely important institution for the whole of Scottish society and being a sacrament it was carefully regulated by the courts spiritual. The canonical minimum age for marriage was fourteen for a man and twelve for a woman, though this was of little relevance to the lower levels of society whose marital age was determined more by the economic ability to establish a household. Multiple marriages were common in Scotland, with widows and widowers usually remarrying, so that major age differences often existed between husband and wife. Despite losing its sacramental status at the Reformation, the kirk insisted weddings should take place publicly, 'in the face of the congregation', and even greater efforts were made to regulate marriage and sexual behaviour through the kirk sessions. In a legal context, many canon law prescriptions were transferred from the pre-Reformation courts spiritual into the civil Commissary Courts which, from 1564, dealt with marital matters. The crown's assumption of jurisdiction led to friction between the courts and the Kirk, for example over the exact grounds for divorce. In a social context, marriage was treated more as an alliance between kin groups than a choice by individuals. For most levels of Scottish society, especially those with property, pre-nuptial negotiations were complex, involving fathers, or senior male relatives, bargaining over the tocher (dowry) and the marriage portion.

Agreements and betrothals made when the couple were young children were often broken as kin alliances changed. In the pre-Reformation period, the 'forbidden degrees', or extensive list of prohibited partners, ensured that before 1560 nearly every Scottish noble required an ecclesiastical dispensation to marry, providing a subsequent loophole whereby an unwanted marriage was annulled. Such flexibility disappeared under the kirk which gradually imposed its norms upon Scottish society. Women, such as Lady Glenorchy during the 1560s and 1570s, took the lead in arranging their children's marriages, sorting out possible partners and judging the couple's likely compatibility, and sometimes a female 'match-maker' was used as a formal go-between. In theory within this patriarchal society, husbands ruled their wives and their households; in practice many wives directed affairs, such as the countess of Moray and Argyll, whose second husband was criticised for allowing himself to be hen-pecked. Wife-beating was a problem the kirk sessions sought to reduce, though within limits it remained socially acceptable. Though the song's focus was upon the misalliance, rather than the beating, the 'Wee Cooper o Fife' in the ballad was able to beat his well-born wife, because she was not used to working with her hands, nor was she willing to do so. Women were perfectly capable of their own violence and in 1535 Alison Rough and her daughter Katherine murdered Katherine's thrice-married and much older husband. Alison was drowned, but Katherine, being pregnant, escaped execution, and after the birth fled to England and became the wife of the Protestant exile Alexander Alane.

The wedding celebrations were an exclusively courtly spectacle and the following day the marriage took place in the chapel of Holyrood Abbey, literally built into the royal palace extensively refurbished to provide suitable accommodation for the newly-weds. Both bride and groom wore white and Hamilton, the king's cousin and master of ceremonies, had been given sixteen ells of white damask flowered with gold for his outfit, because he was one of three earls being belted to add an extra flourish to the occasion. Demonstrating his effortless confidence, James decided his young queen should be crowned on her wedding day instead of waiting until the birth of her first child. In a more spontaneous gesture, 'the King transported himself into the Pallais, thorough the Clostre, holdynge all-wayes the Qwene by the Bodye . . . tyll he had brought hyr within her Chammer'. At the subsequent banquet with its fifteen courses, the heralds proclaimed the royal titles, with James insisting his wife's 'largess' take precedence and then nonchalantly dismissing his own with the comment, 'it souffysed to cry hers'.[4] James' natural sense of theatre enabled him to find this disarming way of dismissing the English claims to sovereignty over Scotland which no-one had been impolite enough to mention at the wedding.

The positive benefits of the union between the two neighbouring realms were elegantly celebrated in Dunbar's poem *The Thrissill and the Rois*. The image of the rose, the symbol of the Virgin Mary and the goddess Venus, allowed the court poet to elaborate upon Margaret's virtues and offer a sharp moral reminder to her husband that his days of dalliance should be over. The vernacular song 'Now fayre, fayrest off every fayre' gave a joyous polyphonic celebration of Margaret's imperial blood, singing,

> Welcum the rose bothe rede & whyte
> welcum the floure of oure delyte
> oure sacrate [sacred] joy syne [then] from thee beme
> welcum of Scotland to be quene.[5]

The elaborate conventions of courtly love and Arthurian romance with the knight striving to prove himself and win his lady made an obvious focus for the tournament which occupied the following days. As an impressive jouster the new earl of Arran displayed his chivalric accomplishments, so recently recognised by his noble title.

At the end of the tournament most of Margaret's English entourage departed, having striven not to be impressed by the five days of celebrations, and tried to avoid mental comparisons with the dowdy court of the elderly widower, Henry VII. With £6,125 spent, the cost was enormous, though, with the exception of James' new father-in-law, fellow monarchs held such expenditure as money well spent. James had shown Scotland could stage a spectacle packed with the latest European fashions, replete with ostentatious display combining courtly music, poetry and drama with the stylised aristocratic pleasures of joust and chase. Since the Scottish king wanted to be taken seriously, such a show was expected by members of the exclusive and expensive 'club' of European rulers.

The intangible benefits of spectacle helped increase the sense of national identity and associate the regions with royal policy. Although

---

[4] Cited and discussed in L. O. Fradenburg, *City, Marriage, Tournament* (Madison, WI, 1991), 105.
[5] Cited and discussed in Fradenburg, *City, Marriage, Tournament*, 109. The song is not now attributed to Dunbar.

Edinburgh was the setting for the main event, other burghs put on pageants when the queen visited. Margaret made a ceremonial entry to the royal palace sites of Stirling and Linlithgow, the archiepiscopal seats of Glasgow and St Andrews and the leading eastern burghs of Dundee, Perth and Aberdeen. As all Tudors revelled in formal deference and stately pageantry, Margaret enjoyed these occasions and especially the new dresses. In the first few months she had been badly homesick before settling in Scotland and enjoying a carefree three years before beginning her royal and female duty of producing heirs.

The royal wedding provided one of the high points of James IV's reign, its confidence and panache showing how far the realm had come since the trauma of his father's killing. Having survived the early crises, the king had found himself in smoother waters and had taken personal control without any awkward break in regimes. As yet, there were few signs of the longer-term problems caused by the weakness of royal finances and the disruption created by crown interference in the regions. James' initial good fortune had helped him develop sound judgement and a relaxed style allowing him to work easily with the magnates. He had proved himself as a warrior leader, a bringer of justice and was set fair to secure his dynasty with a legitimate heir. Based on the brimming self-confidence noted by the Spanish ambassador who recorded, 'He esteems himself as much as though he were lord of the world', James had fashioned himself into the archetypal ideal of a medieval king.[6]

---

[6] Cited and discussed in N. Macdougall, *James IV* (Edinburgh, 1989), 287.

CHAPTER 3

Strutting the European Stage: James IV (1503–13)

J ames' marriage marked a staging point in his reign. The long backward
   shadow cast by the union of the crowns in 1603 obscured its contemporary relevance. In the dynastic lottery, James' marriage brought interesting possibilities since Henry VII did not remarry after his wife's death
and he had lost his elder son, Arthur. The Scottish king had a place in the
English succession for his children or even himself should Henry, Prince
of Wales die. When he was conducting Anglo-Scottish diplomacy, this
put a useful card in James' hand.

The Stewart succession was the more pressing matter for most Scots
who wanted their king to fulfil his primary duty of providing a male heir,
if possible with time to reach maturity before inheriting. James did not
appear in a hurry and, even after the death of his first three children with
Margaret, he had none of Henry VIII's paranoid dread about successfully
fathering an heir. To the great rejoicing of the kingdom on 21 February
1507 the queen was delivered of a son, though mother and baby were seriously ill and James travelled to Whithorn on foot to implore the aid of St
Ninian. The king and queen later returned to the shrine to give thanks
for the saint's intervention, but their son died the following February. It
was not until 12 April 1512, when the future James V was born, that the
Stewart dynasty was secured.

INCREASING CONTROL OVER THE CHURCH

The king already had seven illegitimate children being raised in a royal
nursery in Stirling Castle, and he designated for the church Alexander,
his son by Marion Boyd, to continue his strategy of using the royal family
to draw the church closer to the crown. Alexander, having been carefully

educated, was sent to Italy, the cultural centre of Europe, where he was tutored by Erasmus, the most glittering star in the humanist firmament. The quiet and short-sighted boy endeared himself to his teachers as he developed into an excellent scholar with a profound love of music. Following the death of James, archbishop designate of St Andrews, and sooner than the king planned, Alexander was nominated to the vacant diocese. Although only eleven years old, Alexander showed every sign of becoming a good churchman, making this appointment less scandalous than the uncle he replaced. The swift insertion of his son as Scottish primate indicated that James would not relinquish the lucrative revenues of the archdiocese, nor slacken his grip upon Scotland's ecclesiastical hierarchy. Such a policy provoked no major outcry from the papacy or the Scottish church. The two dominant churchmen, Blackadder at Glasgow and Elphinstone of Aberdeen, were king's men and knew how royal expenditure outstripped normal revenue.

The use of ecclesiastical benefices to provide salaries for royal administrators had a long pedigree and did not automatically produce bad ecclesiastics, as the bishop of Aberdeen's own career proved. An already creaking system was placed under greater strain by the increasing use of dispensations to permit church revenues being held without entering the necessary sacramental or regular orders. The fight over the church's plum prizes could be intense as in the three-year battle between Dundas, a Hospitaller knight, and Paniter, the royal secretary, over the Preceptory of the Hospitallers at Torphichen. In recommending his secretary James employed underhand tactics, accusing Dundas of associating with the English and not being fit for a Scottish benefice. No paragon, Paniter had had an affair with Margaret Crichton, the illegitimate daughter of Princess Margaret, the king's aunt, producing a son who later became bishop of Ross. Margaret, having been conveniently married in 1506 to an Edinburgh burgess, developed a career based in the capital, subsequently acting as a customs collector. Although opposing Alexander's appointment on canon law grounds, Elphinstone was sufficient of a pragmatist to calculate that the support of a strong king whose conventional piety was a conspicuous aspect of his rule was worth a slice of the church's revenues.

The pope was a major player in European diplomacy whose dual role as Italian prince and spiritual head of Christendom complicated his relations with other rulers. For a small kingdom on the European periphery, Scotland conducted a remarkable quantity of business in Rome and the Stewarts kept on good terms with the Holy Father. James had already received several marks of papal esteem, the Golden Rose in 1491 followed

Figure 3.1 The Scottish crown, sceptre and sword of state. [Historic Scotland]

by a sceptre in 1494, and Julius II, the warrior pope, appropriately sent a sword of state in 1507 (see Figure 3.1). Two years later a similar sword and hat were given to Poland–Lithuania, ranking Scotland in papal esteem alongside that far larger kingdom. During a magnificent High Mass in Holyrood Abbey on Easter Sunday James was presented with the sword, scabbard and embroidered belt, along with a hat, now lost, probably embroidered with a golden dove decorated with pearls, symbolising the Holy Spirit. Alongside the crown, the sceptre and sword formed the Honours of Scotland, carried as visual symbols of majesty and authority, remaining in use today.

The papal gifts signalled Rome would continue to allow James to nominate to Scottish benefices and in 1508 the unexpected death of Robert Blackadder, drowned whilst on pilgrimage to the Holy Land, left the archbishopric of Glasgow vacant. The nomination of James Beaton indicated that Scottish archbishops would continue to be drawn from the ranks of trusted royal servants and this appointment marked the beginning of the dynasty of clerical Beatons who played a central role within the Scottish church and government. The vacancy allowed James to extract concessions from the archdiocese of Glasgow over its jurisdictional feud with St Andrews, to prevent that rift from getting worse. When the lucrative diocese of Moray became vacant, it went as a reward and substantial future salary to the invaluable administrator, Andrew Forman. Royal service was manifestly the ladder for ecclesiastical preferment and as the reign progressed the higher ranks of the church increasingly resembled a department of government.

In the case of the secular dioceses the king was primarily interested in political control, but when he turned his eye to the regular orders in Scotland he saw massive financial resources in monastic hands. The abbeys, holding much of Scotland's best land, boasted the largest incomes in the kingdom and were to become an essential supplement to royal income. The first step was to exploit the commendator system, whereby a person could become an abbot without joining the appropriate monastic order. As the chronicler Abell observed, this led candidates for the headship of religious houses to seek to impress within the king's chamber rather than the monastic chapter, where their appointment should have been decided. When the abbey of Dunfermline was given 'in commendam' to the king's natural son Alexander, archbishop designate of St Andrews, his youth ensured its revenues went straight into royal coffers; an example of direct and blatant exploitation. In order to relieve the royal purse and supplement the income of some of its servants, bishops were also made commendators. A further stage was reached in Kintyre when the Cistercian abbey of Saddell was suppressed on the spurious grounds of its total decay. The site was given as a free barony to the bishop of Argyll who promptly constructed a castle to boost political control over an area of doubtful loyalty, thereby removing one of the few monastic foundations in the southern Highlands and cutting patronage to the school of West Highland sculpture associated with the abbey.

A NATIONAL CHURCH

One step removed from the rivalry between St Andrews and Glasgow, Elphinstone was the prime mover behind an important stage in the evolution of a national Scottish church. He oversaw the production of the Aberdeen Breviary in 1507, giving Scots a distinctive liturgical year and inculcating a profound sense of national pride. By introducing or upgrading feast days for eighty-one Scottish saints and including brief accounts of their lives and miracles, this consciously moved away from too-close adherence to the Sarum Use of England. The Aberdeen Breviary and Martyrology (see Figure 2.1) reflected an existing groundswell of appreciation for native saints, part of the enthusiasm for saints' cults then sweeping through Europe.

The great pilgrimage centres at St Andrews for Scotland's patron saint, Whithorn for St Ninian and Tain for St Duthac, were regularly visited by James IV. The queen's devotion to her name saint and, like many women, her use of St Margaret's 'sark' or shirt to ease her childbirth highlighted Dunfermline Abbey and Glasgow's St Kentigern was strenuously promoted by Archbishop Blackadder. Despite their links with St Columba, Dunkeld, Inchcolm and Iona remained of regional rather than national significance, as did Strathfillan with the relics of St Fillan. Local shrines, such as St Adrian on the Isle of May and 'Our Lady of the Hamer' at Whitekirk, were boosted by James' visits. Royal pilgrimages underscored the unifying and socially levelling dimension of late medieval devotion, with king and commoner alike travelling penitentially on foot or attending Mass on St Columba's day. As a national focus St Andrew's saltire was a flag all could follow into battle and a sense of Scottish identity was revealed in 1508 when the French-bred Berault Stewart directed that his heart be buried at Whithorn. Expatriate Scots founded altars to St Andrew and St Ninian in churches in Bruges, Danzig, Bergen-op-Zoom, Copenhagen, Elsinore, Dieppe and Regensburg.

During this period, the Dominicans and Franciscans attracted more lay donations than the monastic orders. With the Observance movement sweeping Europe, turning Observant Friars into the new spiritual heroes, James IV chose Observant Franciscans as his confessors and founded a new convent at Stirling in 1494, also helping establish the houses at Ayr, Perth, Jedburgh and Elgin. Having moved from the lax regime of the Augustinian canons at Inchaffray to the tough Observant Franciscan house at Jedburgh, the chronicler Adam Abell recorded his gratitude to the royal patron of his new order. Franciscan spirituality was particularly associated with the hugely popular devotion to the Passion of Christ and the friars had helped introduce from Bruges the cult of the Holy Blood. The capital's Holy Blood guild commissioned an elaborate banner which depicted a bleeding Christ, the instruments of the Passion, alongside a Franciscan's knotted cord belt and a rosary delicately embroidered in vivid colours.[1] Passion devotion was closely linked to the cult of the Virgin Mary, especially through the image of the Pietà, with Mary as Mother holding her dead Son on her lap. These themes reverberated through contemporary literature, producing poems celebrating Mary such as Dunbar's 'Hale, Sterne Superne' (star on high).

By contrast, in royal dealings with the Blackfriars concern for reform took second place. James gave strong support to David Anderson, the Dominican provincial from 1499 to 1511, but his term of office brought stagnation to that order. Urban dwellers in particular relied upon the friars to provide a range of burgh services from praying for their souls and hearing confessions to mending the town clock. It did not go unnoticed within the tight-knit burgh society, nor did it escape criticism, that the Conventual friars, and occasionally even the Observants, ignored their Rule by acquiring property. Like a steady drip, such behaviour eroded confidence in the ability of the regulars to reform their orders or uphold the high standards of holiness enshrined in the monastic life, propelling some Scots to look outside conventional or orthodox routes for the path to sanctity.

REBELLION IN THE WESTERN HIGHLANDS AND ISLANDS

The most serious crisis James faced in the second part of his reign was the long-running rebellion in the Highlands and Isles; a disaster waiting to happen. Those regions never achieved a high enough priority to merit regular royal visits nor was the king sufficiently interested to learn the local patterns of power in order to impose feud settlements. Despite James' love of the sea, he did not acquire the habit of island-hopping on a galley and mounting a naval expedition to the Isles, involving considerable trouble and expense, made frequent royal progresses to the western seaboard impractical. Though the 1504 Parliament tried a legislative solution, in practice the judicial system was operated by, and for, Argyll and Huntly, in the king's name. Although part of the normal method of employing magnates to govern the regions, while the king governed the

---

[1] The Fetternear Banner is now in the National Museum of Scotland.

magnates, within the Highlands this policy lacked the options available in Lowland regions, such as using alternative peers or ecclesiastical lords, or direct contacts with the lesser nobility. The cost and difficulty of travel to attend the royal court discouraged Western chiefs from making the effort for little apparent gain. One of the greatest losses following the lordship's forfeiture was the disappearance of the Council of the Isles, previously offering regional consultation and settlement of disputes. Most other Scottish regions were represented by at least one magnate sitting on James' council, providing his subjects with a key point of contact between king and localities. For the Western Isles, the national political arena was too remote to act as a replacement for the Council of the Isles and any 'representation' on the King's Council came through Huntly and Argyll.

The instability following the demise of the lordship had been exacerbated by the vagaries of royal policy when granting charters. Since the Lords of the Isles had issued charters, holding land by charter was not a novelty for Highland chiefs, though concepts of legal ownership differed from those held in the Lowlands. Without a Lowland-style framework of legal conveyancing and enforcement through the law courts, Highlanders accepted the validity of 'sword right', or possession by capture and occupation. The clan system, with a chief maintaining fighting men to defend clan land and raid rivals and enemies, formed an integral part of Gaelic social and economic structures. The spoils or *creaght* taken during raids permitted a redistribution of resources from one clan to another and, through hospitality and gift-giving, from the top to the bottom of society. Stewart kings, hoping to draw the chiefs into the Lowland feudal system, had generally granted charters to those in occupation, with Clan Campbell turning charter acquisition into an art form, squeezing every benefit from adopting charters, without losing the flexibility of existing without them. The lordship's forfeiture followed by James IV's revocation, requiring a repurchase of new charters, had not commended the feudal approach to the Western chiefs. This was a minor inconvenience compared to the bestowal of contested lands to more than one recipient. Between 1495 and 1507, the comparatively lucrative lands of Trotternish on the north-eastern peninsula of Skye, previously part of the lordship, suffered a bewildering series of grants. They were given to both Dunvegan and Lewis branches of the MacLeods, to their bitter rivals the MacDonalds of Sleat and to the Clanranald MacDonalds, who were establishing themselves on the Uists at MacLeod expense. Finally, following the rebellion, Trotternish was included in the package of lands acquired in 1507 by Huntly. It is hard to identify any coherent policy behind these grants and a similar record of land-distribution within the

Lowlands would have produced uproar. The crown's dereliction of 'good lordship' fatally undermined the region's stability.

The immediate provocation for rebellion lay in the expansionist drive west into Lochaber and Ross-shire fuelled by previous royal rewards to Huntly and his allies. They brought extreme instability of tenure, feuding and raiding to the invisible frontier running along the Great Glen as the Western clans pushing east clashed with clans from the Central and Northern Highlands pushing west. When rebellion flared, James, with his face now turned firmly towards Europe, could no longer be bothered to deal with it personally and his firm hold on the Lowlands enabled him to delegate the task. In 1500 and 1501 Argyll and Huntly had been appointed Lieutenants in the Highlands with semi-regal powers, which increased their regional rivalry. The rebellion offered a prime opportunity for the ambitious Huntly to demonstrate his indispensability in the Highlands and extend his influence out to the Western Isles. Argyll's position was compromised by his family ties with the major chiefs of the Western Isles, normally a source of strength. Young Donald Dubh, the earl's nephew and grandson of the last Lord of the Isles, had been 'liberated' from the Campbell castle of Innischonnell to become the rebellion's titular leader. Its main leader was Torquil MacLeod of Lewis, Argyll's son-in-law, and his brother-in-law, Hector MacLean of Duart, was also involved.

Donald Dubh was a figurehead for the supposed restoration of the Lordship of the Isles, though the pattern of raiding suggested a different agenda: inflicting damage upon the crown and Huntly. Stewart-controlled Bute was an easy target for the galleys of the southern Isles and the island took three years to recover. A naval expedition sailed from Dumbarton in 1504 to capture MacLean of Duart's castle on Cairn na Burgh, near the modern Fladda lighthouse in the Treshnish Isles, a stunning military feat, if actually accomplished. The second target was Badenoch, a strategic artery in the Huntly-dominated eastern Highlands. In 1506 the earl and his allies finally took the fight to Lewis when a substantial naval expedition equipped with royal artillery stormed MacLeod's Stornoway castle and re-captured Donald Dubh. Y Mackay, based on nearby Sutherland, assisted Huntly and was rewarded with royal recognition for his 1415 charter for Strathnaver, originally granted by the Lords of the Isles. The Grants of Freuchie, close Huntly allies, gained Castle Urquhart, centrally placed on Loch Ness, controlling the passes to Lochalsh and Skye. Giving a free hand to Huntly and his friends ended the rebellion, whilst storing up future trouble. After their recent experience, the chiefs of the Western Isles might have been forgiven for failing to distinguish between holding land by sword right or through a title bestowed by crown charter. With the royal military and judicial systems dominated by the earls of Huntly and Argyll, the advantages of becoming fully integrated into the Scottish realm were hard to find.

EXECUTING THE LAW AND CONSULTING THE REALM

The Highlanders' experience was at odds with the glowing report of James offering justice to all levels of society. The Spanish ambassador commented that the Scots dared not fight among themselves because, 'They have learnt by experience that he executes the law without respect to rich or poor'.[2] Riding on judicial circuit or down to the Borders was part of James' normal routine, and he did it well. That this was not exclusively a selfless pursuit of justice can be seen by the income gained through selling remissions for crimes. However, in the Lowlands much was forgiven of a ruler who was seen to execute justice and was tough in the Middle or Western Marches in best 'Jeddart (Jedburgh) justice' fashion – hanging thieves and asking questions afterwards. James IV's 1504 Eskdale expedition, in the company of the English Warden, Lord Dacre, was more than an ostentatious law-and-order campaign, mixed with a generous allowance of hunting. While there was work for the hangman, the executions of Border reivers had a deeper purpose. As the English Warden watched, and perforce approved, James wielded the sword of justice, one of the distinguishing attributes of a sovereign, thereby asserting Scottish sovereignty over the Debateable Lands. A good dinner prepared by his master cook and Lord Dacre swallowing humble pie left the king well satisfied with his judicial expedition.

James carefully picked his councillors for their political significance, achieving a broader geographical spread and greater balance than his father's council. He was able to be much more eclectic with his favourites and courtiers; learning from his father's reliance upon unpopular cronies and their fate at Lauder Bridge, the king generally separated his policy-makers from his familiars. A rigid division between work and pleasure did not emerge because James was on easy terms with most of his councilors; sharing their aristocratic interests, such as horse-breeding with Arran who ran his own stud at Kinneil, enabled the king to relax with his nobility. In typical Renaissance fashion, the king was fascinated by many

[2] Cited and discussed in N. Macdougall, *James IV* (Edinburgh, 1989), 287.

branches of knowledge, esoteric and mundane. Much to the chagrin of William Dunbar, the king willingly funded the alchemical experiments of John Damian, abbot of Tongland, including the search for the elusive quintessence that would turn all to gold. The court poet got his own back by immortalising Damian's supposed attempt to fly, launching himself from the western walls of Stirling castle and ignominiously landing in a midden up to his eyes in the glaur.

A marked feature of the period after 1496 was that only three parliaments were called and their main business was judicial, such as the forfeiture of rebels from the Isles in 1502 and 1504. Since the king was perceived to be consulting the political nation in other ways neglect of this formal institution did not provoke a wave of opposition. The crown recognised that taxation was one of the slowest and least efficient methods of raising royal revenue and other financial devices produced better results without needing the consent of the Estates. Alternative bodies offered channels for representative consultation avoiding the all too public arena of parliament. Enlarged sederunts at the Council or a General Council attended by a substantial portion of the nobility were used at key junctures such as the discussion of the English treaty in March 1503, renewing the French alliance in February 1512 and examining in April 1513 how France might be assisted. James consulted via one of these councils or conventions during most years of his adult reign, thereby replacing the fifteenth-century reality of annual parliaments with the appearance of being permanently accessible. If the loss were felt, it did not generate vociferous complaints.

JAMES' GUNS AND SHIPS

Like his grandfather and father, James was smitten with artillery, developing James III's French train and importing the latest cast-bronze cannons with their new metal shot. The king viewed cannon as essentially offensive weapons, rather than static defensive protection and the trunnions cast on bronze cannon were mounted on carriages capable of crossing rough country, reducing time and expense. Experts from France, Germany and the Netherlands acted as gunners and established a Scottish foundry in 1511. In Edinburgh Castle on the west side of the Palace Yard (now Crown Square), a House of the Artillery stood where Robert Borthwick, the 'master melter' in charge, made large cannon such as the matching 'Seven Sisters'. As much an exhibition centre as a workshop, it allowed James' guests to stroll across the yard from the splendid new Great Hall to view the cannon, including the veteran Mons Meg resplendent in her cover decorated by Galbraith, the court herald-painter. James amassed substantial cannon enabling him during the Flodden campaign to equip his navy, send guns to aid O'Donnell in Ireland and take seventeen cannon to England, comprising great curtals, culvereins, sacres and serpentines with a range of shot from 4 to 5lbs up to 60lbs. Military hardware on such a scale was extremely expensive, especially on campaign: even in 1496–7, two weeks of artillery in the field cost £743 11s 6d. Though the art of using artillery effectively on the battlefield was in its infancy, cannon were essential in siege warfare and they had considerable psychological value as a deterrent and morale booster. James regarded them as a priceless part of the equipment of a Renaissance warrior prince, and was not concerned about their cost-effectiveness.

The creation of a Scottish royal navy was a more expensive and grandiose addition to James' offensive weaponry. Between 1505 and 1507, when the main ship-building programme got underway, approximately £5,000 p.a. was spent, rising to an average £8,700 for 1511–13, almost a third of annual royal income, with a total bill of around £100,000. In June 1506 when the four-masted, 600–700-ton ship named *Margaret* after the queen and Scotland's saint was towed into the Forth, she had cost about £8,000. The pride of the fleet was the *Michael*, finally battle-ready in 1512 and which, at around 1000 tons, was by far the biggest capital ship in British waters and the likely model for Henry VIII's *Great Harry* constructed the following year. Pitscottie's figures might not be as exaggerated as first thought: the *Michael* probably cost around £30,000 and 240ft full extension from bowsprit to stern sails would fit contemporary naval construction. She carried a crew of 300 men whose wages alone cost 10 per cent of the crown's annual income. A dozen bronze cannon and three great 'basiliks' were placed on board as well as hand weaponry for fighting at close quarters, the main business of a capital ship.[3]

The navy's core of four large ships included the *Treasurer* and the *James* and they were supported by a number of smaller craft and, when necessary, by privately-owned merchantmen captained by James' friends, the Barton brothers and Andrew Wood. The ships and the shipyards acted like a magnet to the king who was frequently slipping down to the docks rewarding those labouring there with drinksilver. Despite sporting his Admiral's gold whistle and chain James was hard-headed enough to leave command of real naval expeditions to others. The specially-constructed yard on the Forth at New Haven became the centre for royal

---

[3] Figures taken from Macdougall's discussion in *James IV*, 223–46.

shipbuilding with its own chapel dedicated to the Virgin and St James. The Pool of Airth, near the modern Kincardine Bridge, was reconstructed to offer an anchorage further up the Forth securely behind the fortifications on Inchgarvie, the island at the Queensferry narrows. Naval developments boosted the economies of the Lothian shore, provoking a struggle for control over Newhaven between Edinburgh and Leith in which the capital's court influence helped it win. The naval base at Dumbarton continued in use, but there had been a decisive shift from Clyde to Forth, emphasising that James was constructing a North Sea fleet with Europe firmly in mind (see Map 3.1).

The main purpose of James' navy was to offer a new offensive option and strengthen his hand in the diplomatic game, particularly in relation to the perennial triangle of Scotland, England and France. The European context was understood by the French who were suitably impressed by the Scottish navy. When their ambassador dined on board the *Michael* his comment that there was not such a powerful ship in Christendom was more than diplomatic flattery. By naming the vessel after the warrior Archangel and launching her in 1511 close to the feast of Michaelmas, James was probably making a nod towards his plan for a crusade against the Ottomans. Talk of crusading remained part of the vocabulary of international relations, periodically utilised by all European rulers; fighting a common enemy had always offered an escape from the tangle of internecine warfare within Christendom.

THE POWER OF DISPLAY

Though harbouring no doubts himself, James wanted to convince the rest of Europe he was a monarch capable of holding his own among the crowned heads of Christendom. This would be facilitated by creating a permanently convincing setting for his court. Since foreign dignitaries mentally graded royal palaces, one good palace was not enough, especially as monarchs remained peripatetic, not least in the interests of hygiene. Thanks to his predecessors, a number of fine royal residences were already in existence, giving James IV the option of upgrading instead of constructing palaces from scratch. Although the king spent so much time travelling, the spread of frequently-used royal palaces was geographically limited. The major residences were Holyrood Palace and Edinburgh Castle in the capital, with Linlithgow Palace halfway down the road to the great bastion of Stirling Castle. Across the Forth lay Dunfermline Abbey and Palace and, about fifteen miles further into Fife, the hunting lodge

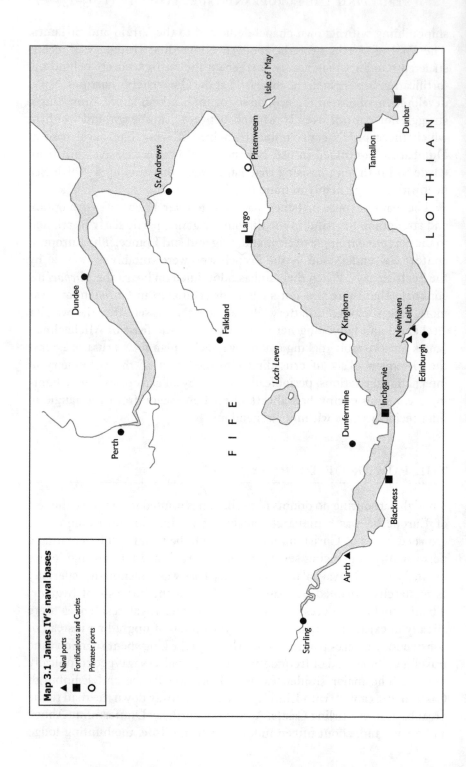

Map 3.1 James IV's naval bases

Naval ports ▲
Fortifications and Castles ■
Privateer ports ○

Isle of May

St Andrews ●

Pittenweem ○

Dundee ●

Largo ■

Falkland ●

Tantallon ■

Dunbar ■

L O T H I A N

Loch Leven

Kinghorn ○

Newhaven
Leith ▲

F I F E

Dunfermline ●

Inchgarvie ■

Edinburgh ●

Perth ●

Blackness ■

Airth ▲

Stirling ●

which became a palace at Falkland. Towards the end of his reign, the king was building new lodgings at the ancestral Stewart castle of Rothesay on Bute. Though James, having bedded down on a table top in Elgin during his famous non-stop ride to Tain, might not be pernickety about where he slept, the queen preferred to travel in state and with a proper wardrobe, which might entail thirty-five carts for her dresses.

Despite, or even because of, his casual style, James also relished the dramatic, set-piece occasions and ceremonies and he spent lavish sums on the Great Halls in Stirling, Edinburgh Castle, Linlithgow and Falkland. At a time when European rulers were withdrawing to private chambers and abandoning the medieval-style hall, James emphasised its place within the palace and filled his halls with the latest in fashionable Renaissance decoration. The stone corbels running from the surviving hammer-beam roof in Edinburgh Castle were so precocious in their classical design, features not seen in France until 1515, that it has been doubted they were made in James IV's reign, even though the cipher IR4 and a flower pot containing thistles and roses are clearly visible. Recently restored, the Great Hall of Stirling Castle, the largest ever built in Scotland, gives a picture of the magnificent public face of court life. It was the grandest secular building in the kingdom with its great height, imposing full-length bay windows illuminating the dais, five large fireplaces for heating and linked to the adjacent royal apartments by an attractive bridge, helping form a courtyard. Set on the highest part of the castle rock, this 'King's House' (now the King's Old Building) had magnificent views to the west. The new forework for the castle with its multi-turreted gatehouse made a favourable impression upon visitors by its overall symmetry and the elegant ashlar facing. Despite its defensive appearance, the triple portal echoed the classical motif of a Roman triumphal arch. Throughout the royal works, the masons freely used the latest fashions from Italy and France though their eclecticism prevented the buildings from being slavish reproductions of any single model. In their architecture, design and furnishings the royal palaces reflected the sense of confidence generated by the patron, the king himself.

An intermixture of features, incorrectly juxtaposed as 'medieval' or 'Renaissance', was characteristic of the spectacular tournaments staged in 1507 and 1508 on the themes of the Black Lady and the Wild Knight. The intended audience was international and exclusive, though the capital's inhabitants witnessed some of the fun. The elaborate and formalised articles of jousting illuminated in gold were dispatched with the Marchmont Herald who took to France the glad tidings of the birth of the first Prince. The call to the best knights in Europe to attend was also sent to England, Denmark, Spain and Portugal. The tournament's main

Figure 3.2 Andrew Myllar's printing colophon, punning upon his name, 1508. [NLS]

purpose was the communication, through stylised imagery and performance, of the chivalric themes of knightly prowess and courtly love thereby
enhancing the glory of the monarchy. Its usefulness as battle training was
reduced by the emphasis upon the ritualised individual jousts, rather than
the group mêlée. Hating to sit still, James took a starring role playing the
Wild Knight armoured in black opposite the Black Lady who was prob-

Scotland's first printing press

Scotland's first printing press was established in Edinburgh in 1507 when a royal patent was granted to Walter Chepman, an Edinburgh merchant and notary with good court connections, and Andrew Myllar, who had probably learned the printing trade in Rouen. Their shop in Blackfriars Wynd in Edinburgh's Cowgate produced books with the distinctive windmill colophon, punning on Myllar's name (see Figure 3.2), and their first title was that well-established favourite, *The Maying or Disport of Chaucer*. Bishop Elphinstone was able to get his handsome Aberdeen Breviary into print and the two printers produced a range of literary best sellers, with the contemporary poet William Dunbar benefiting from having his poems printed. Although Chepman and Millar's business folded and Scottish printing did not properly establish its hold for another half-century, the main impact of the printed book upon Scotland was felt through book purchases and the activities of book sellers bringing in volumes printed abroad. Throughout Europe, the political and religious potential of printing had not yet been fully appreciated by ruler or church, but the explosion of printed material following Luther's Revolt in 1517 showed how important this new, universal medium would be.

ably the negress taken from a captured Portuguese ship. Yellow, purple, grey and green were the group colours worn in the 160 ells of Flemish taffeta purchased for costumes. The wild men accompanying the Wild Knight sported goat skins and stag horns and arrived on dragons carefully constructed of canvas and feathers, possibly an allusion to the Highlanders and Islanders so recently in rebellion. Genuine clansmen did participate, noticeable because they were prepared to draw blood; not standard practice in the choreographed battle scenes. While the name 'Arthur' chosen for the baby prince and the generalised themes of chivalric romance contained a coded message about claims to a British heritage, the tournament's allegories did not provide a commentary upon recent political events. The tournament's judge, Seigneur de la Bastie, duly recognised the great valour of the Wild Knight, allowing James to distribute gold and silver weapons to those knights who had distinguished themselves. Even Dunbar, who still had not obtained the benefice for which he was constantly asking, consoled himself by writing a poem, incorporating much of sexual innuendo, to 'My ladye with the mekle lippis', the negress who had stolen the show.

CHOOSING THE AULD ALLIANCE

During the last decade of his reign James' eyes remained firmly fixed upon the European political arena and he took as full a part in international relations as he could. Having any role in that complex diplomacy was itself a feat for a small kingdom like Scotland, and the king played his limited hand with skill, with more success in European power politics than in his recreational card games. Securing northern Italy was the central issue, as the French military push across the Alps to hold Milan was blocked by the Spanish kingdoms of Aragon and Castile, who held southern Italy. In 1509 the French victory over the Venetians at Agnadello dissolved the League of Cambrai, bringing the pope, France, Spain and the Empire together. In its wake, Pope Julius II, alarmed at the threat to Italy posed by this new 'barbarian' invasion of the peninsula, gathered a 'Holy League', and by 1511 the Holy Roman Empire, Aragon–Castille, England and Venice alongside the Swiss cantons, with their invaluable mercenaries, were lined up against France.

Scotland came under increasing pressure to make a firm choice between the two camps. Since the French needed allies, they offered enough concessions to make it attractive for Scotland to renew the auld alliance in 1512. Although placing Scotland in the opposite camp, James had been careful not to antagonise the pope completely, refusing to allow Scottish churchmen to attend the council called by the French in 1510 in defiance of the papacy. Well versed in separating the pope's role as an Italian prince from his headship of the Western Church, the Scottish hierarchy showed little concern over James' diplomatic alignment, even when it led to the monarch's excommunication in 1513. Being at odds with the emperor, who ruled the Netherlands, was of much greater significance for Scottish economic welfare and it was a serious blow to Scots merchants when their trading privileges were removed. Unfortunately for the trade figures, in his foreign policy calculations the Scottish king placed economic considerations near the bottom of the list.

During an era of war, the exuberant confidence and pride James displayed and on which he traded in power politics would continue to be taken seriously only if the Scots were willing to fight. To sustain his credibility, James had to be prepared to go to war and the French were anxious their diplomatic ally should contribute to their campaigns. Though no official Scottish contingent fought in northern Italy, many individual Scots, especially those already in French service, distinguished themselves in that theatre. While the French looked for the deployment of the Scottish navy, they also expected their ally to undertake the traditional contribution to the auld alliance by invading England.

James' marriage alliance had brought formal peace with England and, during the reign of his father-in-law, the Tudor state was prudently kept out of European warfare. The accession of Henry VIII in 1509 completely changed that stance by bringing to the throne a young king obsessed with the mirage of French conquest emulating his predecessor, Prince Hal. Having little interest in Scotland, the English king failed to offer James an incentive to retain the Anglo-Scottish alliance. A number of incidents, which good will might have defused, were allowed instead to fester. The Scots had a serious grievance over the failure of the English authorities to track down the killer of the Scottish Warden of the East March, murdered on a day of truce. With less justification, James made strong diplomatic protests about Andrew Barton's death and his ship's capture in a fight off the Humber. Such incidents were remembered on the field of Flodden, making both sides less inclined to give quarter. Relations between the allies deteriorated when the Westminster Parliament asserted English sovereignty over the kingdom of Scotland. Concurrently, Louis XII had dispatched 100 puncheons of new wine to keep his Scottish ally sweet. In the spring of 1513 James was probably still willing to consider peace with England, but Dean West's embassy brought nothing of substance, conveying the impression that English friendship was sufficiently valuable in itself. By contrast, the promised privileges such as naturalisation rights for Scots in France, French money and experts had been delivered. It was difficult to argue against the wisdom of holding to the old alliance, even though it led to war.

THE FLODDEN CAMPAIGN

In the summer of 1513 when it became clear that fulfilling his treaty obligations would mean war, James was left with several options about where and when to fight the English. His navy, with a substantial quantity of artillery, was sent to join the French fleet to prevent the return across the Channel of Henry VIII's expeditionary forces. Rather than sailing down the heavily-patrolled English east coast, it went north in July via the Pentland Firth to the Atlantic ports of France. The fleet's subsidiary mission was to assist in an Irish diversionary campaign organised by O'Donnell and it sailed into Belfast Lough and bombarded the English stronghold of Carrickfergus Castle. Though it was sound tactics to attack the Tudor state in Ireland where it was vulnerable, the castle did not fall.

The Scottish fleet was delayed long enough re-supplying in Ayr to miss its rendezvous with the French. Lack of experience managing a war fleet led the Scots to be over-ambitious, and they missed the only chance for Scottish naval power to make a difference in European warfare during the sixteenth century.

A large army assembled to invade England, with Scots arriving from all over the kingdom to fight for their king, including Mackay of Strathnaver who marched his clansmen down from Sutherland. In all Scottish regions the war against the English was popular and Argyll's Gaelic poet expressed a national sentiment in his specially-composed incitement to battle, *Ar Sliocht Gaodhal*, calling for 'no gentle warfare' against the 'Saxons' and valiant defence of 'our native country'.[4] The 1513 campaign was an opportunity for the king to test his latest military hardware and the newly-cast cannons from Edinburgh formed part of the impressive artillery train pulled by 400 oxen over the Lammermuirs to Coldstream and across the Tweed into England at the start of the fourth week of August. All that pushing and shoving was rewarded when, after six days of bombardment, Norham Castle fell, and the smaller strongholds of Wark, Ford and Etal followed shortly afterwards, leaving Berwick as the only English strength in the area. Now brought to a successful conclusion, this was the same strategy pursued in 1496 and 1497. Aware the campaigning season was virtually at an end, in the past the Scots would have withdrawn across the border having achieved their objective. In 1513, knowing he had a large, well-equipped army and French money to sustain the campaign, James was extremely confident. A pitched battle appeared to be a manageable risk.

During James IV's reign the Scots had adopted the successful European battle tactics used by the Swiss and German mercenaries in the Italian wars involving pikemen, whose weapon was 18–22 feet long, drawn up in a large square. The formation was extremely difficult for an enemy to break, since it could switch to face any direction with several ranks of pikes protruding from each side. Training was needed to maintain a tight, disciplined formation, especially on the move, for a square once broken left the individual pikeman with an unwieldy weapon, virtually useless at close quarters.

The weather at the start of September was atrocious and the English northern militias summoned to face the Scottish invasion encountered serious difficulties assembling. The Scots took up a strong position on Flodden Edge, placing their artillery well, so making a frontal assault

---

[4] *Bardachd Albanach: Scottish Verse from the Book of the Dean of Lismore*, ed. W. J. Watson (Scottish Gaelic Text Society, Edinburgh, 1978 ed.), 158–67 at 158–9.

extremely hazardous. Taking a great gamble, Surrey, the English commander, marched his tired and hungry army around the Scots, outflanking them and forcing James to move across Branxton hill with insufficient time to reposition his artillery. On Friday, 9 September in the late afternoon, the Scottish squares advanced down the hill, some troops removing their shoes to get a grip on the muddy slope. The manoeuvre disrupted two squares and, having lost their formation, Scottish pikes were no match for the shorter, manoeuvrable English bills.

The most intense fighting was between James' square and Surrey's own retinue with the Scottish king killed within a few yards of the English standard. With very few prisoners taken in the slog of the hand-to-hand fighting, the Scots stood and died with their king and, at a conservative estimate, 5,000 Scots were killed including nearly all the peers. The English were too exhausted to pursue the remnants of the Scottish army. The campaigning season was too far advanced even if Henry VIII had altered his fixation with the French theatre to invade Scotland. James' body, found some time after the end of the battle, was brought down to London where Henry, having checked with the pope about the burial of a royal excommunicate, interred his brother-in-law in St Paul's Cathedral. Mindful of her personal loss, the English queen, Katherine of Aragon, wrote a sympathetic letter of condolence to her sister-in-law, Margaret Tudor, queen of Scotland.

THE WARRIOR KING'S LEGACY

If James had to choose a way to die, he might have settled for the field of Flodden because he regarded himself as a Renaissance warrior prince. The ruler campaigning in person remained a feature of sixteenth-century warfare, sometimes bringing disaster as at the Hungarian defeat by the Turks in 1526. Where James was at fault was in refusing to accept the personal consequences of the new military tactics he had so enthusiastically embraced. The use of artillery and pike formations made the armoured, mounted knight redundant and it had become essential for a commander to remain as a tactician, keeping apart from the hand-to-hand fighting for as long as possible. As king, James should have concentrated upon his role as the army commander, but he refused to relinquish his self-image as a brave knight leading the charge. Although no general can ever fight a perfect engagement, in his first and last full-scale, pitched battle in overall command, James started and stubbornly remained in the wrong place, a decision that cost him the battle and his life.

However, the king did not lose his kingdom and his defeat should not negate the considerable achievements of his reign. He successfully convinced his fellow rulers and his subjects that he was a warrior prince and his substantial investment in military and naval equipment gave Scotland a high standing in international relations. James employed a similar mixture of panache and expenditure to display his regal status and convincingly to strut the European stage. During his reign, the kingdom experienced a Renaissance flowering in most branches of the arts, thanks in part to the lavish patronage at court. James' natural self-confidence and relaxed style of ruling allowed him to govern the realm with apparent ease, being on good terms with the magnates and consulting them regularly in Council, though less in parliament. Personal charisma helped the king build a reputation in the Lowlands as an accessible king, but that charm was not exercised frequently enough in the former Lordship of the Isles to mitigate the mess following the forfeiture. Stewart ambition to control the entire kingdom outran royal power to implement direct rule and whilst the *laissez-faire* attitude worked tolerably well in the Northern Isles, the Highlands and Islands suffered from ill-considered interventions that further disrupted regional politics.

In common with most Renaissance monarchs, James lived well beyond his means and the crown could not afford the expenditure of the closing years of the reign. With the cost of European warfare spiralling, even the entire kingdom could not produce the resources to sustain a military and naval force of international significance. To remedy his financial problems and augment royal power, James turned to the other pillar of Scottish society, the church, bringing it as close as possible to the crown and firmly steering towards their convergence. James' policies significantly decreased the chances of a successful root-and-branch reform of the church as an institution, despite the individual efforts of Bishop Elphinstone. The death at Flodden of Alexander, archbishop designate of St Andrews, was an elegiac moment for the Scottish church, removing any possibility of an adult and dedicated Scottish primate of royal birth opposing the crown's drive to absorb ecclesiastical resources and manpower into its administration. The fact that the boy was fighting on the battlefield beside his royal father indicated how far things had already gone. In the long run, James' domestic policies were to prove a more significant legacy for the kingdom of Scotland than his defeat on the battlefield.

PART TWO

Renaissance Monarchy Triumphant

CHAPTER 4

The Survival of Renaissance Monarchy: James V's Minority (1513–28)

In Stirling on 21 September 1513 a toddler dressed in his best clothes survived a series of boring ceremonies in which he was not even allowed to play with the large toys offered to him. It would be another fifteen years before the young James V would get his hands, metaphorically at least, on the sceptre and the sword of state or feel that he was the one wearing the crown. Before 1528, the power to rule was held by a series of regents or those wielding vice-regal authority. Despite James V's tender age, there was no suggestion that he or the Stewart dynasty should be replaced. After his younger brother Alexander, duke of Ross, had died, if James himself had not survived, the succession would have gone to the duke of Albany and then to Arran (see Table 2.1), which added spice to their involvement in Scottish politics. James V remained in Stirling, at the centre of the kingdom, inside its safest fortress which dominated the routes into Scotland north of the Forth. The most pressing concern in 1513 was whether an invasion force would be outside the gates before long and although no English army came, the threat was real enough. After James' own death thirty years later, Scotland did experience prolonged warfare, devastation and English occupation.

THE AFTERMATH OF FLODDEN

News of the defeat at Flodden travelled fast across Scotland, though for many women there would have been the agonising wait to find if their men were coming home. The queen had a poet to write lyrical lines about overcoming her grief and making a new life, but with every Scottish region mourning its dead, the national casualty list dissolved into individual tragedies, such as the loss of the laird of Garthclone and his son in

Galloway, or three sons from Lord Glamis' family. All social ranks were found on the death roll, from the lowly Patrick Scott who laboured in Strathearn to the mighty Argyll who had led Clan Campbell into battle. Those who survived gave thanks, with a standing cross being erected in Lorn by Campbell of Lerags (see Figure 4.1), and told their personal tales, as in the north-east, where Black John, standard-bearer for the Keiths, related how he had been taken prisoner but had hidden the blue silk banner from the English inside his clothes. The grief was not confined to Scotland. Erasmus wrote a moving elegy for his pupil Alexander, archbishop designate of St Andrews, who had died beside his royal father. He lamented, 'What hadst thou to do with the war-god . . . thou who wast consecrated to the Muses, nay, to Christ himself?'[1]

After the shock of the news, the women did what they always had whilst their men were at war, and got on with managing things at home. At local and regional levels these unsung heroines ensured the country was kept running. The Edinburgh customs, for example, were collected by Janet Paterson and Margaret Crichton. Although the Act of Twizelhaugh, made by James IV before the battle, had specifically granted to those who fell serving their country a smooth succession without the usual payments for the heirs, much Council business in those initial months dealt with inheritance issues.

At Flodden, a political generation had been lost and their replacements lacked that vital ingredient of experience in political life. The frenetic in-fighting during the next years owed much to this deficit as an entire generation cut their political teeth on each other. Despite the high casualty list, the government and administration continued without major disruption. At the administrative level it was, as usual, the clerics who kept business moving. James Beaton, archbishop of Glasgow, became Chancellor following the death on the battlefield of his fellow archbishop whilst Patrick Paniter, who survived Flodden despite being in charge of the artillery, continued as Secretary. Crucially, Bishop Elphinstone with his legal mind and vast administrative know-how kept the ship of state afloat and he was the obvious man to become primate of the Scottish church. Such an appointment was never straightforward and, before his nomination was confirmed in October 1514, Elphinstone died and was buried in a striking Renaissance tomb in the chapel sanctuary of his beloved King's College. If he had lived to become head of the Scottish church, Elphinstone might have introduced major reform;

---

[1]   Cited in T. G. Chalmers, 'Stewart, Alexander (c. 1493–1513)', *Oxford Dictionary of National Biography* (Oxford, 2004) [http://www.oxforddnb.com].

Figure 4.1 The Cross erected by Campbell of Lerags in Argyll, 1516. [RCAHMS]

such a task was beyond those who subsequently became archbishops of
St Andrews.

Following 1513, Scotland swung between two alliances, remaining
with France or seeking friendship with England; the various Regents

represented the different international alignments. Since it was a minor theatre of war, European diplomacy took relatively little interest in Scotland, concentrating upon the Italian campaigns. The victory at Marignano in 1515 ushered in a decade when French military power reached its high point until the defeat at Pavia and Francis I's capture. Always aspiring to, though never reaching, the major league of Francis or Charles V, Henry VIII and Cardinal Wolsey kept their eyes on continental developments and refused to be distracted by Scotland. They remained in a permanent quandary about whom to use as their chief agent, whether to back Henry's sister, Queen Margaret, or Angus.

During the minority, a combination of the international dimension to Scottish politics and the landed interests of the main protagonists placed the political spotlight upon the upper reaches of Clydesdale and the Borders. The minutiae of their regional politics had a disproportionate effect upon national policies thanks to the instability and fragmentation of central political power. In the Clyde valley Arran felt his powerbase threatened by Angus, who had begun to expand into Ayrshire. Angus and the Humes were Borders-based and Albany had a claim to lands in that region. Since the East and Middle Marches straddled the main invasion routes and the Middle and West Marches were the foci for cross-border raiding, their significance for the triangular diplomacy between Scotland, England and France was obvious.

THE PRIMATE OF SCOTLAND

The appointment to the metropolitan see of St Andrews paid scant attention to the needs of the Scottish church, illustrating instead the complexities of political in-fighting and the seamier side of ecclesiastical promotion. There was a plethora of candidates from the various interest groups seeking to influence the papacy to accept their nominee. The queen and the lords of the Scottish Council sometimes backed different men, and Albany and Francis I were lobbying for their candidate, whilst Henry VIII, as uncle of James V, also ran his own men. The pope made his nephew, Cardinal Cibo, administrator of the archdiocese as soon as he heard of the vacancy. On Elphinstone's death Gavin Douglas, court poet, provost of St Giles and son of 'Bell-the-Cat' Angus, grabbed St Andrews Castle as a way of strengthening his claim. Not to be outdone, John, prior of St Andrews, the current head of the Hepburns, besieged and captured the castle. The archbishop of Glasgow wanted to move archdioceses, but the successful candidate in the end was Andrew Forman.

With a career pattern and aspirations remarkably similar to Cardinal Wolsey, Forman was not an obvious compromise choice, described by his rival Gavin Douglas as 'yon euyll myndyt Byschop of Murray'.[2] Since he had been an avid supporter of the war against England, he was blamed for Flodden. Nothing deterred, the bishop of Moray employed his diplomatic expertise to negotiate his way into the see, placating the Pope by offering to exchange his newly-acquired French archbishopric of Bourges with Cardinal Cibo. Having spent half a year in Pittenweem Priory carefully keeping out of sight and mischief, Forman finally secured control over the archdiocese in February 1516. To balance Forman's appointment, Gavin Douglas was promoted to Dunkeld, though he had an equally tricky time getting established. On his first visit to the cathedral, he was shot at from the steeple by the troops of Atholl's brother, Andrew Stewart, who claimed the see. Like his secular counterparts, this ecclesiastical lord found that having the patronage and the paperwork was not enough; it was still necessary to win in the locality.

THE STRUGGLE FOR THE REGENCY

On the face of it, the immediate problem of who was to act as regent for James V seemed straightforward. In the provisions of his will James IV had left Queen Margaret as the official guardian of her son, with the standard proviso that this would continue as long as she remained a widow. There were two obvious problems: Margaret was a woman and, worse still, she was an English woman. As a counter-balance it was assumed the queen regent would be a figurehead, particularly since she was preoccupied with carrying James IV's posthumous child, which all hoped was another son to strengthen the slender line of succession. Although Margaret talked about being a good Scotswoman with only the young king's interests at heart, her private, begging letters to Henry VIII belied her public words:

> If I were such a woman that might go with my bairn in mine arm, I trow I should not be long from you, whose presence I desire most of any man . . . I am so super-extended that I doubt that poverty shall cause me to consent to some of their minds which I shall never do without your counsel, as long as I have a groat to spend.[3]

[2] Cited and discussed in P. Bawcutt, *Gavin Douglas* (Edinburgh, 1976), 12.
[3] Cited in P. H. Buchanan, *Margaret Tudor, Queen of Scots* (Edinburgh, 1985), 93.

The alternative candidate for regent was James IV's nephew and the nearest adult male relative, John, duke of Albany, born and raised in France after his father's banishment by James III. The choice of regent carried with it a foreign-policy alignment in addition to the gender and personality of the two contenders. Scots assumed Albany would continue to serve his French royal master, and Margaret would be under the direction of her brother, Henry VIII. Scotland gained a respite when France and England agreed a truce and in August 1514 made peace, sealed by a marriage alliance sending Mary, Margaret's younger sister, to wed the elderly Louis XII. Any prospect of family ties uniting the Scottish, English and French courts quickly faded. The Scottish Queen Mother appeared in a strong position in the regency race, having borne a son in April and received backing from the council meeting in July. A month later she had lost that support and an enlarged council, with sixty-one attending, deposed her from the regency. Despite the show of unanimity, Scotland was split with neither side strong enough to impose its will, resulting in a messy stalemate as rival parliaments were called – the queen's supporters meeting in Perth; her opponents in Edinburgh.

The apple of discord was a handsome nineteen-year-old, whom Margaret had married in a secret ceremony in Kinnoull church, near Perth. The marriage of any queen had international as well as domestic implications, which made a clandestine wedding before the normal year of mourning was passed a precipitate act at the least. Possibly provoked by her younger sister's upstaging marriage to the French king, Margaret made her own choice, before an unwelcome match was negotiated by her brother. With its well-known dire consequences, Margaret transmitted her tendency to marry in haste and repent at leisure to her own grandchildren Mary, Queen of Scots and Henry, Lord Darnley. Knowing it would provoke one of Henry VIII's rages, Margaret had not summoned the courage to mention her wedding until 1 September, though her second husband, Archibald Douglas, 6th earl of Angus, was a strong Anglophile. The Scottish political community felt a sickening sense of *déjà vu* when they heard Margaret had married a Douglas. Lord Home asserted that, by marrying, Margaret had forfeited her position and the vacancy could be filled by the Council, appealing to James IV's will and the contractual nature of Stewart rule:

> We have shown heretofore our willingness to honour the Queen contrary to the ancient custom of this kingdom. We have suffered and obeyed her authority the whiles she herself kept her right by keeping her widowhood . . . Now she has quit it by marrying, why

should we not choose another to succeed in the place she has voluntarily left? Our old laws do not permit a woman should govern in the most peaceable times, far less now when such evils do threaten.[4]

REGENT ALBANY

Unfortunately, the Frenchman with extensive military experience, whom the Council wanted for the job, was not immediately free to occupy the regency. In the tradition of the *princes étrangers* within early modern France, the duke was busy serving the king and this prior commitment to French service formed the backdrop to all his visits to Scotland. Contrary to the rumours assiduously circulated by the English, Albany had no ambitions to take the throne nor did he make serious efforts to reconstitute his Scottish estates, because thanks to his Auvergne lands, his long-term future was located firmly in France. From the Scots' perspective, this gave him the advantage of being aloof from domestic rivalries, with the disadvantage of making him dependent upon the public purse for his activities as regent, supplemented by generous subsidies from the French which arrived with strings attached. The accession of Francis I in January 1515 changed French policy, opening the way for Albany's first period of regency. The acceptance of his authority in Scotland was demonstrated when the sceptre and sword of justice were carried before him, and Albany processed into parliament wearing his ducal coronet and mantle, after which the nobles gave him their bodily oaths of allegiance. A flood of cases seeking redress came before the Council, such as that of the Edinburgh widow Janet Paterson, whose previous legal decree had failed to prevent interference with her lands. Protecting the widows and fatherless was emblematic: justice was being re-established with the return of stability.

By contrast, Margaret, Angus and their supporters felt aggrieved at their treatment. Drummond, Angus' grandfather, had rashly 'waffed his sleif at an harralde, and gave him upon the breast with his hand'.[5] Since it was treason to lay violent hands upon the Lord Lyon, King of Arms, Drummond was stripped of heritage and goods and warded in Blackness Castle. Angus' uncle Gavin Douglas also found himself in prison in the

---

[4] Cited and discussed in R. Marshall, *Scottish Queens 1034–1714* (East Linton, 2003), 89–90.
[5] Cited and discussed in W. K. Emond, 'The Minority of James V, 1513–1528' (unpublished University of St Andrews Ph.D. thesis, 1988), 78.

sea-tower of St Andrews Castle after his efforts to secure the archdiocese by main force. Margaret, who had wept and pleaded with Albany on behalf of Drummond and Douglas, was herself having difficulties securing the revenues from her dower lands and faced an acute shortage of money.

The real battle between Albany and the queen lay over the control of James V. The showdown came at Edinburgh Castle when the queen ordered the portcullis lowered and, more like a fishwife than a queen, shouted through its bars at those who had come to take her sons, after which she retreated to Stirling Castle with the boys. To demonstrate he meant business, Albany arrived with troops and Margaret finally conceded, playing the drama to the end by handing the keys to James V who passed them to Albany. Losing contact with her boys was a bitter blow for Margaret, whose maternal instincts were strong. The attempt by Angus and Hume to rescue them from Stirling and take them to England confirmed Albany's belief the queen could not be trusted to have access to her children. Though heavily pregnant, Margaret managed to engineer a daring escape from Linlithgow and later fled into England.

Albany now felt secure enough to deal with the Humes, who had been in treasonable correspondence with England and, taking a substantial force to the Merse, he systematically destroyed their strongholds. He was boosted by news of the great victory at Marignano in September 1515 which put the French back in control in northern Italy and he celebrated at the newly-captured castles of Fast and Dunglass. The following January he was again in the field facing down a rebellion led by Arran. When the Regent displayed the royal standard at 'Kittycrosshill', an unknown location, close to Glasgow, thereby turning rebels into traitors, Arran and his fellow 5,000 rebels decided not to fight. By March a policy of reconciliation had brought both Arran and Angus back onto the Council, though Gavin Douglas believed that Albany harboured 'capitalle and dedelie inimye to me and all my hous'.[6] Similar leniency was not afforded Lord Hume and his brother who, having been pardoned, again took up arms and on 8 October 1516, as a clear example to others, they were executed for treason and their heads displayed on Edinburgh's walls. Unlike other European kingdoms, such a final measure was not common in Scotland, leading to a bloodfeud between the regent and the Humes, exacerbated by the fear that Albany, as the newly restored earl of March, would permanently undermine Hume dominance in their heartland. The French regent, conscious of their military significance, devoted much effort to bringing the eastern Borders firmly under his control.

---

[6]　Cited and discussed in Bawcutt, *Gavin Douglas*, 1.

Scotland's place in Christendom visualised

The strength and the residual self-confidence of the kingdom in its place within Christendom were displayed in dramatic visual fashion in the magnificent heraldic ceiling of St Machar's Cathedral in Aberdeen, designed around 1520, probably by Alexander Galloway, canon of the cathedral, and crafted by James Winter of Angus. It had three rows, containing a total of forty-eight carved and painted shields, representing the European monarchs, the Scottish church and the Scottish nobility, with Old and New Aberdeen and the University giving local pride due place. Indicating its symbolic position at the heart of the kingdom, the church, headed by the arms of Pope Leo X, was afforded the central row. Here was the national institution in all its power and glory, with the thirteen archbishops and bishops of Scotland and the prior of St Andrews and University of Aberdeen representing its monastic and educational wings. The Holy Roman Emperor headed the north row, on the sinister side heraldically, containing the secular rulers of Europe with France being given second place, then Spain, relegating England to fourth position in a subtle heraldic snub, increased by giving the Tudor king his three leopards, though pointedly not including the quartering with the lilies of France normally shown on English royal arms. The south row, heraldically the dexter and more important, was devoted to Scotland, beginning with James V's arms with the closed imperial crown above them, the only European king to be depicted on the ceiling with this style of crown. The king's arms were followed by those of St Margaret of Scotland which in another deliberate snub was as close as the Queen Mother got to her own shield, and then by those of the duke of Albany as regent followed by the major Scottish magnates. This vision of ordered unity, with its careful integration of sacred and secular and its hierarchy of jurisdictions demonstrating how the regional, national and international levels fitted together, might have seemed to observers in 1520 somewhat removed from the reality of their faction-torn kingdom. However, it remained an ideal to which they could aspire and which most Scots assumed was obtainable, once their Stewart monarch reached his 'perfect age'. With some justification, they assumed that the current disorder was the superficial froth which bubbled up during a minority and even with that lying on the surface, the main business of life continued relatively unhindered.

The high point of his regency came in November 1516 when Albany was formally recognised by parliament as second person in the realm. When they registered his father's annulment, thereby removing any possible doubt about his legitimacy, the Estates performed an interesting piece of tidying for Albany. The consequence of his success in imposing order was his return to France in June and the treaty of Rouen he was able to negotiate whilst there. This fully offensive and defensive alliance tied Scotland more closely to her old ally, making it difficult for Scottish foreign policy not to dance to the tune piped by Francis I. Whilst it owed much to Albany's own skills, the initial success of the regency was also a tribute to the underlying strength of Scotland's Renaissance monarchy.

A few days after Albany had embarked from Dumbarton in 1517, Queen Margaret crossed the border from England and had a frosty reunion with Angus. The sacred setting of Lamberton church might have prevented one of the couple's famous shouting matches, but it did not reduce Margaret's resentment at her husband's previous behaviour. Following her hasty flight into England, she had narrowly survived the birth of their daughter, also named Margaret. Angus had then refused to accompany her to London, returning to repair his fortunes in Scotland and conduct an affair with Catherine Stewart, a former fiancée. Henry VIII was indulgent to his sister; they had kissed and made up over her second marriage and she had revelled in the amusements of the Tudor court, replenishing her wardrobe at her brother's expense with twenty-two dresses of cloth of gold. She could not refuse to return to Scotland when Henry insisted she do her duty as an Englishwoman. The Scots, assuming that was her role, imposed heavy restrictions upon Margaret's access to James V, all the more precious to the queen because Alexander, her other son, had died the previous year.

SLIDING INTO FACTIONALISM

In his absence Albany had left Arran and his second-in-command, Antoine de la Bastie, to run the country. Not possessing the duke's quasi-regal authority, they struggled to do the job. Attention remained concentrated upon the Borders, since central control in the French interest was essential to block English attempts at destabilisation and infiltration, orchestrated by Lord Dacre, who later described himself as a 'fiddling stock to hold Scotland in cumber and business'.[7] In a revenge

---

[7] Cited in C. McKean, *The Scottish Chateau* (Stroud, 2004 ed.), 82.

killing for the executions of Lord Hume and his brother, their kinsmen murdered de la Bastie in September 1517. The strategically important Priory of Coldingham also saw the violent deaths of two priors in as many years, with David Hume murdered in 1518 and to re-establish Hume dominance Robert Blackadder was killed by Hume of Wedderburn, accompanied by sixty Englishmen. All along the Borders the situation appeared to be sliding dangerously out of control and national politics became focused on this region, allowing many other parts of Scotland to go their own way. Angus' attempts to re-establish Douglas power in the Marches were viewed with great suspicion because he remained in contact with the Humes and the English. In the western borderlands, the Maxwells emerged as the main bastion against English raiding, filling the vacuum left by the deliberate reduction of Douglas authority. Angus' continued control over his wife's dower lands of Ettrick Forest and Newark Castle led to further problems and marital rows, despite an agreement made in Council in November 1518 to guarantee Margaret a proper income. Angus also faced the intense rivalry of Arran, who deliberately snubbed him and his offers of Douglas assistance to run the country. Their mutual antagonism created two factions where Hamilton and Douglas landed interests collided, especially in the upper Clyde valley, and with major lords joining one or other faction, their feuds were added to the explosive mixture, as when Glencairn's support for Angus pushed Montgomery into backing Arran.

A tug-of-war over the provostship of Edinburgh which had developed between Arran and Douglas of Kilspindie provided the spark that caused a political explosion. On 30 April 1520 the burgh became the arena for armed confrontation. When the Hamilton faction found themselves trapped in the Dominican convent on the Cowgate, Gavin Douglas, bishop of Dunkeld, attempted to mediate. However, many had come prepared for a fight, including the archbishop of Glasgow who had, according to Pitscottie, a breastplate hidden beneath his garments revealed by its jangle when he emphasised a point by slapping himself on the chest. In the subsequent 'cleansing of the causeway', the fighting in Edinburgh's High Street drove the Hamiltons out of the burgh. Amidst the Douglas triumph, members of the Hume family retrieved from Edinburgh's walls the desiccated heads of the 3rd Lord and his brother and took them for burial. The deaths in the fracas of Sir Patrick Hamilton and the Master of Montgomery created later bloodfeuds though, thanks to Gavin Douglas' intervention, Archbishop Beaton kept his life. A full-scale battle was averted on May Day morning, even though the

Table 4.1 The political fortunes of the five major noble families

Family Name	Hamilton	(Lennox) Stewart	Douglas	Campbell	Gordon
Earldoms	Arran; Duke of Châtelherault	Lennox (Lord Darnley)	Angus; Douglas; Morton	Argyll	Huntly; Sutherland
Powerbase	Lanarkshire; Clyde–Forth corridor. In the line of royal succession.	The Lennox. Glasgow and Clyde. In the line of royal succession.	Borders; Angus	Argyll, West and Central Highlands	North-east; Northern Highlands; Sutherland
Chronology					
1. James IV transition 1488–95	Minor. No significant part in 1488 events. 1st cousin of James IV. Helps rapid rise at court.	Lord Darnley supports prince. 1489 In rebellion. 1490 Restored as Earl of Lennox.	5th Angus (Bell-the-Cat) supports prince. 1491 Death 9th Douglas – last of Black Douglases. 1492–7 Chancellor. 1493–5 Controls regime.	1488 2nd Argyll supports Prince James. 1488–92 Chancellor.	2nd Huntly does not support prince.
2. James IV adult rule 1495–1513	1503 Created 1st Arran at royal wedding.		1497–1513 Out of favour.	1495–1513 Master Royal Household (becomes hereditary). Royal Lieutenant in West and serves Crown.	1497–1501 Chancellor. 1501 Death 2nd Huntly.

Section	Lennox	Angus	Hamilton (Arran)	Argyll	Huntly
					3rd Huntly Royal Lieutenant in Highlands. 1507–9 Major rewards.
3. James V minority 1513–28	1513 2nd Lennox killed at Flodden.	1513 5th Angus' 2 eldest sons killed at Flodden.	Naval commander and takes fleet to France in Flodden campaign.	1513 2nd Argyll killed at Flodden.	3rd Huntly survived Flodden.
		1513 Death 5th Angus. 1514 6th Angus marries Margaret Tudor, Queen Dowager.	Royal Lieutenant in Borders.	1514 3rd Argyll Justice-General (becomes hereditary).	Royal Lieutenant in North.
				Royal Lieutenant in West and serves Crown.	
		1520 Clash with Hamiltons – 'Cleanse the Causeway' in Edinburgh.	1520 Clash with Douglases – 'Cleanse the Causeway' in Edinburgh.		
					1524 Death 3rd Huntly; succeeded by grandson, ward of Queen Margaret Tudor.
		1525–8 6th Angus controls James V.			
	1526 3rd Lennox tries to free king. Killed by Hamilton of Finnart. Start of Hamilton–Lennox feud.		1526 1st Arran's illegitimate son Finnart kills Lennox (Arran's nephew). Start of Hamilton–Lennox feud.		
		1527–8 Chancellor.			
4. James V adult rule 1528–42		1528 James V attacks 6th Angus.	1529 Death 1st Arran.	1529 Death 3rd Argyll.	Huntly close friend and favoured by king.

Table 4.1 (continued)

Chronology (cont.)

Family Name	Hamilton	(Lennox) Stewart	Douglas	Campbell	Gordon
James IV adult rule 1528–42	Hamilton of Finnart close to king.	1532–43 4th Lennox in voluntary exile in France.	1528–42 6th Angus in exile in England.	4th Argyll not close to James V but continues to serve.	Gordons gain control Sutherland through marriage.
	2nd Arran – heir presumptive to Scottish throne. Close to king.				1537 11th Sutherland succeeds.
	1540 Finnart executed.				1542 Huntly Lieutenant of Borders.
5. Mary, Queen of Scots minority 1542–58	1543–54 Governor of Scotland.	1543–4 4th Lennox returns to Scotland. Switches from French to English alignment, opposite of Arran.	1544–5 6th Angus switches from English to French alignment. Returns and leads Scots at victory Ancrum Moor.	Pro-French, supports Beaton and Mary of Guise.	Pro-French and supports Beaton, Mary of Guise.
	1543 Switches from English to French alignment.	1544–64 Exile in England.	1548 Death 3rd Morton, succeeded by son-in-law (6th Angus nephew).		1546–62 Chancellor.
	1548 French bestow dukedom of Châtelherault.	1544 Marries Margaret Douglas, 6th Angus' daughter.	1548–50 4th Morton prisoner in England.		

	1554 Châtelherault hands over Regency to Mary of Guise.	In England and not directly involved	1557 Death 6th Angus. Succeeded by great-nephew; long minority. 4th Morton signs 1st Protestant Band.	1557 4th Argyll signs 1st Protestant Band. 1558 Death 4th Argyll.	1554–7 Loses favour and Great Seal, though keeps title of Chancellor.
6. Reformation Crisis 1558–60	Châtelherault formal head Lords of the Congregation. Arran (eldest son) active leader.		4th Morton Leader Lords of the Congregation.	5th Argyll Leader Lords of the Congregation.	Stays on sidelines and only joins Congregation in April 1560.
7. Mary, Queen of Scots personal 1561–7	Châtelherault and Arran advisors.	Lennox remains in England.	4th Morton advisor.	Close advisor to queen. Her brother-in-law.	Advisor.
	1562 Châtelherault in background; Arran declared insane.		1563–6 4th Morton Chancellor.		1562 4th Huntly in rebellion, defeated, died and forfeited.
	1564 Major threat from return of Lennox, and Darnley marriage.	1564 4th Lennox returns to Scotland.			1563–5 Sutherland forfeited, and in voluntary exile in Flanders.
	1565 Châtelherault in rebellion, then voluntary exile in France.	1565 Son, Darnley, returns and marries Queen Mary.		1565 Rebels over Darnley marriage.	1565 5th Huntly restored.

Table 4.1 (continued)

Family Name	Hamilton	(Lennox) Stewart	Douglas	Campbell	Gordon
Chronology (*cont.*) Mary, Queen of Scots personal 1561–7		1566 Darnley involved in Rizzio murder. 1567 Murder Darnley. 4th Lennox goes to England.	1566 4th Morton involved in Rizzio murder. Exile in England. 1567 4th Morton Leader of Confederate Lords against Queen and Bothwell.		1566–7 Chancellor. 1567 11th Sutherland poisoned by Sinclairs, succeeded by minor.
8. Civil Wars 1567–73	Supports Queen's Party. 1570 Archbishop John Hamilton organises assassination of Regent Moray. 1573 Signs Pacification of Perth.	Leader King's Party (James VI is Lennox's grandson). 1570–1 4th Lennox Regent. 1571 Killed.	1567–72 4th Morton Leader King's Party. Chancellor.	1567–71 Leader Queen's party. 1571 Settles with King's party.	1567–73 Leader Queen's party. 1573 Signs Pacification of Perth.
9. James VI minority 1573–88	1575 Death of Châtelherault.	1576 Death in England of Charles, 5th Lennox.	1572 4th Morton Regent. 1572–8 4th Morton Regent; 8th Angus (Regent's nephew) becomes prominent.	1573 Chancellor; Death of 5th Argyll.	

		1573–8 Feud with 6th Argyll.	1573–8 6th Argyll feud with Regent Morton.	1576 Death 5th Huntly; succeeded by minor.
		1578 Loses power.	1578 Leads coup against Morton.	1578–80 6th Huntly tours continent. Strong Catholic sympathies.
1579 Hamiltons forfeited and driven into exile.	1579 Esmé (grandson 3rd Lennox) comes to Scotland.	1579 Leads campaign against Hamiltons.	1579–84 Chancellor.	
	1580–1 Created Earl and then Duke of Lennox. Very close to James VI.	1581 Executed for Darnley's murder.		
	1583 Death of Duke of Lennox.	1580s 8th Angus fluctuating fortunes.	1584 Death 6th Argyll, succeeded by minor.	6th Huntly good relations with James VI.
		1588 Death 8th Angus.		

Hamiltons arrayed in fighting formation on Boroughmuir. With the capital paralysed by violence, self-help became the order of the day in Fife, with eighteen nobles agreeing to prevent factionalism disrupting their shire. A compromise was reached in Edinburgh when Arran and the Burgh Council signed a bond guaranteeing that whilst he remained in the burgh, Angus would not be allowed entry. As everyone recognised, this was no way to run the country and a plea was sent to France for Albany's return.

The duke sailed into Gareloch in November 1521 with a specific agenda. There was a basic consensus that domestic order needed to be restored and the first stage, gaining control over the person of the king, was easier than before, thanks to Margaret's changed attitude. The Queen Mother viewed Albany as a potential ally who could assist her against her husband, Angus. The duke was related to the Medici family who currently held the papacy, and could bring diplomatic pressure upon Leo X to grant Margaret the annulment she craved. The English king, whose marital troubles were yet to come, having adopted a high moral tone when Margaret suggested ending her marriage, blocked any moves in Rome. Henry regarded his sister's friendship with Albany as a betrayal of English interests and spread malicious rumours that there was more to the relationship than a political alliance. Angus, having withdrawn to Ladykirk on the Tweed, enabling him to step into England at a moment's notice, eventually surrendered to Albany and was sent into exile in France, taking his daughter Margaret with him. His uncle, Gavin Douglas, was left stranded in England where Margaret, who blamed him for her own and Scotland's woes, wrote to her brother, 'he has bene the caus of all the dissention and trobill of this Realme', adding with a vindictive flourish, 'sen I helpit to get hyme the benefice of Dunkeld I sall help hyme to want the samyn'.[8] In September 1522 Douglas died of the plague and was buried in London, probably giving the Scottish queen a nasty glow of satisfaction.

The hardest part of Albany's agenda was to persuade the Scots to mount a campaign against the English as part of Francis I's European strategy. By his constant insistence there could be no peace unless Albany was removed from the country, Henry VIII merely strengthened the duke's case. The Scottish lords continued to fear the English king would send his forces to 'protect' his nephew, making French help necessary. However, they were wary of being used as a catspaw for France and with the Scottish army in the West March and Carlisle reputed to be

---

[8]   Cited and discussed in Bawcutt, *Gavin Douglas*, 20.

defenceless, they still declined to venture across the border. These set-backs made Albany angry and frustrated and he was reputed in such moments to snatch his bonnet from his head and throw it in the fire; with some exaggeration, Lord Dacre reported the regent had expended a dozen bonnets. Albany returned to France in October 1522 to explain to his royal master the Scots' reluctance to attack the English. At the end of September the following year, he brought 4,000 French men-at-arms, 1,000 hackbutters, 600 horses and some artillery. Having failed to take Wark in November, the whole effort disintegrated since it was too late in the campaigning season. Feeling that during his Scottish regency he had been like a hawk mobbed by crows, a disillusioned Albany departed from Scotland for the last time in May 1524. Further French plans for the Scottish front vanished following the crushing defeat at Pavia and the capture of Francis I in February 1525. The Italian campaigns under-mined Albany's permanent legacy, leaving his spells as regent as short interludes of order amidst instability, instead of a sustained period of French-assisted good rule for Scotland.

THE STRUGGLE FOR CONTROL OVER KING AND COUNTRY

In the 1520s attention within Europe was becoming focused upon the revolt of Martin Luther, a relatively obscure German professor, which was tearing a serious rent in the fabric of Christendom. News of events, now labelled the early Protestant Reformation, arrived in Scotland via France and the Netherlands with the educated elite and government circles receiving much of their information via Paris, probably filtered through the Sorbonne's disapproval of Protestant ideas. A more favourable evaluation and direct exposure to Lutheran doctrines was transmitted through east-coast trade links with the Low Countries. When the Scottish Parliament took it upon itself in 1525 to pass an Act against heresy, it treated the problem more as one of contamination from external sources than an internal threat, target-ing merchant ships and foreign traders importing heretical literature and ideas. Scotland's position on the fringes of continental Europe seemed a positive advantage when Christian orthodoxy needed to be upheld.

Patrick Hamilton sought to reduce his homeland's relative isolation by returning from Protestant Germany. An enthusiastic convert to the Lutheran doctrine of justification by faith alone, he spread the new ideas among his noble kinsmen and within St Andrews Priory and University. This provoked a heresy trial in 1528 and an opportunity, which Hamilton embraced, of becoming the first Scottish martyr for his faith. Being a Douglas, Angus was less inclined to intervene on Hamilton's behalf in the ecclesiastical proceedings. Patrick's constancy during the poorly-managed six-hour-long execution left a considerable impression upon onlookers, especially his fellow Augustinian canons, ensuring 'the reik of Maister Patrik Hammyltoun . . . infected as many as it blew upoun' with heresy.[9] Not realising this was the beginning of a threat to its control over the country's beliefs, the Scottish church showed little inclination to diversify into persecution, preferring to concentrate upon reforming ecclesiastical abuses.

Much to Margaret's fury, Albany's departure in 1524 had opened the way for Angus' return from France via London. She could not completely block his power, even though she had been recognised once more as regent and had the support of the anti-Douglas faction. As a consequence of their marital breakdown the Queen Mother was left with a passionate hatred of her husband and fights over money and the custody of their daughter further poisoned their relationship. Her long-awaited divorce finally arrived in 1528, freeing Margaret to make the same mistake of remarriage and regret, her third husband being Henry Stewart, who had been serving in her household. When Angus first re-appeared in the capital the queen trained Edinburgh Castle's cannon on his retinue, killing four bystanders when a shot was fired. With Henry and Wolsey regarding Angus as a more reliable tool than Margaret, Scotland witnessed the bizarre situation in 1524–5 of two pro-English factions at loggerheads, with each camp attempting to employ parliament to autho-rise its position. Since no scheme which excluded Angus would work, in the parliament of February 1525 Margaret had to swallow the bitter pill of accepting him as one of the governing team, alongside Arran, Lennox and Argyll.

The bloodless solution to the previous impasse had proposed control over the king and government being rotated quarterly among the four magnates, with Angus given first turn in order to conclude a truce with England. In retrospect such naivety appeared to push trust beyond rea-sonable limits, though it is unlikely that Angus planned his coup from the beginning. When the time came in November 1525 for Angus to pass on his charge, he simply retained James V.

[9] *The Works of John Knox*, ed. D. Laing (6 vols, Edinburgh, 1842–64), I, 42.

DOUGLAS RULE

Throughout his period of dominance, Angus believed himself indispensable to English policy, a view not shared in London. With the French threat from Scotland in abeyance, Henry VIII and Wolsey, by design or default, were content for their northern neighbour to remain weak and pro-English. Since 1513 there had been little sign England desired a peaceful alliance, being happier to destabilise Scottish domestic politics. Their successful wrecking tactics included Lord Dacre's constant Border raiding in peacetime and the wartime punitive expeditions. Being labelled an Anglophile, though failing to deliver visible gains from friendship with England, did not endear Angus to his fellow Scots and during his adult rule had a significant negative effect upon James V's own foreign policy.

Being too fearful to trust others, Angus struggled to inspire their trust in return and could not establish a basis for co-operation or reconciliation. He attempted to sustain his regime solely through his kin, though for a man so conscious of his 'name', Angus exhibited a curious neglect of his own dynastic duty of producing a male heir. To consolidate his control over government Angus placed his kinsmen in key offices. Making a break from the line of clerical appointees, Archbishop Beaton lost the Great Seal, with Angus himself eventually becoming Chancellor in 1527. His uncle Archibald was Treasurer and returned to being provost of Edinburgh. In close proximity to the king and able to keep watch on him, Angus' brother, George, was appointed master of the household, with James of Drumlanrig master of the wine cellar and James of Parkhead master of the larder. Between June and September 1526, a rush of over a hundred grants of offices, pensions, wards and non-entries followed a formal royal Revocation. Since Angus proved incapable of attracting the loyalty of fellow magnates such a traunche of patronage failed to construct the broad basis of support the Douglas regime needed. The earl also alienated those who had given their support in 1525 against the queen, such as Argyll and Lennox, who along with Glencairn and Cassillis ceased attending the Council, thereby dangerously reducing its regional representation. Instead of political accommodation and reward, Angus employed threats as a way of ensuring compliance. He gave/or withheld remissions for past crimes, holding over Arran his ten-year-old treason at Kittycrosshill, whilst allowing Moray to obtain his pardon for an attack on Huntly in Perth in 1524. Not featuring on Angus' political agenda nor sucked into the maelstrom of

---

The Gaelic learned orders and the *Book of the Dean of Lismore*

Within late medieval Gaelic society the main bearers of cultural traditions were the hereditary learned orders (*aos dána*), families of specialists transmitting their particular skill, poetry, history, music, medicine, law, carving and other decorative arts and crafts, to succeeding generations. These families developed extremely close links with the church, holding benefices and acting as notaries and priests, exemplified by the MacGregors of Fortingall in central Perthshire between 1512 and 1526. One family member, James, Dean of Lismore (d. 1551), collected poetry and other items into the *Book of the Dean of Lismore*. It contained the work of Irish and Scottish professional poets in the strict bardic forms of Classical literary Gaelic, and featured amateur poets from the surrounding nobility, such as Iseabail ní Mheic Cailein, countess of Argyll, who composed courtly love poems, and MacGregor's neighbour, Duncan Campbell of Glenorchy, who contributed more bawdy verses. The *Book* was written in a Scots-based orthography, demonstrating the tri-lingual skills of the learned orders who acted as cultural bridges and translators between the Scots- and Gaelic-speaking worlds as well as operating with ease in the intellectual and ecclesiastical language of Latin.

---

national politics, Highland Perthshire experienced a cultural flowering with the production of the *Book of the Dean of Lismore*, the most significant Gaelic literary manuscript surviving from the entire period.

Angus lacked a long-term strategy and, inexplicably, failed to plan for the time when James V would rule in person. He did possess a talent for political tactics and an ability to take those opportunities which presented themselves, allowing him to exploit the dynastic complexities of the Stewart succession (see Table 2.1) for his short-term gains. Should the king die, Arran, as the grandson of James II, headed the nearest male line within Scotland, though his family's claim was overshadowed by the divorce of his first wife, a matter which dogged the Hamiltons for another fifty years. The line might then pass through Arran's sister to his nephew, Lennox. Having settled his own difficulties with Angus, on 4 September 1526 Arran took the field against his nephew, who had been attempting to free the king from Douglas control. At the end of the skirmish near Linlithgow, Arran was found weeping over Lennox's corpse, calling him 'The wyssist man, the stoutest man, the hardiest man that ever was bred in Scotland'.[10] What undermined this moving display of grief was that Lennox had been killed by Arran's eldest illegitimate son, Hamilton of Finnart. Since it was believed that their earl had died after being taken prisoner, the Lennox Stewarts remained at feud with the Hamiltons for the rest of the century. Finnart's belated and perfunctory penance in 1531 and endowment of Masses for Lennox's soul did not cancel the blood debt.

For Angus, the death of Lennox had the beneficial effect of temporarily cowing any opposition since Lennox had technically been in rebellion. Since Angus had also turned a blind eye or half-heartedly pursued other killings, this gave an overall impression that there was no impartiality in the administration of justice, the touchstone of good rule. When Cassillis was murdered at the end of August 1527 on Prestwick sands, his killer, Campbell of Loudoun, was not outlawed for over a month and then not apprehended. Having buried their chief in Maybole church, the Kennedys vowed their revenge under the Cassillis 'dule' (gallows) and oath-swearing tree. This feud added a further complication to Ayrshire politics, already riven by the continuing Cunningham–Montgomery antagonism. It directly affected national politics when Eglinton, one of Angus' main supporters, could not be brought fully into government for fear of alienating Glencairn, who was pursuing Eglinton for his kinsman's murder. The general mood was expressed in the dark and brooding feel of the Mass 'Ferra Pessima' for five voices, probably composed in the mid-1520s by Robert Carver. Its title was taken from the biblical story of the return of Joseph's torn and bloodied coat of many colours to his father Jacob who assumed his son had been eaten by wild beasts. Contemporaries, aware Scotland was herself being torn apart, regarded the maintenance of justice as the only secure way out of the tangled maze of feud and faction linking local, regional and national political life.

Angus, far from secure even in his own backyard of the eastern borders, had to travel with a sizeable retinue as protection against the Humes, who resented his encroachments. His backing of the Kers in the Wardenship of the Middle March brought opposition from the Scotts, who caused a serious scare at Darnick in 1526 when the royal party was surprised by Scott of Buccleuch and in the fight Ker of Cessford was killed. Angus countered by conducting a series of judicial raids to impose order upon the Borders, with even the English acknowledging the region was more peaceful.

[10] *The Historie and Cronicles of Scotland . . . by Robert Lindesay of Pitscottie*, ed. A. J. E. Mackay (3 vols, STS, Old Series 42–3, 60, Edinburgh, 1899–1911), I, 320.

Bell, book and candle

In addition to judicial raids, Border reivers faced the Church's strongest censure when the archbishop of Glasgow issued the following excommunication in 1525. Applying a specific curse to each part of the body and every activity, this comprehensive sentence withdrew access to the sacraments and condemned the sinners to Hell, unless they repented and did penance.

I curse thare heid and all the haris of ther heid, I curse thare face, thare ene, thare mouth, thare neyse, thare tounge, thare theith, thare cragis (necks), thare schulderis, thare breystis, thare hartis, thare stomakis, thare bakis, thare armys, thare leggis, thare handis, thare feyt, and everilk part of thare bodys behynde, within and without; I curse thame gangand, I curse thaim rydand, I curse thame standand, I curse thame sittand, I curse thaim eittand, I curse thaim drynkand, . . . I curse thare wyiffis, thare bayrnis and ther servandis participant with thame in thare evil and myscheiffus deidis; I uayry [wary = curse] thare cornis, thare catall, . . . thare horsis, . . . thare hennis, thare chalmeris, thare beddis, . . . thare bernys, thare byris, . . . and all the gudis and houssis that are necessar for thare sustenatioun and welefare. . . .

I dissevir and partis thame fra the kirk of God . . . I interdyte all and syndry the kyrkis . . . that thai cum to or remainis in fra all messis sayng and celebration of divine service and ministratioun of the sacramentis of halykirk except the sacrament of baptisme allanerly; and thare bodeys at happinis to dee under this cursing and interdictioun to be cassyn furth to doggis and beistis and nothir to be erdit in kirk nor kirkyard . . . I forbyd and inhibitis al preistis and kirkmen under the pane of the gret cursing to schryif [shrive] or absolve thame of ther synnis quhil thai be first assoilyeit [absolved] fra this cursing; I forbid . . . al Cristin man and woman til have ony cumpany with thame . . . I discharge al bandis, actis contractis . . . and fynaly I condampne thame perpetualy to the deip pott of hell to remane with Lucifere and Baelzebub and al ther fallowis devillis of hell . . . and as the sounde of this bell gais fra your eris and the lycht of this candle fra your sycht sa mot thare saulis gang fra the visaige of god almychty and ther gude fame fra the warld quhill tha forbeire ther oppin synnis . . . and mak satisfactioun for ther misdedis and cum to the boissum of haly kirk to ressave and do pennance for the remission of ther oppin synnis.[11]

[11]   *St Andrews Formulare, 1514–46*, ed. G. Donaldson and C. Macrae (2 vols, Stair Society 7 and 9, Edinburgh, 1942–3), I, No. 229.

Both Lennox and Scott of Buccleuch had been attempting to free James V from the hands of the Douglases. Though not under close physical restraint, the constant supervision irked the teenager who knew he was being treated like an item of royal regalia, carefully polished and preserved, but purely symbolic. His scholarly education was interrupted when Angus dismissed his tutor Gavin Dunbar, though James, preferring his chivalric training to his academic studies, might have been grateful. Sir David Lindsay later recalled his part in the king's upbringing, teaching James music and dancing as well as playing games with the boy and tenderly caring for him.

> Quhen thow wes young, I bure the in myne arme
> Full tenderlie, tyll thow begouth to gang,
> And in thy bed oft happit the full warme,
> With lute in hand, syne, sweitlie to the sang:
> Sometyme, in dansing, feiralie I fland;
> And, sumtyme, playand fairsis on the flute.[12]

As he grew older, James developed a profound and abiding aversion to his stepfather, giving the king a further bond with his mother, to whom he remained close. As a way of occupying his attention and energies, the Douglases had encouraged the boy to indulge himself, especially by taking a precocious interest in sexual pleasure. In later life the king was noted as being sparing in his diet and infrequently drinking wine, though he showed little sign of moderating his sexual appetite. He had boldly taken the initiative in 1526, making a bond on his own behalf with Lennox, 'as we war ane privat person . . . by [without] ony wertu of prilegis of soverantye'.[13] James attempted to slip away from Linlithgow with the earl, and Lennox's death shortly afterwards was a blow to his hopes, teaching him how to watch and wait.

JAMES' ESCAPE

James' expectation that a more active role in government would follow his sixteenth birthday sparked a major row with Angus at the Easter Council

---

[12] Cited from *Dreme*, verses 8–13, and discussed in C. Edington, *Court and culture in Renaissance Scotland: Sir David Lindsay of the Mount (1486–1555)* (East Linton, 1995), 18.
[13] Cited and discussed in Emond, 'The Minority of James V, 1513–1528', 504.

of 1528. Though not best pleased by his mother's recently-announced third marriage, James used it to extract concessions from her: she would sign over Stirling Castle, part of her dower, to him in return for the marriage's formal recognition. Probably on the spur of the moment, James took his chance to escape from his Douglas captivity at the end of May. He had raised the royal standard and received the backing of sufficient lords to assume the government of the country a month later. He placed his former tutor, Gavin Dunbar, archbishop of Glasgow, into the chancellorship. When the Douglases refused to enter ward, the September parliament forfeited them. Having been carried along on the wave of his freedom, James found it much harder to be completely rid of his former warders. His campaign against Douglas strongholds was not a success: he was left staring at the pink sandstone walls of Tantallon Castle from the ditch protecting his cannon. Twenty days of battering and the drummers playing the march 'Ding Doun Tantallon' had not brought the walls tumbling down like Jericho. It was not exactly the dream start to his personal reign for which he had hoped.

The prolonged instability of James' minority had made all levels of society keenly aware of the need for a robust system of justice and one which curbed those exploiting their local and regional power. Scots assumed an adult monarch would perform that function and James found himself with a realm willing to accept harsh measures as the price of firm rule. Even if it required the surrender of some local jurisdictional autonomy, a central court had become an increasingly attractive notion.

The young king had experienced a difficult, and artificially prolonged, childhood making it extremely hard for him to trust others and giving him a wary aloofness at odds with his father's excessively relaxed style. For all the problems since Flodden, the kingdom was intact, free from direct external threats, and its underlying framework had proved strong enough to withstand fifteen turbulent years of royal minority. Scotland's Renaissance monarchy had survived and the country was ready to resume its confident stance.

CHAPTER 5

Courts and Clergy: James V (1528–37)

In 1528 the foundations of the Stewart monarchy were relatively secure, despite the battering they had experienced during fifteen long years of minority and factional strife. Once the focus and patronage of an adult ruler returned, the glitter and style of a Renaissance court were quickly re-established. Alongside the monarchy's residual strength, James inherited a reservoir of good will among his subjects, who would tolerate many things in the name of firm rule. They hoped and expected an active king would bring justice back to the regions. However, the legal systems in Scotland were creaking and a growing consensus among the legally trained recognised a new approach was needed. They welcomed the establishment of the College of Justice in 1532 which helped transmute 'justice' into 'the rule of law', and marked a milestone in the development of Scotland's judicial system and the emergence of a legal profession. The clergy were central to this process and to the general stability of the kingdom. James V's personal rule saw the convergence of crown and church with a hybrid growing from that conjunction that sustained the governance of the kingdom for the next fifty years. As that church–crown hybrid grew, the chance of successful Catholic reform diminished. There was an ironic twist to English carping that James was a 'priest's king'; it was a neat inversion of the reality that the clergy were very much the king's priests.

PUSHING THE MINORITY INTO THE PAST

Having escaped from the Douglases, James established his personal rule by demonstrating it was his actions and decisions that counted, instead of those done in his name. If the break in 1528 had been quick and clean, the reign would have gone more smoothly, but the protracted struggle to expel Angus and the looming presence of the Douglases sitting across the border left a sense of unfinished business. A deal was finally mediated by the Provincial of the Observant Franciscans, though, curiously, it was Angus who walked away. Eventually, in May 1529 the earl crossed the border into exile in England where he was to remain for the rest of James' life. When general remissions were granted to 146 Douglas supporters among the lairds and lower ranks the messy episode came to a ragged ending. James never forgave Angus and his associates and nourished a grudge against those who had not immediately recognised his authority in July 1528. For the rest of his reign, James savoured his cold dish of revenge, never quite banishing the minority to the past.

With greater patience and less bitterness, the king tidied up another of the minority's legacies: his mother. Immediately after his escape, she and her husband had provided refuge at Stirling, bringing thanks for Henry in the form of the title Lord Methven, the only peerage of the reign. Personal relations between mother and son remained relatively good, though increasingly distant. There was friction on two fronts: Margaret was an advocate of a pro-English policy whilst James pursued a French bride and alliance; Margaret's permanent marital problems, particularly her desire to divorce Methven, created further tension. His mother's complaints about having no money, especially to spend on clothes, also provided a constant irritant. During James' stay in France, Margaret even tried to flee to England, though she was stopped at the border. Judging from the satirical sketch in his 1534–5 account book of the Queen Mother playing bagpipes, the Treasurer had endured Margaret's financial moans and, like the rest of the court, was not overly sympathetic. Greater harmony prevailed in Margaret's closing years as Mary of Guise, with consummate tact, succeeded in encouraging her mother-in-law to adopt the role of regal figurehead. The Queen Mother died of a stroke in 1541, lamenting to her confessors that she had fallen out with her second husband, Angus. One abiding sorrow was that she had not seen her daughter, Lady Margaret Douglas, who had been brought up in the English court with Princess (later Queen) Mary Tudor, a friendship with major consequences for future Anglo-Scottish relations.

THE ARRIVAL OF A CONFESSIONAL FRONTIER

Anglo-Scottish relations remained tense thanks to the Queen Mother's counter-productive advocacy of England's cause and continued English support for the Douglases. The Scottish king was unlikely to be wooed into cordiality by his uncle's assumption that James should automatically follow his advice, and be grateful it was being bestowed. However great James' irritation, he could not risk another English invasion and considerable effort was expended on maintaining peace, if not friendship, with England during the 1530s. This task was made especially difficult following Henry VIII's break with Rome; it introduced a new confessional border within the island of Britain.

When the question was raised of what to do about the schismatic English, the Scottish king found himself at the heart of European planning. Ruling the best gateway onto the British mainland, James was an essential component in any invasion schemes. This increased the kingdom's prestige with its ally, France, and made the Emperor and other European rulers take more notice of Scotland. There was a danger Scotland would go to war with England whilst those rulers cheered loudly from the sidelines without sending their promised backing. This explains the extreme caution in 1536–7 when the Pilgrimage of Grace rocked the Tudor state, proving, in retrospect, the best opportunity for a Catholic attack, though by the time it was organised the moment had passed. Thanks to the confessional border, James dramatically increased his bargaining power with the papacy, and every last concession was squeezed from Clement VII and Paul III. English upheavals sent to Scotland a stream of religious and political exiles and encouraged Scots in trouble for their heretical views to go south, such as the talented musician and Franciscan friar Robert Johnson. With Henry VIII feeling insecure while Scotland held the opposite religious stance to his own, the exiles loomed ever larger in his mind, contributing to the outbreak of war in 1542.

A LIVELY RENAISSANCE COURT

Freed from Douglas control, the royal household re-emerged as the centre of a lively court and a magnet for those seeking cultural patronage. The mix of chivalric and Renaissance culture thriving under James IV quickly re-appeared, exemplified in Sir David Lindsay's dual role as court poet and Lyon King of Arms. James, who enjoyed music, inherited many royal musicians, such as the trumpeters of the Drummond family, from Italy before adopting a Scottish name and serving three Stewart monarchs. They were part of the musical establishment playing the 'loud' instruments for public occasions outside or in the great halls,

The music of Robert Carver

Robert Carver, c.1488–1568, an Augustinian canon at the Abbey of Scone, was the premier Scottish musician of the first half of the sixteenth century, and from his compositions five Masses and two votive antiphons have survived in his Choirbook (see Figure 5.1). Making major demands upon singers, his complicated polyphonic music would only have been performed by large, well-trained choirs attached to the Chapel Royal, major cathedrals and churches boasting a 'sang schule'. The antiphon, *O Bone Jesu*, was scored for nineteen voices, possibly to compliment the nineteenth year of James V's reign, and was a mature work of great architectural sophistication with a massive dramatic impact when all the voices were marshalled together. Carver's Masses included the only British example to follow the continental fashion of the cantus firmus *L'homme armé*, giving an indication of the composer's broad range of musical sources and knowledge which also incorporated English material. The fragments surviving from Carver's fellow composers reveal that 'musick fyne' was flourishing within pre-Reformation Scotland.

distinguished from those playing 'soft' instruments in the private setting of recreational music within the chamber. In that intimate context, since the king had a good ear and could sight-read music, he played the lute and took part in the singing, though his voice was described as 'rawky and harske'.[1] Music and dancing went together, especially during celebrations, and in common with much of court life were heavily influenced by French models and fashions. Whilst little secular music remains, some of the sacred music James would have heard has survived, such as David Peebles' 'Si quis diliget me' (If anyone loves me, he will observe my words), whose deceptive simplicity disguised the complete mastery of the composition. Outwith the court, the cathedrals, collegiate churches and larger burghs had sufficient musical resources to display the polyphonic beauty of contemporary liturgical music and the sophisticated repertoire performed at Lincluden collegiate church, Dumfries, can be glimpsed in the Dowglas/Fischar part book.

The architectural splendour of the court was enhanced by a remarkable architect with a wealth of new ideas who constructed for James

---

[1] Cited and discussed in A. Thomas, *Princelie Majestie: The court of James V of Scotland, 1528–1542* (Edinburgh, 2005), 92.

Figure 5.1 Robert Carver's Choir book, c. 1503–46. [NLS Adv MS 5.1.15]

magnificent royal apartments to rival the best in Europe. Sir James Hamilton of Finnart might have sauntered off the pages of Machiavelli's *Prince*, with all the attributes of an Italian Renaissance man: a highly talented architect and designer, a great admirer and collector of cultured and beautiful objects, including women, he was also a skilled soldier and ruthless politician. He nursed an exceedingly high opinion of himself and exuded ambition, seeking to overcome his illegitimate birth and become heir to his father's title and estates. 'The Bastard of Arran', as he was known, was prepared to fund the royal building works in the expectation that a grateful monarch would legitimise and support him, and pay most of the construction costs later.

Finnart undertook most of the building work in the 1530s on the royal palaces at Linlithgow, Stirling, Holyrood and Falkland, and on Blackness and Rothesay castles, the house at Crawfordjohn, the 'New Inns' within the Priory of St Andrews and the lodging at Balmerino Abbey, on the south bank of the Tay, for the sickly Queen Madeleine. His reconfiguration of Linlithgow, shifting the entrance to the south and developing a greater sense of symmetry and proportion, gave the palace a new character. The eye-catching, three-tiered, 'wedding-cake' fountain, with its water flowing from the imperial crown at the top, created the feel of an open-air Renaissance courtyard in its combination of intimacy and public space. The overall effect elicited Mary of Guise's tactful observation there was not a finer chateau in France.

At Stirling, Finnart created a mini-palace within the existing one, building a new series of royal apartments surrounding an enclosed courtyard, the 'Lion's Den'. The king and queen each had three perfectly-proportioned rooms with large windows, serving as an outer chamber, a presence chamber and a bed chamber with inner and outer galleries. The apartments created the physical layout for formalised court routine, guarding access to the monarch by limiting entry to the presence and bed chambers. Into the high ceilings of the presence chambers were placed the impressive and amusing Stirling Heads, carved portraits on wooden roundels depicting members of the court, including the Queen Mother. With a strongly classical theme, the statues of the three external facades portrayed deities, the virtues and the arts and one of the king and Finnart himself.

The interior furnishings were equally lavish with the same blending of medieval and Renaissance styles and motifs, especially in the tapestries imported from Flanders and northern France. The traditional *mille-fleurs* of the unicorn tapestries hung alongside those depicting epic scenes from classical mythology giving the impression of painted murals. Alongside magnificent buildings and furnishings, James wanted excellent palace grounds to pursue that deeply-ingrained Stewart passion for hunting. With an imperiousness displaying no regard for the law, he dispossessed the tenants to enlarge the parks at Holyrood and Falkland. After his death the notorious illegality of these actions caused the Court

Craignethan Castle

Craignethan Castle stands above the gorge of the Water of Nethan in Upper Clydesdale and Hamilton of Finnart was fortunate to have a greenfield site in 1531 on which to construct his fine country villa, inside a defensive box. With the land falling away steeply to the river, natural defence was available on three sides whilst the western approach was overlooked and needed protection from cannon fire. Using his Italian experience, Finnart built a thick western wall with a deep ditch, into which he placed a caponier, a vaulted stone-roofed gallery with loopholes that provided cover fire for the ditch – a startling innovation in Scotland. Two towers to the east and a surrounding wall completed the box, safely enclosing the luxurious lodging. Being lower and squarer than contemporary tower houses, it was more like a magnificent bungalow, compact yet remarkably spacious. It was split by a cross wall separating the two parts of the household in a horizontal version of 'upstairs-downstairs', with noble accommodation on the right and service quarters on the left. Uniquely for that period, the entrance led straight through a lobby into the magnificent, barrel-vaulted hall, approximately a double cube in proportion, with a large minstrels' gallery. Big windows lit the room and provided comfortable window seats with stone polished to resemble marble. Finnart's chambers led off the hall, carefully designed for maximum comfort with en-suite facilities and central heating from the chimneys for the kitchen and hall running behind the chamber walls, as well as its own fireplace; his secure little charter room could only be accessed from a stair inside his private chamber. Finnart had designed an elegant country house with a sense of light, air and symmetry permeating the noble rooms and with a high degree of 'finish' in the dressed stone surrounds and spacious built-in cupboards; even the drainage and sewage systems were well planned, running down into the Nethan. This castle, effortlessly combining comfort and defence and filled with clever design details, reflected the Renaissance eclecticism and flamboyance of its skilled architect.

of Session to offer redress to the injured parties, for 'the wele of his grace's saule'.[2]

Although revelling in Renaissance display, James did not share his father's great passion for a navy, being content to use French gifts such as

---

[2] Cited in R. K. Hannay, *The College of Justice*, ed. H. MacQueen (Stair Society Supplementary Series I, 1990), 308 at n. 3.

the *Salamander* or captured ships like the *Mary Willoughby*. Without the focus of royal interest and funding, Scotland's shipbuilding industry did not progress, remaining largely at the level of boat building and ship repairs and servicing. As the Low Countries led the way into semi-industrialised ship production, the kingdom fell even further behind, with deleterious consequences for Scotland's mercantile fleet. For a country with such a strong maritime tradition, this was a serious missed opportunity, though reticence over a substantial royal navy was extremely prudent given how far the crown's finances were already stretched.

'JEDDART JUSTICE'

In the opening years of his personal rule, James, conscious of the need for firm gestures to re-establish justice, stamped his authority upon the Borders. Before going to France, he personally led expeditions into the Borders in 1529, 1530, 1532, 1534 (twice), 1535 and 1536. The Middle and West Marches, in particular the 'Debateable Lands', had generated English complaints and given an excuse for Lord Dacre to make retaliatory raids into Scotland. The Armstrongs remained troublesome, since Maxwell, who held their bonds of manrent, proved unwilling or unable to bring them to justice. When John Armstrong of Hollows Tower and Gilknockie and his band answered the summons in 1530 to appear before the king in Teviotdale, appeals for mercy were ignored and they were hanged. Pitscottie transformed this into the romantic legend of the ballad 'Johnie Armstrang', subsequently made famous by Sir Walter Scott. In an instance of poacher turned gamekeeper, John Johnstone captured George Scott of Bog, described in the *Diurnal of Occurrents* as a great thief who burned woman and children in their homes. Making the punishment fit the crime; Scott was tied to a stake and burned alive. Though labelling such summary methods 'Jeddart (Jedburgh) justice', contemporaries approved of these law-and-order raids and the harsh imposition of justice. In Sir David Lyndsay's moral tale of the royal hound 'Bagsche', condemned to hang without confession, the dog received a pardon. Since royal pardons were in very short supply, this was probably intended as a reminder to James to exercise the regal virtue of mercy in addition to executing justice.

James had cleared the way for his raid by placing in ward the Border magnates and on their release insisting they signed general bands to keep good rule over their subordinates, to deliver them to justice and to remove malefactors from their lands. The penalty for failure was loss of lands, and human pledges were taken for the good behaviour of their kinsmen from those not landholders. The traditional tough line in the Borders was expected of an adult monarch and applauded by those who had bewailed its absence during James' minority. For the rest of the century, Jeddart-style justice and general banding were regarded as viable policies for dealing with unruly regions.

NO EASY PATH TO INTEGRATION

Tough or rough justice was not applied throughout the kingdom in James' reign, with little notice being taken of the bitter internecine feud in Orkney and Caithness among the Sinclairs, bringing the last pitched battle on Orkney soil. Since their acquisition, the crown had not found, or seriously investigated, a satisfactory method of governing the Northern Isles – out of sight remained out of mind. Whilst the bishops of Orkney had proved important, there was not a consistent policy of backing their authority against the regional power of the Sinclairs, formerly earls in Orkney and holding the earldom of Caithness. When Lord Sinclair was a minor, the Sinclairs of Warsetter, on the island of Sanday, had taken effective control in Orkney. Once of age and having failed to achieve restitution through legal means, William, aided by his cousin John, earl of Caithness, attempted to re-assert himself by force. Landing on the mainland with several hundred men in June 1529 the mainland Sinclairs were met at Summerdale by Orcadians under the command of Warsetter's illegitimate son. The brief and bloody skirmish left Caithness dead and Lord Sinclair in captivity. The crown displayed an almost total lack of interest despite the fact William had been enforcing the rule of law.

To add insult to injury, in 1535 Warsetter's son was legitimised, knighted and granted a royal charter for his Sanday lands. In a manner perfectly suiting Adam Abell's moralising, the ruthless Sir James, who had terrorised Orkney, met a terrible fate: he committed the mortal sin of suicide by running stark naked into the sea. In 1540 after the royal visit to the Northern Isles, the courtier Oliver Sinclair, from the Rosslyn branch of the family, was given the tack of royal lands in Orkney. The gift to a courtier did not signal direct central intervention and integration, despite the naming of the judicial offices in Scots terms rather than with their traditional Orcadian titles. The battle of Summerdale had demonstrated how difficult it would be to impose a new order upon the Northern Isles from the outside. The feud between Caithness and Orkney, and the internal struggle among the Sinclairs, continued to disrupt northern Scotland for decades to come.

Although the king paid more attention to events in the West Highlands than the Northern Isles, the results were little better. Throughout the royal minority, Clan Campbell was led by the 3rd earl of Argyll (named *Cailean Mailleach*, Colin Lumpy-Brow, because his forehead crinkled when he grew angry), who held sweeping powers as Lieutenant of the West. The earl and his brother, Campbell of Cawdor, expanded their power in the Western Highlands and the Isles, combining raiding and force with the gentler tactics of making bonds of manrent and marriage alliances. Although married to the Cawdor heiress, and taking her Moray inheritance and its territorial designation, Cawdor also sought further territory in the west, bringing him into conflict with his brother-in-law, MacLean of Duart, whom he killed in 1523 when they were attending court. Existing tensions in Kintyre increased to the point of rebellion when Argyll, as Chamberlain, was instructed to increase royal rents, instead of using the former MacDonald lands to build up co-operation and support. This was a glaring example of short-term financial pressures driving out long-term strategic considerations: Stewart rulers through- out the sixteenth and into the seventeenth centuries pursued policies based upon the mirage of making a profit from the Highlands.

When rebellion flared in 1529, the king rejected Cawdor's grandiose plans to suppress it though forces were gathered for a royal expedition. The show of might proved sufficient to bring MacDonald of Dunyvaig and MacLean of Duart back to obedience, and by appearing in person in Council, MacDonald neatly turned the tables on the newly-succeeded 4th earl of Argyll. MacDonald's extravagant offer to clip Argyll's wings and drive him from his own shire was not tested, but he was reinstated whilst the earl lost Kintyre. MacDonald and MacLean demonstrated their loyalty in 1532 by raiding the Isle of Man and capturing two English ships. James personally accepted the 'gift' of the *Mary Willoughby*, and sailed it back to Dumbarton, making it the largest vessel in the royal fleet.

Though appearing to operate a classic 'divide-and-rule' strategy to exert royal control over the Hebridean chiefs, neither James V nor his successors discovered or manufactured a viable alternative to employing Argyll in the southern section and Huntly in the northern part of the Highlands to enforce royal justice and authority. The crown was unwill- ing, and probably unable, to devote sufficient attention and resources to filling the power vacuum created by the forfeiture of the Lordship of the Isles and directly ruling those regions. In 1531 another option, previously employed with Border chiefs, was tried, when MacDonald's young son, James, was sent to court as a hostage to be educated by the Dean of Holyrood. The path of integration into the Lowland aristocracy had been

Figure 5.2 The tomb of Alexander MacLeod in St Clement's church, Rodel, Harris, prepared 1528. [Historic Scotland]

voluntarily and extremely successfully trodden by Clan Campbell who had mastered the art of operating in both worlds. However, the integration of a region, and its political conformity through acculturation, required more than one boy's formation; there was no concerted attempt by persuasion or force to draw other Gaelic chiefs to court or involve them in Lowland society. The artistic self-confidence displayed in Alexander MacLeod's tomb in St Clement's church on Harris (see Figure 5.2) demonstrated the Isles were no backwater in need of 'culture'. In common with most Stewart interventions in the Highlands and Islands, royal policy remained at the mercy of competing priorities, finance or power, with the underlying problem being a lack of consistent interest.

THE COLLEGE OF JUSTICE

James V had conformed to his father's model of carrying justice around the kingdom by conspicuously attending justice ayres, especially in the Borders. Taking royal peace and protection to the regions was at best a partial solution to stem an increasing flow of individual petitions pouring into the centre, directed to Parliament and to the king and his Council. The parliamentary committee of Auditors of Causes and Complaints made valiant efforts to wade through the wave and the Council sat 'in session' more regularly to cope with its judicial business. The regular attendees at the Council Sessions and on the parliamentary committee, by combining legal training with extensive experience, were emerging as professional judges. The slow evolution of practice, procedure and personnel culminated in the formal creation of a central civil court in 1532. In institutional terms the records demonstrate the continuity, since the start of the Court of Session merited an enlarged capital letter within the Council records, though not a new register. However, the foundation of the College of Justice marked an important legal milestone and gave an essential focus to the development of the Scottish legal profession.

As its name implied, the College was a corporate body of judges deliberating together in a central unitary court which rapidly developed into a powerful, supreme court in civil matters having full cognisance over all civil causes and the exclusive right to determine certain matters. At its inception, instead of its modern counterpart the criminal law, it was the consistory jurisdiction of the ecclesiastical courts that formed the opposite of the civil jurisdiction of the Court of Session. The College comprised fifteen Senators or judges, half clerical and half lay, led by a clerical President. Though not a Senator, the Chancellor was entitled to sit and a number of Extraordinary judges were also appointed by the crown. After an Act of Parliament in May 1532 and following long negotiations with the papacy over financing, in 1535 the College was formally erected by papal bull, though its endowment had to wait until 1540.

Although the foundation was not solely a money-making device, from the start James intended that some funds granted by the papacy would be employed elsewhere. The eminently pragmatic solution to the pressing problem of justice was probably devised by the legally-learned Chancellor, Gavin Dunbar. His scheme, which had native roots, paralleled European developments introducing central courts and placing greater reliance upon Romano-canon law, the *ius commune*. The first President of the College was Alexander Myln, abbot of Cambuskenneth, whose legal experience had begun in the church courts and continued as a Lord of Session in the King's Council. Like most of his fellow Senators, the President carried both experiences across in an unbroken line into the College's work. The first surviving legal reports from the Court of Session found in *Sinclair's Practicks*, now considered the work of John, rather than his older brother Henry, cover decisions in the 1540s and reveal the court applying the *ius commune* whenever Scots domestic law did not express a contrary rule. The Sinclairs were appointed Senators in James' reign and later followed each other as President. This highly-educated pair were career lawyers for whom ecclesiastical benefices provided a steady income allowing them to pursue a wide range of humanist and literary interests and own extensive libraries. Henry's great love of books can still be seen in the expensive tooled-leather bindings and distinctive name stamps on his volumes, such as the fine 1532 edition in Greek of the Patristic Father, Basil the Great.[3]

The lawyer-clerics were not a separate group from those 'men of law' not in holy orders; it was a choice of personal career route. Legal learning acquired in formal university training or through practice in the courts gave them a shared expertise and group solidarity which distanced them from other judges deemed to be insufficiently learned upon matters of law. By separating upper and lower ranks of 'men of law', the Court of Session's naming of advocates to act as general procurators of the council encouraged the emergence of two defining characteristics of a legal profession: control over entry and subsequent discipline over entrants. The College's foundation gave vital momentum to the emergence of the Faculty of Advocates, encouraging the gradual evolution of a recognisable profession in Scotland and their close and continuing association with Edinburgh was being forged by these sixteenth-century developments. The eight advocates, named as procurators, predictably formed an interconnected group with most having been educated at Orléans, and possessing strong ties with Edinburgh, either as burgesses or members of the burgh's Trinity collegiate church, or linked to Stirling's Chapel Royal. Their interests were not confined to the law, being part of a core of self-aware, learned men in the capital and the court who gave dynamism to Scottish cultural life. Having been part of Mair's circle of illustrious logician-philosophers in Paris, the procurator and cleric Robert Galbraith was also a poet and author of an important legal manuscript, the *Liber Galbraith*. His post as treasurer of the Chapel Royal in Stirling and long association with the court did not prevent him from being a burgess of Edinburgh, with a house close to the Tolbooth that became a centre of legal activity. However, all this came to an untimely end in 1544 when he was murdered in Greyfriars churchyard because of a dispute with a fellow burgess.

[3] Edinburgh University Library *Dd 4 16 Basil*; T. A. F. Cherry, 'The library of Henry Sinclair, Bishop of Ross 1560–65', *The Bibliotheck* 4 (1963), 13–24.

THE FIFE CIRCLE OF ROYAL SERVANTS

In law as elsewhere in royal service, the reign of James V did not see a parting of the lay and clerical routes. Entering the 'service nobility' had long been an attractive, if somewhat precarious, route for the upwardly mobile, particularly those of laird stock or peers' younger or illegitimate sons. There was no need for individuals to opt for a single route until relatively late in their career, since many benefices could be held by those in minor orders. David Beaton, the future cardinal archbishop, following the well-trodden path of education and ecclesiastical benefice picked up the commendatorship of Arbroath Abbey while training as a diplomat and royal administrator, not receiving major orders until his consecration as bishop of Mirepoix in 1536.

A younger son of Beaton of Balfour, a Fife laird with Angus connections, local links helped David start his career and remained important when he became a patron himself. Two Beaton uncles had achieved success in royal service using a clerical and a lay path, with James rising to become archbishop of Glasgow and then St Andrews, and David of Creich becoming James IV's Keeper of Falkland Palace and Treasurer. Their nephew David, having grown up at Balfour Tower, followed the progress of his Markinch neighbours, Sibbald and Lundie of Balgonie, both of whom served as Treasurers, a post later occupied by Kirkcaldy of Grange living a few miles away. David's maternal kin, the Monipennys, originated in Fife's East Neuk, with Sir William distinguishing himself as an ambassador for James IV whilst his cousins, the Duries, from Leven, held the abbey of Dunfermline. When Beaton was archbishop of St Andrews, a cluster of royal officials were settled within strolling distance of his country residence at Monimail, with Henry Balnaves and then the Melvilles at Halhill and Sir David Lyndsay at the Mount. Since many of James V's activities in the 1530s centred on and between the three burghs of Falkland, Cupar and St Andrews, this part of Fife achieved considerable political importance.

With few great magnates, the sheriffdom of Fife was dominated by its lairds from whose ranks emerged this stream of royal servants. The lairds' self-confidence, deriving from their continued presence at court, helped their daughters marry 'up' into the peerage as did Janet, daughter of Beaton of Creich when she wed the 1st earl of Arran, and her sister Grizel when she married Lord Lyle. James V's particular liking for hunting within Fife allowed the Beatons to bolster their local position, and the bond with the king increased when Elizabeth became his mistress. Easy access to the king was a boon for other Fife lairds giving them a chance to demonstrate their loyalty and catch the king's attention by sending presents when he was in the vicinity, such as the rabbits supplied by the laird of Earlshall.

ECCLESIASTICAL WRANGLES

The successful clerical career of James Beaton, becoming archbishop of St Andrews and primate of the kingdom, was marred by his clashes with Gavin Dunbar, archbishop of Glasgow. The jurisdictional dispute between the archdioceses continued to disrupt the Scottish church, hamstring concerted or co-ordinated action and hamper national reforms. James V's consistent support for his former tutor and current chancellor greatly strengthened Glasgow whilst his relations with Beaton deteriorated badly after the clash over the funding of the College of Justice, which Dunbar had masterminded. Beaton was warded in St Andrews Castle and James wrote critical letters to the Pope seeking to have him tried. In response to royal pressure, the papacy had agreed a prodigious sum could be extracted from the Scottish church as an annual tax of £10,000, in addition to three tenths levied on benefices worth more than £20 a year. Since the two taxes were to run concurrently for three years, this would remove a quarter of prelates' incomes. The compromise of a lump sum of £72,000 and £1,400 annually towards the judges' salaries left the king taking most of the money and the judges fighting hard for their incomes. As part of this financial settlement, James pushed Archbishop Beaton into calling a Provincial Council of the Church, the first since 1470, which met for a week in the Blackfriars Hall in Edinburgh during March 1536. Dunbar's formal protest regarding this infringement of Glasgow's exemption from the primate's authority exemplified the obsessive concern with jurisdiction characterising Scotland's bishops. Given the spread of Protestantism in Europe and the concurrent activities of the English Reformation Parliament, reform of the Scottish church should have been top of the agenda, but the fundamental issues of reform and heresy were not addressed.

ROYAL APPOINTEES AND THE CHURCH–CROWN HYBRID

James, enjoying his bargaining power, made no serious effort to alter an ecclesiastical system working so much to his advantage. It was no accident that the pope formally recognised in 1535 the Scottish crown's right of nomination to clerical appointments and permitted a twelve-month delay during which the crown enjoyed the temporalities. This concession enabled the king to expand his father's policy of placing family members in lucrative benefices, a practice which became notorious when James' five surviving illegitimate sons were placed in the wealthiest commendatorships in the land: James (i) taking Kelso and Melrose; James (ii), St Andrews; John, Coldingham; Robert (i), Holyrood; and Robert (ii), Whithorn. To make room for these appointments two abbots were made bishops, and the hot-tempered prior of St Andrews, Patrick Hepburn, who had produced even more illegitimate children than James V, received Scone Abbey and the diocese of Moray. Though it benefited the hard-pressed royal treasury this major reshuffle of top ecclesiastical posts damaged the spiritual leadership of the regular orders and the dioceses.

Having royal appointees in charge of monasteries was not disastrous in every case. Remaining a royal servant throughout, Robert Reid, appointed abbot at Kinloss, did take the Cistercian habit. By careful regulation and particularly an educational programme which brought the humanist Giovanni Ferrerio to teach the monks, Reid organised monastic reform. Like Elphinstone's reforms in the previous reign, Reid could regenerate the particular patch under his direct control, but was unable to spread reform outwards through the monastic orders, let alone the whole church. Spiritual renewal came to Scotland in the conventional guise of new cults. Existing devotion to the Holy Cross found a new location at Peebles, given archiepiscopal blessing in 1530. Musselburgh became the Scottish site of the Virgin of Loretto, an Italian cult that had swept across Europe. Its resident hermit, Thomas Doughty, attracted many pilgrims, including Mary of Guise. His success also brought mockery and derision from the evangelical earl of Glencairn whose verses attacked Doughty's 'miracles' and the Franciscans in general. With a decidedly practical piety accompanied by civic pride, Janet Rynd added a hospital in the 1530s to her husband's foundation of Magdalen Chapel in the Cowgate, Edinburgh, where her tomb still lies. Her benefaction exemplified the continuing devotion flowing through well-worn channels of Catholic piety, though humanist and evangelical voices condemned the externalised and 'superstitious' aspects of some religious practices.

The notorious placement of James' sons in the wealthiest abbeys was the starkest example of the convergence of church and crown at the highest levels. A hybrid grew from that conjunction which drew upon ecclesiastical and royal authority, personnel and finances, making it impossible to distinguish between the two sources. For a Stewart ruler, this permitted the level of expenditure necessary to sustain a Renaissance monarchy and govern the realm, without placing additional pressure upon the kingdom's subjects. The hybrid's existence blocked major reform of the institutional structure of the church and gave the crown a vested interest in resisting change. Whilst spiritual vitality remained evident within many areas of pious practice, it was not easily channelled into the church's institutional structure where new life was so badly needed.

FRENCH BRIDES

What the Stewart monarchy also needed to sustain it during the 1530s was a legitimate heir, and that meant a royal marriage, though in his protracted search for a bride, like his father, James V showed no sense of pressure. Although the Treaty of Rouen negotiated by Albany during his minority had made provision for a French bride, childhood arrangements could be diplomatically forgotten or overturned if they no longer suited an adult ruler. Having fathered a handful of illegitimate children, James could be relaxed about providing an heir for Scotland. The choice of queen would provide the clearest indication of his diplomatic alignment and a dowry was the main chance of obtaining a substantial foreign subsidy. Being a reigning monarch of a small but significant kingdom, James' choices in the European marriage market were plentiful and improved by the favourable position Scotland enjoyed after England's break with Rome. Eighteen candidates were considered, including Margaret Erskine, the one mistress whom James took to his heart. Since she lacked a substantial dowry and was already married, that scheme did not last long. Obtaining a papal annulment for a royal marriage was a sensitive issue in 1536: Margaret was not destined to become Scotland's Anne Boleyn.

With the importance of the auld alliance, a French match had always been the favoured option and a series of diplomatic missions had been sent to secure an agreement. Whilst anxious to strengthen his Scottish ties, Francis I was reluctant to marry Madeleine, his sickly daughter, to James V, proposing instead Marie de Vendôme accompanied by a large dowry, the Order of St Michael and other inducements. The Scottish king accepted and on 1 September 1536 sailed from Leith with a substantial train, including his organist and his 'broudstars' or embroiders, essential for the forthcoming round of appearances. By leaving the kingdom for what proved to be a nine-month holiday, James demonstrated a high level

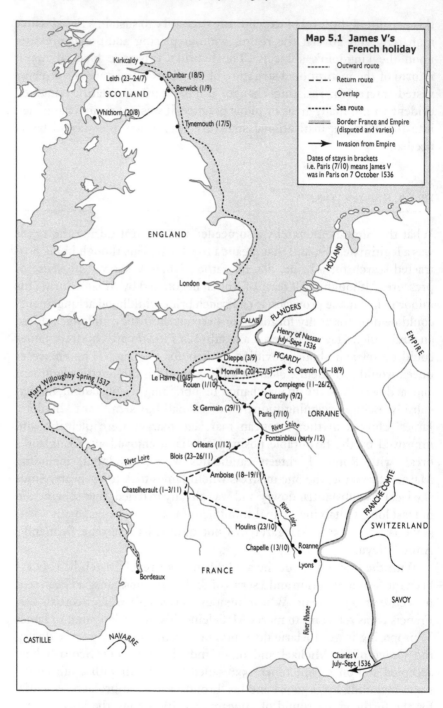

Map 5.1 James V's French holiday

- - - - - - Outward route

- - - - Return route

———— Overlap

.... Sea route

Border France and Empire (disputed and varies)

→ Invasion from Empire

Dates of stays in brackets i.e. Paris (7/10) means James V was in Paris on 7 October 1536 of confidence that the country's affairs could run smoothly without him and his subjects would not exploit his absence. The vice-regents he left in charge managed the realm in his absence, keeping the administration quietly ticking over and those magnates, who had initially accompanied the king, did not create any trouble when they returned to Scotland.

After arriving in Rouen, James visited Marie de Vendôme at St Quentin in disguise and, having been less than impressed, decided to change his bride. Whether this version of events is accurate, it proved a good moment for James to press Francis I to agree to a marriage with Madeleine because, to the French, James was coming to their aid when they were facing the emperor's attacks. The betrothal took place at Amboise on 26 November and James enjoyed a tour of the Loire chateaux, before making his entry into Paris on 31 December with the status accorded a dauphin of France. The following day he was married to Madeleine in Notre Dame Cathedral in a magnificent ceremony rounded off with a dinner eaten off gold and silver tableware and all the pomp and display he could possibly have desired. Even after the fortnight's wedding celebrations had finished, James lingered in France, receiving a cap and sword from the pope. The newlyweds finally arrived back in Scotland in May 1537, though the queen fell ill and two months later died in James' arms. Scottish rejoicing turned to mourning and Lindsay's celebratory poem became an epitaph, describing the king's and kingdom's loss.

With no hesitation and almost unseemly haste, another French bride was sought and James proved fortunate because a month before Madeleine's death, the duke of Longueville had died, leaving his widow Mary of Guise as a most suitable candidate. Francis I, equally anxious to secure the Scottish alliance, proved willing to furnish a second dowry and ignore Henry VIII's suit. Whatever her personal misgivings about remarrying and leaving her son in France, Mary of Guise calculated she had a better chance of living into old age as the wife of James V than that of Henry VIII. When told of the English king's interest she is said to have joked about the small size of her neck. In June she sailed from France, landing in Fife, and entering St Andrews to a welcome staged by Sir David Lindsay. At the abbey gate, a cloud opened to reveal an angel bearing the keys of Scotland for its new queen; it was a prophetic entry, because this Frenchwoman would subsequently rule the realm for a decade and die in its capital.

When he returned to Scotland after his extended sojourn in France, James was brimful of confidence and self-belief, though Madeleine's death cast a temporary shadow over the brightness. The new supreme central court provided an extremely positive postscript to the lawlessness of his minority. Its existence began the process of redefining the meaning of 'justice' with the College's foundation having profound effects upon the judicial process, the lawyers and the style of Scottish governance. In 1537 the Scottish king was at the very height of his prestige, having cut an even more impressive figure upon the European stage than his father. His enhanced status flowed in large measure from the French alliance and from King Francis, who had treated him with the respect due to a fellow monarch and accorded him the dignity and warmth reserved for a son. His father-in-law had also accepted the tiresome parenting duty of paying the bills, covering the expenses for James' stay, the elaborate wedding and the fleet home. When a second French bride was needed, Francis did not permit grief for his daughter's death to delay James' marriage to Mary of Guise. For king and country, the auld alliance was proving extremely beneficial, delivering all that had been promised and spreading Scotland's reputation throughout Europe. Francis' diplomatic generosity was in sharp contrast to the paltry offers and hectoring tone emanating from Henry VIII, who had never learnt the art of being gracious and was not going to start with his nephew.

Domestically, James was able to rest on the substantial financial cushion provided by ecclesiastical taxation, in addition to the generous French dowries. Even the economy was surging forward, with domestic stability and the ever-closer ties with France giving a noticeable boost to Scottish trade. Through the church–crown hybrid James could draw upon the wealth, authority and institutional strength of the church, as well as relying upon its personnel to staff his administration. The royal court and the new civil court now depended upon ecclesiastical finance and in both the 'king's priests' played a central role.

CHAPTER 6

Imperious Majesty: James V (1537–42)

T he statue on the north-east corner of the palace apartments at
Stirling Castle portrayed James V as a stern-looking man in court
dress, resting one hand on the dagger at his belt and the other on his
flowing beard. The distinctive profile with its long sharp nose can be seen
with a clipped beard on the gold ryal coin of 1539 and in the painting
alongside Mary of Guise, where his expression is less intimidating. In his
portraits, James conveyed the majesty of kingship through the force of his
personality. In the king rested the power to command and be obeyed and
he held the authority to execute. Touching his 'whinger' or dagger probably recorded one of the king's characteristic gestures, but it also referred
to the sword of justice, wielded by the monarch. It was reported that
James told some bishops, 'I shall reforme you, not as the King of
Denmark by impreasonment does, neyther yitt as the King of England
does, by hanging and heading: but I shall reforme yow by scharpe whin-
garis.'[1] As James V's reign progressed, there was plenty of respect and the
'dread' due a king, but less of the warmth and love his father inspired.

IMPERIAL DISPLAY

Their French holiday had given James and his companions a nearly inex-
haustible supply of ideas about Renaissance court life. French cultural
norms were borrowed, not slavishly copied and, thanks to the confidence
injected by the trip, they became translated into a distinctive Scottish
vernacular style. In their architecture and furnishings, the royal palaces
displayed extensive French and Italian influence, with many nobles

---

[1] *The Works of John Knox*, ed. D. Laing (6 vols, Edinburgh, 1846–64), I, 83.

following suit by constructing their own 'chateaux'. With the benefit of hindsight, Bishop John Leslie in his *History of Scotland* pinpointed the country's adoption of French fashion in building, banqueting and behaviour, following James' marriages, as the primrose path leading to the kingdom's moral and financial ruin.

Boosted by his French experience, James gave a higher priority to displaying the 'outward signs of majesty'. Though there was not a substantial increase in formality in Scotland, at times James felt court etiquette too restraining, and he disguised himself and mingled with his subjects, encouraging the epithet of the 'poor man's king' and the legends of the 'guidman of Ballengeich', subsequently exploited by Sir Walter Scott. A range of symbolic and heraldic artefacts, from coins to plaques, paintings and the remodelled crown, were consciously employed to express James' imperial majesty. The core symbols of regal authority were the Honours of Scotland (see Figure 3.1) and in 1536 James ordered the length of the sceptre to be increased. The royal crest was adapted to include the lion holding the sceptre, in addition to the sword he already carried. By adding an imperial crown to the Scottish thistle and the saltire a specifically royal version of each symbol was produced. Four years later the prestigious contract to remodel the damaged imperial crown was gained by John Mosman, whose goldsmith's workshop and dwelling on the High Street are better known today as 'The John Knox House'. A few days after the newly-modelled crown had been delivered, James wore it at the coronation of his heavily-pregnant queen, Mary of Guise, held with due pomp at Holyrood on 22 February 1540.

The court's imagery remained rooted in its chivalric culture, visually expressed through heraldry. On the imposing new gateway into Linlithgow Palace the eye was immediately caught by the four roundels displaying the European chivalric orders of which James was a member: the English Garter; the French St Michael; the Golden Fleece from the Emperor; and his own thistle and St Andrew collar. James probably contemplated establishing a Scottish chivalric order; the Order of the Thistle with a proper foundation and statutes did not yet exist, though James was shown wearing a thistle collar in the portrait painted with Mary of Guise. The royal arms were further modified, with the unicorn supporters given a flagstaff bearing a saltire banner as can be seen at Holyrood Palace (see cover illustration).

The new imperial image of the monarch was widely circulated when a gold coin was issued; since its high value precluded everyday use in Scottish markets, the ryal was essentially a vehicle for publicity. The new 'Bonnet piece' made in 1539 offered a different image of James V from

Armorials

In his capacity as Lyon King of Arms, Sir David Lindsay completed his splendid Armorial in 1542, Scotland's earliest extant Register of Arms, providing the model for the later Seton and Forman Armorials (see Figure 8.2). This beautifully illustrated record of the arms of Scotland and its nobility celebrated heraldry as the language of chivalry, including the arms of the Nine Worthies, that mix of biblical, classical and medieval warriors: David, Joshua, Judas Maccabeus, Julius Caesar, Alexander the Great, Hector of Troy, Charlemagne, Arthur and Godfrey of Bouillon, who appeared for the rest of the century in royal pageants or decorating castles, as at Crathes. Though mostly in the vernacular, the Armorial chose to celebrate noble virtue in a Latin prefatory verse, linking humanist and chivalric ideals. Complying with the 1540 Parliamentary Act demanding 'the memor of tratouris suld remane to the schame and sclander of thame that ar cummin of thame and to the terror of all vthiris to comit siclik in tymes cuming' Lindsay included the arms of forfeited traitors. Loss of honour was a very serious matter in sixteenth-century Scotland and the negative side to James V's imperial majesty turned treason into a more heinous crime carrying a heavier penalty.[2]

the youthful full-face portraits of the king, with the mature monarch portrayed in stern profile with his prominent 'Roman' nose and wearing a court bonnet holding a regal circlet and his thistle collar across his chest. The pose and profile were similar to Francis I, his father-in-law, whose nose also boasted imperial proportions. When making their own heraldic displays, loyal subjects were quick to adopt the new representations, such as the Newbattle Abbey font with its six heraldic shields. By communicating in the language of heraldry, the vernacular shared by Europe's rulers and nobility, and recognised and 'read' by all Scots, the imperial message spread far and wide across the realm.

MANAGING THE ROYAL FINANCES

Imperial display carried a hefty price tag and, like his fellow Renaissance rulers, James spent to the limits of his income and beyond. The king was

---

[2] The Armorial is now in the NLS; see also C. Edington, *Court and Culture in Renaissance Scotland. Sir David Lindsay of the Mount* (East Linton, 1994), 37–41.

fortunate in having the financial cushion afforded by ecclesiastical taxation and his French dowries. He also benefited from an improvement in Scottish trade which surged in the 1530s, lifting the economic gloom though not reaching a boom. James developed the habit of taking freely, holding fast what he had acquired and giving sparsely, thereby ensuring there was sufficient money to spend on major projects and maintain a cash reserve. Instead of hoarding like his grandfather, this James spent prodigally, like his father, on his favourite schemes and used methods of collecting revenue both kings had previously employed. At their heart lay the exploitation of crown lands, increasing royal holdings and raising rents and feus. Royal administrators made strenuous efforts to ensure lands technically belonging to the crown paid their way and they achieved a marked improvement in the length and value of rentals from Strathdee, Braemar and Cromar in the eastern Highlands. As had been the case in Kintyre in 1529, such financial exactions often incurred a high political cost. Since Stewart monarchs continued to believe a pot of gold waited in the Highlands and Islands, this mythical financial incentive helped drive the monarchy's efforts to enforce stability beyond the Highland Line.

Another method of increasing revenues from crown lands was direct exploitation of their resources such as the gold mine at Crawfordmuir, which produced a good return and supplied the metal to refurbish the crown. A handsome profit of around 2,000 merks came from the royal sheep flocks whose success provoked a pompous homily, that James ignored, from the English ambassador about not derogating one's nobility through dirtying one's royal hands with vulgar trade. James V did make widespread use of his father's device of compositions to avoid recognition of lands, managing with the standard Act of Revocation, issued first in 1537 and confirmed in parliament in 1540.

The pressure to raise money remained manageable, thanks to two substantial sources of income: the French dowries and the church. In total, Francis I paid out £168,750 (Scots), a huge windfall for his son-in-law. Placing his illegitimate sons as monastic commendators brought at least £10,000 and possibly four times that sum. During his reign James taxed his subjects directly thirteen times, raising £52,000, with most of the burden falling upon the church and, to a lesser extent, the burghs, with nobles relatively lightly taxed by comparison. Disguising the crown's extremely shaky financial underpinnings, the unprecedented availability of the church's wealth gave James a financial cushion and, equally vital for fiscal stability, the regular payment of a steady income. Though income was buoyant, expenditure kept pace, since James had no intention of stinting himself. Like his fellow rulers, James spent the money as long as it was there, never questioning whether this level of expenditure was sustainable.

In addition to her substantial dowry, Mary of Guise brought the Scottish court a steadying female presence and a sense of stability, counterbalancing her husband's ingrained Stewart restlessness. She settled into the public role of Scottish queen with grace and ease, though privately she sorely missed her son in France. Mary fulfilled her wifely duty by securing the succession with the birth of two sons, James and Robert, in 1540 and 1541 respectively, and a daughter in 1542. Her generosity of spirit and delicate tact enabled her to re-incorporate the Dowager Queen Margaret and as a royal family they shared the 1541 tragedy of the two princes dying within hours of each other. Despite that domestic and dynastic blow, Mary had proved an excellent choice as a queen consort, personifying the French alliance and adding her own lustre to the imperial court of Scotland. She was later to prove she could also rule the kingdom.

CAREER COURTIERS

As befitted a Renaissance monarch, James V could be generous, though he did not enjoy a reputation for distributing patronage or largesse with an open hand. If he had lived, he might have elevated some contemporaries to the peerage, though he had shown few signs of parting with royal lands to provide endowments and only made one land grant from the forfeited Angus estates. Such a policy of retention did not bode well for career courtiers looking to establish their own noble dynasty with matching titles and lands. The richest pickings were still found in ecclesiastical benefices and James exploited these to the full to reward his servants. Even in this lucrative field the pool of available resources was reduced, thanks to the king's own illegitimate sons taking so many commendatorships. A crop of the illegitimate sons of peers were anxious to make their fame and fortune at James' court, but their poverty and pushiness, as well as their birth, made them unpopular. The 'Bastard of Arran' (Finnart) was the most flamboyant of these lay courtiers but Campbell of Lundie, the natural son of the 1st earl of Argyll, who became royal treasurer, was witheringly described by Gavin Douglas as a 'bastard bribor quhilk had not 5s worth of good of his aun'.[3]

---

[3] Cited and discussed in A. Murray, 'Sir John Campbell of Lundie (d. 1562)', in *Oxford Dictionary of National Biography* (www.oxforddnb.com).

Making a bad situation worse in Angus

The crown's search for money and predatory courtiers seeking land made a bad family situation a lot worse in the 1530s. Their internal difficulties had made the Lindsays of Crawford soft targets. The 6th earl, having lost the dukedom of Montrose bestowed upon his father by James III, fell at Flodden before siring a legitimate male heir. The earldom quickly passed from his uncle to his cousin, leaving two Dowager Countesses both at loggerheads with the new 8th earl. The 'wicked Master' of Crawford, his son, was found guilty in 1531 of imprisoning his father and attacking his kinsman, Lindsay of Edzell. The 8th earl, previously convicted of oppressing the Dowager Countess of Montrose, then faced investigation by the Council over the rights of the 6th earl's widow. Once his rental books were produced, eagle-eyed royal lawyers discovered the previous earl had not been served correctly as heir, meaning non-entry payments were owed from 1513. The crown demanded £1,000 in back payments and insisted Crawford cover his tenants' dues. The Court of Session also declared the king's right to select sub-vassals and to sell that right to its assignees. With no room for manoeuvre, Crawford lands were mortgaged or sold, with estates bought by prominent rival courtiers. Another major beneficiary was Edzell, who obtained the right to the earldom that the Wicked Master had been forced to surrender and in 1542 succeeded as 9th earl, provoking a raid upon Finavon Castle and Glenesk by the Wicked Master's son. The earldom reverted to the senior branch in 1558, though the formidable Katherine Campbell, Edzell's widow, continued to dominate the region for a further twenty years. The two branches of the Lindsays remained at loggerheads, and the feuds engendered in the shire lasted into the next century.

The regional politics of Angus and the Mearns were dislocated as a result of direct crown intervention during the 1530s. Having been part of the landed powerbase of the earls of Angus, the region was of especial interest to the king and he was determined the Douglases should not rebuild their client network. The internal difficulties of the house of Crawford made them extremely vulnerable, leading to a royal demand for a substantial composition (see the box on making a bad situation worse in Angus, above). Lawyers exploited the king's feudal rights and courts to alter the earls' relationship to their tenants and benefit the crown. The entire process undermined the political balance of the shire allowing court rivalries to enter directly into the struggle for predominance in

Forfarshire. Thanks to their court connections royal servants such as David Beaton, abbot of Arbroath and future cardinal, Secretary Erskine of Brechin and William and David Wood of Bonnyton and Craigie were able to lead instead of follow the regional peers – the earls of Crawford, and Lords Ogilvy and Gray. Along with Campbell of Lundie, all of these career courtiers succeeded in their ambition to create a noble house based in Angus. James V's main aim of permanently dismantling the Douglas network failed, and the earl of Angus was able to rebuild his affinity during the 1550s. However, the pattern of predatory courtiers undermining weak peers proved more durable, becoming a common feature of the court's relationship with the regions.

TRIALS AND EXECUTIONS

Those in favour at court seized any opportunity to establish a local power-base or enrich themselves. James tolerated this 'help yourself' approach provided it was not at the expense of the crown and permitted the sharper rivalries that emerged and the attempts not simply to displace and disgrace an opponent, but to seek his death. By the late 1530s, a treason charge mentioning aiding the Douglases became 'code' that the king would permit an opponent to be executed. In a political culture used to seeing nobles forfeited, warded or exiled, James' refusal to exercise clemency added a ruthless edge to his rule.

In 1537 James displayed the negative aspect of his assertive imperiousness. He was firmly committed to the French alliance and determined to obliterate the Douglas ghost and its pro-English associations. For some time he had been suspicious of Angus' contacts with his sister, Janet, Lady Glamis. In 1529 rather than a remission, she was offered the chance to leave the country on pilgrimage, though probably because of her young children, she did not go abroad and, consequently, was put to the horn in 1530. Two years later and at the same time as the moves against the earl of Crawford, she faced a charge of poisoning her husband when the Angus power structure and the wider connections of the Douglases in the region had come under specific and exacting crown scrutiny. Janet appeared to have weathered the storm and was allowed to remarry, but in July 1537 she was convicted on two counts of treason: attempting to poison the king and communing with her Douglas brothers. Although probably guilty of the latter charge, the poison plot was improbable and her son's confession was obtained under duress. The sentence for poisoning was burning and she was executed forthwith, providing a tragic and romantic end for the beautiful woman of later legend. Her son, Glamis, had his death sentence commuted to imprisonment and her husband should have gone free, if he had not fallen to his death escaping from Edinburgh Castle. James was probably not in a merciful mood, since it was only ten days after the death of Queen Madeleine; he chose not to intervene rather than vindictively commanding Lady Glamis' burning.

Three days earlier he had been equally implacable, allowing the Master of Forbes to be executed for treason where the charge of a plot to kill the king was flimsier than Lady Glamis' alleged poisoning. The trial was part of Huntly's campaign against Forbes to gain control in Aberdeen. The king displayed a callous indifference to the Master's fate and to the use of a treason charge, with its death penalty. James might have been copying his Uncle Henry, though he displayed none of the intense paranoia of the Tudor king and had no need to dispose of excess wives. Reversing the previous expectation that the penalty would be commuted to exile or imprisonment the Scottish king probably wanted to convince the political community that traitors would be executed, bringing his realm into line with the European norm. Emphasising the heinousness of treason, as the 1540 parliamentary statute did, was primarily a way of enhancing the majesty of the crown. The underlying message was more disturbing with a form of negative patronage coming into operation. Instead of rewarding an individual or faction, James permitted them to dispose of their political rivals using trumped-up treason charges. Since he did not grant out the forfeited estates, the crown reaped the financial benefits, with the Treasury gaining an extra £5,770 from the Glamis confiscations.

A straightforward charge and traditional method of punishment faced Otterburn of Reidhall. In 1538 he was suddenly dismissed from his office as Lord of Session and king's advocate for communicating with the earl of Angus. Given the events of the previous year, Otterburn was grateful to escape with a crippling fine of £2,000, imprisonment in Dumbarton Castle and a brief internal exile to Fife. His usefulness to the king as a diplomat, especially on embassies to England, facilitated his rehabilitation. Fortunately for this lawyer, pro-English sympathies and a rumoured link with the Douglases did not prove fatal.

The most high-profile treason trial was that of Hamilton of Finnart, a self-made man destroyed by enemies within his own kindred. While his half-brother, Arran, had accompanied the king on the 1540 circumnavigation of Scotland, Finnart had been busy working on Rothesay Castle and Stirling Palace. Being in the direct line of succession after the two baby princes, the young earl had begun to take his place in royal counsels, determined to recover his father's power and influence. In Arran's opinion, Finnart had stripped the earldom's assets and sought to become head of the Hamilton kin. During the voyage Arran probably took the chance to persuade James to abandon the wealthy Finnart. Not suspecting the seriousness of his position, Finnart remained nonchalant when arrested for treason, relying upon his familiarity with the king and his architectural services. During his colourful career he had made many enemies, especially among his kin; so no-one came to his aid. Finnart's recent involvement in Beaton's anti-heresy campaign might have made him a target and those wanting reform were well represented on the panel finding him guilty. Having gone to Seton Castle, the king was deliberately absent from Edinburgh, removing the possibility of a last-minute mercy plea. Finnart was executed at the capital's Mercat Cross, protesting, 'If he had been as good a servant to God as he was to the king, he had not died so shamefully'.[4] His forfeiture brought the crown treasure, beautiful goods and lands worth about £5,000, with silver chapel furnishings magnificent enough to be re-engraved for Prince James.

In Finnart's case, James had pointedly let justice take its course. Allowing the exhumation of the body of the distinguished lawyer Leslie of Innerpeffer to face a charge of *lèse majesté* relating to a conspiracy in 1529 smacked of vindictiveness. Perhaps Leslie's extensive Angus connections had brought him into conflict with the king when the political face of the shire was being reconfigured. James' hard-faced indifference to the fates of these 'traitors' gave a nasty sheen to his final years. His negative patronage acted like a bridle controlling court factions, adding a fatal outcome to the political game of 'ins and outs'. Imperial majesty was manifested in the iron fist of punishment as well as the velvet glove of display; imperial shaded into imperious.

THE ANTI-HERESY DRIVE

The court's mood – that examples should be made – was echoed by that prince of church and court, Cardinal Beaton. With his extensive French experience, Beaton probably took his cue from Francis I's post-*Placards* (1534) policy combining a crackdown on overt evangelicals with limited toleration of humanist reformers. Despite being a Cardinal, Beaton could only implement a rigorous policy once he held the Archbishopric of St Andrews following his uncle's death in February 1539. By the end of the

[4] Cited and discussed in C. McKean, *The Scottish Chateau: the Country House of Renaissance Scotland* (Stroud, 2001), 91.

first month, Beaton had rounded up a gaggle of heretics and burned five of them. Though repression might suit his autocratic temperament, the cardinal treated persecution as a political tactic to be employed when necessary, and with an eye to its effect upon the papacy and his persistent demand for full legatine powers. Whilst occasionally wanting to parade his orthodox credentials before a European audience, the king was not filled with a persecuting zeal in defence of the true faith, resembling his father-in-law, Francis I, rather than his brother-in-law, Henry II. In common with most late medieval Christians, James combined conventional piety with an enjoyment of anti-clerical plays and poems. As Beaton realised, his royal master's support would be turned on and off according to circumstance; one day the king would joke about sending Scottish bishops to face his English uncle; the next, he would attend a heresy trial.

One of those collected in Beaton's sweep was Thomas Forret or Forrest, Augustinian canon of Inchcolm and vicar of Dollar in Clackmannanshire. Making little effort to disguise his views, he had taught his parishioners every Sunday from an English bible and probably composed a vernacular children's catechism. In addition to their spiritual needs, he attended to their practical ones by constructing the 'Vicar's Bridge', still standing at Pitgober, to give easier access to church. He annoyed his fellow clergymen by refusing to charge mortuary dues, the highly unpopular taking of 'the cow and the uppermost cloth'. During the interview censuring Forret's biblical teaching, Crichton of Dunkeld remarked, 'I thanke God, that I never knew what the Old and New Testament was! Therefore, Deane Thomas, I will know nothing but my portuise (breviary) and my pontificall': it later circulated as a proverb, 'Ye are like the Bishop of Dunkelden, that knew neither the New Law nor the Old Law'.[5] When Beaton was looking for heretics and particularly those unlikely to recant, Forret was an obvious target and, along with four others, he was burned on Edinburgh's Castlehill in February 1539. Most heretics collected in the sweep preserved their bodies and instead 'burnt their bills', or list of accusations, thereby recanting.

The anti-heresy drive allowed Beaton to score points against his political and ecclesiastical rival the archbishop of Glasgow by sending a friar and his legally-trained secretaries to help conduct the Glasgow heresy trial and insist upon the execution of the guilty. However, this was not a comprehensive drive to investigate and root out all dissent. Whatever he

---

[5] *David Calderwood's History of the Kirk of Scotland*, ed. T. Thomson (8 vols, Wodrow Society, Edinburgh, 1842–9), I, 126–7.

urged elsewhere, Beaton was very selective in his own backyards of Angus and the Mearns and in Fife, where there was increasing support for church reform and evangelical views among the nobles and lairds and within St Andrews University.

If the image of a united episcopal bench bloodthirstily intent upon eradicating heresy was one of Knox's imaginative creations, a facade of unity was presented in the stage-managed trial of Sir John Borthwick. Receiving advance warning, this soldier and royal servant had safely escaped to England. In his absence a trial was held at St Andrews in May 1540, gaining maximum publicity and a large attendance of spiritual and lay lords present for Prince James' baptism. If there was a covert strategy to push into exile those with unorthodox views, it might explain the unofficial list of heretics from one of Knox's stories, telling how the king rejected the clergy's list, declaring the clerics would not come between him and his nobles and friends. The germ of truth in the tale might be that the king had been tempted by gaining the forfeitures of heretics.

THE CIRCUMNAVIGATION OF THE REALM

Grand schemes flowed naturally from a court saturated with imperial thinking and display, and the mid-summer circumnavigation of James' realm in 1540 encompassing Scotland and enclosing it with an imperial sweep was a remarkably grandiose gesture: surprisingly, no royal propagandist was organised to provide a suitable travelogue. The purchase in 1538 of four clocks and a compass for the flagship suggest some forward planning to allow the king and the young noblemen in his train, nearly all 'twenty somethings', to have their naval fling. A military expedition was to be combined with a luxury cruise, in a similar mixture to Border raids where hunting and other leisure activities accompanied a military and judicial purpose. The circumnavigation was no rush to the Isles to regain lost control, though the brief rebellion of 1539 led by Donald Gorm MacDonald of Sleat had probably concentrated minds and ensured the expedition set sail heavily equipped with artillery and soldiers. A former master of artillery, Methven, was in charge of the expedition's preparations, having retained royal favour despite his stormy marital relations with the Queen Mother. He assembled sixteen vessels, with the fleet's flagship, *Salamander*, named after the personal emblem of its donor Francis I. Other items included the king's expensive green-cloth sea garments, the sixteenth-century equivalent of waterproof jacket and trousers.

Alexander Lindsay's *Rutter*

Giving the first known series of navigational directions for the entire Scottish coast, Alexander Lindsay probably compiled his *Rutter* in preparation for James V's circumnavigation of 1540. It supplied the different courses needing to be set and the main 'kennings', those visual markers seen from the sea enabling the calculation of position and distance (see Figure 6.1). More accurate than the few available sea charts, it contained information about the hazards of Scotland's coastline, such as directions how to sail around the 'Bore' between Orkney and Dunscanby Head. The *Rutter* finally appeared in map form in 1583, incorporated into Nicolas de Nicolay's map printed in Paris. Scottish navigational knowledge, acquired by experience and transmitted orally, was largely found among the sea-faring community, especially the 'good coasters', called as expert witnesses by the Admiralty court. The *Rutter* signified a major development and its accurate information was highly prized. Maritime knowledge and maps were guarded by governments and were the target of spying activities by their enemies. John Elder, the self-professed 'redshank' (Highlander) spy, had sailed the northern and western coasts of Scotland in his youth, giving him the mapping expertise he was able to sell to the English, and the French, courts.

The expedition was delayed to await the birth of the king's first legitimate child. In April, the king had accompanied the queen on a journey in easy stages from Stirling to Falkland, stopping at Dunfermline Abbey to pray and make an offering at St Margaret's shrine, the protectress of the royal family and of women in childbirth. Mary of Guise moved to St Andrews, with James arriving a few days later, having ordered some velvet as a present for his wife because, as her portrait by Corneille de Lyon revealed, she looked very fine in a black velvet dress. To tempt her palate or keep the king happy, oranges were sent by Dundee merchants, as well as the usual food presents of fish and meats for the royal table. English mariners shipwrecked in Orkney and a poor Northland man gave the king the latest news about the expedition's first ports of call and other entertainments were provided, such as 'dugemen' dancing on the beach and 'cachpule' or hand tennis matches. After a fortnight of waiting, James left for Edinburgh only to return post-haste the next day for the birth of his son, Prince James, on 22 May 1540.

Having celebrated the heir's safe arrival, the royal party embarked at Leith on 13 June, and having circumnavigated his kingdom, the king landed at Dumbarton, arriving back in Edinburgh on 6 July. With near-permanent

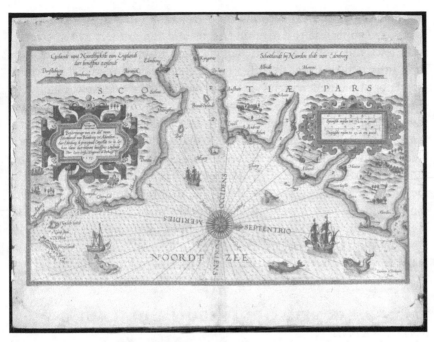

Figure 6.1 Waghenaer's map of the Firth of Forth and east coast, showing at the top the 'kennings' or landmarks as seen from the sea, 1583. [NLS EMS.s.100]

light to see the coastline making the voyage safer, the long summer days and light nights also improved on-board conditions. Sixteenth-century ships were not designed for passengers to lounge on deck, though music was available from the organ brought for the voyage. Orkney was the first destination, with the convoy stopping at Kirkwall, to be entertained by the Bishop. Probably following Lindsay's *Rutter*, they sailed round the northern coast and called at Lewis where Rory MacLeod met the king. The Trotternish peninsula on Skye was the next stop since it was the site of the Macleods of Dunvegan and Harris' feud with the MacDonalds of Sleat. The royal expedition had the serious purpose of transporting overwhelming military force into such locations, enabling James to command the attendance of the Highland and Island chiefs. Having arrived, Mackay of Strathnaver, MacLeod of Lewis, MacLeod of Harris, the Captain of Clanranald, MacDonald of Glengarry, the MacLeans of Duart and of Coll and the brother of MacDonald of Dunyvaig became enforced guests for the remainder of the voyage and were then placed in ward in the Lowlands until they provided hostages for their good behaviour.

In line with previous Stewart policy, special attention was paid to the southern Hebrides and its close links with the Firth of Clyde. The vice-admiral of the expedition, the Master of Glencairn, was left in Kintyre to supervise the royal garrisons and cannon left at Dunaverty, and Stewart of Bute was given artillery for Dunyvaig and Port Ellen on Islay. In 1539 the Master's brother had become bishop of Argyll and commendator of Saddell, with its recently-constructed castle. It was hoped to spread Cunningham authority across the Clyde from Ayrshire to Kintyre, thereby having loyal Lowlanders to watch Clan Donald's southern branch and provide an alternative to Argyll's power in the area. Though blocking his expansion into Kintyre, James did not entirely snub the Campbell earl, granting him the regality of Abernethy near Perth. Despite promising beginnings, nothing substantial came from the southern Hebridean initiative and after the spectacular circumnavigation, the Western Highlands and Islands again dropped off the agenda. With Clan Donald South concentrating its attention upon expansion in Antrim, no major rebellion forced the Western Isles back onto James' agenda.

TRIANGULAR RELATIONS: SCOTLAND, ENGLAND AND FRANCE

The Scottish king's attention was occupied by foreign policy, as peace between France and the Empire brought the chance of a united front against the English schismatic. This European re-alignment, rather than events in the British Isles, dramatically increased the tension between Henry VIII and James V. In 1539 frantic defensive preparations were made in England to face an invasion across the Channel. Henry VIII had the added worry of a Scottish attack across his northern border since he found it impossible to believe James' declaration, 'He wold never breke with the King his uncle during his life'.[6] However, Henry found little to offer to avert the threat and his ambassador had the thankless task in 1540 of repeating English arguments urging the Scottish king to abandon the papal cause. Kept waiting before his first audience as James attended Mass surrounded by his lay and spiritual lords, Sir Ralph Sadler might have realised he would be wasting his breath. The ambassador did not receive an aggressive rebuff of his embassy, being tactfully escorted by two Anglophile courtiers, indicating that while James would not break with Rome, he was prepared to live with a confessional border: something Henry could not accept.

[6] Cited and discussed in J. Cameron, *James V: The personal rule, 1528–42* (East Linton, 1998), 288.

The English king had become obsessed with the religious exiles in Scotland and the issue continued to sour relations. Convinced of his own powers of persuasion, Henry decided a meeting with his nephew would solve all outstanding problems and pressed on with preparations for a joint royal visit to York in 1541. James prevaricated, regarding this as one more round in the diplomatic game, and when there was a rumour of a kidnap plot, decided to stay away. Having waited in York for a fortnight, a furious Henry stomped off south convinced he had been dishonoured and duped. Relations were not improved by James' gift of hawks accompanied by a somewhat cheeky letter. With this second substantial grievance added to the exile issue, the two countries slid down the slope to war. When Henry, seeking to relive his glory days, went on campaign in France in 1542, he demanded assurances the Scots would not attack. Since any such assurance broke his French alliance, the Scottish king refused and an Anglo-Scottish war had come again. Ominously, the assertion of English suzerainty over the British mainland was dusted down and the archbishop of York sent to investigate his archives to prove English jurisdiction in Scotland in readiness for inclusion in the pamphlet justifying the war.

With less aggression than his father had shown in 1513, James V made the sensible choice that repudiating the French alliance was too high a price to pay for continuing a tension-filled peace with England. War was precipitated by Henry's unwillingness to risk leaving his border, now a confessional as well as a political frontier, without a guarantee of non-belligerence. Since the triangular configuration of diplomacy guaranteed Anglo-Scottish relations included France, James had to confront the consequences within the British mainland of Henry VIII's desire to campaign in France. At such crisis points, the Scots and their king recalculated the pros and cons of the French alliance, deciding whether its many tangible benefits compensated for war with their neighbour in Britain. In 1542 the calculation produced a strong affirmative answer based upon the king's Francophile perspective and the anti-English mood of the country; despite later myths, James led a united nobility and country into war.

Although Henry was anxious to concentrate upon France, he accepted the English axiom that Scotland would be overawed by a display of military might. A large raid was planned whose aim was to bring destruction and instil terror. Such raids faced the dilemma that to achieve the maximum devastation over the largest possible area, a substantial force had to be divided into smaller groups that were vulnerable to mobile and quick-witted opponents. With each nation catching the other at a temporary disadvantage both the Scottish victory at Hadden Rig and the

English one at Solway Moss fitted this pattern. In terms of loss of life, equipment and honour, the Scottish defeat was far more serious than the English one but, because of its association with the death of James V, Solway Moss acquired a military significance it did not merit. In that battle the Scots were defeated by those eternal enemies of time and tide, supplemented by the outstanding tactics of the English commander who used his local knowledge of the Solway to perfection.

Three weeks after the humiliation of Solway Moss, James was dead. By associating these two coincidental events a meaning has been manu-factured distorting the death, the defeat and, in some respects, the entire reign. Starting with Pitscottie, moving to Knox and Buchanan and passing into the historical record, an explanatory chain been forged whose first link was the assumption that James died because of Solway Moss. Before he died, James fell ill with severe vomiting and diarrhoea, most probably because he had contracted a virulent disease, possibly cholera. Following his wife's advice and probably his own better judgement, he had not led the raid into England himself, but had been in the Borders with his troops. An army provided the most efficient breeding ground for disease and one possible carrier was the thirty-five-year-old Atholl who had died of the 'pestilence' during the campaign. James had managed to visit Linlithgow to see Mary of Guise, who gave birth to their daughter Mary on 8 December. Government business slowed down around 6 December, with the last entries in the registers of the Privy Council and Court of Session a couple of days later. The king retired to his favourite palace of Falkland, dying there on 14 December, though the colourful deathbed scenes recounted by the chroniclers cannot be trusted, nor is there authentication for the much-quoted prophecy, 'it cam wi' a lass and it'l gang wi' a lass'.[7]

The death of the king brought the general uncertainty of a minority added to the pressures of being at war, though most Scots men and women would find their daily lives continued much as before. Some, such as the Douglas and the Lyons families, probably breathed a sigh of relief and the churchmen might have hoped for less taxation, whilst the loss of continuous royal visits to Fife would have affected the livelihoods of the boatmen at Kinghorn. Though Scotland was at war with its southern neighbour and had recently suffered a humiliating setback, it was the age and gender of James' successor, rather than the military situation, that created the biggest threat from England. In a dynastic context James was

---

[7] *The Historie and Cronicles of Scotland . . . by Robert Lindesay of Pittscottie*, ed. A Mackay (3 vols, STS, 42–3, 60, Edinburgh, 1899–1911), I, 407.

not blessed with much luck, succumbing to a fatal disease when he was only thirty years old, after having lost both his legitimate sons the previous year. Although he had been siring children since his teenage years, the delays over his marriage and the loss of his first wife meant his first legitimate child was only born two years before his own death. Despite hanging on the thread of a sickly infant daughter less than a week old, the Stewart succession did continue because James had completed the dynastic duty of supplying a legitimate heir. Whatever the problems to come, when he died the kingdom was stable and had become used to firm and effective government.

RENAISSANCE MONARCHY TRIUMPHANT

The reigns of James IV and V saw the self-confidence of the Scottish monarchy and nation at one of its highest points. With a heady mix of chivalric pride and Renaissance bravura, the kings of Scots and their courts displayed their assurance through their diplomacy, their architecture, their naval hardware and their imperial crown. The strength of this self-belief supported the kingdom through the political mess after the heavy defeat at Flodden and the fifteen long years of minority. It encouraged and supported a vibrant cultural flowering in poetry and literature as well as music and architecture. Despite the loss of the patronage of the Lords of the Isles, Gaelic literary culture remained healthy and the unique monumental sculpture of the West Highlands continued.

During this period, the European orientation of Scotland became even more marked as political and cultural ties with France were drawn closer, even if the marriage of the thistle and the rose had brought a period of alliance with England. Though unable to replicate the military and naval capability built up by James IV, his son enjoyed an equivalent standing within Europe, thanks to an extremely favourable international situation following Henry VIII's break with Rome. James V gained a powerful lever with which to extract concessions from the papacy, enabling him to complete his father's moves to propel the institutional structure of the Scottish church along a converging path with the crown. The resulting hybrid of church and crown sustained the Scottish monarchy, allowing it to spend well beyond its means without facing serious domestic repercussions.

With contrasting styles, but similar effects, both adult monarchs were able to work with the great magnate families. The exception was the Lords of the Isles who were forfeited in what proved to be the end of their lordship. The fragmentation of Clan Donald led to the southern branch concentrating their attention upon expansion in the north of Ireland, adding a new dimension to the inter-relationships of the British Isles. The instability of James V's minority had witnessed intense struggles between the Houses of Douglas, Hamilton and Lennox Stewart, and had begun the dynastic rivalries and feuds that bedevilled the remainder of the century (see Table 4.1). Argyll and Huntly had been less immediately involved in these internecine struggles, being preoccupied with extending their own power within the Highlands, though remaining important forces within national politics.

Despite their imperial style, the Scottish kings did not seek to build an empire nor to force political integration upon their kingdom. They employed the traditional approach of extending regal authority and bringing justice by personally visiting a region, with the trips to 'daunt' the Western Isles falling into this pattern, though they had little long-term success. After an initial assertion of royal jurisdiction, the Northern Isles continued their lives largely untouched by directives from the south. Governing the regions through the major nobles, who were then answerable to the king, remained the underlying method. It was frequently counter-productive for the court and central administration to take too close an interest in a region, with their increasing interventions destabilising local politics and making, instead of resolving, feuds. Attitudes towards dispute settlement were evolving and the demand for, and creation of, the Court of Session, a central civil court with national jurisdiction, gave a strong indication that a wind of change was blowing and the decentralised attitude to governance within the regions might disappear. In the summer of 1542 these appeared as small clouds upon the horizon as Scotland basked in the sun, enjoying the luxury of an adult king ruling in his prime. The following winter saw a very different prospect as James V's sudden death catapulted a baby girl onto the throne.

PART THREE

The Battle for Britain

CHAPTER 7

Wars for Britain (1543–51)

The succession of a female heiress altered the diplomatic triangle by turning Scotland into an inviting prize for France or England. During the next two decades, a battle was waged for supremacy within the British mainland. Henry VIII made little secret of his desire to control the person of Mary, Queen of Scots, whilst her mother, Mary of Guise, was determined to safeguard the dynastic rights of her child and protect Scotland's links with France. As the focus of the Habsburg–Valois struggle slowly moved north from Italy to the borders between France and the Holy Roman Empire and the Netherlands, the British mainland became more important. In the 1540s and 1550s the fate of Scotland was of international interest and the European and British contexts merged into a single struggle: the battle for Britain.

International involvement added an extra ingredient to the Scottish domestic mix, placing in opposite camps those in favour of an English or a French alliance. For the first time, supporters or opponents of church reform introduced an ideological ingredient to the struggle. Although reformers usually made common cause with the Anglophiles, there was no neat equivalence of pro-English and pro-reform opposing pro-French and anti-reform. With the benefit of hindsight, King Henry VIII had two great chances in 1513 and 1542 to annex Scotland and he missed both of them. The defeats of Flodden and Solway Moss and the deaths of James IV and James V apparently left a defenceless country at the mercy of the English. However, in both instances the Scottish front was part of a larger war and Henry assumed Scotland would present few difficulties once France was defeated. The English king was so intent upon achieving a glorious and resounding triumph in France that the real victory in Scotland could not divert him. The shadow cast by the Rough Wooings has distorted 1542: at James V's death the security of England was the top priority and ending the Scottish military threat was sufficient for Henry. The abundance of high-ranking prisoners taken at Solway Moss and the presence of the exiled Douglases and the disgruntled earl of Bothwell gave the English an opportunity to deal with Scotland on the cheap. These 'assured lords' promised to pursue an Anglophile policy and, by introducing ecclesiastical reform into Scotland, remove Henry's deep-seated worry about the confessional border. The lords were also committed to supporting a future marriage between Mary, Queen of Scots and Edward, Prince of Wales, and a full Anglo-Scottish alliance.

Before Flodden, James IV made his will and left provision for the government of the kingdom in the event of his death. Deciding not to risk his royal person in battle, James V had neglected this task and he was then caught on campaign by disease, war's marching companion. The nature of the late king's wishes became a matter of controversy in the first months of 1543, when Cardinal Beaton presented himself as the interpreter of the king's mind in his final days. The sole thing on which all Scots agreed was that the infant Mary was their new monarch. Within Scotland, while Mary's right to succeed was not questioned, there was a struggle over the regency. Their experiences of Margaret Tudor were fresh enough for Scots to be wary of another foreign queen as regent and the Queen Mother sensibly chose to bide her time. Arran, recognised as heir presumptive in 1536 before James had legitimate children, was the obvious candidate, though he was vulnerable because doubts might be raised about his legitimacy. If he were disqualified, Lennox would be heir to the throne and their dynastic ambitions made the two men and their two kindreds bitter rivals for the remainder of the century (see Tables 2.1 and 4.1). Whatever lay in their inner thoughts or secret prayers, neither Arran nor Lennox attempted to wrest the throne from Mary: well aware of the number of children dying before their majority, both waited to see if the young queen would survive.

ARRAN AS SOLE GOVERNOR

The initial struggle for the regency largely took place behind closed doors. In December a regency council of Beaton, Arran, Moray, Argyll and Huntly was proclaimed, though, at the start of the New Year, it was superseded by Arran's appointment as sole governor, later confirmed by parliament. Since Beaton and Arran had quarrelled and at one meeting had to be physically separated, a private deal brought the chancellorship for the cardinal. In return, Beaton probably agreed to surrender the notarial instrument allegedly recording James V's wish to exclude Arran from any regency council. The arrangement did not last, and at the end of January the cardinal was arrested and imprisoned.

Arran was a quintessential dynast, acutely aware of his leadership of the House of Hamilton and prepared to live and die in its cause. He had no compunction in destroying Finnart, the Hamilton 'usurper', moving quickly and decisively in 1540 as he was to do at the start of 1543 when the regency was at stake. By contrast, he normally adopted a 'wait-and-see' approach, delaying until the last minute to show his hand, a practice sometimes costing him dearly, though avoiding disastrous mistakes. Better at tactics than strategy, he was a born bargainer, trying to be all things to all men and he was sometimes swayed by the last person to whom he talked. Always tacking with the wind, he followed a zig-zag course, making it impossible for his allies to trust him to hold a steady line or see through a policy: a reputation that, once acquired, seriously undermined his effectiveness.

Although Arran was charged with being inconstant, he was not incompetent and becoming sole governor was an impressive achievement. His positive actions were assisted by two negative factors: distrust of Henry VIII's intentions, which speeded up a decision to appoint a single governor instead of a committee, and dislike of Cardinal Beaton, which produced a coalition willing to support Arran. At the coalition's heart were the evangelical courtiers willing to ally with England to achieve their programme for ecclesiastical reform. Once Arran was firmly in place, he broadened his coalition by welcoming home the Solway prisoners, reversing the forfeits for treason made at the end of James V's reign, and freeing Donald Dubh (Black-haired) MacDonald of the Isles.

Surprisingly, given their past rivalry with the Hamiltons, the Douglases joined Arran's coalition. Lady Margaret Douglas, the new governor's wife, helped welcome back to Scotland her relatives Angus and his brother, Douglas of Pittendreich, who returned after a fourteen-year exile during which they had led English forays into the Scottish borders and advised Henry VIII on Scottish matters. In the complex manoeuvring of 1543, Pittendreich employed his considerable charm, intelligence and energy, alongside his talent for deviousness, to counter Cardinal Beaton and help re-establish a Douglas presence in Scotland and, whatever his labyrinthine negotiations, remained immensely loyal to Angus and his Douglas kindred. In the event, it was Pittendreich's dynastic legacy rather than his political skills which had the greatest effect upon Scottish history. In 1543 he contrived to marry his son James to Morton's youngest daughter with a settlement securing the earldom for them, and his elder son later succeeded to the earldom of Angus. Two earldoms, Angus and Morton, for his own family was a substantial dynastic achievement for a younger son, and in 1573 it resulted in the last Douglas ascendancy in Scotland.

ARRAN'S 'GODLY FIT'

In a similar pattern to James V's minority, there were many switches in alignment in the first decade of Mary's reign, making the politics of the period swirl like a kaleidoscope in front of the eyes. During 1543 in particular there was a complete revolution of fortune's wheel, with the French alliance to which James V had adhered being abandoned in favour of an English alliance, which in turn was rejected to come full circle with the reaffirmation of the auld alliance with France. Equally volatile was the composition of the group holding political control: Cardinal Beaton spent the first few months in prison, gained his release and ended the year dominating political affairs. The political alignments of Arran, Angus, Lennox, Argyll, Huntly and Moray all altered in a confusing round of coalitions. This produced a high level of tension and mistrust throughout the country. The French ambassador's first impression of Scotland in 1543 was that the Scots were under arms

> for all the friends of one faction mistrust all those of the other
> faction. So much so that not merely is the nobility in arms, but
> churchmen, friars and the country people only travel through the
> countryside in large companies all armed with pikes, swords and
> bucklers and a half pike in their hands, which in this country is
> called a lance.

The state of the country induced the visiting Papal Legate to add his jeremiad, 'this realm is so divided and confused and full of heresy, that, unless God provide for it, we shall shortly hear of Scotland what we have heard of England'.[1]

The new element of confessional allegiance was emerging as a political factor, but ideological commitment was merely one from a number of considerations and did not constitute the decisive voice later commentators, like Knox, assumed it held. By supporting Arran, the evangelical

---

[1] *Two Missions of Jacques De La Brosse*, ed. G. Dickinson (SHS, 3rd ser., XXXVI, Edinburgh, 1942), 9–10, 23.

group at court were able to advance their cause through government measures. Henry Balnaves acted as Arran's secretary and it was hoped he might become a Scots version of Thomas Cromwell. The most significant step in the evangelical programme was the Parliamentary Act of 1543 authorising the reading of the Bible in the vernacular. Moved by Maxwell and Ruthven, with Balnaves presenting arguments in its favour, it hit vociferous opposition from the first estate, led by the archbishop of Glasgow. The clergy, already on strike and refusing to administer the sacraments in protest against Beaton's imprisonment, were mollified by the concession forbidding theological debate on the Scriptures.

No instantly recognisable line had yet emerged between authorised reform and moves beyond orthodoxy. When John Grierson, the Dominican provincial, commissioned three friars to preach throughout Scotland he did not anticipate the evangelical tone of their sermons. Religious passions were stirred in precisely the way the ecclesiastical hierarchy were seeking to avoid and the abbey at Lindores and the friaries in Perth and Dundee were attacked. In May the Blackfriars convent in Perth was invaded and the common pot containing the friars' dinner removed and subsequently paraded around the burgh. Tangled motives lay behind this piece of street theatre, with economic grievances combining with a criticism of the friars' lifestyle and possibly an attack upon supporters of orthodoxy. If the cooking-pot incident could be laughed off, a harsher fate awaited three Perth men in January 1544 who were hanged for mocking a statue of St Francis.

By mid-April 1543, after being prohibited from preaching, two of the Dominicans, Gilyame and Rough, left the order and this reversal for the evangelical programme signalled Cardinal Beaton's gradual recovery of political influence. The abbot of Paisley, recently returned from France, worked on his brother, Arran, persuading him to stop supporting ecclesiastical reform and to reinstate Beaton. As early as June, the Council issued orders against ballads, such as those adapted by the Wedderburn brothers of Dundee to spread the new theological opinions. In September in Stirling's Franciscan church, Arran formally renounced heresy and swore to uphold the monasteries, allowing the cardinal to shepherd this high-profile lost sheep back into the fold of Mother Church. The governor was taken to Dundee in November for the religious crackdown following the iconoclastic attacks in the burgh and the following month parliament passed an act against heretics.

Amongst the groups wanting substantial ecclesiastical reform, a broad spectrum of beliefs and a variety of views existed as to how reform should be implemented and what form it should take. Anti-clerical and especially anti-monastic opinions formed part of the vernacular humanism of many Scottish *literati*, even those in clerical orders. Those recognisably 'evangelical' in Scotland had adopted *solafideism*, the central Lutheran tenet of justification by faith alone, and their movement was built upon private contacts and family networks, such as the group descended from the fifteenth-century Lollards of Kyle. Since reading the vernacular Bible was their central activity, the circulation of Nisbet's manuscript translation into Scots had a considerable impact. English biblical translations produced in the wake of Henry VIII's break with Rome found their way north, joining the polemical literature produced for the European Reformation coming in via the east-coast ports. Scottish evangelicals, like their European counterparts, looked to the political authority of the crown as the main hope for change, though it is not clear how many envisaged full-scale reform outside of Catholic orthodoxy. The disappointment of 1543 was a salutary lesson; having grabbed the first opportunity to use government power and achieved a small advance towards their programme, the evangelicals suffered a severe backlash and quickly reverted to the conventicle as their focus rather than the royal court.

CHANGING ALLIANCES AND ALIGNMENTS

Boosted by the return of the 'assured lords', the large turnout of nobles at the parliament of March 1543 authorised peace negotiations with England and an Anglo-Scottish marriage treaty. The ambassadors' instructions contained a firm refusal of the offer to raise Mary, Queen of Scots at the English court and permitted no compromise over Scotland's sovereignty. In July the Scots team completed two treaties at Greenwich, one bringing peace and the other the marriage of Mary Stewart to Edward Tudor. Henry agreed to most of the Scottish terms, assuming that an English-style religious reformation was underway that would remove the confessional frontier and that eventually the marriage would dissolve the political boundary. By the time the treaties were ratified at Holyrood in August, the Governor was co-operating with Beaton and was prepared to re-align foreign policy to favour France. The Scottish parliament's repudiation of the Greenwich treaties in December made Scotland's return to the auld alliance explicit.

The end of Arran's 'godly fit' and the repudiation of the English alliance provoked a series of political re-alignments. In his military career Lennox had marched under the banner of France for years, before returning to Scotland in 1543. Acting in the French interest he secured

Dumbarton, the strategic key to the Clyde, and supported the successful campaign which moved Mary of Guise and the infant queen to Stirling. However, responding to Arran's public change Lennox switched sides in the autumn. The French ambassador, recognising Lennox as the chief trouble-maker in Scotland, advised Francis I to recall him. It was too late; by the end of the year the Anglophile faction was led by the unlikely pairing of Lennox and Angus. Though both had been absent from the country, they retained considerable support from regions such as Ayrshire, Fife and Forfar, and earls, such as Marischal, Glencairn or Rothes. The Angus–Lennox faction was outwitted and outnumbered in January and when Lennox tried to fortify Glasgow in the spring, Arran acted decisively and took the city by force. Henry VIII rewarded Lennox for turning his coat by marrying him to Margaret Douglas, his niece and Angus' daughter, and granted him a Yorkshire estate, making him the first Scotsman to hold English lands since the Wars of Independence. By combining dynastic links to the Scottish and the English thrones, this marital alliance and the children it produced proved of immense significance within British politics (see Table 2.1).

While factions struggled at court, a major clan battle, later called *Blàr na Lèine* (the field of shirts), took place in July 1544 at the end of the Great Glen where Clan Ranald ambushed and killed a party of 400 Frasers. They had formed one section of Huntly's troops returning from raiding Clan Ranald's lands in Moidart during the latest episode in the Gordons' drive westwards. Clan Ranald's disputed leadership had given the Frasers, backed by Huntly, the chance to support Ranald *Gallda* (stranger), who had been reared amongst his Fraser maternal kin. At his inauguration as chief, Ranald ruined the hospitality and acquired his clan by-name 'Ranald of the hens' by commenting that chicken could have replaced the oxen being prepared for the feast. The release of John of Moidart, held since James V's circumnavigation, allowed him to re-establish himself as Clan Ranald's chief and he led them and their allies, the Camerons, MacIains of Ardnamurchan, MacDonalds of Glengarry and Keppoch, to victory against the Frasers. Preoccupied with national affairs, Huntly could not avenge the Frasers and suffered further humiliation in April 1545 when western clans swept east in a month-long raid around Castle Urquhart on Loch Ness, held by the Grants, also Huntly clients.

Within the southern Highlands, Argyll faced military pressure as the Clyde became a front line in the Anglo-Scottish war. Lennox's powerbase in the West made him useful in English plans to stir up trouble in the Highlands and Islands and disrupt Argyll's contribution to the Scottish military effort. Arran's generous, if short-sighted, release of Donald Dubh allowed him to step from prison, where he had spent most of his life, onto the international stage. With most of the Hebridean clans rallying to him and the old Council of the Isles reconvened to determine policy, Donald became the figurehead for the final attempt to revive the Lordship of the Isles. If the rebellion had succeeded, Henry VIII's formal agreement with Donald might have posed a serious threat to the Scottish kingdom's integrity. Although a major force of 4,000 men and 180 galleys was collected in Dublin ready for an assault, nothing materialised since Lennox was used on the Borders instead of commanding the Islesmen's attack on the Clyde. Donald died of fever and after quarrelling over money the clansmen sailed home. The sorry debacle marked the end of any dream of returning to the past glory of the lordship.

FIRE AND SWORD

Francis I having played a long and risky waiting game was vindicated when the auld alliance was reaffirmed in December 1543. He was fortunate Mary of Guise had worked tirelessly and spent her own money keeping the French cause afloat and helping Beaton. English diplomacy and its much trumpeted marriage alliance had flopped and the Scots had made Henry look foolish. Though the English king employed military might to bring revenge and force Scotland into a marriage alliance, he remained more interested in France. An alliance with the emperor encouraged Henry to launch an attack, optimistically dubbed the 'Enterprise of Paris', once more relegating the Scottish front to second place. The keynote of the English campaigns of 1544–6 was destruction, with Henry's instructions directing his fire-and-sword policy against the Borders, the Lothians and Fife, 'not forgetting among all the rest so to spoil and turn upside down the cardinal's town of St Andrews, as the upper stone may be the nether, and not one stick stand by another, sparing no creature alive within the same.'[2]

During his brief 1544 campaign, the English commander combined land and sea operations to great effect; he sailed into the Forth, landed his army in four hours at Newhaven and took Leith by storm. Having unloaded his heavy artillery, he turned to Edinburgh, parts of which were

[2] *Hamilton Papers*, ed. J. Bain (2 vols, Edinburgh, 1890), ii, 326, and discussed in M. Merriman, *The Rough Wooings: Mary Queen of Scots 1542–1551* (East Linton, 2000), 144.

Privateering and piracy

During the sixteenth century, Scots privateers and pirates had a fearsome reputation as they preyed upon shipping in the North Sea and off the Atlantic coast of France. As part of the chain of international alliances, Charles V declared war upon Scotland in 1544 and for the next six years the Scots gained far more in privateering than they lost in legitimate trade with the Low Countries, or so those in the Netherlands believed. Particularly badly hit was the great Dutch herring trade in the North Sea. The theoretical distinction between privateering, an extension of hostilities against an enemy's ships authorised by government-issued letters of marque and reprisal, and piracy, the indiscriminate capture of vessels, was extremely blurred in practice. Scotland's Admiralty court dealt with privateering, judging whether a captured ship was a lawful prize, and dealing with the recovery of merchandise stolen on the high seas. The court was entitled to a tenth of the value of a prize, a profitable business for the admiral, and the rest of the 'pillage' was divided according to clear rules, with the captain receiving the best piece of artillery, the master the best anchor, the boatswain the top sails, the gunner the broken powder and gunner's gear chest and bullets, the barber the barber's chest and the cook the whole cooking utensils, with the rest sold and the proceeds divided among the crew.[3] The line between trading, privateering and piracy had been frequently crossed in James IV's reign by the ship owners, Andrew and Robert Barton, and their letters of reprisal of 1506 against the Portuguese were still being used in 1561. The Bartons had operated down the east coast of Britain from Leven and the Firth of Forth, while many compatriots used the French Channel ports such as Rouen and Dieppe or the Atlantic port of Brest as their bases. In the western sea lanes, Allan MacLean of Gigha, *Ailean nan Sop*, became famous for his exploits in seizing ships, and the poem celebrating the sea raids in bardic verse written by the kinsman he had imprisoned, Hector MacLean, *An Cléireach Beag*, won his release.

burned, though the castle held out. The English army completed its task by marching back to Berwick destroying all in its path. Lord Seton's beautiful gardens and orchard in East Lothian were devastated, and the bell and organ were stolen and the woodwork burned in the collegiate

---

[3] *The Practicks of Sir James Balfour of Pittendreich*, ed. P. G. B. McNeill (2 vols, Stair Society, 21 and 22, Edinburgh, 1962–3), II, 640–1.

church next door. On the coast every seaworthy vessel from Stirling downriver on both sides of the Forth was taken. Lands belonging to Douglases were among those to suffer, a piece of English carelessness that brought Angus and his kinsmen back to the Scottish side. Insult was added to injury, when the following year the English sacked Melrose Abbey and despoiled the graves of Angus' ancestors.

Heavy raids continued in the winter of 1544–5 and in February Scots forces led by Angus ambushed 5,000 English troops at Ancrum Moor. Whilst the victory gave a major boost to Scottish self-confidence and punctured the English sense of invulnerability, its strategic significance was slight. A second campaign of destruction arrived in September 1545 with Kelso as its main target. The surrounding countryside of the Merse and Teviotdale suffered especially badly with the destruction of seven monasteries; sixteen towers; five market towns; two hundred and forty-three fermtouns; thirteen mills and three hospitals[4]. Across much of southern Scotland where the harvest was burned and the livestock taken, those amidst the smoking ruins blamed Arran and Beaton for not defending them against the English. Despite the resentment, there was no political alternative; the cardinal retained the whip hand in policy-making. Angus, so long vilified as the arch-traitor and Henry's pensioner, revelled in the patriotic glory of his victory at Ancrum Moor. Meanwhile, Lennox replaced Angus as the long-term exile and English courtier.

GEORGE WISHART'S PREACHING TOUR AND DEATH

Whilst Beaton's crackdown on heresy in the winter of 1543–4 had put the evangelicals back where they had been in 1540, the high-profile preaching of George Wishart injected enough leadership and cohesion to create a new momentum. By offering a more clearly articulated theology derived from the Swiss Reformers, Wishart brought breadth and depth to the movement. Returning from exile in England he went into Angus, close to his Kincardineshire roots. His sermons on Romans stirred up a Dundee audience, including the Earl Marischal, who offered to defy the cardinal on the preacher's behalf. Wishart's incendiary public preaching repelled some, whilst others, like John Knox, were inspired.

The preacher concentrated upon making an explicit theological challenge to the established church; his lay supporters in Ayrshire offered a

---

[4] Figures from J. Dent and R. McDonald, *Warfare and Fortifications in the Borders* (Scottish Borders Council, Melrose, 2000), 19.

starker and more political challenge. They placed him in the pulpits of their parish churches, by force if necessary. Under the protection of the local evangelical families of Campbell of Cessnock and Lockart of Bar, the congregation heard Wishart's sermons in the comfort of their parish church at Galston, up the Irvine valley. At both Ayr and Mauchline Wishart chose to avoid armed confrontation by delivering his sermon in the open air. When Campbell of Loudoun, sheriff of Ayr and Melrose Abbey's bailie for Mauchline, barred the church entrance, lairds such as Campbell of Kinzeancleuch and his teenage son were willing to attack their kinsman to gain entry. Instead, in the picnic atmosphere of a hot summer's day, Wishart stood on top of a dyke at the moor's edge and his three-hour sermon reduced to tears the laird of Shiel whose wicked life was reputedly transformed by his conversion.

The fight between the Glasgow and St Andrews cross-bearers

One particular incident in the long-running antagonism between the archbishops of St Andrews and Glasgow was recorded by Knox in his *History*. He wrote a 'merry' account of the 1545 fight, in which he displayed a fine range of rhetorical skills, with the alliteration and the carefully paced dramatic narrative building up the humour of the situation.

> Cuming furth (or going in, all is one) att the qweir [choir] doore of Glasgw Kirk, begynnes stryving for state betuix the two croce beraris, so that from glowmyng (scowling), thei come to schouldering; frome schouldering, thei got to buffettis, and from dry blawes, by neffis and neffelling (fisticuffs); . . . and assayis quhilk [which] of the croces war fynast mettall, which staf was strongast, and which berar could best defend his maisteris pre-eminence; and that thare should be no superioritie in that behalf, to the ground gois boyth croces. And then begane no litill fray, but yitt a meary game; for rockettis war rent, typpetis war torne, crounis war knapped (cracked), and syd gounis mycht have bene sein wantonly wag from the one wall to the other. Many of thame lacked beardis, and that was the more pitie; and therefore could not bukkill other by the byrse (grab by the beard), as bold men wold have doune.[5]

---

[5] *The Works of John Knox*, ed. D. Laing (6 vols, Edinburgh, 1846–64), I, 146–7; discussed in K. D. Farrow, *John Knox: Reformation Rhetoric and the Traditions of Scots Prose, 1490–1570* (Bern, 2004), 270–2.

By preaching in public Wishart was offering open defiance to the ecclesiastical authorities, though he persuaded his followers not to resort to violence and the two-handed sword carried before him by the immensely proud John Knox was purely symbolic. Though Archbishop Dunbar was curiously lax about stopping Wishart's preaching in his archdiocese, Cardinal Beaton would not suffer such opposition and Wishart knew and accepted he was a marked man once he went to plague-striken Dundee, and then to East Lothian. He was arrested in the laird of Ormiston's house and taken to St Andrews for trial. Predictably, he was condemned as a heretic and was executed in front of the episcopal castle with the reconciled cardinal and archbishop of Glasgow reportedly watching together over the eastern blockhouse wall. As Wishart had intended, his death gave a martyr's seal to his cause, underlining his unequivocal message about the primacy of scripture and the Swiss Reformed interpretation of the sacraments. The Scottish political situation remained too unstable for a sustained campaign of persecution against the evangelicals and Beaton was too canny a politician to embark on such a risky course.

CARDINAL BEATON'S ASSASSINATION

Superficially, Cardinal Beaton appeared to be running Scotland with ease. In fact, he had to work hard to maintain control and hold together his anti-English coalition. Wishart's trial had taken place against a background of tension between laymen and clerics in government. Many of the frustrations of these war years were blamed directly upon the cardinal: the constant drip of English propaganda targeting Beaton was having some effect. Henry VIII's personal animosity had encouraged several conspiracies and Beaton had to move warily around the country. His unwavering advocacy of the French alliance increased his political vulnerability since his much-repeated promises of substantial French aid were not honoured. Francis I's top priority was the recovery of Boulogne after its capture by the English in 1544, though some resources were released for Scotland after peace with the emperor removed the problem of fighting on two fronts on French soil. Protracted French negotiations with Henry eventually produced the Treaty of Camp in June 1546, but that was too late to help the cardinal.

The plots against Beaton were a backhanded compliment to his success in presenting such a convincing facade of control, since the Anglophiles and their English allies could think of no other way of securing political power and reinstating the policies of Arran's 'godly fit'. The plan was more than an assassination plot; it involved a coup d'état seizing St Andrews Castle. The foreign policy motivation was obvious and the underground network involved in previous English conspiracies was represented by Kirkcaldy of Grange and the Master of Rothes. The plotters also had personal and local axes to grind since the closely-related group of Fifers all knew Beaton of old, and had reason to dislike his dealings, with Rothes' son being on exceptionally bad terms after a property dispute. A tangle of feud and confessional conviction led Melville of Carnbee, Wishart's personal friend, and Leslie of Parkhill to exact revenge for the preacher's death.

Under cover of the building works, eighteen men entered St Andrews Castle on 29 May 1546. Having killed the doorman and evicted the guards and workmen, they took possession of the castle. Found in his chamber, Beaton's pleas were ignored and he was stabbed to death with his body later being displayed over the wall as proof for the crowd of bewildered St Andrews citizens below. The conspirators had done precisely what they had planned: Beaton had been killed and they held St Andrews Castle. The next moves had to be made by others.

THE SIEGE OF ST ANDREWS CASTLE

Political assassination could not be countenanced and Governor Arran moved swiftly following Beaton's death. Within two days his brother, the abbot of Paisley, was granted the temporalities of St Andrews and started on the wearisome task of gaining possession of the archdiocese. The chancellorship went to Huntly, the first layman, apart from Angus during his ascendancy, to hold it for fifty years, thereby tying the earl and the Queen Dowager more closely to Arran's regime. By a series of deals the governor gained the support of or neutralised most Anglophiles. Those closely associated with the Castilians were politically isolated, with Rothes leaving for exile in Denmark. By eliminating his dominating influence, Beaton's death gave Arran political elbow room. The military side was less successful; the governor besieged St Andrews but perched on rock by the sea, the castle was hard to storm. Arran's eldest son, having been part of the cardinal's household, was in the castle at the time of the murder, and he was too valuable a political asset for the Castilians to release. To modern eyes the siege of St Andrews in 1546 appears a curious affair, with much coming and going in and out of the castle, which was not tightly encircled. Considerable military effort was expended, including an attempt to mine through solid rock which the defenders neatly

foiled with their own countermine. However, proceedings were dominated by that particular Scottish talent for fighting and negotiating at the
same time.

The relaxation of the siege permitted some Anglophiles and evangelicals to join the Castilians, the most famous of whom was the schoolmaster John Knox with his two pupils, arriving in April 1547 when English
intervention was believed to be imminent. During the delay confirming
the archbishop's appointment, ecclesiastical authority in St Andrews had
devolved to Sub-Prior John Winram, vicar-general of the diocese. A supporter of reform who had published a vernacular catechism the previous
year, Winram attempted to follow the pattern of intensive preaching and
disputation that had produced reformation in the Imperial and Swiss
cities. He permitted the Protestants, Rough and Knox, to preach in
St Andrews' parish church, provoking controversy with the burgh's
friars and leading to a formal disputation in the university college of
St Leonard's. Few shared Knox's views, expounded in his first-ever
sermon, that the Church of Rome was Antichrist and only scripturally-
commanded ceremonies should be used in church. Like Winram, most
believed the established church could still undergo moral, administrative
and theological reform. Arousing further clerical opposition, Winram
also permitted a form of evangelical Mass, giving the laity communion
wine as well as the wafers. This experiment in local urban reform was terminated by the castle's capture, removing the Castilians to French prison
or the galleys. Winram was untouched and continued up until the
Reformation crisis of 1559–60 to work for internal reform.

Negotiation worked for Arran at Dumbarton Castle, the key to the
western approaches. By offering terms, the governor won over its captain
and persuaded Lennox's brother, Robert Stewart, to join him with the
promise of restoration to the bishopric of Caithness. The Hamiltons were
adept at manipulating ecclesiastical benefices for themselves and using
them to gain political support. By such political deals, Arran held his
coalition together, preventing major defections to the Castilians. He made
strenuous efforts to obtain a papal pardon for Beaton's murderers and by
December 1546 this appeared to be working, with supplies running low
and disease sweeping the castle.

European and British politics were transformed by Henry VIII's death
in January 1547 followed three months later by that of Francis I: it
marked the changing of a political generation. The substantial English
aid sent to the Castilians alarmed the new regime of Henry II in France.
He secretly dispatched French galleys to St Andrews, where they placed
some cannon on St Salvator's tower and from sea and land pounded the

castle into submission. It was a French masterclass in the swift reduction of a fortified position.

SOMERSET'S SCOTTISH STRATEGY

In an important change to English priorities, Edward VI's uncle, Protector Somerset, concentrated resources upon Scotland and was even willing to treat Boulogne as a bargaining chip to further his Scottish campaign. He calculated upon the Habsburg–Valois struggle resuming, preventing France from intervening in Scotland on a sufficient scale to ruin his plans. Consequently, in late summer 1547, the English invaded Scotland. Assuming the invaders would arrive via the central route through the Middle Marches, rather than marching up the east coast, Arran had failed to hold Pease Pass, near Dunglass. He did have an excellent defensive position on the River Esk, just outside Musselburgh, on which to deploy his army of around 25,000 men, one of the largest armies gathered in Scotland. Somerset used his naval arm to pound the Scottish flank and the English army's mercenary force of mounted hagbutters, the greater experience derived from continental warfare and superior co-ordination of its infantry, cavalry and artillery won the battle of Pinkiecleugh and killed around 10,000 Scots.

Bagpipes

The first unambiguous reference to the use of Highland bagpipes occurred in a French history of the 1540 wars in Scotland where the author commented that Highland troops who served under Argyll at Pinkie were encouraged to fight by hearing the sound of the bagpipes. Buchanan explained their military context in his *History*: bagpipes had replaced the trumpet on the battlefield. With several different varieties of pipe common in Scotland, the precise evolution of bagpipes and their music is unclear, but by about 1600 they emerged associated with the MacCrimmon family of pipers under the patronage of the MacLeods of Dunvegan. A branch of the MacCrimmons based in Balquhidder in 1574, probably pipers to the Campbells of Glenorchy, have recently been discovered. Though surviving versions were developed later, this period created the *ceòl mór* (the great music) of the bagpipe, reflecting the martial setting of its origins with battle-tunes and marches, gatherings, salutes and laments, and a similar formality of composition to classical Gaelic verse.

Having gained a resounding victory, celebrated with much beer drinking in the English army, Somerset adhered strictly to his preconceived plan and moved to Leith, then withdrew his large army, devastating farmland on the way. Since the failure to take Edinburgh proved a key factor in losing the war, that mistake proved far more costly than Arran's defeat at Pinkie.

Part of Somerset's grand strategy was to win Scottish collaborators by capitalising upon the ideological reasons for Anglo-Scottish co-operation. Though evangelical reformers had looked to England since the break with Rome, no simple equation can be made between evangelical theology and 'assuring' with the English. Having become an integral part of the English government's approach since the 1530s, propaganda played its part in the English invasions. Without a properly established printing press or government-sponsored authors, Scotland could not easily reply in kind. The English appeal was based upon a union of the two realms and Somerset's *Proclamation*, distributed before Pinkie, insisted co-operation was in Scots' best interests. In his *Epistle* the following year a glowing picture was painted of a joyous union, cemented by the marriage of Edward and Mary, with the two kingdoms basking in divine approval for their 'godly' conjunction and reformed religion.

Henrisoun, an Edinburgh merchant, was convinced of this case and in a series of tracts written from his base in London tried to persuade his fellow countrymen of its merit. In his *Exhortation*, he pressed the case for a united Britain where Scots and English were no more: all would be equal Britons. Other Scots leapt for their pens to reject such ideas, Lamb producing *Ane Reasonyng*, refuting unionist arguments, and the anonymous *Complaynt of Scotland* making a stirring call to patriotism. Even without these re-statements of the glories of Scottish independence, most Scots had no difficulty remembering the English claims to suzerainty within the bombastic justifications for Henry VIII's 1544 and 1545 campaigns. Such arguments remained part of the debate for English audiences throughout the 1540s and resurfaced at the end of 1548 in propaganda for Scotland.

As Henrisoun complained bitterly to Somerset, it was impossible to make the case for equal union while the English army were harrying even those Scots who had assured. Here lay the nub of the problem, creating an English Pale brought an invading and occupying army and to the Scots these actions shouted much louder than printed words. Occasionally slipping on a velvet glove and penning a fine line in unionist rhetoric could not disguise the iron-fisted intimidation needed to sustain English garrisons. At the time the propaganda probably only convinced those

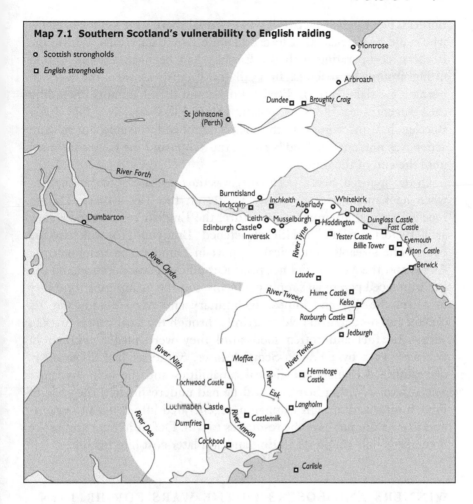

Map 7.1 Southern Scotland's vulnerability to English raiding

- o Scottish strongholds
- ☐ English strongholds

already nearly persuaded. However, in retrospect the identification of the 'Edwardian moment', when God had provided an opportunity for a union of the two kingdoms, achieved great significance for the Protestant understanding of the mid-century. Cecil's personal campaign experience in the English army taught him Scotland could not be conquered into union and he concluded that English actions needed to match their words if the kingdoms of the British mainland were ever to come together.

Somerset's grand strategy was to create an English Pale in Scotland. Pre-selected sites with the new style *trace italienne* fortification were garrisoned with light cavalry. By adding forts at Lauder, Haddington and Broughty Ferry, most of south and east Scotland became a war zone, feeling the continual pressure only previously experienced in the

Borders. For English success it was essential there were sufficient Scots who could be persuaded or forced to supply such garrisons. Within the Borders, co-operating with the English had been an age-old option fitting around local feuds. In 1548 the English assisted the Kers in burning Catslak Tower in Ettrick Forest and its inhabitants, including their seventy-year-old kinswoman, Dame Elizabeth Ker, Old Lady Buccleuch. Consorting with the enemy might be forgivable, but such an action was not, and the feud between the Scotts and the Kers continued until the end of the century.

Of the 'assured' Scots, Lord Gray was the most useful to the English, when he handed over Broughty Castle on the Tay estuary. Having repelled several attempts at recapture, the English constructed a new artillery fort on Balgillo Hill, christened 'Bragyng Trouwble' by the Scots. The sizeable evangelical support in Dundee and neighbouring Angus and the Mearns did not produce sufficient co-operation and the garrison faced perennial supply problems, severely hampering its ability to patrol the Tay and impose its military and naval dominance. Its captain and his garrison held on grimly through the hard winter of 1549 with little fuel and rotten food until they were finally overrun in February 1550 by a Franco-Scottish force. Somerset had disastrously overestimated England's logistical capabilities and the help his cause would receive within Scotland and he had underestimated the scale of French intervention. His campaign degenerated into a war of occupation that he did not have the resources to win. Defeat in Scotland broke Somerset's hold on power in England and later cost him his life.

WINNERS AND LOSERS IN THE WARS FOR BRITAIN

The collapse of the English war effort was relatively swift. Warwick, who had replaced Somerset, got the best terms he could from France. As with any complex international conflict, sorting out the peace was a convoluted affair, requiring a series of different treaties. France and England came to terms in March 1550 in the Treaty of Boulogne that comprehended Scotland. The following December, Scotland's long war with Charles V came to an end in the Treaty of Binns. The Scots also needed a separate treaty with the English, concluded at Norham in June 1551, setting up a special boundary commission to sort out the Debateable Land around Liddisdale. A year later a line was drawn on the map and a dike constructed on the ground removing, at least in theory, any confusion about rival territories or excuse for raiding.

If Somerset lost the war, then Henry II won it. He gambled by pouring resources into Scotland to evict the English and to gain ascendancy over them on Scottish rather than French soil. France recovered Boulogne and brought Scotland into her protection. One crucial ingredient in French success was that the Scots had directly asked their allies for help. Knowing it weakened his own authority as governor, to his credit Arran still issued the invitation, and his actions ensured Scotland was not forced into a dynastic, and possibly political and religious, union with England. The French responded with troops, munitions and money and the immediate task of expelling the English was achieved. They were able to call the tune in Scotland, because they had been prepared to pay the piper, if not the 'million of gold' Henry II estimated in 1558, then probably at least £1m (Scots) and 2,500,000 *livres tournois* spent in 1549 alone.[6] Guided by Mary of Guise's local knowledge, French pensions and honours were liberally bestowed upon Scots nobles, winning the key tussle for the loyalty of Argyll and Huntly, who enjoyed their pensions and proudly displayed their chain of 'cockles', the coveted Order of St Michael. Though these material inducements sweetened Scotland's political elite, they did not affect the fundamental choice. Most of the political nation did not want union with England and to avoid it, they were prepared to become a French client, to allow their queen to be raised in France and to postpone consideration of the implications of her marriage to the Dauphin. Henry VIII's bullying and Somerset's unionism had driven the Scots straight into the arms of the French.

They signed the Treaty of Haddington, taking Mary, Queen of Scots to the French court in 1548 to enjoy a pampered and carefree upbringing as a favourite of her future father-in-law, while he contemplated the longer-term battle for the entire British Isles. Henry II boasted to the Ottoman Sultan:

> I have pacified the kingdom of Scotland, which I hold and possess
> with such authority and obedience as I do in France, to which two
> kingdoms I am joining another, namely England, which by
> perpetual union, alliance and confederation is now under my
> control . . .[7]

During the war Henry II's willingness to intrigue in Ireland, looking to open another front there, demonstrated that his vision extended across

---

[6] Figures from Merriman, *Rough Wooings*, 367.
[7] Cited and discussed in Merriman, *Rough Wooings*, 37.

the whole of the British Isles with Scotland as the central component. As the 1550s unfolded, that remained the ultimate goal with the person of Mary, Queen of Scots as the key dynastic element to the plan.

For the six years between 1544 and 1550 the Scots had taken a hammering. Destruction had been the goal of Henry VIII's campaigns and the south-east of Scotland from Edinburgh to the Borders had been devastated. Somerset's garrisons vastly extended the area vulnerable to raiding (see Map 7.1), and Inchcolm and Inchkeith on the Forth and Broughty Ferry on the Tay had harried east-coast shipping. Dundee had suffered particularly badly from the physical and economic effects of war and plague and, as late as 1582, it appealed for special consideration over taxation because of its experience during the 1540s. The financial burden of the war had fallen most heavily upon the church and to pay its war taxes, the feuing of church lands had accelerated. Ecclesiastical buildings and furnishings had been prime targets and some clerics had fled their parishes and others had been killed. The report in 1556 on the roofless, ruined state of many churches in the Merse indicated that recovery would take decades, not years.

The general level of human suffering during the wars was considerable, though most was not recorded. A few were fortunate to receive some compensation, as the £3 6s to a poor Dumbarton woman whose cattle had been slain. The country faced a subsistence crisis and serious inflation and the parliaments of 1551 and 1552 sought to regulate the prices of foodstuffs and manufactures because shortages had driven up prices. Measures introduced to build up food stocks such as forbidding the slaughter of lambs or young fowl and a ban on hunting with guns indicate the government was out of its depth when faced with the long-term disruption of agricultural production brought by the wars.

At the end of the conflict, probably to his own surprise as well as that of his compatriots, Arran was still governor of Scotland and would glory in his elevation to duke of Châtelherault, a status normally reserved for members of the immediate royal family. His place as second person in the realm was reaffirmed in parliament and he continued to enjoy the use of the royal palaces and access to royal patronage. On his coat-tails, a flock of Hamiltons were securing themselves in their new offices and benefices. As Arran knew, much of the political power and the strategic planning for Scotland had crossed the seas to France along with the young queen. Henry II's protection was accompanied by a close scrutiny of Scottish affairs, channelled through Mary of Guise and a succession of French advisers.

The cost of six years of unremitting, year-round warfare, the worst on the British mainland during the century, had been horrendous. As well as the 10,000 who perished at Pinkie and the other battle casualties, large numbers died as a result of the diseases and starvation brought in the armies' wake. At great cost the Scots had learned much about the latest arts of warfare, though they could not afford to stay in the arms race and fund the military hardware. They had proved good soldiers, and in the future, this very saleable skill helped many Scots earn their living abroad. The material destruction and the economic dislocation would take decades to restore and in cases such as the Border abbeys would never be put right. The blight on the kingdom and the burden of reconstruction were eased by the warm glow of victory which fostered relatively mag-nanimous treatment towards the 'assured'; collaborators were hit hard in their pockets, with Lord Gray paying £1,000 for his composition. The evangelicals, in particular, felt contaminated by their treasonable association with the invaders and kept their heads down for the next few years. Most Scots displayed a great resilience at the end of the wars. They remained profoundly self-confident, savouring the knowledge they had beaten the English; that is, with a little help from their friends, the French.

CHAPTER 8

Franco-Scotland (1550–60)

On 7 July 1548 in the nunnery outside Haddington whilst troops were besieging the English garrison there, the Scots and French envoys had signed the treaty that betrothed Mary to the Dauphin and brought Scotland under the protection of Henry II. The French king had been as good as his word and had furnished the necessary troops, supplies and finances and the military pressure on the front in northern France that compelled the English to withdraw from Scotland. He had then actively intervened in the peace negotiations, ensuring no English garrisons remained and the war with Charles V was ended. The Scots happily shared in the great triumph at Rouen in 1550 depicting Henry's achievements and did not cavil when they watched the banners portraying the forts of Haddington, Broughty Ferry and Inchcolm being carried in the march as if they were exclusively French victories. The auld alliance had again served its purpose of being a successful antidote to the English.

As the Scots appreciated, Henry II was not doing this solely for the sake of auld lang syne. He had seized the dynastic chance of incorporating Scotland into a French empire through a marriage alliance. From the moment of her accession, Mary's future wedding would carry her kingdom as a most handsome dowry for her husband. Mary's claims within the English succession were a bonus allowing Henry II to think realistically about a Franco-British empire. At best, given the doubtful legitimacy of Henry VIII's daughters, Mary could claim the English throne directly, at worst his son and daughter-in-law could place a dynastic pincer on England's northern and southern borders. Despite being a chancy business, the French knew to their cost how a similar dynastic gamble had extended Habsburg power to encircle their own country.

MARY OF GUISE'S VISIT TO FRANCE, 1550–1

Many Scottish nobles watched the Rouen parade, having accompanied the Queen Mother on her return to France. To the surprise of most observers, Mary of Guise had not travelled with her daughter in 1548, staying in Scotland until hostilities ended. Despite once more being an extremely eligible widow, there was no sign that Mary would remarry. Her Guise brothers realised it was essential to their plans she remain in Scotland rather than being married to a European prince. During 1548 Mary had exhausted her own resources funding the Scottish nobles for their military contributions, doling out cash incentives to retain their loyalty and employing bonds of manrent binding the aristocracy to her. In the midst of the military campaigns, she had smoothed the rubs between French and Scots with her political skills and knowledge of the Scottish political scene. This apprenticeship at the centre of Scottish government impressed the nobility, proving she was not a Queen Mother in the mould of Margaret Tudor. As had the duke of Albany during James V's minority, Mary offered an impartiality in domestic disputes that Governor Arran manifestly lacked, and many were willing to support the Queen Dowager. When she finally returned to France to see her family she took a substantial train of nobles with her. Though this was no 'brainwashing' expedition, the French king lost no opportunity to dazzle the Scots with his power and prestige and impress upon them that he was a generous and caring protector of the northern kingdom. In 1550 Henry II cherished the Scots political elite, something his English namesake had conspicuously failed to do in 1543. Following the lavish hospitality shown to James V in 1536, Scottish nobles expected such treatment in 1550 and they recognised a golden opportunity to reap the rewards of their monarch's dynastic position, as they were to do again in 1603.

Mary held extended discussions with the king and his advisers about future policy towards Scotland. Since it was essential to French strategy that Mary, Queen of Scots actually married the Dauphin, this was facilitated by her upbringing in company with her future husband and the rest of the Valois children in the royal nursery. While possession of the bride had been accomplished, peaceably bringing the kingdom as her dowry required long-term involvement in Scotland. A consistently pro-French regime was needed to follow the direction set by Henry. Despite his French duchy and generous pension, Arran's government did not match that job description, and he was induced to promise to relinquish the governorship when Mary came of age. The French *Parlement*, rather than the Scottish Parliament, declared the Scottish queen did not have to wait for

Embroidery

The art of needlework was an essential part of female education for all levels of society, vital for running any household. For men, sewing was a craft and in Dundee four of the prestigious Nine Trades, the tailors, cordiners (shoemakers), glovers and skinners, as well as bonnetmakers plied a needle for their living. Exclusive professional embroiderers worked at the royal court and for the nobility, producing high-quality finished goods and creating and drawing out embroidery designs on canvas or linen later embroidered in a noble household and categorised as ladies' 'works'. These intricately-worked pieces provided colour and elegance to brighten interior furnishings, such as the red woollen hangings with applied black silk embroidered in yellow and blue silks (in the National Museum of Scotland). The use of names or initials, heraldry and emblems, some with complex puns or allusions, alongside flowers, animals and other decorative patterns, communicated specific messages as well as reflecting chivalric and Renaissance tastes. Being a large and prestigious item of furniture, beds attracted embroidered hangings: the bed valances made by Katherine Ruthven for her marriage in 1551 to Campbell of Glenorchy, displaying the couple's arms, initials and the story of Adam and Eve, are probably the earliest surviving example of Scottish embroidery (in the Burrell Collection, Glasgow). Possibly linked to Katherine Oliphant's wedding was a fine carpet, covering a table, not the floor, embroidered with her arms, initials and an elephant, punning on her name. Psalm verses were stitched around the borders and biblical texts illustrated the panels, with one of St Paul offering Timothy a glass of wine (1 Tim. 5: 23). Much surviving Scottish embroidery has been attributed, usually incorrectly, to Mary, Queen of Scots, such as the later Perthshire valances depicting the story of Daniel. Needlework was an abiding pastime for the queen, especially in her English prison, where she produced the famous Oxburgh Hangings. Ecclesiastical vestments were heavily embroidered by professionals and the Blairs College set were probably worked in southern German, rather than by a royal hand. Clothes were greatly enhanced by embroidery and 'blackwork' can be seen on the earl of Moray's shirt in his wedding portrait of 1562 (see Figure 8.1), the sort of effete French fashion attracting Richard Maitland of Lethington's criticism.

her twelfth birthday: she came of age during her twelfth year beginning on 8 December 1553.

Since Mary would remain in France alongside her future husband, finding Arran's successor had added significance because this regency would effectively be permanent. The lesson of James V's minority was that Albany had been acceptable because he was a Stewart, despite regarding himself as the king of France's man in Scotland. When left in charge, Albany's deputy had been murdered: not a good precedent for a Frenchman as viceroy. When the regency decision was taken in 1551, the Scots made it plain a Frenchman was not to their taste – they preferred the Queen Mother, whose candidature was strongly supported by her Guise brothers. It was to her credit that she was willing to do this duty for her lineage and her country, though it necessitated leaving her children and, in the event, she never saw her daughter again. She faced the added sorrow that, as she started back to Scotland, her son fell ill and died in her arms. The 1550–1 visit proved a watershed in her life, placing her firmly on course for the regency of Scotland. That visit also confirmed the arrival of a peaceful period for Scotland, with noblemen able to concentrate upon rebuilding and noblewomen upon running their households and enjoying the art of needlework (see the box on p. 178).

Arriving back in Scotland late in 1551, the Queen Mother tactfully managed the delicate task of handling the governor. Having bargained hard and extracted from Henry II a good price for his demission of office, the new duke of Châtelherault departed with grace. On 12 April 1554 in front of parliament sitting in the Edinburgh Tolbooth Mary of Guise was formally invested. Significantly, it was the representative of the French king, Scotland's protector, who placed on Mary's head the crown of Scotland, and put the sceptre and sword of state into her hands. The new Regent rode triumphantly back down the Royal Mile with the Honours borne before her and the Scottish nobility clattering alongside. Mary might well smile on that day, for the dozen years since James' death had been hard, yet, largely by her own efforts, Henry II's Franco-British policy and the direction of Scotland were securely in her hands.

FRANCO-BRITAIN VERSUS ANGLO-IMPERIAL BRITAIN

A sense of urgency was added to Mary's installation as regent by events in England threatening her long-term dynastic strategy. In a blow to

French interests, at the death of Edward VI the brief reign of Lady Jane Grey was swiftly overturned by Mary, the daughter of Henry VIII and Catherine of Aragon. For most of her life Mary Tudor had looked to her mother's relatives, especially Emperor Charles V, and to make matters worse, the English queen contracted a marriage to Charles' son, Philip of Spain. France faced complete encirclement by her Habsburg enemy and Scotland shared a border with this Anglo-Imperial regime. The children from that marriage would relegate to obscurity the claim of Mary, Queen of Scots to the English throne, reducing the Franco-British strategy to tatters. At the start of her regency Mary of Guise was faced with a crisis: in the short term, a hostile England, with war a near certainty; in the long term, the end of her daughter's hopes of the English throne.

At this juncture the British Isles became one of the foci of European politics, with the main Habsburg–Valois war zone migrating from Italy to the French borders with the Holy Roman Empire, the Low Countries and into the English Channel. The French triumph during the Rough

Crossing the North Channel

During the 1550s sea traffic across the North Channel from the west of Scotland to the north of Ireland increased as the pace of Scottish settlement in Antrim and the mercenary and commercial trades quickened. Forming a boundary between the Stewart monarchy and the Tudor state, the North Channel had few of the attributes of the land border. Its sea lanes brought the Western Isles close to the Isle of Man and the northern Irish coast (see Map 1.1) and when wind and tide were favourable it took a couple of hours to cross from Kintyre to Antrim, and on a clear day beacon fires could be seen across the water. Clan Donald south, the MacDonald branch holding Islay and Kintyre, had spread into the Glens of Antrim. During the sixteenth century, the MacDonalds dramatically increased their holdings by successful campaigns of conquest and colonisation. Since the thirteenth century many Islesmen served the Irish chiefs as soldiers or *gallowglasses* and settled in the country. The seasonal migration of Scottish mercenaries or *redshanks* greatly increased as the Tudor conquest of Ireland pressurised Gaelic Ireland. The food and wealth saved or brought back to the Western Highlands and Islands from these mercenary bands made a major impact upon their economic well-being. The climate changes upon these marginal areas became particularly noticeable from the 1550s, encouraging further Scottish migration and colonisation on the more fertile Irish lands and helping ease the subsistence burden upon their homelands. The most celebrated influx of Scottish mercenaries arrived in Ulster during 1569 as dowries for two Scottish women, Agnes, Lady Dunyvaig, who married the O'Neill chief, and her daughter Finola, wed at the same time to the O'Donnell chief. Easy links across the North Channel maintained the Gaelic cultural flow between the two countries, allowing men from the Scottish learned orders to receive training in Ireland and a few Irish poets to visit Scotland. The largely unregulated trade between the Isles and Clyde ports with Dublin, Drogheda and Carrickfergus in primary products, such as timber, was also flourishing. Particularly through mercantile contact with Chester, this was part of the general traffic running down the western sea lanes of the 'Inner Sea' of the islands of the Atlantic archipelago and hence to the Atlantic coasts of France and Spain (see Map 9.1). The possibility of exploiting the Irish link for diplomatic and military advantage floated in and out of the Scottish monarchy's consciousness. The Campbells were the most convenient bridge for Scottish rulers and that clan's involvement in Lowland, Highland and British politics ensured that the North Channel remained a significant factor in relations between Scotland, England and Ireland.

Wooings, giving them the upper hand in the Battle for Britain, was negated by the Imperial gain of England as the dowry kingdom for Philip of Spain. Having battled for over fifty years for European dominance, both Valois and Habsburg courts hoped the addition of an extra kingdom would tip the balance decisively in their favour. The dynastic accident leaving England and Scotland with reigning queens appeared to make the Battle for Britain the decisive one within Europe.

Fighting had resumed between the Emperor and Henry II in 1552 and the Scots narrowly avoided having to declare war on the Netherlands. From 1554, they were far more concerned about the threat of Spanish and Imperial troops invading Scotland since, with both sides entrenched within the British mainland, the Anglo-Scottish borders might have become one of the main Habsburg–Valois battlegrounds. Though less likely, the North Channel sea frontier might be exploited by the English troops and naval vessels stationed in Ireland to threaten Scotland's west coast. Having emerged from the battering of the Rough Wooings, Scotland was in poor shape to face another invasion.

During the mid-1550s when she was planning Scotland's defence against the threat of Anglo-Imperial invasion, the regent faced a major problem. There was an urgent need to refortify key strongholds because the forts constructed by the English and the French during the Rough Wooings had been dismantled. Though the castles of Edinburgh and Stirling required repairs, as did Leith, Inchkeith and Dunbar to protect the Forth, it was the lack of any fortified strength in the Borders that most concerned Mary and D'Oisel, appointed Henry II's Lieutenant-General in Scotland. After grandiose plans to fortify Kelso were dropped, attention concentrated upon Langholm. The other shortage was troops, most of whom had gone to fight in the battles on France's northern border with the Netherlands. When hostilities had been resumed in 1552, about 3,000 Scots had entered French service, including units commanded by Ruthvens and Frasers, the great mercenary families of later years.

Money was needed to prepare Scotland for war and that was in chronically short supply. As part of his 'golden handshake' in 1554, Châtelherault had been relieved of his debts, leaving Mary of Guise with a deficit of £31,184 12s 6d. Setting up a separate French household in 1554 for Mary, Queen of Scots was expensive and this had taken most of Guise's own revenues as well as a Scottish subvention. In an acute form, the regent faced the permanent Stewart dilemma of where to find extra resources to finance military preparations. In Mary's case the extensive refortification required was ruinously expensive and not something Scots were accustomed to treating as a defensive necessity. That Stewart financial standby, the golden goose of the church, was finding it increasingly difficult to lay eggs. Much of its land had already been feued, with major consequences for the social and economic life of the realm. The church had suffered badly during previous wars and its resources and posts had been utilised to bolster political support leaving very little spare cash within its wealthy system. Since the ecclesiastics had become exceptionally late payers of their taxes, it was hard to extract finance quickly from the church.

Even when a substantial tax was granted, such as £20,000 in 1555, collecting the contributions remained a perennial problem; the regent sought to tackle it by improving tax assessment and record-keeping. As the sole business of the meeting, the Lords of the Articles proposed to the 1556 Parliament that a new roll be made listing taxpayers' overall worth, instead of the traditional 'auld extent' of their lands. Taking the sort of inventory compiled for one's last will and testament would, some complained, set a winding sheet before their eyes. A tax on goods and wealth rather than the outdated valuation of land was an extremely radical pro-

Feuing and the transfer of church property into lay hands

It is difficult to overestimate the quiet revolution that transferred church property into lay hands during the sixteenth century. Many families established their dynasties and their hold on lands previously owned by the medieval church which they acquired either by direct transfer or by feuing. At St Boswells in Roxburghshire, Marion Cochrane was able to secure the holding in 1557 where she had the 'kindness', being nearest kin to the previous occupier, and had entered as tenant through customary inheritance. She received her feu charter from Melrose Abbey for one and three quarter husbandlands (about forty-five Scots acres) though not before the Dean of Glasgow had bought the lands of Lessudden then sold them at a profit. The feu gave Marion legal recognition of her rights and the all-important heritable possession allowing her holding to be passed to her daughter, Christian. Nearly two thirds of the feus of Melrose Abbey lands went to sitting tenants, who, like Marion, faced high initial costs with the down payment, an annual feu duty higher than the previous rent and periodic grassums or payments to the proprietor. For some, though by no means all, the feu charter brought future prosperity.

At the opposite end of the country, the Burnett family were small barons with an estate near Banchory on Deeside who had lived for 250 years on a *crannog* (dwelling on an artificial island) on the Loch of Leys. It was the marriage in 1543 of Alexander to Janet, daughter of an Arbroath canon, which transformed the family's fortunes. Two years later Cardinal Beaton, Arbroath's abbot, gave them a charter of the lands of Pittenkeir because they had protected the monastery against its oppressors. Janet's dowry enabled construction to begin on the tower house at Crathes. For the next forty years they employed the Bell family of masons, equipped their home with oak furniture made by the Aberdeen wood-working school and, finally, painted their ceilings with the latest Renaissance fashions. Thanks to obtaining church lands a new group of landowners were created who altered the social and political mix within localities and regions.

posal. If such tax records were available, it would be easier to introduce a yearly tax. Those Scots with French experience had seen that country's tax bill substantially increase and feared a similar outcome. There was sufficient opposition to the regent's plans that, after three days' debate, they were dropped. In a rare tactical error, she had not explicitly linked the tax to the refortification programme and had failed to allay fears this was the thin end of a large tax wedge. The lesser nobility spearheaded the opposition and, looking back to their fifteenth-century forbears, chose parliament to voice their grievances. Although the reported figure of 300 was probably an exaggeration, on such a contentious national issue the lairds came en masse to Edinburgh, as they were to do again for the Reformation parliament of 1560.

STEPPING OUTSIDE THE CATHOLIC CHURCH

The Scottish church had been left without clear leadership following the murder of Cardinal Beaton and the death two months later of his Glasgow rival, Archbishop Dunbar. There was a two-year gap before the new archbishop of St Andrews took possession of his see, and at Glasgow James Beaton was not consecrated until 1552 after two other nominations had foundered. The decade had opened with a heresy trial. Archbishop Hamilton, having finally secured his diocese, demonstrated his authority by Adam Wallace's trial and execution. This self-taught layman, from the Kyle district of Ayrshire with its long tradition of anti-sacerdotal heresy, had been working in East Lothian within the St Andrews archdiocese. Wallace had benefited from the laird of Ormiston's practice of giving his co-religionists employment as a tutor. There were strong links between the heretical families of Lothian and Ayrshire and their homes hosted the evangelicals' meetings to read their bibles and discuss the theology of salvation. Wallace had gone an important step further; he was accused of preaching without licence and baptising his own child. Constantly appealing to Scripture as the sole authority during his trial, Wallace explained the absence of a 'true minister' made him baptise his child. This was totally different from the common justification for lay baptism of a sick child when a priest was not immediately available: Wallace was asserting he was part of a separate 'true church'. Having definitively and unambiguously stepped outside the bounds of the institutional church, Wallace can be designated as the first native Protestant within Scotland. Few fellow evangelicals in 1550 wanted to follow him across that Rubicon, though the next few years saw profound changes in the evangelical movement as a recognisable Protestant identity emerged.

For the first half of the 1550s, the ecclesiastical authorities left most evangelical laymen and women alone and they remained quiet and unobtrusive. There was neither a campaign to root out heretical views nor a wave of iconoclasm or open defiance. It was safe enough for Glencairn to walk out of Wallace's trial, telling the bishop of Orkney and his fellow clergy to take responsibility for the condemnation. Although his younger brother had been tried for heresy in James V's reign, Glencairn had little fear in 1550 he would be accused. With the mood of reconciliation following the Rough Wooings, reform dropped its unpatriotic tag and the pro-English association of evangelical opinions was finally broken when Mary Tudor returned England to the Catholic fold, thereby dissolving the confessional border existing since 1533.

The dramatic reversal of fortune for English Protestantism following Mary Tudor's accession also sent into exile on the continent a significant number of Scots. John Knox, having worked in the Church of England since his release from the French galleys, was forced to flee. Along with other Scots already in Europe, he gravitated towards the English exile congregations, especially the one settled in Geneva, the city of John Calvin. The shared exile experience and the 'British' outlook it fostered helped shape Scottish Protestantism. The products of that exile congregation, the Geneva translation of the Bible and the Form of Prayers or *Book of Common Order*, as it became known, were the liturgical and literary foundations upon which Scottish Protestant culture was subsequently built.

OBSTACLES TO ECCLESIASTICAL REFORM

Anglo-Scottish Protestant relations flourished in exile, though the same was not true of the two Catholic churches within the British mainland. The disappearance of the confessional frontier did not presage a new era of joint initiatives for Catholic reform. A golden opportunity to reinvigorate Catholicism throughout the British Isles was missed because Scotland was tied to France and England to the Imperial interest. From 1555 church unity was weakened by the virulent anti-Habsburg policy pursued by Pope Paul IV, including a personal vendetta against Cardinal Pole in England. Ecclesiastical co-operation between the English and Scottish hierarchies might have generated the impetus for a thorough reform programme in Scotland and helped mitigate the policy of persecution in England. If they had formulated a common programme, both institutions would have been stronger when facing their respective crises in 1559. Being constructed during the 'in-between time' in European Roman Catholicism, after reconciliation with the Protestants had been blocked by the Council of Trent's first session and before a Counter-Reformation programme had been fully articulated, the reforms introduced by Archbishop Hamilton and by Cardinal Pole shared many characteristics. Despite similarities, they remained determinedly separate, a weakness that contributed to Catholicism's defeat in both British kingdoms in the next decade.

Shortly after he had established himself in St Andrews, Hamilton, as primate of Scotland, called a Provincial Council in 1549 and further Councils met in 1552, probably 1556 and in 1559. Since doctrinal discussion was largely avoided in these councils, the theological cracks within the church appeared bridgeable. To those clerics inside the church trying to introduce it, consensual reform looked an achievable goal: the worldly cleric grimly defending his privileges seemed a greater obstacle than the heretic. Thanks to the Scottish-born archbishop of Armagh, the decrees of Trent's first session were sent to Scotland, though no prelate from Scotland had attended. The archbishop of Cologne's reforming measures promulgated a decade earlier combined with the first Tridentine decrees to shape the Scottish Provincial Councils' statutes.

This reforming legislation had two targets: lax clerical morality and lay and clerical ignorance. Clerical discipline was a perennial problem, allowing past measures simply to be reissued concerning concubinage and abuses such as providing for the clergy's children from the church's patrimony. Scots waited to see how far the assembled higher clergy would alter their own lifestyles to match their fine pronouncements. Acknowledging more recent humanist and evangelical criticism, regular preaching became a priority and provision was made for sermons from bishops or their deputies. Though the decrees were eminently worthy, tightening clerical discipline and providing a limited educational programme to deliver longer-term improvements, they lacked two crucial ingredients for a successful reform programme: religious zeal and a viable method of enforcement. Specifically, there was a deafening silence on the subject of visitations, the time-honoured method by which Council decrees were implemented. Visiting was essential if changes to the behaviour of the diocesan clergy and of the regular orders were to be introduced and monitored. Since no alternative mechanism was put in place, the implementation of reform rested upon individuals' energy and conviction, a less than adequate provision, given the personnel of the Catholic hierarchy.

The financial, organisational and career structures of the late medieval Scottish church were geared to funnelling resources to its higher reaches and producing high-flying clerics capable of staffing the royal administration, ecclesiastical and civil law courts, universities and church management. The production of bishops who could run the country and administer their dioceses had become a fine art. The best were well educated, frequently steeped in canon and civil law, making them eminently useful, and busy in royal service. The worst had been given a meal ticket and licence to live as they chose in order to sweeten a political deal with a noble relative. Since the system had virtually selected out the qualities of spiritual leadership which might have inspired and mobilised a reform programme, it was predictable that no member of the episcopal bench emerged in the 1550s in such a role. The growth of the church–crown hybrid, tailored so well to the needs of Scottish governance, created a crushing weight of vested interest, an immovable object blocking fundamental, systematic ecclesiastical reform.

Three clerical Johns based in St Andrews, Winram in the Augustinian Priory, Douglas in the university's St Mary's College and Grierson, the provincial general of the Dominicans, represented the strands of Catholic reform seeking to revitalise the Church during the 1550s. Following the premature end of his 1547 attempt at local urban reform, Winram concentrated upon the priory, raising the recruitment of Augustinian canons to the highest levels of the century; a pool of talent which after the Reformation flowed into the kirk's ministry. As its provost, John Douglas led the refoundation in 1555 of St Mary's College as a humanist academy for clerical training with particular stress upon biblical study. One of Douglas' deputies was Richard Marshall, a highly-qualified English Dominican whom Grierson had welcomed to St Andrews when he had fled from Henry VIII. The provincial general of the Scottish Dominicans, himself a product of Elphinstone's reforms at Aberdeen, attempted to reinvigorate his order along Erasmian lines and to help the wider church do likewise. In addition to attending the Provincial Councils, held in the Edinburgh Blackfriars' splendid hall, he summoned Dominican chapters to implement reform. Marshall provided an important element within this plan, educating future preachers and drafting 'Hamilton's' Catechism, the most positive and significant achievement of the 1552 Provincial Council.

The Catechism's reforming and conciliatory tone was particularly noticeable in the article on the contested doctrine of justification, reflecting the pre-Tridentine co-operative humanist spirit present during the Lutheran–Catholic dialogue in 1546 at Regensburg. Though it could be interpreted as a conciliatory gesture by the evangelicals, the absence of any reference to the pope owed far more to the Scottish conciliarist tradition. The heavily clericalist tone of Catholic reform and the general disinclination to treat the laity seriously, regarding them as sheep needing to be shepherded back to the fold, would have alarmed evangelicals. Such a blind spot was later identified by the Catholic apologist Winzet as one of the most serious failings of the pre-Reformation church. The hierarchy showed little sense of urgency and did not recognise the need to confront key theological issues. It was not until 1558 that Abbot Kennedy's *Compendius Tractive* appeared, giving a reasoned defence of tradition and the most impressive refutation of the Protestant argument for Scripture alone.

THE ESTABLISHMENT OF 'PRIVY KIRKS'

Meanwhile, the evangelicals were moving from conventicles to the establishment of 'privy kirks'. Having organised and hosted the conventicles, the lairds fostered greater communication between them, producing an embryonic awareness of being a national movement. Being essentially a lay initiative, the movement had been located in households and utilised kin and social networks, such as the reform-minded network spreading from Perth to adjacent shires, facilitated by the marriages of the six daughters of Lord Ruthven. Evangelical contact followed routine interchanges by word of mouth and travel between friends and relations. An active participant in this intercommunication was the middle-ranking Ayrshire laird Campbell of Kinzeancleuch, whose constant riding from Ayrshire to the Mearns, Perthshire, Fife and Lothian did not spark domestic arguments since his wife was an equally ardent evangelical. Knowing he was travelling on behalf of the cause, Elizabeth did not produce 'ill-cooked kail' when he returned late for his supper, as other wives would have done.[1] Within their household she confidently interpreted the Scriptures, having no hesitation in correcting some less well-informed men.

The growing strength of evangelical organisation was revealed when John Knox slipped back into Scotland in the autumn of 1555 on a private visit. On the lookout for Protestant clergy to give them spiritual guidance and the benefit of Protestant sacraments, the lay leaders persuaded him to conduct a preaching tour. Based in lairds' and merchants' houses and comprising exhortations and discussions, this did not imitate Wishart's very public preaching. Although sermons remained

---

[1] John Davidson, 'A Memorial of the life of two worthye christians, Robert Campbel, of the Kinyeancleugh, and his wife, Elizabeth Campbel', in *Three Scottish Reformers*, ed. C. Rogers (Grampian Club, London, 9, 1876), 111–12.

important, Knox also administered communion. By receiving the sacraments from a Protestant minister, the conventicles separated themselves from the established church, self-consciously shifting their identity to become 'privy kirks', congregations of the faithful gathering in private within Scotland. During his many discussions, Knox hammered home the same message: attendance at Catholic worship was forbidden, because the Mass was idolatrous. He condemned the practice of Nicodemism – privately holding evangelical opinions whilst publicly attending Mass. Despite Knox's best efforts, this remained a debateable point among Scottish Protestants. It was a major step to make a clean break by stopping attending one's parish church. Many were not convinced of its necessity or were not willing to risk a conviction for heresy. Despite being strongly urged to stay and offered full protection from arrest or trial by Argyll and his Campbell kinsmen, Knox returned to Geneva in May 1556.

THE REGENT'S VIEW OF JUSTICE

Both peers and lesser nobility might have been suspicious of two of the regent's policies appearing to undermine their power within the regions, inhibiting the kind of protection Argyll had offered to Knox. In a sweeping act the practice of bonding was abolished in 1555, specifically removing any link between a bond of manrent and the granting of lands, tacks, pensions or other economic inducements. Despite its universal language, the lack of an outcry suggested the legislation had two particular targets: it relieved the regent from paying pensions previously given in bonds to build support for the French cause; equally, it prevented Châtelherault in the future from employing the same device to undermine her authority. Mary of Guise hoped it would also stifle the overtly political bonding with a precise aim, developed during the Rough Wooings. Even with its limited targets, this policy had a strong whiff of centralist sentiment.

An even more authoritarian strategy, verging on a colonial approach to governing Scotland, was present in the regent's views about the lax administration of justice in the local courts. In a private letter Mary of Guise explained to her brother:

> my determination [is] to see justice take a straightforward course,
> and they find me a little severe, they will not endure it, and say
> that these are laws of the French, and that their old laws are good,

which for the most part are the greatest injustices in the world, not in themselves, but from the way they are administered.[2]

Although sensitive to Scots' fears, the regent believed she recognised more clearly than the Scottish nobility the true nature of justice and she had the benefit of her French experience to help them see the best path to follow. She viewed her role as bringing 'a young nation to a state of perfection'. She introduced a tough new law against perjury, with piercing of the tongue for those guilty of bearing false witness, and a type of 'law court sanctuary', making it more heinous to murder the defender or pursuer in a court case. This attempt to minimise the violence of local feuds and ensure their settlement in an exclusively legal context was part of a deliberate policy of inserting 'public', central and royal justice into the kin world of 'private' justice and conflict resolution.

The regent possibly had Huntly in mind when she wrote of the great lords who were obstructing justice. In her ascent to power, the 4th earl had been one of Mary's most significant supporters and he had received a range of rewards. These had included the coveted lands of the earldom of Moray, which led to a tussle for control over Clan Chattan, the confederation of clans with bases in Strathspey and Badenoch, who were the key to further westward expansion. Huntly had been using his Lieutenancy of the North and his royal commissions of fire and sword to justify the execution of Cameron of Lochiel, MacDonald of Keppoch and the Captain of Clan Chattan. In each case this removed an impediment to Gordon plans to dominate Moray and expand their control into Lochaber. Following the manoeuvre whereby the countess of Huntly had executed Mackintosh, Captain of Clan Chattan, when Mary of Guise and her entourage were in France, the regent probably put Huntly on warning he was to act with due procedure and follow government instructions properly, especially in his 1553 commission to deal with Clanranald and Clan Cameron. The earl's campaign was a disaster, being abandoned beside Loch Ness because his Lowland horsemen from Aberdeenshire refused to enter such unsuitable terrain. Since he did not trust himself alone with the Mackintoshes of Clan Chattan who made up his Highland infantry, Huntly had no option but to march home.

[2] Mary of Guise to the Cardinal of Lorraine, 13 Jan. 1556/7, *Papal Negotiations with Mary, Queen of Scots*, ed. J. H. Pollen (SHS, 1st ser. 37, Edinburgh, 1901), 427–30 (at 430); discussed in P. E. Ritchie, *Mary of Guise in Scotland, 1548–1560: A Political Career* (East Linton, 2002), ch. 5.

The regent was not forgiving and Huntly crashed from grace, being imprisoned in Edinburgh Castle from October 1554, though his sentence of exile was commuted to a large fine. What hurt far more was having the Great Seal removed and bestowed upon du Rubay, the French Vice-Chancellor. Having lost his Moray and Orkney lands, salt was rubbed in Huntly's wound when Sutherland, his kinsman, was granted the bailiery of Moray in August, renewing his previous links with that province. In the New Year, Huntly wrote a grovelling letter to D'Oisel, seeking his good offices with the regent to remove her 'ewyll opponzeone of my serwice touerts hyr grace.'[3] Having made her public example of the 'Cock o' the North', Mary relented; at Stirling Castle on 30 March 1555 Huntly gave caution, before being packed off to Jedburgh to police the Borders. Although working relations were resumed between the regent and the earl, his treatment rankled sufficiently to explain his lukewarm support for her during the crisis of 1559–60.

In characteristic Stewart fashion, as part of her extended progress during the summer of 1556 the regent personally brought justice to those shires where Huntly held sway: Inverness, Ross, Banff, Aberdeen and particularly Moray. Aberdeen's entertainment bill indicated where the burgh council believed the real power in Scotland lay: not accustomed to wasting its money, the council expended £20 on wine, spices and candles, including lavish provision for D'Oisel in addition to Mary of Guise. This talented Frenchman, who formed the other half of the regent's formidable team, was regarded as the most powerful man in Scotland and, as Huntly had recognised, the best person to restore him to favour. The regent's visit gave Huntly a chance to show off his splendid new palace incorporated into Castle Huntly at Strathbogie. The castle was dominated by its new round tower whose design was probably influenced by the earl's visit to France and possibly by the castle profiles in the Duc de Berry's *Très Riches Heures*. The furnishings were as magnificent as their architectural setting, with silk, velvet and gold-embroidered coverings and curtains in yellow, crimson, blue, green and violet. In the hall there was a crimson cloth of state embroidered with gold under which the earl would sit and velvet cushions for the comfort of the ladies and gentlemen in the chambers and bed chambers where access was restricted.

In direct competition was Balvenie, where Atholl, Huntly's son-in-law, had also placed a fine new Renaissance lodging within a medieval castle. It was situated about a dozen miles from Strathbogie and better located

---

[3] Huntly to D'Oisel, 4 Jan. 1555, *Scottish Correspondence of Mary of Lorraine*, ed. A. I. Cameron (SHS, 3rd ser. 10, Edinburgh, 1927), 395–6.

Figure 8.1 A conjectural reconstruction of Balvenie Castle, as it might have appeared when Mary of Guise visited in 1556. [Charles McKean]

than the nearby Gordon castle of Auchindoun to command the key routes to Elgin, the Spey river, the Moray Firth and the Cabrach pass through the Grampians. Marital kinship had not diminished the rivalry between Huntly and Atholl, whose influence blocked any extension of Gordon power to the south. In the early 1550s it found expression in competitive building, with Atholl's lodging presenting an even more elegant frontage than Strathbogie to welcome the regent. The carefully-contrived entrance to this stately dwelling had delicate oriel windows and heraldic mountings, displaying in bright tinctures the royal and family arms and the motto 'Furth Fortun and Fil thi Fatris' (Forth fortune and fill thy coffers) – not perhaps a sentiment the regent was anxious to encourage. Mary of Guise would have found more acceptable the pious tag 'Christ is my hope' that adorned the doors to the new stair towers in the courtyard.

The regent also stopped at Elgin, a burgh with many fine houses and a well-developed sense of its own elegance as the seat of the rich and prestigious diocese of Moray. A cultured appearance could be deceptive, for the previous year there had been a serious affray during Vespers in the cathedral when the Dunbars and Inneses fought, with blood spilt 'in the presence of the sacrament' itself. Among those involved were Alexander

Dunbar, the abbot of nearby Pluscarden, and his kinsman David, dean of Moray and at least two others in holy orders. They claimed their clerical privilege and were sent for trial to the bishop's court rather than the royal criminal court. To contemporaries divine justice judged the deeds at Elgin Cathedral when a terrible storm hit Moray devastating the crops and killing livestock. Whether through church or civil jurisdiction, it was proving difficult for the regent to ensure human justice followed as straight a path as divine retribution appeared to do.

On progress or in the capital, the regent acted as if she were an adult ruler in her own right. When able to devote herself to enforcing justice she was successful, using the tried and tested methods by which Stewart monarchs had imposed their authority. The Borders furnished a litmus test of good order and in 1554 the regent made a sweep through the Eastern Marches administering justice, collecting hostages and unsuccessfully trying to resolve the feud between the Scotts and the Kers. The murder in 1552 of the Warden of the Middle March, Scott of Buccleuch, in Edinburgh's High Street had carried Border feuding to the regent's doorstep. Despite her Fife origins, Janet Beaton, Buccleuch's wife, displayed the full 'Border spirit' when she led 200 Scotts (of Buccleuch) to the Kirk of St Mary of the Lowes in Yarrow and seized Ker of Cranston in revenge for her husband's murder. Such dramatic action made a rousing ballad, but it deeply offended Mary of Guise's sense of order and justice, though her merciful intervention ensured charges were eventually dropped.

Buccleuch's death, leaving his young grandson as heir, created a power vacuum in Teviotdale, encouraging the regent to employ as Warden in the Middle March a series of men without a strong local base who were closely supervised by her government. Though it did improve the day-to-day administration, it proved less effective than the traditional method of relying upon those with substantial local power. Further central direction brought the stationing of a troop of French light horse in the Borders to repress thieves. The local population regarded them as a burden and a nuisance and the resulting abuse of the French provoked a Parliamentary Act in 1555 protecting Scotland's allies from verbal harassment. In Border affairs, the regent appeared over-anxious to assert royal rule and by communicating directly with the English wardens she concerned herself with a level of detail better left to those at her command. Her intervention shifted discussions to the level of diplomatic negotiations, bypassing the normal wardens' exchanges, in favour of instructions sent through the French ambassador resident in London, or involving the English ambassador in Paris.

Acute tension caused by the international situation and the expectation that Scotland and England would shortly be at war made cross-border co-operation near impossible and raiding difficult to stop. The judicial, rather than offensive, role of the French horse troop was not obvious to the English, who became alarmed. The cold war existing between the Habsburg and Valois power blocs encouraged hot exchanges on all their mutual frontiers. Early in 1557 fighting resumed on the border between the Low Countries and northern France. Philip of Spain's pressure upon his wife, Mary Tudor, to join the war, was successful in July. The English declaration of war against France hardened Scottish attitudes, leading to a series of destructive raids across the border.

When in the autumn of 1557 the Scots gathered a substantial army to assault Wark Castle, Lieutenant-General D'Oisel wanted the target to be Berwick. The Scottish nobility stuck to the strategy employed since James IV's reign of a limited, destructive raid undertaken at the close of the campaigning season and the softening of the defences on the middle route across the Tweed. In mid-October, with bad weather, disease and desertion among the troops and news of English preparations at land and sea, the Scottish commanders opted to disband the army rather than attack, leaving Mary of Guise and D'Oisel furious. The Queen Dowager was reported to be weeping in anger and frustration and D'Oisel, like Albany before him, wished he were back in France. Though the military impact of England and Scotland on the overall struggle was actually slight, France lost face badly over the Scots' decision.

THE NEW PROTESTANT LEADERSHIP

Following Knox's departure in 1556, the Protestant initiative returned to lay hands with the leadership moving up the social ladder as peers of the realm became more actively involved, thereby altering the movement's political profile. Seeking to persuade or pressurise the Queen Regent into authorising a programme of church reform, the Earl Marischal and Glencairn asked Knox to write an open letter in what were for him conciliatory tones. The Ayrshire peer presented it to Mary of Guise whose flippant dismissal of the tract put Knox's literary nose severely out of joint and laid the foundations of his deep enmity towards the regent. In the game of move and counter move the Catholic hierarchy resumed their heresy proceedings; safely absent abroad, Knox was condemned and his effigy burned in Edinburgh.

The noble leadership of the emerging Protestant movement was passing to a group of younger men joined by ties of kinship and age. Argyll's son, Lorne, was brother-in-law to James, commendator of St Andrews, and Erskine was cousin to them both. Their youthful enthusiasm tinged with impatience drove the campaign of increasing pressure upon the ecclesiastical authorities to make concessions. In December 1557 a bond was signed outlining their intentions and backed by the political weight of Morton and the veteran earls, Argyll and Glencairn. The 'First Band', as it later became known, was like the bonds of maintenance routinely given to dependents by nobles, promising their 'whole power, substance and very lives' in support. The bond's unusual aspect was its religious language and the confessional nature of the feud, as protection was extended to 'the haill congregatioun of Christ' against 'Sathan and all wicked power that does intend tyranny or truble against the foirsaid congregation'.[4] This compact noble faction had a specific programme: setting up an alternative style of worship, with 'faithful' ministers preaching and administering the sacraments, that would be defended against suppression by the ecclesiastical hierarchy. Notice was also given that the signatories and their followers would refuse the ministrations of the Catholic Church, possibly including a tax strike: the clean break Knox had been urging the previous year. Significantly, the clause normally found in bonds, excepting action against royal authority, was not included.

The actions accompanying the First Band were less radical than its language. In most feuds or power struggles, Scots nobles engaged in trials of strength, making moves indicating they were serious, while remaining open to negotiation. The Protestants, assuming the regent would allow pressure to be applied upon the ecclesiastical authorities, hoped the clerical reform party could still engineer substantial changes to the church. Rather than iconoclastic demonstrations, the gatherings for sermons previously held within households quietly became more open and public. These limited local reformations in areas of existing strength were a sign of increased militancy by the Protestant faction, but they also revealed its relative weakness. Archbishop Hamilton immediately recognised this challenge to ecclesiastical authority. He dispatched his kinsman to Argyll with personal messages and a letter to persuade the elderly earl to forgo his support for the preacher publicly expounding heresy in his household. Scotland's primate begged his brother-in-law not to place him in such a difficult position, declaring everything could be worked out in

4 *The Works of John Knox*, ed. D. Laing (Edinburgh, 1846–64), I, 273–4.

a quiet deal. Employing the negotiating language of regional politics instead of doctrinal debate, he appealed to Argyll's responsibility to his lineage, urging the earl not to put his noble house in danger. Argyll chose religious discourse for his reply, sending back a resounding refusal to compromise in the language of a confession of faith. No longer interested in private deals, the chief of the Campbells demanded public acceptance of the moves towards reformed worship.

Demonstrating he was deadly serious, the archbishop had a well-known Fife cleric, Walter Mylne, executed for heresy. It was a public relations disaster, with the eighty-year-old Protestant welcoming his chance to witness through martyrdom, making the ecclesiastical authorities look less like defenders of the faith than callous prelates selecting a soft target. The St Andrews citizens expressed their disapproval by refusing to supply the executioners with materials leaving them, it was alleged, to cut the archbishop's tent ropes for cords to tie Mylne to the stake. The heresy trial also formed part of the church's internal struggle, forcing many whose views resembled Mylne's to sit on the bench condemning him. If the experience was intended to bring them into line, it signally failed; probably contributing to the willingness of senior clerics, such as Winram and Douglas, to abandon the Catholic ship the following year.

In Protestant rhetoric the enemy was the Catholic hierarchy and not the regent's regime. However, the campaign of pressure rested upon the political power of Protestant nobles within their localities and employed the standard methods of regional politics to achieve its aim. Since the dispute was not a regional feud, but an ideological stance that had national and international implications, it destabilised the political equilibrium Mary of Guise had constructed during her regency. Though not yet in complete opposition, the regent was faced for the first time by a noble faction with a specific goal.

THE WEDDING OF MARY, QUEEN OF SCOTS

Putting the oxen before the cart was how some Scots described the situation, explaining to the regent in 1557 that since her daughter had not yet married the dauphin, Scotland should not be expected to behave as if the union with France had taken place. A wedding, the sooner the better, would bring stability to the kingdom and certainty over who was their 'lord'. Such mixed messages for the French were the result of the Scots' attempt to steer a difficult course. They worried Henry II might heed the advice he was receiving that France would be better served by marrying

Mary to a French duke, enabling the couple to rule in person in Scotland. This would be a less prestigious match, bringing a French ruler without his own resources at a time of acute danger from the Anglo-Imperial marriage partnership south of the border. On the other hand, the Scottish peers wanted to preserve as much independence for the kingdom in the short term when finalising the marriage provisions and in the longer term when the union of the crowns of Scotland and France became a reality. Pushing for the marriage and at the same time flouting French orders was not completely unreasonable; it was attempting to extract as much as possible from a weak hand. In the heady days of the 1530s when James V found both his brides in France, the Scots could boast they were partners, albeit junior ones, with the French. In the 1550s a colder reality prevailed when the best that could be secured was that Scotland's lass would marry France's lad and take her kingdom as dowry.

Mary of Guise skilfully employed Scottish opinion to put pressure upon Henry II and Scottish commissioners came to France to finalise the details for the wedding on Sunday, 24 April 1558. Breaking with tradition, the Queen of Scots wore white, the colour of mourning in France, and had a splendid dress with a long train borne by two girls, diamonds around her neck and a gold crown on her head. The service at Notre Dame in Paris was the opening of several days of court celebration where the beauty of the Queen Dauphiness was celebrated in a setting of almost unparalleled magnificence.

A few days before the wedding, at the behest of Henry II, the man who had been a kindly father to her for years, Mary had signed three secret documents. They contained provisions in case she died without children transferring to France her rights to her kingdom and the English succession, reimbursing the revenues Henry had spent on Scotland and nullifying those clauses in the formal treaty between France and the Scottish Estates running counter to these arrangements. When the ink dried on these papers, Henry II had achieved the main section of his dynastic strategy: whatever befell Mary, Scotland would become part of the French empire. These were the fruits of the victory he had won against the English in the campaigns of 1548-50. With a sense of great security, he could look, hope and plan for the next part of the struggle for Britain: the prize of the throne of England.

In Scotland, Mary of Guise, the co-architect of Franco-Scotland, knew that, with her daughter safely married and the crown matrimonial secured for the dauphin, her main task had been accomplished to her great satisfaction and relief. Despite the handicap of being a foreign woman, she had managed the transfer of power from Arran and had

Figure 8.2 Francis II of France and Mary, Queen of Scots, in the Forman Armorial.
[NLS Adv MS 31.4.2]

established her own authority, ruling more like an adult Stewart than any other sixteenth-century Scottish regent. She had faced an extremely grave threat from a hostile England under Philip and Mary, though was fortunate no serious warfare resulted. The problems of defence had underlined Scotland's dependence upon the French military machine. The Scots were unable and unwilling to shoulder a massive increase in government expenditure or the consequent overhaul of the taxation system to fund refortification. Easy recourse to ecclesiastical cash was no longer possible, since immediate funds had been drained by James V, the burdens of the Rough Wooing and the Hamiltons helping themselves. Despite extensive feuing of its lands, ecclesiastical resources remained formidable and the church–crown hybrid continued to sustain royal governance, but altering the church's course took time. From a different perspective, that was precisely the problem facing both Catholic reformers and the emerging Protestant movement. The gap between the two groups was widening as the Protestants formed privy kirks and began a campaign of political pressure, though hope still remained in 1558 that consensual reform was possible. The rise of religious opposition and the signs of discontent with French-style justice and with French advisors, soldiers, coins and fashions appeared to be containable problems. Ironically, it was the regent's success in creating a Franco-Scotland which made her vulnerable. Throughout the 1550s Henry II's willingness to commit time, money and effort to Scotland depended upon the kingdom becoming part of the Valois empire and the stepping stone for Franco-Britain. Whilst for Scots being part of a semi-detached Franco-Scotland under the permanent rule of Mary of Guise might be acceptable, Franco-Britain was a different proposition. What no-one could predict in 1558 was how the next two years would change Europe and the British Isles and that Scotland would be embroiled in revolution.

CHAPTER 9

Reformation by the Sword (1555–61)

There were more than enough funerals between 1558 and 1560, as monarchs, alliances and allegiances met their end. The deaths of kings and queens had exact dates but the demise of inanimate ideals, concepts and loyalties, though less precise, were as deeply mourned, as in Sir Richard Maitland's famous, 'Quhair is the blyithnes that hes beine'.[1] Sixteenth-century observers realised they were living through 'trublous' times, though no-one knew how long changes would last or whether the wheel of fortune would spin again. Royal funerals followed each other in rapid succession; the deaths of Charles V in Spain in 1558 and Henry II in France a year later closed the era of Habsburg–Valois wars that had dominated international relations for the previous half-century. The deaths of Mary Tudor in England in 1558 and Mary of Guise in Scotland in 1560 facilitated a diplomatic revolution within the British Isles. The death of Mary, Queen of Scots' husband, Francis II, at the end of 1560 brought an adult monarch back to Scotland to rule. During these two years Scotland had undergone a successful rebellion giving the Protestants political power and making Roman Catholic worship illegal. The auld alliance was no more and Franco-Scotland was buried with Mary of Guise.

THE GRAND FRANCO-BRITISH STRATEGY

The news of the death of the queen of England on 17 November 1558 changed Scotland's political outlook. By dissolving Philip of Spain's authority in his wife's realm, it removed the Habsburg–Valois frontier

---

[1] *Maitland Quarto*, ed. W. A. Craigie (Scottish Text Society, 9, Edinburgh, 1920), 15.

from the Scottish border. In its place the confessional border between England and Scotland reappeared allowing Scottish religious dissidents to find a sympathetic ear and a refuge in the south. That eventuality paled into insignificance beside the change to Mary, Queen of Scots' status, as a dynastic clean sweep became possible: the enticing prospect of being queen of Scotland, France and England. For the following decade the English succession became a fixed star in Scotland's firmament, at times outshining domestic politics, especially for Mary, Queen of Scots herself.

Having no heir of her own body, Mary Tudor reluctantly recognised her half-sister, Elizabeth, as her successor, though the countess of Lennox fostered the rumour that the English queen had considered her son, Darnley. The serious doubts about Elizabeth's legitimacy heralded a grander stage in the Franco-British strategy of Henry II and Mary of Guise. When seeking the pope's support for their plans, the French king presented a strongly Catholic case for Mary, Queen of Scots as the nearest legitimate heir in blood, emphasising that in canon law the marriage of Elizabeth's parents, Anne Boleyn and Henry VIII, had never existed and their child was illegitimate. It was vital that Mary's case as Catholic Europe's choice for the English throne should not be weakened by religious concessions and Henry II became more intransigent when dealing with French Huguenots and Scottish Protestants. Following the momentous peace treaty of Câteau–Cambrésis in April 1559, concluding the protracted Habsburg–Valois wars, there had been talk of France and Spain sinking their rivalry and mounting a joint offensive against Europe's heretics.

In the context of this grand Franco-British strategy, the opportunity to stake a claim to England had arrived a little too soon: there had been no time for the King Dauphin and Queen Dauphiness to consolidate their authority in Scotland and an exhausted and bankrupt France needed peace with an equally tired and penniless Spain. The new priorities immediately reduced the regent's room for manoeuvre when dealing with the Protestant faction and increased the chance of Scotland becoming a launching pad for a campaign to capture the English throne. James IV's great army in 1513 had dreamt of a glorious exploit and a suitably destructive campaign on English soil; it had not envisaged conquest. Speculating about invading England, or providing a safe base from which French troops might do so, required a major shift for Scottish thinking: it altered the range of possible futures and presented a new set of variables to Scots calculating their political course. From recent experience Scots understood how a French military machine might operate in their kingdom and though it was a reasonable price to pay in 1548–50 to evict the English occupying forces, the realm was no longer in danger. The possible presence of a substantial French army in 1559 presented an entirely different proposition. While there was an obvious distinction in Scottish minds between rejecting the grand Franco-British strategy and repudiating the auld alliance, this was not a division the regent could accept. In her view the Scots had been enjoying French protection for the past decade, and in return they should surrender a modicum of independence to further a strategy from which all would benefit.

THE END OF RELIGIOUS CONCILIATION

The immediate casualty of the Franco-British drive was the chance of religious conciliation. In Scotland, as in France, those championing an irenical policy faced mounting pressure from Protestants moving further into the open and as it became politically expedient to suppress heresy, these *politiques* also found themselves squeezed from the other side. Requiring an orthodox front for papal consumption, Mary of Guise could not countenance public concessions over worship. This blocked the area on which Scottish reformers of all shades were willing to open negotiations. Without the regent's backing, there was equally no chance by 1558 of constructing a consensus to drive other reforms through the church. As the theological issues crystallised, the common ground between the various types of reformer was rapidly shrinking. The superficially straightforward call for a disputation to clarify matters immediately encountered the fundamental divide about theological authority. With one side demanding the matter be judged by Scripture alone, and the other insisting upon the inclusion of Tradition, it was virtually impossible to bring Protestant and Catholic disputants to a debate; the abortive disputation in Ayr between the Catholic abbot and the Protestant minister underlined the difficulty.

The best hope for progress lay in the final Provincial Council meeting in March 1559. Catholic reformers attempted to hijack the agenda by presenting a petition in the name of the laity to the regent. Probably written by clerics, it reflected their view of the priorities for humanist-style reform, emphasising the goal of a moral and educated clergy conscientiously performing their duties and not oppressing the laity with financial exactions. Common prayers in the vernacular were acceptable and priority was given to preaching and providing doctrinal explanations, such as the Council's 'Twapenny faith', a short pamphlet giving a simple exposition of the eucharist. At the same time, there was sharp condemnation for the verbal and material attacks upon church sacraments and ornaments. The Protestants had previously presented a petition to parliament, demanding communion in both kinds, services in the vernacular, the right to interpret the Scripture and the suspension of the heresy laws to allow for 'tenderness' of conscience. Accompanying the petition, a Protestation denied responsibility for 'any tumult or uproar . . . and if it shall chance that abuses be violently reformed that the crime therof be not imputed to us'.[2] The gap between the sides had become a chasm.

On the first day of the New Year, an ominous warning of future direct action was posted on the doors of friaries. Reputedly from the poor, widows, orphans, bedridden and disabled, with quasi-legal formulae it had given notice to the mendicant orders to quit the hospitals by Whitsun and allow the 'real' beggars to receive the alms. The imagery and rhetoric of this 'Beggars Summons' drew heavily upon the established genre of anti-mendicant literature and its call for social justice widened its appeal.

The dragon of 1558: portents and providence

Throughout the summer of 1558 after sunset a fire was seen to rise from the Forth and to spread over Edinburgh. Many were afraid to keep a fire in their homes in case the two blazes joined and burned down their houses. Alongside the fire in the morning, a dragon was seen settling on the top of David's tower in Edinburgh Castle, rising into the sky, fighting the seven stars and finally vanishing. In November the fire appeared again, provoking prayers and preaching. When the 'alteratione of religion' followed a few months later with the destruction of the Perth Charterhouse and other religious houses, the portent's meaning became clear to contemporaries. Early modern Scots assumed many natural phenomena were portents, giving them warning of events to come. Divine or diabolical power was at work in the world, altering its normal course and chroniclers noted down and interpreted such unusual events. Post-Reformation theology dismissed the protection of the saints and downgraded personal guardian angels, placing more stress upon the direct providential hand of God intervening in the happenings of daily life, for nations as well as individuals.[3]

---

[2] *John Knox's History of the Reformation in Scotland*, ed. W. C. Dickinson (2 vols, Edinburgh, 1949), I, 148–58 (at 157).
[3] Memo of Dragon NAS, RH9/17/4.

The aggressive language disguised a limited reform, though rejecting the mendicant ideal, it only demanded the removal of hospitals from the friars' control.

The Provincial Council ended in stalemate; failure to win its backing forced leading Catholic reformers, such as Winram, to break with the established church and openly join the Protestants. For purposes of legal indemnity, Reformation changes were subsequently deemed to have begun in March 1559, before any open hostility between the sides. The Council's close and the Easter celebrations marked crucial turning points and the first cleric to preach publicly in defiance of the government was Alexander Gordon, the recently appointed bishop of Galloway. After the Regents' proclamation that a traditional Easter should be kept, the manner of celebrating the festival, attending Catholic Mass or a Protestant service, became a public declaration of religious allegiance. However, though tension mounted, the Easter festival did not produce a flashpoint.

Increasingly, Protestant momentum brought confrontation closer, especially as it collided with the almost immovable object of ecclesiastical vested interest. The existence of the church–crown hybrid increased the political dimension of any direct challenge to the pre-Reformation church. In the limited areas where Protestants enjoyed overwhelming local support and protection, their preachers occupied church pulpits: elsewhere privy kirks continued to meet in households. Communication networks kept the different regions of Protestant strength, and especially their lairds and burgesses, in touch with each other. Though lesser nobility and burgh authorities were not often involved in national politics, the universal issue of religion drew together a party from a cross-section of local elites. Religious conviction was one of the few causes capable of uniting feuding kindreds; a shared Protestantism enabled the Leslies to co-operate with their Fife rivals, the Lindsays.

THE WARS OF THE CONGREGATION

Catching many unawares, an iconoclastic outburst tipped the balance from crisis to confrontation. On 11 May 1559 in St John's church in Perth, John Knox, recently arrived from the Continent, preached a sermon on the text of Christ cleansing the Temple. Putting actions to the words, the Protestants violently 'cleansed' the church and attacked all the burgh's friaries and the Carthusian house of royal foundation. The violence of the outburst flowed in part from existing tensions within the burgh community as the craftsmen struggled to gain a political voice and a feud over the office of Provost raged between the Ruthvens and the Grays. Perth was in an ambivalent position, unlike the overtly Protestant Dundee or Ayr, able to accomplish controlled local reformations directed by their town councils in their accustomed role managing the burgh's religious affairs. Perth provided a perfect example of an area where Protestants were growing in confidence, without being locally dominant. While the Perthshire hinterland, especially fertile Strathearn, held a significant group of Protestant lairds with interests in the burgh, there were Catholic and conservative elements within shire and burgh. When encountering local opposition, the Protestant strategy of constantly pushing to open the door of reform might easily switch into kicking it down.

For the regent, what happened in Perth was simply a riot, and she summoned troops to deal with such civil disorder. Thanks to the excellent Protestant communications system, 2,500 men from Ayrshire under Glencairn marched cross-country to defend Perth's new religious stance. An agreement was reached by negotiation and the burgh opened its gates to Mary of Guise. Determined to make an example, the regent badly overplayed her hand by summarily removing the Protestant Ruthven as provost, by stationing four companies of troops on the burgh and by ostentatiously restoring the Mass. The boisterous entry of her forces into Perth, during which a Protestant laird's young son was accidentally killed by a hagbutter, further embittered the situation. The Protestants called foul and mobilised and, crucially, persuaded Lord James Stewart and Argyll, who had been part of the Regent's negotiating team, to abandon her and join their co-religionists. The two young men became the leaders of the newly-designated 'Lords of the Congregation' and proceeded to rally their fellow Protestants.

The Congregation's aim was simple: they would spread their local reformations around the country by arriving in force to assist local Protestants, where they existed, with the task of 'cleansing' the churches and instituting reformed worship. Where there was reluctance, as at Aberdeen, the neighbouring 'gentlemen of the Mearns' paid the burgh a visit to ensure the Burgh Council instituted religious changes. The ecclesiastical capital, St Andrews, was one of the first burghs to be reformed in this manner along with the other East Neuk ports. The regent was not idle: when the archbishop of St Andrews arrived at Falkland Palace to tell her what had happened to his city, Mary of Guise dispatched forces to march up the River Eden towards St Andrews. Meanwhile, a small Protestant contingent came marching to meet them, stopping on the Hill of Tarvit, high above the recently-reformed burgh of Cupar, and watching as the French troops and artillery deployed. The Protestant communications

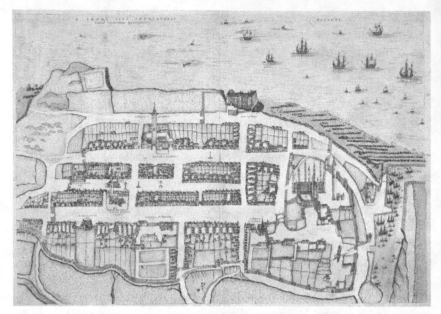

Figure 9.1 A bird's-eye view of St Andrews by John Geddy, c. 1580. [NLS MS 20996]

network saved the day, though Knox, present as the army chaplain, saw a different hand at work, declaring, 'God did so multiply our number, that it appeared as if men had rained from the clouds'.[4] Reinforcements from the rest of Fife, Dundee, Perthshire and Lothian arrived in time to bluff the regent's commanders into negotiating a truce. Knox was not entirely wide of the mark: though mediated through kinship networks, the willingness to come when called was motivated by religion.

Those who supported the regent and the status quo were less efficient at mobilising their kinsmen, friends and allies. Catholic mobs did not gather, as in France, to oppose Protestant mobs in urban streets, and when specifically targeted by the Protestants, burghs made no concerted efforts to protect their friaries, which were integral parts of urban communities. Limited protection against Protestant force was possible, as at King's College, Aberdeen where armed students defended their chapel, though this did not prevent the 'cleansing' of St Machar's Cathedral next door. Edinburgh citizens did not welcome the Lords of the Congregation in the autumn of 1559, but neither had they manned the gates against them. Pleased when Protestant forces were forced to withdraw, there was talk in the burgh markets about helping the Frenchmen

---

[4] *John Knox's History*, I, 183.

cut the throats of the heretics. Looking to the French to end the rebellion gave many Scots an excuse to sit on their hands and watch what transpired.

This attitude was particularly noticeable among the Catholic peers, with few making an active contribution to the regent's efforts. Huntly remained protecting his northern territories, possibly because he remembered the regent's treatment in 1555, or because his Protestant brother, the bishop of Galloway, persuaded him not to enter the main fight. Quentin Kennedy did an excellent job of convincing his nephew, Cassillis, to support the Catholic cause, but in Ayrshire the Kennedys were surrounded by Protestants and cut off from easy access to the east. Similarly, Eglinton and his Montgomeries had too many regional enemies to risk marching out of the area. With the Hamiltons controlling Paisley, Sempill was besieged in his castle by the Congregation's forces, rendering him unable to assist the regent.

During the crisis the Catholic ecclesiastical hierarchy quickly switched into salvage mode; hiding valuables, feuing land and turning to friends and kin for protection. Individuals, like the commendator of Dunfermline, joined the French troops in Fife whilst the bishop of Dunblane was captured and imprisoned by the Congregation, but neither in defence nor attack were the prelates effective. Though clerics had died aplenty fighting the English at Pinkie, during the Wars of the Congregation they did not mobilise. Catholic clergy and supporters faced intimidation rather than martyrdom for their faith as this limited rebellion followed the traditional Scottish pattern, with care taken by all sides to avoid unnecessary spilling of blood or the creation of future bloodfeuds (see the box on intimidation, p. 208).

Although Protestant forces had a wave of initial success in bringing Reformation changes to the main burghs and parts of Lowland Scotland, they could not sustain these local religious settlements. A group of enthusiastic localities had nearly, but not quite, forced their agenda upon a reluctant or indifferent kingdom. The Protestants might have achieved enough if this struggle had remained a Scottish affair and followed the pattern of limited rebellion by demonstrating a clear agenda backed by a determined show of armed force. The Congregation's regional gains might then have produced significant royal concessions and an end to the matter. However, this was an uprising in Franco-Scotland and its declared cause was religious reform, an international conflict entering an especially decisive phase throughout Europe; a Protestant rising in Scotland could not be treated as a little local difficulty.

Intimidation

In their drive to 'cleanse' the realm of false religion, the Protestants targeted images rather than people and in a symbolic demonstration the debris from the iconoclastic destruction at St Andrews was burned on the site of Mylne's execution as a heretic the previous year. Although avoiding making martyrs, where they had local control, the Protestants were not gentle with known Catholic supporters. Probably in fear of his life, the elderly Dominican Provincial-General was forced to make a comprehensive recantation by the newly-formed and aggressively-assertive St Andrews Kirk Session. Possibly because of his involvement in Mylne's trial, Grierson's grey hairs were no defence against the humiliation in March 1560 of standing in front of the parish congregation and renouncing idolatry, the pope, the Mass, images, the cult of saints, vows of chastity and transubstantiation. The central tenets of the old orthodoxy had become the articles of the new heresy. Convinced of their grasp of theological truth, the Protestants had few qualms about pressurising others to acknowledge it.

By steadfastly treating this militant opposition as a political rebellion, the regent gradually gained the upper hand. Having forced the Congregation into attempting a coup d'état, they failed to hold the capital or make their deposition of her authority stick. In the late summer Mary of Guise had received a total of 1,800 French reinforcements – not enough to crush the rebellion speedily, but sufficient to force the Congregation onto the defensive. Being professional soldiers, the French troops could remain in the field while the Congregation's forces could only be used for limited periods or called up in rotation. Both sides turned to external help: the regent from her brothers in France, the Congregation from the new regime in England.

INTERNATIONAL INTERVENTION

The reaction to their respective pleas for help was determined by the totally unexpected death of Henry II following a jousting accident whilst celebrating the peace of Câteau–Cambrésis. Losing an adult king at the height of his powers was a severe blow to France, and brought his fifteen-year-old son, Francis II, to the throne with Mary becoming queen of France and her uncles, the Guises, placed in pole position. Superficially, this appeared to shoot Scotland to the top of the French agenda, with the prospect of increased aid for the regent and maximising the threat to England. In practice, sending help to their beleaguered sister became more difficult for the Guises because it appeared more like favouritism for one's kin than sound policy defending French interests. Absorbed by her new position, Mary, Queen of Scots did not over-exert herself to send assistance to her mother. With growing religious unrest and the problems of demobilisation and state bankruptcy, there were enough domestic troubles to distract the Guises; though unable to make it a top priority, they tried to help their sister. Faced with escalating domestic crises, Henry II's grand Franco-British strategy was no longer sustainable and, when push came to shove in 1560, Franco-Scotland would be sacrificed for the sake of France.

In the summer of 1559 following Henry's death, the Congregation received a sympathetic hearing in England, but little in the way of assistance. As in France, a new monarch occupied the throne and faced an unstable religious situation. The Congregation were fortunate in finding an ally in Cecil, Queen Elizabeth's Secretary and chief advisor. Viewing the Tudor state within the context of the British Isles, he was receptive to the idea of an Anglo-Scottish alliance. He needed to persuade his queen to intervene in Scotland on behalf of the Protestant rebels: a proposition running counter to Elizabeth's natural instincts. Using the threat that Mary, Queen of Scots posed to Elizabeth's crown, he finally convinced the English Privy Council and queen in December 1559 of the need to fight a preventive war in Scotland against the grand Franco-British strategy. An English fleet was immediately sent to blockade the Forth and stop French reinforcements from landing. In the meantime, Cecil had been free with his advice concerning the Congregation's conduct of their campaign. With one eye on his own queen's sensibilities and the other on the Congregation's limited support, he urged a switch from the Protestant rhetoric of reforming the church to a patriotic justification of resistance to French domination.

To provide an aura of legitimacy to the Congregation's rejection of the regent and all things French, the open support of the duke of Châtelherault, the 'second person of the realm', was required. In a nifty piece of cloak-and-dagger work, English agents spirited Arran, Châtelherault's eldest son and heir, from under French noses. Once back in Scotland, Arran's safety and his convinced Protestantism persuaded his father to declare for the Congregation. Given memories of their rapaciousness when previously holding power, it was a mixed blessing to have the Hamiltons so prominently on board and the Congregation had the sense not to make Châtelherault regent for a second time. As Mary of Guise frequently remarked, this was treason and her officials drew up a legal case against Châtelherault. However, she did not appreciate that, whatever the letter of the law said, in Scottish minds campaigning against a regent was not the same crime as facing the monarch on a field of battle. Successful sedition, especially during a royal minority, was politics pursued by other means and did not generate in Scotland the odium it produced elsewhere.

Playing the patriotic card allowed the Congregation to tap into Scottish unease with the Franco-British strategy. Its existence gave plausibility to their argument that, taken together, all the little signs of increased influence added up to the start of a French takeover of Scotland. When Argyll sat in council with the West Highland clan chiefs, he gave them a history lesson of how Brittany had been absorbed into the French state. He warned the same thing was happening in Scotland:

> the France ar cumin in and sutin down in this realm to occupy it
> and to put furtht the inhabitantis tharoff, and siklik to occupy all
> uther menis rowmes pece and pece, and to put avay the blude of
> the nobilite.[5]

Whether convinced by this scaremongering, prepared to follow Argyll as their lord or simply liking a good fight with someone else paying, MacDonald of Dunyvaig, MacLean of Duart and other chiefs added their clansmen to the Congregation.

For those caught in the middle, warfare was always bad news. Janet Watson, a widow, complained later she could not pay her dues because, when defending her field against soldiers stealing her corn and trampling her crop, she had been violently 'dung down' and injured badly enough to need carrying home in a blanket.[6] Turning it into elegant verse, a depressed Sir Richard Maitland wrote in his New Year poem for 1560:

> I can not sing for the vexatioun
> Of Frenchemen and the Congregatioun,
> That hes maid trowbill in this natioun,
> And moneye bair biging:
> In this New Yeir I sie bot weir,
> Na caus to sing.[7]

[5] Hamilton to Regent, 29 Sept. 1559, *Scottish Correspondence of Mary of Lorraine, 1542/3–60*, ed. A. I. Cameron (SHS, 3rd ser. 10, 1927), 427.
[6] NAS Livingstone papers RH15/12/2.
[7] *Maitland Quarto*, 15.

Admiral Winter and his English crewmen battled the sea storms to sail up to the Forth and were sighted off Fife Ness in January 1560. With French reinforcements storm-bound in their ports, this constituted the first Protestant wind, saving the British mainland for Protestantism, twenty-eight years before the Armada sailed. By halting the French advance before it reached the Congregation's eastern base at St Andrews and making French troops retreat to the safety of Leith fort, the presence of the English fleet transformed the immediate military position. For at least one Scot, receiving help at this critical juncture brought reconciliation with the old enemy. The moment he sighted the English ships, Douglas of Lochleven forgave his father's death at English hands at Pinkie.

Further English assistance was guaranteed by the Treaty of Berwick signed in February 1560 between Elizabeth and the Congregation. This remarkable document was the product of a new approach to Anglo-Scottish relations: instead of being one side of the triangular relationship with France, they were treated as part of an exclusively British strategy. In the immediate situation, additional military assistance to the Congregation arrived when an English army was met at Prestonpans with a warm welcome. Since Mary of Guise's French reinforcements were nowhere to be seen, many neutrals concluded it was time to join the Congregation and the April band agreed at Leith was packed with signatures, including the Catholic Huntly. By failing to storm the Fort at Leith, the joint Anglo-Scottish forces did not cover themselves with military glory. This proved of little consequence, because the combatants wanted to negotiate and talks began immediately following Mary of Guise's death.

As Mary of Guise lay in Edinburgh Castle dying of dropsy, Scottish magnates, including her enemies, the Congregation's leaders, came to make their personal peace. Their visits reflected the respect in which she was held, and demonstrated the Scottish elite's attitude towards limited rebellion: their quarrel was political and religious, not personal. Though the regent had steadfastly refused to surrender, she had lost the Wars of the Congregation. For the first time since the Treaty of Haddington, her countrymen had failed to send sufficient resources to save Franco-Scotland. Eighteen years of the regent's hard work in Scotland was being destroyed. However, as a mother, Mary of Guise had achieved her dynastic ambition: Mary, Queen of Scots was also queen of France, and her claims to the English throne remained intact. Once France, freed of its domestic troubles, was strong again, there would be chances to renew the auld alliance and possibly resurrect the grand Franco-British strategy.

Having already lasted for twenty years, the current situation represented a reverse in the Battle for Britain between France and England. Neither Mary of Guise nor anyone else in 1560 could be certain this was a final defeat for France.

THE PROTESTANT TRIUMPH

In July 1560 the Treaty of Edinburgh was signed by the English and French diplomatic teams, agreeing their respective troops would withdraw from Scotland. Going with barely a whimper, the Franco-British strategy was in ruins and the auld alliance was replaced by amity with England. The regency was over, ending Mary, Queen of Scots' minority in practical if not in strict constitutional terms. In the summer of 1560, Scotland faced a prolonged period of absentee monarchy while Mary carried out her prime duties as queen of France. Having been briefly distracted by events in Scotland, the rest of Europe returned to their own affairs.

The Congregation's leaders assumed the government of the country and in the name of their monarchs called a parliament. Despite having been specifically excluded by the treaty provisions, religion was on the agenda and Protestant lairds flooded into the capital to ensure there was no backsliding. Not normally counted as part of the Three Estates, the lesser nobility appealed to fifteenth-century precedent, though they cited the wrong act. Legal niceties counted for little when over a hundred lairds appeared and joined the urban Protestants among the representatives of the twenty-two burghs, all determined to make the voice of the localities heard. Protestant supporters had the victory euphoria to push through a legislative reformation, though their political vulnerability prevented them from getting too carried away. A ringing Protestant Confession of Faith was adopted, with some nobles, such as the aged Lord Lindsay, adding their personal testimony, 'I have lived many years. I am the eldest in this company of my sort. Now that it hath pleased God to let me see this day when so many nobles and others have allowed so noble a work, I will say with Simeon, "Nunc dimittis" '.[8]

The Parliamentary Acts abolishing the pope's jurisdiction and forbidding the celebration of the Mass and other Roman Catholic sacraments

---

[8] Randolph to Cecil, 17 Aug. 1560, *Calendar of State Papers relating to Scotland and Mary, Queen of Scots, 1547–1603*, ed. J. Bain et al. (13 vols, Edinburgh, 1898–1969), I, 885–6; discussed in M. H. B. Sanderson, *A kindly place: living in sixteenth-century Scotland* (East Linton, 2002), 155.

radically shifted Scotland's official doctrinal position and recognised Protestant services as the only legitimate form of worship. As an institution the Catholic church remained intact, leaving untouched the structure of the church–crown hybrid. Designed not to rock the political boat, this produced a remarkably conservative programme, avoiding matters touching property, resources and organisation. The sweeping changes proposed in the *First Book of Discipline* to use the old church's wealth to fund the establishment of the Protestant kirk were rejected by the Convention of Estates at the end of 1560. A similar conservative reticence prevented any tampering with the constitution: there was no suggestion Queen Mary might be replaced and a diplomatic silence was maintained on the precise relationship between the new Protestant government and their absent monarch. Neither a political nor a social revolution was permitted to ride into Scotland on the coat-tails of religious reformation.

The diplomatic revolution bringing alliance with England proved permanent because a temporary re-alignment was able to solidify. France was so preoccupied with domestic troubles and subsequent civil wars it was unable to recover its position as Scotland's permanent ally: a dramatic reversal for the victor of the wars for Britain during the 1540s. The old triangle of Scotland, France and England that had dominated three centuries of diplomacy within the British mainland disappeared, making Anglo-Scottish relations bilateral or the dominant strand within a different, and exclusively British, triangle comprising Scotland, Ireland and England (see Map 9.1). In their correspondence during the wars of 1559–60, the Congregation and Cecil had expressed their shared belief in a lasting Anglo-Scottish amity founded upon common geography, common religion and common interest. More ambitious hopes were behind the July 1560 agreement to pursue joint action in Ireland made between Argyll and the English queen. If successfully implemented, such co-operation would have transformed the British Isles, though neither the warmth of the amity nor the Irish adventure survived beyond the honeymoon period of 1560. For the remainder of the century, Scotland and England did manage to limp along in tandem and this lesser achievement did create an important pre-condition for James VI's accession in 1603 to the English throne.

As part of that 1560 summer of hopes, the Scots made a valiant effort to forge closer links with England in the manner they knew best: a marital alliance. Scots from across the political spectrum were willing to support the suggestion that Arran, Châtelherault's son, should marry the queen of England. The long letter sent south expounding the benefits of a unified Protestant British mainland demonstrated that Scottish self-confidence

Map 9.1 The Atlantic archipelago

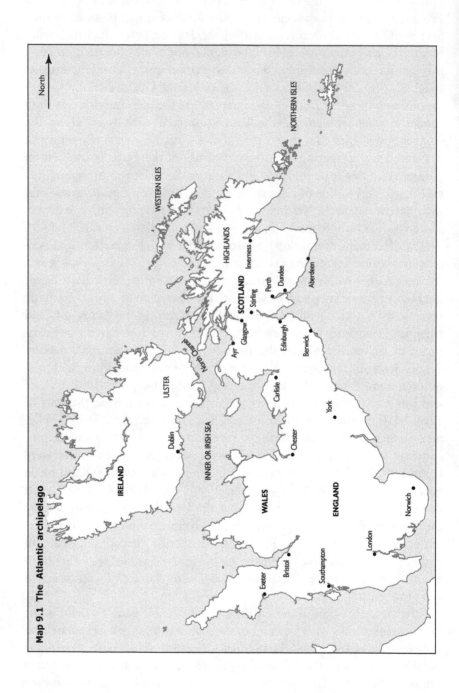

had bounced right back and exposed a high level of diplomatic naivety. Though not revealed until December, Elizabeth's instant rejection rendered the idea a non-starter. At the end of 1560 the last royal death of this two-year period changed Scotland's position once again. Having caught an ear infection which developed into a brain abscess, the young Francis II sickened and, despite devoted nursing by his wife and mother, died on 5 December 1560. Mary, devastated by the loss of her childhood companion and her beloved husband, thought little during her mourning of the political implications: as the Venetian ambassador commented, she 'has lost France and has little hope of Scotland'.[9] Her countrymen and the rest of Europe started to recalculate their options.

The years 1558–60 brought revolution to Scotland. It was radical and conservative at the same time, reflecting the two wings of support obtained by the Congregation in their struggle against the regent. One wing comprised those, in standard medieval and early modern fashion, who were prepared to support change in order that things might remain the same. Concerned the French would alter Scotland out of all recognition, they fought to keep the realm's governance in Scottish hands and along current lines, even being prepared to ally with England to achieve their goal. The other wing had their sights firmly on religious reform. In 1559, those wanting church reform had been forced to make their choice. Some, following Erasmus' footsteps forty years earlier, decided Christendom's unity was too high a price to pay for reforms and remained inside the Roman Catholic church. Most Scottish reformers joined the Protestants and opted to use force to implement their programme. As a result, the kingdom became officially Protestant and Franco-Scotland was destroyed; since neither change was reversed, Scotland was never the same again. A series of contingent events, not least the succession of royal deaths, allowed the Scottish revolution to happen and altered the face of Europe sufficiently to permit it to endure. Reflecting at the end of the decade, Douglas of Lochleven, who had fought with the Congregation and knew its weakness only too well, attributed its success to the hand of God, 'Surely it was thy wark, for it wes thy hand that wrocht the same, for we were na cumpany.'[10]

---

[9] Cited and discussed in A. Fraser, *Mary, Queen of Scots* (London, 1970 ed.), 137.
[10] Cited and discussed in Sanderson, *Kindly Place*, 171.

CHAPTER 10

Reformation by the Word (1560–88)

Having found themselves in political power in the summer of 1560, the Protestants were faced with the momentous task of establishing a new ecclesiastical institution. They were both blessed and cursed by the fact that taking over the entire existing church structure had not been an option. On the one hand, they were able to make a fresh start without the encumbrances of the medieval benefice system or the necessity of accommodating reluctant or hostile clerics; this gave the Scottish kirk a different complexion from the magisterial reformations in Europe and in England. On the other hand, they faced a severe of lack of resources, with the new kirk's funding being a constant problem well into the seventeenth century that created permanent friction with the government. The intermeshing of the pre-Reformation church into Scottish society and especially the existence of the church–crown hybrid guaranteed that major transfers of wealth from the pre-Reformation church system entailed significant political consequences. The kirk also faced a shortage of ministerial manpower, only getting close to its basic goal of a minister in every parish by the end of the century.

THE TERRITORIAL PARISH SYSTEM

The one area of the prc-Reformation church completely adopted by the Protestants was the territorial parish system including the parish church buildings. The kirk was founded on this local unit and grew out of the reformations in the localities, some of which had occurred during the Wars of the Congregation. The absorption of the parish system reflected the fundamental assumption the kirk was a national church with comprehensive coverage across the kingdom, linking to a Scottish identity in

a way developed under its predecessor: all Scots were within the jurisdiction of the Scottish kirk. The parochial focus heavily reinforced the
territorial nature of the Scottish ecclesiastical organisation tying it tightly
to geographical boundaries at local, regional and national levels. Though
using a new framework, the kirk shared with its predecessor a more
efficient and comprehensive national organisation than that available
to the Scottish crown. Once properly organised with connections
through the hierarchy of church courts from kirk session to General
Assembly, this afforded the kirk massive organisational strength which
the seventeenth-century Covenanters could adapt to govern the country.
Shifting the emphasis away from the ecclesiastical hierarchy and back to
the parish and localities fulfilled one of the ideals animating pre-
Reformation Scottish reformers. Placing the parish and the congregation
at the heart of the kirk's system reflected the 1550s Scottish pattern of
privy kirks and the continental model of urban Reformation of small city-
states, such as Geneva. Since Scotland was an extensive, rural kingdom,
this had drawbacks; placing a considerable burden upon burghs to act as
local and regional centres disseminating reformation.

The adoption of parish units was part of the conservative aspect of
religious change, bringing minimal organisational disruption at the local
level by retaining existing boundaries. In the Highlands, in particular,
some parishes covered a vast expanse of territory as much as twenty
miles across, with scattered settlements throughout, and a parish church
located anywhere within the parish bounds. Location and ease of access
became crucial issues following the changes in the pattern of worship.
Instead of being present during Mass, held in assorted locations at a
variety of days and times with specified days of obligation, parishioners
were expected to attend their parish church every Sunday at a set time,
with doors locked against latecomers. Getting the parish community
together in one place at one time caused logistical problems when the
parish was in an awkward location, as at Eilean Fhianain in Loch Sheil in
Moidart, across the water on the holy isle associated with St Finan.

In addition to their location, the architecture and interior furnishings of
parish buildings provided another set of obstacles. Having seized the buildings, sixteenth-century Protestants were not faced with a national building
programme; they chose to adapt rather than rebuild. Major alterations
were made to church interiors, with walls being whitewashed and all altars
and the rood screen removed to leave a clear space with a pulpit, joined
eventually by fixed seating or pews. In addition, the almost chaotic plethora
of religious provision found in late medieval Scotland was removed, with
an exclusive concentration upon the parish as the local unit with the parish

church as the sole location for congregational worship. Those church buildings not required for parish worship, including great cathedrals such as St Andrews, were abandoned. The availability of buildings that could be converted to alternative uses and of high-quality dressed stone was a considerable boon to sixteenth-century housing stock. Many houses in South Street in St Andrews display the building materials taken from the cathedral at the end of the road. This contraction cut away in dramatic and drastic fashion the provision from the religious orders, the chapels, the extra clergy of the chantry priests, and the religious guilds, all of which had been associated with praying for the dead, the saints and saying Masses, three of the top targets on the Protestant hit list.

KIRK DISCIPLINE

One consequence of the kirk's exclusive focus upon the parish was to increase the power of local elites, particularly through the exercise of discipline. The kirk session operated as the lynchpin of the kirk's system of discipline, although technically it was the lowest of an ascending hierarchy of new church courts. James Melville expressed the centrality of discipline, the third mark of a 'true church', for the kirk's very existence,

> that discipline was maist necessar in the Kirk, seeing without the saming, Chrysts Kingdome could nocht stand. For unless the Word and Sacaraments war kiepit in sinceritie, and rightlie usit and practesit be direction of the discipline, they wald soone be corrupted. And therefor certean it was, that without sum discipline na kirk, without trew discipline, na rightlie reformed kirk; and without the right and perfyt discipline, na right and perfyt kirk. [1]

The kirk session proved the most successful institutional innovation of the period with the greatest direct impact upon the lives of Scots for the next couple of centuries. Drawing upon traditional patterns of local governance, particularly the burgh and barony courts, it also gained strength from being part of a national system providing an appeal procedure and furnishing overall direction and cohesion. By overseeing the people within its parish bounds as part of a national system, it signalled the

---

[1] J. Melville, *The autobiography and diary of Mr James Melvill*, ed. R. Pitcairn (Wodrow Society, Edinburgh, 1842), 280.

broader movement towards a more territorial, and less jurisdictional, approach to governance. The moral regulation enforced by kirk sessions chimed with the ideals of civic and civil religion and becoming an elder merged with the classical 'republican' concepts of serving the public good. The empowerment of local elites through their membership of the session had a significant effect upon Scottish society and its politics, especially within the regions of Lowland Scotland.

From the beginning of their operation, sessions insisted individuals appear in person and not through proxy, thereby cutting professional lawyers out of the disciplinary process and making it quick and cheap by comparison with other law courts. Being based within the locality was essential to the kirk sessions' success: they were a local court meeting in the parish church and dealing primarily with congregational matters. When summoned, members of the community were usually prepared to attend as penitents or act as witnesses, especially to their neighbours' behaviour. Since the session was concerned with the reconciliation of sinners, alongside their punishment, the traditional techniques of arbitration played an important part in its functioning. It also proved an extremely effective way of marginalising those whom local society did not wish to include. During the subsequent witch craze this had serious consequences for some older women who had fallen foul of their local communities. Offering self-regulation at parish level, the session brought the advantages and disadvantages of tight local control.

The discipline exercised within the parish covered the regulation of religious practice and belief, such as running the pre-Communion examination and the enforcement of moral standards, particularly regarding sexual behaviour. The biblically-based moral code reflected values which the social elite and a sufficiently broad section of the local community found acceptable. While many Scots found it personally difficult to live up to those standards, they did want them enforced, particularly upon other people. They were willing to exert pressure upon their neighbours to safeguard communal welfare, such as the insistence an unmarried mother disclose the father's identity to make the man support the child, rather than the local community. Kirk sessions operated less of a double standard in such matters than society in general, since, whenever possible, the man was pursued for fornication as well as the pregnant woman. Without this passive consensus, the system would not have functioned nor achieved greater efficiency than contemporary secular courts. Such close supervision at local level delivered a high degree of parochial conformity and uniformity: they were the main mechanisms turning Scotland into a Protestant country.

Since the spread of Protestantism within the Highlands relied less upon the parish system than the informal structures of the households and the learned orders, kirk sessions were not well developed and key aspects of Lowland Protestant culture did not find their way into the Gaelic-speaking parts of the country. This divergence from the Lowland 'norm' of ecclesiastical structure and its attendant culture was regarded with increasing suspicion and consequently the Highlands became labelled as 'irreligious' and 'uncivilised'.

PROTESTANT CLERGY

The parish was the new focus for the Protestant clergy, especially in the Lowlands. Although the congregation was given an enhanced theoretical role in the Protestant sacraments and inclusion within the kirk courts, the removal of the vast clerical estate, and especially the sacerdotal priesthood of medieval Catholicism, did not signal a complete triumph for the laity. It was not only the exasperated monarch who thought that new presbyter might be old priest writ large. Under Protestantism, the clergy ceased to form an estate within the kingdom and developed into a tightly-organised single body with many professional characteristics, earning a salary, controlling entry through training and examination, and self-regulation through the higher church courts.

From the start the kirk set its face against the mingling of ecclesiastical and secular occupations characteristic of the pre-Reformation church that had produced the church–crown hybrid. With some difficulty it extracted ministers from a legal role and Robert Pont was the last of the old generation able to continue as a Lord of Session. The qualifications for, and job description of, a minister became precise, having the cure of souls in a particular parish with a predominant emphasis upon the task of preaching. The principle of bishops forming a separate order of clergy was rejected and in the 1570s and 1580s the argument was extended into a positive adoption of ministerial parity. Instead of moving up the clerical promotion ladder as the medieval higher clergy had done, Protestant ministers moved around parishes, thereby altering general attitudes towards geographical and social mobility. All parishes were equal, though it appeared in practice some parishes, especially in major burghs, were more equal than others. Those burghs tended to function as centripetal forces drawing ministers into a congenial 'centre' of like-minded enthusiasts, instead of their designated centrifugal role of sending clerical expertise out into the 'dark corners of the land'.

One highly visible change was the official arrival of the minister's wife and family. Despite the abuse of being clergy's whores faced by the first generation, the minister's wife developed a significant role within the local community. In the 1580s the wives of Edinburgh's banished ministers played a prominent part in protests against Arran's regime (see p. 313). In common with other emerging professional groups, ministers' families intermarried, forming clerical dynasties and forging links with legal and medical families thereby helping to increase the social diversity of the Scottish elite.

Despite endless practical problems, the parish level of the kirk presented no theoretical difficulties. The same was true of the national level of the new ecclesiastical organisation. In December 1560 there was a national gathering in Edinburgh which prosaically called itself a General Assembly. This body, composed of both ministers and laity, particularly the Protestant nobility, rapidly settled into an institutional existence, meeting twice a year and legislating for the 'universal' or national church through its Acts. Growing from the excellent communications network which had evolved during the days of the privy kirks and the Wars of the Congregation, it reflected the deep commitment to the Reformation as a national enterprise. This did not preclude an equally profound awareness of being a member of the European family of Reformed churches and an integral part of the entire Protestant movement, standing together against the Roman Catholic foe. Doctrinal solidarity was continually reinforced during the sixteenth century by personal and written communication with continental leaders such as Beza, Calvin's successor in Geneva, the French Huguenot church and the Calvinists in the Netherlands and Holy Roman Empire in addition to existing contacts with Scots abroad and English Protestants. Scottish enthusiasm for Europe continued to contain a significant religious dimension and despite its parochial organisation, there was nothing parochial about the kirk's outlook.

In organisational terms the regional level provided the kirk with endless headaches and caused most controversy. The General Assembly did not require designated resources to function, being an occasional institution like Parliament which it resembled. When called, people came to the Assembly for a week or fortnight with expenses paid at local level, if at all. Regional synods and later district presbyteries could operate on a similar basis, but there were no immediately available resources to fund a middle level of the ecclesiastical polity, previously supplied by bishops and dioceses. Discussion about a solution focused upon two needs: the regular day-to-day governance of the kirk above the parish level and the careful oversight of the clergy, one of the weaknesses of the pre-Reformation church. The initial response of the *First Book of Discipline* was the logical extension of the territorial principle, dividing the country into ten, roughly equal, regions, each to be supervised by a Superintendent. These individuals were given extensive powers and expected to 'plant kirks' and supervise the parishes in their region, with their performance subject to the General Assembly's scrutiny. The Superintendent's job description, which expected the superhuman and verged upon the impossible, indicated points of future tension. A Superintendent was required to visit his region for ten months of the year whilst maintaining constant preaching and a link with the particular congregation in the burgh in which he had his base. The association of being a minister with having a full-time preaching role and 'cure of souls' or pastoral links to a congregation sat uneasily with the demands of regional supervision, but reflected a fear the 'lordliness' of previous bishops might creep into the kirk by the back door.

Due to a lack of resources, the Superintendent system was never fully implemented and the 1560s witnessed a patchwork of provision at this middle level with functioning Superintendents in Fife and Strathearn, Argyll, Lothian and Tweeddale, Angus and the Mearns, Glasgow and the West working alongside the bishops of Orkney, Caithness and Galloway, all of whom had joined the kirk and continued to act in their dioceses, and finally with a series of ad hoc Commissioners appointed by the General Assembly to cover other parts of the kingdom. Despite the exacting demands of the General Assembly, in most instances the individuals made a good job of a difficult task.

This temporary stopgap was a mishmash of a system and prompted the search for a better and more permanent solution. An agreement, appearing to solve the resources problem by tapping into the existing dioceses, was made in 1572 at Leith. As they became vacant, Scotland's sees would be filled by Protestant ministers, exercising powers similar to the Superintendents and subject to the General Assembly. In addition, they would be expected to serve a particular parish and have a 'chapter' or ministerial advisory group to assist in the running of their diocese. The arrangement rapidly fell into disrepute because those individuals who became bishops were sucked into the existing patronage system and found themselves serving two masters – their patron, usually Regent Morton or another member of the higher nobility, and the General Assembly. Since patrons expected to receive land grants and pensions from the diocesan store, these bishops acquired the agricultural nickname of 'tulchan' bishops, referring to wrapping calfskin around straw, producing a tulchan or dummy calf, to convince the cow to continue producing milk.

One method of preventing the formation of a new version of the church–crown hybrid was to emphasise the rigid separation between the ecclesiastical and civil spheres and make oversight exclusively a matter of collective responsibility. Although rejecting a hierarchy of individuals on the episcopal model, the hierarchical principle was retained using a collective body, which had medieval precedents, in the strong conciliarist tradition and in monastic governance, especially of the Dominican chapters. It was proposed presbyteries would operate at district level, with ministers and elders gathering for regular meetings in the designated burgh or burghs. First envisaged in 1578 in the *Second Book of Discipline*, three years later a pilot scheme of thirteen 'model' presbyteries was introduced as a precursor for ambitious plans for near countrywide coverage, never fully implemented. The scheme formed a central plank of the programme identifying parity of ministers as an important goal in itself. By challenging episcopacy on theological grounds, it sought the outright rejection of bishops as an option for ecclesiastical government. Andrew Melville, the most eloquent exponent of this view, attached his championing of a presbyterian polity to a clearly formulated theory that there were two separate kingdoms: one ecclesiastical and the other civil, co-existing within the realm.

Thus the ordering of the kirk's middle level became the major battleground between the minority, and later adult, governments of James VI and a significant and very articulate section of the kirk's ministers. The debate over its polity reflected broader issues concerning the kirk's political power and its potential power within the realm, and whether that should exist independently from the crown and other reins of authority running through the kingdom. Under James IV and James V, the Stewart monarchy was accustomed to being 'imperial', without a jurisdictional rival, and those rulers had also achieved a high degree of control over the church. The Protestant kirk, with its ambivalent relationship to the crown, recast the problem, helping propel James VI and his counsellors towards an assertion of national sovereignty, including the monarch's role as the 'nursing father' of the kirk. Although the debate in the closing decades of the sixteenth century between presbyterian and episcopalian polities generated an excess of heat over light, all parties agreed it was essential to turn Scotland into a Protestant nation. Making Scots Protestant entailed a profound re-formation of their religious culture, through embedding Protestant worship and patterns of thought and, though rarely acknowledged explicitly, adapting Protestantism to fit the needs of Highland and Lowland Scots; entailing complex processes of inculturation and acculturation.

CONFORMITY TO THE 'WORD'

The Protestant goal was to bring worship and practice in conformity to the 'Word', understood both in the passive meaning of Scriptural authority and the more dynamic sense of the 'Logos' (Word) of Christ. The 'uproar for religion' in 1559–60 had brought fundamental change to the practice of worship in Scotland, often through dramatic and forceful iconoclasm. The destruction of the setting, furnishings and equipment of Catholic worship was a central element within the Protestant message, emphasising the self-consciously radical break with the past and rejection of gradual or compromise reform. Before or during such 'cleansings' items disappeared into protective custody, probably in the hope of restoration when the political situation altered. Aberdeen's burgh council ensured sacred vessels and vestments from St Machar's cathedral went for safekeeping to Huntly. However, when some women looked at a Mass vestment, as the Catholic Queen Mary did after Huntly's forfeiture, what they saw was a piece of luxurious material covered in exquisite embroidery asking to be recycled, in this case into royal bedcovers. In equivalent circumstances looking at sacred vessels, men saw precious metals waiting to be melted down to alleviate cash crises. To avoid the accusation of simply pillaging churches and emphasise the aspect of ritual cleansing, the Lords of the Congregation had ordered the burning of items, though with sturdy practicality they reminded the lairds they commissioned to save anything of future use at Dunkeld and not get carried away and smash the doors or windows that kept the cathedral watertight. Although a rood screen remained in the conservative stronghold of Aberdeen's parish church of St Nicholas until Regent Moray's visitation in 1569, the phase of destruction and removals was generally more speedily accomplished. The artistic loss was immeasurable and very little of the beauty and glory of Scottish medieval church interiors or equipment has survived, though since the Covenanters still found plenty of offensive material to keep them busy, by no means all the destruction took place in the sixteenth century.

For Protestant enthusiasts the artistic destruction had nothing to do with taste or preference; the point was to rid the kingdom of 'idolatry', the worship of anything other than God, which they identified with the use of images, association with the saints, and with the Mass. Since idolatry transgressed the Ten Commandments, the task could not be more serious or urgent. If the destruction brought the relief of cleanliness to a few, for many Scots the removal of visual images would have been shocking and disorientating: no longer able to feel their religion through their

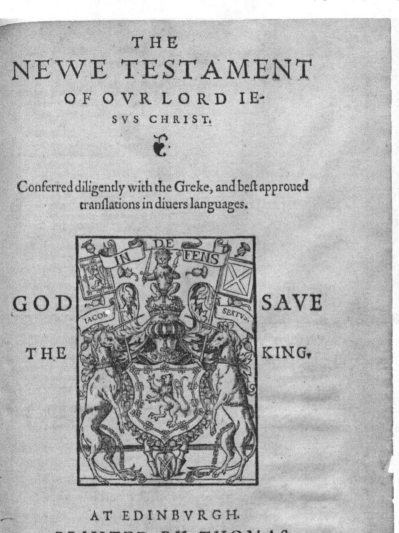

THE
NEWE TESTAMENT
OF OVR LORD IE-
SVS CHRIST.

Conferred diligently with the Greke, and beft approued
tranflations in diuers languages.

GOD ... SAVE

THE ... KING.

AT EDINBVRGH.
PRINTED BY THOMAS
BASSANDYNE.
M. D. LXXVI.

CVM PRIVILEGIO.

Figure 10.1 The title page of the New Testament printed by Thomas Bassandyne, 1576. [NLS]

Figure 10.2 The Tenor singer and the opening of Wood's Psalter, started in the 1560s. [EUL La.III.483.2]

eyes, they would have felt blind. The Protestants sought to fill the vacuum with verbal pictures and with forms of worship that involved the congregation in new ways.

Since a congregation was an essential ingredient in Protestant worship, this brought a new stress upon marshalling lay participation. Neither the preaching of the Word nor the administration of the sacraments, along with discipline the marks of a 'true church', were valid without the congregation's presence and action. Demanding attendance at Sunday worship every week altered a parishioner's religious obligation, and the intense level of enforcement, handled now by the local kirk session instead of a priest in confession or a distant church court, ushered into Scottish life a new ordering of time and space. This introduced Scots to a more rigid form of timekeeping, since it was essential to arrive before the start of the service, marked as before by the tolling of the church bell. The centrality of Sunday as the sole surviving holy day imposed a weekly rhythm superseding the more seasonal rhythms of the liturgical year. Although previous festivals, including Christmas and Easter, ceased to be officially celebrated, the practice of holding a Communion service in the spring partially mitigated the loss of Lent and Easter. The fairs and holiday atmosphere, previously integrated into the observance of a

Psalms and Protestant singing

As a consequence of the introduction of Protestantism, the singing of psalms moved from a highly elaborate clerical activity in the magnificent musical settings of great polyphonic composers to a congregational activity where the words were dominant and the main aim was universal participation. This migration proved an unmitigated disaster for 'musyck fyne', instantly destroying the market for its product and its skills and forcing the composer David Peebles reluctantly to turn his hand to writing psalm tunes. The compositions of those asked to set the metrical psalms into four parts were collected by Thomas Wood of St Andrews and written into at least two sets of illuminated manuscript Psalm part-books. Singing Peebles' four-part tune to Psalm 124, Edinburgh Protestants celebrated the return of their exiled minister in 1583 (see p. 311).

However, by simplifying the music and concentrating upon the words presented in easily memorable form, the psalms became accessible to the laity, especially the non-literate. Because it was sung, the psalter was the section of the Bible most readily memorised in full, and being permanently available in the memory, psalms were used outside formal worship, as 'battle hymns of the Lord' in confrontational and military contexts and in the less aggressive settings of prayer and comfort. Singing was also used as a memory tool for the Catechism, Lord's Prayer and Ten Commandments. The psalms and religious singing were an essential method of disseminating the new Protestant culture, because they cut across the literacy divide. They rapidly became the songs of the godly laity, building upon previous familiarity with the Psalter especially through the Books of Hours. Psalm-singing travelled from its associations with monastic daily worship through the complex musical settings of sung Masses and into the vernacular and simplified music of popular lay songs. The metrical psalms became, and remain, a marker of a distinctively Scottish Reformed identity.

saint's festival, were entirely divorced from an ecclesiastical framework. Continuing to mark out the times and seasons of the year, as in legal terms or special markets, festival days did so in a non-religious context.

In Protestant theology, the purpose of attending Sunday worship was to expose all comers to the 'Word', the chief means of grace and route to salvation, and its proclamation through Bible-reading and preaching was regarded as essential for the conversion of the nation. Although biblical

stories were familiar to Scots, for most listening to readings in the vernacular from the Scriptures was a new experience. Similarly, the heavily
expository style of preaching, beginning a sermon cycle at the start of one
of the biblical books and following it through to the end, was a change
from previous sermons heard from the friars. Religious and intellectual
excitement was generated by this new material and sermons were
expected to be at least an hour in length; not to turn the hourglass
attached to the pulpit was criticised as unacceptable brevity. In an age that
valued oratorical performances, a good sermon became an entertainment
and talking point, at least for a significant minority. As well as the clerical
desire to instruct, weekday sermons in the major burghs reflected a
demand from the 'godly' laity and popular preachers, like Robert Bruce,
gathered 'fan clubs'.

However, with an acute shortage of ministers, many parishes did not
have a weekly sermon. Where the 'reader's service' had to suffice, there
were biblical readings, prayers and psalm-singing, very reminiscent of the
practice of the privy kirks. In the Highlands an informal itinerancy developed with ministers travelling to preach across several parishes or within
their own extensive bounds. Ministers, many drawn from the Gaelic
learned orders, employed traditional open-air venues, such as the
Preacher's Rock by Loch Fyne, to deliver a Gaelic sermon embellished
with bardic language and flourishes.

Having categorically rejected the hallowed use of Latin as a language
for worship, one of the fundamental Protestant requirements was that
each part of the service should be audible and comprehensible, or at least
spoken in the language of the people. In Scotland, that raised the problem
of translation of the Bible and of the liturgical texts and the necessity of
having a native speaker preaching the sermon. The adoption of the
Geneva Bible and the *Book of Common Order* (originally entitled Form of
Prayers), both written in English initially for use in the Genevan exile
congregation, had profound effects upon the Scots language. Though an
edition of the *Book of Common Order* was produced in 1578 using Scots
orthography, it failed to become the norm because English was
sufficiently comprehensible to Scottish readers. Scots never fully established itself as a language of print and the growing divergence between
the printed and written language and its pronunciation had major ramifications for its development. Scots Gaelic faced a greater problem
though the *Book of Common Order* was translated in 1567 by John
Carswell (see the box on the first book printed in Gaelic, p. 229). Future
plans for biblical translation failed to be realised following the deaths of
Carswell and his patron, and had to wait several centuries for their final

The first book printed in Gaelic

The *Book of Common Order* was the Protestant liturgy authorised by the General Assembly in 1562 for use throughout Scotland. John Carswell, Superintendent of Argyll, probably working in the elegant and newly-built Carnasserie Castle in Argyll, produced a Gaelic version, the *Foirm na n-Urrnuidheadh* (Form of Prayers), published in Edinburgh by Robert Lekprevik in 1567, the first book ever printed in Gaelic. Though faithful to the text in best Renaissance style, Carswell's dynamic translation of the *Book of Common Order* transposed the Protestant liturgy into Gaelic culture as well as the language. He employed Classical Common Gaelic, the formal literary language of the learned orders, though in a radical break with tradition, he adapted poetical styles and conventions into his prose translation. He and his fellow Protestant ministers in Argyll coined a new Gaelic vocabulary to express Protestant worship and ministry. Illustrating his appreciation of the practical needs of Scots Gaels, Carswell included a unique poem of blessing for a ship: by then ingrained in Gaelic oral culture, the blessing was recited to Martin Martin on his travels at the end of the seventeenth century. The Superintendent had a profoundly appreciative view of the protective and supportive role of the nobility, in particular Argyll, his patron and clan chief. Carswell subtly altered the military attributes conventionally praised in Gaelic panegyric poems to present the vision of a spiritual warrior fighting for truth and ecclesiastical purity. He made an impassioned plea to the Gaelic learned orders to embrace the medium of print and translate the Bible. Gaelic Protestantism was offered as a unifying factor reinvigorating the shared culture of the Gaels of Scotland and Ireland. Carswell's translation remained an isolated achievement and the dynamism of his Protestant humanism disappeared with his death in 1572. Consequently, the Scottish *Gaidhaeltachtd* did not experience the kind of cultural and linguistic revival that followed in Wales from the 1588 biblical translation.

fulfilment. The accustomed role as cultural bridges of the Gaelic learned orders, many of whom became Protestant ministers, enabled them to make oral biblical translations and interpretations, thereby diminishing the detrimental effects of the lack of printed Scriptures. In Shetland, Norn was virtually ignored, with the Scots-speaking clergy using their language for worship and speeding its dominance as the vernacular of the Northern Isles.

The logocentricity of Sunday worship entailed a large measure of passive participation from the congregation, demanding new skills of quietly sitting and listening. The construction of permanent seating was a slow development though fixed pews gave an opportunity, as the kissing of the paxboard or previous Corpus Christ processions had done, to demonstrate the local social hierarchy. Church seating gave rise to some bitter disputes about relative rankings, with violent incidents such as chopping up a rival's pew. Craft guilds, who had previously sponsored altars and chapels within burgh churches, sat together in special lofts or pews decorated with the craft insignia, as can be seen adorning the galleries in Burntisland church.

Although processions, led by crosses and clergy in their colourful vestments, had disappeared, Protestant services retained the measured and ritualised movement through the internal space of the church. During Sunday worship the penitents in their sackcloth, who had stood at the church entrance whilst the congregation filed into the building, were processed to their places on the repentance stools situated beneath the pulpit. At the appropriate point in the service they gave their public confession of sin and asked the congregation's forgiveness, with those who had completed their penance being reconciled by exchanging a kiss of peace or handshake with the minister and elders and crossing the significant boundary to sit within the body of the congregation. With many similarities to the previous penitential practices and to reconciliation rituals ending bloodfeuds, the symbolism of this ceremony of penance had a reassuring familiarity.

From the seven pre-Reformation sacraments, the Protestants retained two, baptism and the Lord's Supper, though marriage, penance, ordination and confirmation, or their Protestant equivalents, continued to take place within the church. With its obsession about not praying for the dead, the kirk officially adopted a minimalist approach to rituals surrounding death. Though non-ecclesial, the strong religious element of a 'good death' was retained, with Protestant declarations of faith replacing extreme unction. By demand, rather than theological requirement, funeral sermons were preached and funeral processions continued, including elaborate, often heraldic, displays expressing the deceased's social position. Social pressure ensured the continuation of burial inside the church, despite General Assembly acts forbidding it. The social elite indulged in increasingly elaborate tombs, often filling the old side chapels and retaining the kindred's designated space by building a family loft above their burial aisle.

The *First Book of Discipline* insisted sacraments took place 'in the face of the congregation', and children were baptised within the church during a preaching service, thereby uniting Word and sacrament. However, strict doctrine bent to social demand with the continuation of the important social institution of gossips or godparents, transmuted into sponsors for the child. Indicating a tacit awareness of their social, in addition to their religious, significance, a light regulatory touch was usually applied to the celebrations following baptisms and marriages. Although the trappings were different, Scots enjoyed considerable continuity in the marking of their rites of passage.

The greatest care was taken in the administration of the Protestant Lord's Supper to demonstrate how and why it differed from the celebration of the Mass, stigmatised as idolatry. Drama and gesture were freely employed to complement and augment the vitally-important audible words. The deliberate use of ordinary tableware, pewter plates and cups, and sitting together on benches at wooden trestle tables erected in the middle of the building, usually the nave or lay section of the church, gave unambiguous signals of the new communal and congregational focus to the sacrament. It was reinforced by the novel lay experience of receiving the communion wine, not just the wafer. Since the bread and wine were handed from person to person around the table, like an ordinary meal, this provided a dramatic demonstration of the Protestant rejection of transubstantiation, the change through priestly consecration of the bread and wine into the physical presence of Christ's body and blood. Where previously there had been the *corpus Christi* available for adoration on the altar or in the monstrance, the lack of a specific location within the church for the presence of God required a fundamental re-ordering of the sense of, and access to, the holy.

DOCTRINAL UNIFORMITY AND IDENTITY

Though much of the novel theological meaning was expressed within worship and explained in sermons, doctrinal uniformity was too important to be left to the chance these messages had been received. In such a doctrinally-driven reformation, uniformity of belief throughout the kingdom, in addition to conformity in religious practice, was deemed essential. From 1560 adherence to the Confession of Faith had provided one test of being a Scottish Protestant, spreading from the clergy to the laity. In 1581 a specifically anti-Catholic Confession was added to the armoury. Such a stress upon credal formulae encouraged a subscription culture, further linking religious banding to the common Scottish practice of making bonds. Confessional identity and doctrinal uniformity

Catholic survival

Although illegal, Catholic belief and practice survived in post-Reformation Scotland. The Roman Catholic ecclesiastical hierarchy did not greatly aid this process, with lay leadership and initiative proving crucial in the years prior to the missions. Where there was significant local protection, as in South Uist with Clanranald or in the north-east from Huntly and the Gordons, Catholic sacraments and practice could be maintained with comparative openness. For most of Scotland, they retreated to the privacy of the home and, in a mirror image of earlier underground Protestantism, kin networks and the household provided the focus for Catholic survival. Its non-institutional nature enhanced the role of women as transmitters and upholders of the faith. The strongly committed, such as Lady Fernihurst in the Borders, turned their households into centres of religious activity, offering safe havens for priests.

Some Protestants were prepared to ignore or accommodate traditional Catholic practice. The two-sided font surviving at Inveraray, the seat of the very Protestant Argyll, was used, according to local tradition, by the local minister to offer a choice of a Catholic or a Protestant baptism to his parishioners. With the passing of the generation who had known the pre-Reformation church and the arrival of the Counter-Reformation missionaries, Scottish Roman Catholicism entered a new phase.

were expressed and tested through the ability to give correct theological answers and affirmations. Learning those answers via the catechism turned into a prerequisite for acceptance as a full member of the kirk and the catechising sessions on a Sunday acquired great importance for minister and congregation. Demonstrating a basic proficiency in the catechism replaced confirmation and developed the status of a rite of passage for the post-Reformation generations.

A national Protestant identity embraced most Scots since it was defined as much by Catholic beliefs not held as by the basic tenets of Reformed doctrine that were. The clean institutional break with the pre-Reformation church made in 1560 and the establishment of the kirk's Reformed organisation rapidly generated a sense of pride in Scottish achievement, which was particularly gratifying when compared to the lukewarm Reformation of its southern neighbour. By 1572 the General Assembly could refer to its polity as one of 'the best reformed kirks' in

Europe.[2] A dozen years later one Scot confidently declared to his English correspondent that, 'the kingdom of Satan in this country is even at an end'.[3] Thanks to the kirk's claims to be the church of, as well as in, Scotland, this melded with national pride and identity: Scots had an additional reason to hold their heads high in Europe and within the British Isles. During the second half of the sixteenth century, Scottish self-confidence discovered a high religious ranking to replace the loss of international standing following the Battle for Britain.

To Protestants, the open adoption of 'true religion' in 1560 placed the kingdom in a covenant relationship with God, making it a new Israel. As a holy people, the realm had its place in God's great providential purpose and an important role in the struggle between the forces of Christ and Antichrist. Since Antichrist was identified with the papacy and the Roman Catholic Church, this cosmic battle was being waged throughout contemporary Europe. Scots maintained a keen interest in European confessional conflicts, especially the French religious wars, in which a number of Scots fought. In 1572 the St Bartholomew's Eve massacre of Huguenots was particularly shocking because of the continuing close contacts with France and for many of the Scottish elite this was news of friends and of familiar places. Those killings confirmed previous Protestant suspicions that the Roman Catholics were conspiring to destroy them all. The sending of the Spanish Armada in 1588 redoubled this view and the narrowness of the escape heightened the sense of God's protection for his people, encapsulated by Hume's celebratory poem, 'The Triumph of the Lord, after the manner of men'. The consciousness of the cosmic war fought between good and evil encouraged a parallel focus upon the activity of the Devil in the world, linking witchcraft with diabolical machinations and helping create the pre-conditions for the witch prosecutions during the closing decades of the century and reaching a crescendo the following century. Pride in being a new Israel and the apocalyptic framing of Scotland's destiny offered a new dynamic to Scottish identity. Scots could stand united against the enemies outwith the kingdom, perceived as the international 'tyranny of the papists'.

Whilst the kirk made headway in developing a confessional identity, on a personal level Scots refused to adopt a virulent anti-Catholicism. The disruption of kin relationships though religious branding was strongly resisted, with an unwillingness to ostracise one's kindred even persisting

---

[2] Cited and discussed in J. Kirk, *Patterns of Reform* (Edinburgh, 1989), 334.
[3] Cited and discussed in M. Todd, *The Culture of Protestantism in early modern Scotland* (New Haven, CT, 2002), 405.

among the kirk's ministers. In Ayrshire, that hotbed of reform and ecclesiastical radicalism, four kinsmen held a jolly dinner party at the turn of the century; one was a Jesuit missionary in the country illegally, and the other three were prominent Presbyterian clerics from the local community. Although the presbytery issued a reprimand that was the end of the matter: contemporaries acknowledged blood kinship overrode religious division. Throughout Scottish society a tacit distinction was made between an individual's personal beliefs and a public and political religious stance. Napier of Merchiston, whose fervent Protestantism was not in doubt, differentiated between the familial relationship with a Roman Catholic father-in-law and the condemnation of his involvement in the political conspiracy of the Spanish Blanks of 1593.

PROTESTANT AFFECTIVE PIETY

Apart from the 'papists', the kirk faced other enemies within Scotland and this produced a more divisive identity, splitting the 'godly' from the 'ungodly'. Having begun in revolutionary circumstances and experienced a Catholic queen, a strand within the kirk learned to distrust royal authority and slipped easily into a stance of permanent opposition. This embattled view was engendered by ambivalence at the heart of the kirk's ecclesiology. On the one hand, the kirk proclaimed itself the national church for all Scots, working in conjunction with the civil authorities; on the other, it retained the language of the persecuted faithful minority that had sustained the privy kirks. In his sermons, writings and especially in his *History of the Reformation*, Knox perpetuated this sense of being surrounded by enemies and it rapidly struck root in the presbyterian tradition, finding voice in the accounts of James Melville and especially in David Calderwood's *History of the Kirk of Scotland* at the beginning of the seventeenth century.

Being a member of this persecuted and faithful minority was part of the identity of the 'godly', a self-selected group of religious enthusiasts. To demonstrate their conviction and commitment, they applied the yardstick of moral behaviour to distinguish themselves from their necessary 'other'; the 'ungodly'. It became a godly obsession to search for the 'good fruit' that denoted a 'good tree' and offered assurance of election to salvation. The scrutiny of each aspect of daily life and behaviour to discern its providential meaning engendered the mentality underlying the writing of personal diaries which flourished in the next century as life writings developed into an important literary genre. The attention to moral behaviour provided an acceptable entry via the back door for those 'good works' unceremoniously booted out of the front door by the Protestant insistence upon justification by faith alone.

Although the comparison would have horrified enthusiastic Protestants, many of their own devotional traits were similar to those displayed by their late medieval counterparts. The internalised life of piety, originally derived from monastic spirituality migrating into medieval lay, especially female, practice, emerged in fresh attire as the model of Protestant godliness. Intense devotion had always been a minority pastime and was a trademark of voluntary religion, the exertion of extra effort over and above a basic parochial obligation. Whereas previously regulated by a personal confessor, in Protestant guise the searching of conscience was retold to fellow spiritual enthusiasts within a household setting, a practice developed within the privy kirks. Pilgrimage, having lost its physical locations, moved exclusively into the interior world of religious metaphor and became a popular image describing the soul's progress through worldly life. The restless, introspective spirituality of these 'godly' Scots generated intense emotional responses that were freely expressed in wails and tears of sorrow and joy. For women in particular, this affective piety offered a non-institutional outlet for their religious zeal within the secure environment of the home and was the context in which Lady Culross was nurtured during the closing decades of the sixteenth century. Her religious poetry gave expression, at considerable length, to the same strain of piety noticeable among the 'godly sisters' who had formed Knox's pastoral circle both before and after 1560.

CIVIL VALUES

A different and explicitly philosophical introspection also flourished in Scotland, growing from the intense exposure to the Greek and Roman classics in humanist education. Within Scotland, the Classical Republican ideal had a less pronounced urban flavour than in mainland Europe; contemplating the consolations of philosophy in the peace of a garden or rural chateau provided a new framework for the culture of the country house that was evolving at the end of the sixteenth century. Scottish Protestant culture shared many points of contact with the civil values occupying a core strand within the refashioned mental world of the Scottish elite. The maintenance of a moral code, one aim of the kirk's disciplinary process, married with a renewed desire and drive for order within society. Kirk sessions offered an efficient mechanism to impose the social control that urban, and to a lesser extent rural, oligarchies deemed necessary. They believed discipline was not only imposed from without, but should reflect an inner control. The ideals of self-restraint and sober behaviour, though not the avoidance of alcohol, were central to the concept of the good citizen of late Renaissance Europe. Such a man, imbued with civic virtue, would be active in the political process, selflessly serving the common weal of the realm or *respublica*. As in France, civil values in Scotland were strongly linked to humanist jurisprudence and a generally *politique* position which could also emphasise a more ambivalent valuation of politics and a tendency to withdraw from the cut and thrust of court factional life. A variety of intellectual currents, some mutually antagonistic, combined to create a wide stream of late Renaissance civil values that flowed into the strong Neo-Stoical current of the seventeenth century.

CHANGING BOUNDARIES BETWEEN THE SACRED AND PROFANE

As a consequence both of the theological changes and of the loss of the complex corporate entity that had been the medieval church, the boundaries between the sacred and the profane in daily life were redrawn. The area under ecclesiastical jurisdiction contracted with the creation in 1564 of the Commissary Courts which transferred marital, testamentary and debt cases to the civil justice system. Medicine completed its migration from its monastic setting to become a craft and a separate medical profession began to crystallise. Likewise, education moved further from its ecclesiastical roots, though the kirk maintained supervision over the doctrinal views of schoolmasters and the theological training of ministers in universities. Although the kirk was very active in social welfare and provision for the poor, the overall direction of policy became a matter of parliamentary legislation and burgh initiatives. Taken as a whole, this represented a withdrawal of ecclesiastical control over substantial areas of Scottish life. It left the kirk with a tightly-defined area of interest and competence that could be more efficiently supervised than the medieval ecclesiastical sprawl.

Conceptual boundaries also shifted, especially in the consciousness and location of the sacred. Popular belief in sacred space remained remarkably resilient in the face of theological objections, with graveyards not relinquishing their status as holy ground. Despite official condemnation, Scots continued to visit holy wells and trees and use holy objects, such as the charm crystals that retained their healing powers, though in a non-ecclesial context. The penumbra of semi-magical practices tolerated by the medieval church were firmly banished to the realm of 'superstition' and magic. Supernatural beings also had a lean time, with angels managing an endangered existence and other beings assumed to be diabolically inspired. An exception was provided in the Highlands by the continued belief in the fairies, without direct censure from the resident Protestant authorities. Supernatural power remained a very present reality for Scots, with the ready acceptance of diabolical activity and the existence of witchcraft alongside the firm assumption that divine power and God's providence extended to the smallest details of daily living.

The Scottish Reformation combined the dramatic events of 1559–60 with the slow process of confessionalisation. Among the generation of mid-century Scots who had their religious world turned upside down, some would have remained indifferent, while others deplored and a third group welcomed the changes. The continued attraction of Catholic practices after they had been made illegal within the secure environment of the home indicated that many felt bereft by the loss of colours, sounds and smells of traditional worship and the reassuring liturgical meaning woven into the agricultural year. Many missed being surrounded by the intense physicality of the holy, the concrete grace delivered by the sacraments and protection from the army of saints. Others felt liberated by direct access to the biblical text and relished the freedom to pray without intermediaries, reassured that faith would bring their salvation. For them, the spiritual presence of the divine gave a deep sense of God's providential hand guiding the nation and the individual. In whichever way they reacted, Scots continued to be served by their newly-attired parish church and clergy, participating in communal rituals to mark their rites of passage and to guard and guide them through the spiritual and physical dangers they faced.

THE BATTLE FOR BRITAIN

For many European countries the middle decades of the sixteenth century brought a series of crises and turning points: Scotland was no exception. Thanks to the dynastic position of the baby Queen of Scots, her kingdom was briefly caught in the European spotlight and became the battleground between England and France for control over the British Isles, and part of the broader northern theatre of war in the long-running Habsburg–Valois struggle. The direct involvement of the big battalions on Scottish soil demonstrated that Scotland's own military machine could not cope with the latest patterns of warfare. France shouldered most of the military and financial burden on her behalf, and in so doing cushioned the realm from some of the pressures driving other European countries towards state formation. Substantial French subsidies in the 1540s and 1550s preserved the kingdom's independence, though they did little to repair the serious economic dislocation caused by the Rough Wooings. It took decades for the country to recover fully from English occupation.

The eventual ending of the Habsburg–Valois wars in 1559 led to a re-alignment of international politics along confessional lines. The following year witnessed Scotland's own diplomatic revolution, with the end of the old alliance with France and the entry into friendship with England, her old enemy. The French, who had provided the mainstay of Scottish independence against English domination for over 250 years, virtually dropped out of international affairs, becoming preoccupied for the rest of the century with their own civil and religious strife. The familiar trian-gular politics of France, England and Scotland disappeared. This was twice as surprising since the French had decisively won the battle for Britain in the late 1540s and had created a Franco-Scotland in anticipa-tion of a permanent regnal union.

The possibility of Scotland's absorption into the Valois empire was one factor in the successful rebellion of 1559–60 against the absent Mary, Queen of Scots. It brought a religious revolution, in addition to the diplo-matic one, and with it an ideological element into Scottish political life. At a stroke during the Reformation parliament, Scotland became officially Protestant, with the abolition of papal jurisdiction and the removal of its spiritual function from the Scottish church. A new Protestant kirk was put in its place that brought the emphasis back to the parish. The most dramatic, and probably the most unsettling and upset-ting, changes witnessed by most Scots during the sixteenth century occurred during the re-formation of church worship, especially the loss of the liturgical year. In its place the sermon was supposed to reign supreme, but that needed a fully-staffed and educated ministry which remained a goal rather than an achievement. A self-consciously Protestant culture slowly emerged and started to spread throughout Scotland.

The events of 1559–60 were pivotal for the British Isles because the diplomatic and religious revolutions proved permanent. The kirk's cre-ation not only ensured Scotland would over time become a Protestant nation, it helped guarantee a Protestant British mainland. Hopes that

Scottish intervention would bring the kingdom of Ireland within this Protestant fold were not realised, with long-term consequences for the religious diversity of the British Isles. The religious battle for Britain left an internal confessional boundary running through the Atlantic archipelago, with the Protestant mainland separate from a Roman Catholic Ireland. The confessional solidarity of mainland Britain against the common Roman Catholic foe was of critical importance when the Spanish Armada sailed in 1588 as part of a new Spanish-led battle for Britain. A common Anglo-Scottish Protestant culture laid the foundations for a smoother union in 1603 of the Scottish and English crowns.

There was an understandable loss of artistic momentum with the disappearance of a vibrant court during the queen's minority and the long periods of warfare. However, for many dimensions of Scottish culture, 1560 brought a disastrous downturn, with the Scottish church's removal and replacement by the kirk with its different cultural values and limited resources. Although the iconoclastic destruction of artistic objects mattered, the real hammer blow was the colossal patronage deficit. Commissions dried up overnight and, more seriously for the future, the skill base was undermined by the decline of the institutional structure of the medieval church.

In 1561 when Mary was preparing to return to her kingdom it appeared as if the diplomatic and religious revolutions of the previous two years might be reversed. Most Scots heartily welcomed an adult ruler back to the country, despite the handicap of her female gender, and with her the prospect of a return to a lively Stewart court.

PART FOUR

Re-forming the Kingdom

CHAPTER 11

'The Empire of a Woman': Mary, Queen of Scots (1561–7)

To manage the unusual situation of an adult monarch returning to rule the kingdom in person, Scots turned instinctively to the familiar precedent of the end of a royal minority. In common with other minority regimes, what had been done in the ruler's name bore little resemblance to the wishes of the reigning monarch. In 1561, this mismatch assumed the gigantic proportions of a diplomatic and religious revolution and the violent overthrow of the queen's mother and her regime: the question was how much of the 1560 settlement would survive Queen Mary's return. In addition, there was the separate problem of a female ruler. Although from 1542 Scots had been content that Mary should reign, having an adult woman rule in person, being a king as well as a queen, was a new departure. Despite Mary of Guise having gained respect for her proficiency as regent, 'the empire of a woman' was far from ideal. Many agreed with John Knox in his *First Blast of the Trumpet Against the Monstrous Regiment of Women* that it ran counter to the natural order, though very few endorsed his radical remedy of replacing every queen regnant. With their accustomed pragmatism, the Scottish political elite treated Mary as they did male rulers and judged her personality and performance.

Mary's dynastic and female duty to marry and produce an heir was plain, but she was surrounded at the French and Scottish courts by conflicting and contradictory messages concerning sexual love found in contemporary love poetry. In a man's world where women were expected to be subordinate to their husbands, being a married queen regnant placed a severe constitutional and personal strain upon the couple: even the dutiful Philip II of Spain had found it exceptionally difficult to reign in England alongside Queen Mary Tudor. Neither Darnley nor Bothwell was remotely suitable material for a royal consort. The choice of a husband was the one area in which a female ruler could not afford a mistake: Mary twice got it badly wrong and as a result lost her throne. Like her Tudor grandmother, she found it impossible to disentangle her public and private personae or her political and personal judgements and emotions. When she needed to act like a king and not a queen, she could not overcome her training and personality. Selecting her husbands from the kingdom's warring factions and from 1564 onwards repeatedly switching from one policy extreme to another generated a vicious cycle of coup d'état politics. By the final year of her personal reign the Scottish political elite faced the task of separating Mary from her second and then her third husband: desperate times produced the desperate remedies of murder and deposition.

CONSTRUCTING MARY'S GOVERNMENT

The prospect of Mary's return to rule Scotland in person concentrated minds and started the scramble to ensure royal favour. In view of the recent rebellion some, like Argyll, felt the need to make extra declarations of their loyalty and service. On more official missions, two emissaries were dispatched to persuade the Queen of Scots to adopt their policy. The first to arrive was John Leslie, the bishop of Ross, sent on behalf of those Catholic and conservative peers who had deep reservations about the pro-Protestant and pro-English stance of the Edinburgh regime. With Huntly at their head, the message was relayed that if Mary landed at Aberdeen, the north-east would rise and she could sweep south with 20,000 troops in a grand Catholic coup. She declined the invitation, listening instead to her half-brother when he arrived in April to persuade her to accept the diplomatic, political and religious status quo in Scotland. He advised she settle into her natural place at the head of the kingdom, without rocking the religious boat, and in return, she would be able to practise her own faith in private. Having taken advice in France and conducted a prolonged series of goodbyes, Mary finally sailed from her childhood home in July 1561. Arriving in the Forth in the middle of thick haar, arrangements to meet her at Leith were rushed. Some nobles had to ride in haste to the capital, with Huntly needing sixteen post horses to relay his corpulent frame south. The weather was a gift to Knox who prophesied about dark days as signs of a bad beginning with a Catholic queen and worse yet to come. He and a band of Protestant supporters got their retaliation in first by coming down to Holyroodhouse to sing psalms under Mary's windows on her first night back in Scotland. To their fury, the attempt on the first Sunday to storm Holyrood Chapel, where the queen was attending Mass, was blocked by Lord James and Argyll, as Mary's Protestant councillors proved they would uphold their side of the bargain. In response to the fracas, the August royal proclamation, calling for an end of religious strife on the basis of the present settlement, gave the queen's endorsement to the changes already made.

That note of conciliation and inclusion was also struck in the formation of the Privy Council; Huntly was confirmed as chancellor and the anti-English Bothwell included, alongside Lord James, Argyll, Arran and Maitland of Lethington, who had led the Congregation. If one element within the 1559–60 rebellion was a re-assertion of the Scottish peers' place in government, Mary was willing to reassure them by employing the Privy Council. Contemporary perceptions of gender roles and her own temperament encouraged Mary to adopt her mother's consultative rather than her father's authoritarian style. However, unlike her mother, Mary, Queen of Scots did not give the impression she was making the key political decisions independently: the guiding presences of Maitland and Moray were always by her side. With substantial power in the regions, and their Campbell and Douglas kindreds, Argyll and Morton brought aristocratic power to the controlling group.

A PROTESTANT ANGLOPHILE REGIME

Cracks in the rainbow coalition on the Privy Council appeared within months of its formation. There was existing bad blood from Bothwell's activities harassing the Congregation and this produced personal clashes with Arran and Lord James. Arran was in a fragile state after his rejection as a suitor first by Elizabeth and then by Mary. Despite a temporary reconciliation, his dispute with Bothwell continued, with street fighting between Hamiltons and Hepburns in Edinburgh, following which both principals were imprisoned. Arran's behaviour became increasingly strange and he was confined as a madman. This was an exceptionally severe blow personally to his father, Châtelherault, and to the Hamilton dynastic interest. Finding himself languishing at the political margins, the duke, conscious of his French duchy, began to consider a more pro-French stance. After escaping from Edinburgh Castle, Bothwell fled the country, thereby removing another of the personal and political rivals of the ruling clique of Argyll, Lord James and Maitland.

The Scottish queen demonstrated her favour to Lord James in the clearest terms by creating him earl of Mar, and secretly earl of Moray, as a generous wedding present. Rewarding her illegitimate half-brother

Figure 11.1 The wedding portraits of James, earl of Moray and Annas Keith by Hans Eworth, 1562. [Private collection]

with a peerage demonstrated his migration from a clerical commendator to a lay noble and gave him a secure foundation for his ambition to found a dynasty. It marked the symbolic end to the world in which James IV and James V had placed their illegitimate sons in the church. Mary regarded the bestowal of Lord James' noble title in a personal context as part of her strategy to surround herself with a Stewart family group, including her half-brothers and sisters and the family networks of her ladies, the four Maries. In the style of the courtly romances she read, she delighted in becoming involved in a love match. The courtship had been protracted, though the attractive and highly intelligent Annas Keith, eldest daughter of the Earl Marischal, the richest peer in the realm, had everything to recommend her. Lord James' new honours, his place as Mary's close adviser and his switch to a lay career covered any impediment arising from his illegitimacy or clerical status. As the splendid double wedding portrait showed, Annas' classically proportioned face with wide-set, intelligent eyes and a rosebud mouth had a more open and welcoming expression than the cold, haughty look of her husband, with his marked resemblance to James V.

The couple were married in February 1562 in St Giles' with Knox's sermon exhorting them to be moderate in all things and reminding the groom he should continue to support the kirk. This grudging tone was a consequence of the severe falling out between the two men over Mary's private Mass. Knox was equally grumpy about the subsequent party at Holyrood, as the Scottish nobility gathered for the banquets, dancings and maskings just before Lent. The occasion was also used to celebrate Anglo-Scottish amity, with Mary toasting her sister queen in a gold cup gifted to Elizabeth. With this gesture and declaration, as with many others, Mary believed she was successfully wooing her cousin.

On the diplomatic front, the queen, urged on by the Anglophiles, had been pushing for an English alliance recognising her position within the succession. An apparent unity of policy disguised different goals: the queen sought amity and alliance with England as a means to an end; her councillors regarded it as a desirable end in itself. They wanted to make the 1560 diplomatic re-alignment solid and permanent and to guarantee Scotland's safety by forging a united and Protestant British Isles. In the pursuit of her dynastic claim, Mary embarked upon a charm offensive to win the English queen and her subjects, believing if she met Elizabeth she could employ her personal charisma at the meeting arranged for York in the summer of 1562. News from France of Guise's massacre of a Protestant congregation gave the English queen the excuse for not welcoming the duke's niece on English soil. Elizabeth probably breathed a sigh of relief that she did not have to stall Mary's demands for recognition nor face a direct comparison of queens which might not flatter her. Mary felt a personal as well as a political disappointment at the postponement.

CRUSHING THE GORDONS

Finding a free summer on her hands, Mary revived plans for a progress taking her into the 'Cock o' the North's' region. On personal and policy grounds there was no love lost between Huntly and the Protestant Anglophiles. Having been a faithful attendee of the Privy Council, Huntly absented himself from the decision to meet Elizabeth and all subsequent council boards and his excuse of a sore leg was wearing thin. Mary's secret donation of the earldom of Moray to her half-brother made a showdown inevitable. Since their rise in the fifteenth century, the Gordons regarded control over Moray as an essential precondition for their westward expansion. Without control over the shire, their hold became tenuous over the lordship of Badenoch and the clans of the eastern and central Highlands with their reservoir of manpower. The province's considerable wealth was an equally important consideration and previous royal attempts to increase episcopal power or plant a

Stewart dynasty in the earldom had met fierce Gordon opposition. Mary, aware Lord James' grant would raise a storm, initially kept it secret.

The queen did not rush up to Aberdeen, travelling via Stirling, Glamis and Edzell to enjoy entertainment from the Lyons and the Lindsays to compensate for the cold and wet summer weather. As a central element of the royal progress, Mary adopted the Stewart practice of bringing justice to the regions. Top of her legal agenda was Huntly's third son, who, having wounded Ogilvy of Cardell, with whom he was at feud, had compounded his offence by escaping from prison. At the justice ayre in Aberdeen Sir John was ordered into ward and his refusal confirmed Mary's belief the Gordons were defying her authority. To impress her they had made lavish preparations at Strathbogie, including a fully-equipped chapel with the Mass vestments laid out waiting. Mary refused to visit, travelling in an extended arc around Strathbogie, staying at Balquhain, Rothiemay, the castle of Grange and Balvenie, before enjoying Elgin's hospitality. The queen stopped at Darnaway, the seat of the earldom of Moray, choosing to announce its grant to Lord James. The next day in Inverness, she was incredulous and furious when the captain did not open the castle gates, and concluded such defiance meant the Gordons were in rebellion. The surrounding localities rallied to her call and the castle was taken and its captain hanged. Back in the safety of the regional capital, the queen made her formal entry into New Aberdeen on 23 September.

For his part, Huntly seemed incapable of picking the right option and missed opportunities to cast himself on the queen's mercy. He escaped capture at Strathbogie and faced Lord James and the royal army at Corrichie, where most of his followers deserted. Huntly suffered a heart attack, probably as a result of his exertions in full armour, and died a captive on the battlefield. Sir John was executed for treason, many Gordon lairds and allies were forfeited and Strathbogie was stripped of its magnificent furnishings, though Huntly's heir and Sutherland, his cousin, were spared.

As a result of his tactical errors and deft prodding from his enemies, Huntly had drifted into rebellion. No peers supported him and most friends and allies refused to take the field against the queen. Egged on by Protestant councillors seeking Huntly's downfall, Mary's experience proved more exhilarating than fearful. Six months later during his parliamentary trial, she had to sit facing the earl's embalmed corpse propped up in its coffin, followed by the ritual of attainder when his coat of arms was ripped in pieces and struck from the Herald's register. The fears subsequently generated by Huntly's fall were more significant than its immediate consequences. Without any apparent difficulty, the crown had plucked down the north-east's leading magnate. Within the region this proved a flash in the pan and Stewart power did not spread into the political vacuum. Preferring to remain a court politician, Moray failed to establish himself properly in the region and had insufficient time, or inclination, to build a local network to challenge the Gordons. However, the ensuing bitterness between the two families underlay the destructive feud of the 1590s culminating in the murder of the 'Bonny earl o' Moray'. Unlike her father's care in dismantling the Douglas ascendancy in Angus, Mary left the infrastructure of Gordon power and three years later, when she needed it, Huntly was able to pick up the threads of his regional network.

THE GRACIOUS QUEEN

The military outcome of her northern progress did not dissuade the queen from taking to the saddle shortly afterwards to see her kingdom and by September 1563 she had covered 1,200 miles. Possessing some of her grandfather's easy manner, she could turn a visit into a special occasion as at Dripps on Lock Eck in Cowal, and such visits earned her a personal loyalty that withstood later political disasters. During her personal reign, the queen stayed with over eighty different hosts and spent the night with lairds and merchants as well as great magnates. Across the kingdom she charmed hosts such as Durie of Rossend Castle in Burntisland; Ross at Kilravock in Nairn; Kennedy of Bargany at Ardstinchar in Ayrshire and Ogilvy of Boyne at Portsoy in Banffshire.[1] Mary made an excellent job of bringing the royal presence to her subjects: this was the role for which she had been trained in France and she had the part to perfection. She was less adept at learning about the regions she visited or gauging their political temperature. On her hunting expedition to Glen Tilt in Atholl, in search of the legendary white hind, she missed the opportunity to iron out the Robertsons' grievances, or quash the beginning of the feud between the MacGregors and their neighbours that ended in the clan's proscription.

The queen sometimes identified with the locals by pretending to be one of them, though St Andrews' citizens had little difficulty guessing the identity of the six-foot-tall, redheaded 'bourgeois wife' and her troop staying in South Street. Progresses lent themselves to holiday fun,

---

[1] Names and places from E. Furgol, 'The Scottish itinerary of Mary, Queen of Scots', *PSAS*, 117 (1987), 219–31; fiche D3–6.

though neither the travelling nor the dressing up suited everyone. When the queen decreed the entire court should wear Highland dress for the Argyll progress, the English ambassador took fright at the prospect of wearing a plaid and saffron shirt and engineered a recall to England. Mary, wearing the 'Highland' dresses borrowed from Lady Dunyvaig, went to Inveraray to enjoy the hunting and complete her private mission of reconciling her half-sister, the countess of Argyll, with her estranged husband.

Mary's position as dowager queen of France made a marked difference to the Scottish crown's finances. Her jointure was worth about £30,000 (Scots) and covered her household costs without recourse to taxation. Her administration was marked by financial prudence, avoiding the pressures her mother faced when needing either to extract further funds from the Scots or from France. The absence of war or of substantial building programmes made it easier to maintain financial balance. With her dower money, Mary patronised the arts, picking up the threads from her father's court and mother's circle. To Queen Elizabeth's chagrin, Mary's musical gifts made her a better performer on the lute and virginals and with her fine voice the Scottish queen participated in ensemble singing, enjoying listening to the 'sangsteris' and to the instrumentalists playing Franco-Scottish music. As well as his lute-playing, Riccio sang bass and was merely one among many court musicians. The composers, James and his son John Lauder, played the organ and virginals and produced much of the court's consort music. The galliards and pavans served as dances as well as instrumental pieces; the art of dancing having a central role in court life. A more sedate pastime was provided by George Buchanan reading Livy to the queen and his own towering reputation as a humanist poet added cultural lustre to Mary's entourage. Such a cultivated atmosphere was precisely what Scots expected from the court of an adult monarch.

FINANCIAL CONCERNS

The long-term financial position for the crown remained bleak, with customs revenues extremely low, failing to reach half the amount collected in 1542 before the start of the wars. Although the economy had made a slow recovery in the 1550s, it was not generating continued improvement nor additional exports but still relied upon the medieval mainstays of wool and skins. With rising prices and inflationary pressure spreading from the continent, from the mid-century Scots began to experience sharply increasing costs, especially in agricultural products, which rose at more than double the general rate. This was passed on in the cost of food, with a decrease in the size of the wheatloaf purchased for 4d, dropping about a third in weight between 1550 and 1573. With an increasing population, doubling between the middle and end of the century, there were more mouths to feed, leaving the poorest and wage-earners hardest hit. In response to such pressures, the Lowland diet in particular moved from reliance upon meat to dependence upon bere barley and oats as the main staple (see the boxes on diet, p. 10 and fishing, pp. 42–3).

Mary's government looked to the traditional expedient of the church. Severing the tie with Rome in 1560 removed the necessity of persuading the pope to authorise church taxation and a royal edict was sufficient to impose a 33 per cent tax on ecclesiastical benefices. Despite Knox's grumbles about dividing the proceeds with the Devil, the new kirk received a share to pay ministerial stipends. The system of the 'thirds' was a shrewd political compromise keeping each of the parties involved, crown, kirk and benefice-holders, moderately content and avoiding institutional upheaval. By 1565 the system was running properly and producing over £32,000 a year. The regularity of the income was crucial, giving the Stewart monarchy financial continuity. The comptroller, Wishart of Pittarow, devised the scheme and ensured it worked well. A great survey noted down in the Book of Assumptions the precise details of ecclesiastical property and resources, demonstrating the complexities of the pre-Reformation benefice system. Since nearly every Scottish landowner was involved in one way or another, there was no simple and politically acceptable way of unscrambling these resources. Although admirably fit for purpose, the financial data was not exploited further by the royal administration, representing a tax path not taken: an unusual reticence for a European monarchy.

The 'assumption' of ecclesiastical benefices was more than a financial device; it was the logical extension of the existence of the church–crown hybrid in post-Reformation Scotland. As Donaldson noted, there was 'a silent revolution whereby the crown, assuming papal, and more than papal, powers, took into its own hands the disposal of ecclesiastical property'.[2] After the 1560 Act abolishing papal jurisdiction, the crown expanded into that space. The pressing need to provide remedies for day-to-day disputes surrounding benefices, previously settled in Rome, was one reason for the erection in 1564 of the commissary courts. Their other

---

[2] *Registrum Secreti Sigilli Regum Scotorum, Register of the Privy Seal of Scotland*, eds M. Livingstone et al. (8 vols, Edinburgh, 1908–82), i 1556–65, ii.

major areas of competence were debts, marital and testamentary affairs, all of which were suffering from the jurisdictional confusion following the disappearance of the courts spiritual. Based within existing dioceses, the new commissary courts largely adopted the canon law and procedure by which previous consistory courts had operated. The Edinburgh commissary which, in addition to its own regional business, oversaw the other regional courts, found itself under the eye of the Court of Session, thereby producing a national and centrally-directed legal structure. This quiet transition moved substantial sections of Scottish life and business into the non-ecclesiastical sphere and helped redraw the boundaries between sacred and secular business.

THE ENGLISH SUCCESSION AND MARY'S SECOND MARRIAGE

Mary favoured the Protestant lords who had rebelled against her mother because they offered the best opportunity of furthering her goal of being recognised as Elizabeth's heir. In the hopeful mood of 1561 negotiating an alliance, incorporating the renunciation of Mary's immediate claim to Elizabeth's throne in return for recognition of her status as heir apparent appeared straightforward. The task particularly suited Maitland of Lethington's negotiating skills, his close ties with his English counterpart, Cecil, and his own long-term strategy of amity with England, and he made a good start in his initial diplomatic missions. While the postponement of the York meeting was a setback, Elizabeth's strategy of stalling and avoiding naming a successor under any circumstances had not yet become apparent. Since the English persistently hinted that if Mary married someone Elizabeth favoured, this would resolve the matter, the association of her second marriage with the English succession became firmly fixed in Mary's mind.

As a young widow in her early twenties with a kingdom as a dowry, the Scottish queen's next marriage was the talk of the courts of Europe. Even while she was grieving for Francis II, her Guise uncles had seen it as a way of regaining their influence. Catherine de Medici firmly blocked one avenue: she would not permit Mary to marry another of her sons. The most prestigious of the European options was a match with Philip II's son, but the king of Spain remained unpersuaded of the value of securing Scotland; his own marital excursion into the British Isles had been enough. Less glamorous options, such as the Scandinavian royalty, were not seriously considered because Mary became obsessed with the idea her marriage was the key to unlock the English succession.

Elizabeth, when pressed to name a list of acceptable suitors, eventually suggested Dudley, her court favourite and reputed lover. Having ascertained this was not a joke in poor taste, the Scottish Anglophiles knew they had their work cut out to convince Mary to marry a mere knight whose father and grandfather had been executed as traitors and whose own reputation was besmirched. Only a firm promise on the succession and the English parliament's ratification would make the Scottish queen seriously consider the suit. The name that had been half expected in Scotland was Darnley, known by his English-style courtesy title instead of Master of Lennox. Through his father, he was in the Scottish line of succession and through his mother's Tudor blood, in the English succession, second only to Mary's own claim (see Table 2.1). Having been born and raised in England, Darnley had the advantage for succession purposes of being legally classed an Englishman.

Despite twenty years in exile living on his Yorkshire estates, when the opportunity of returning to Scotland arose, Lennox took it eagerly. He was treated extremely generously on his arrival in Scotland, his lands fully restored and being vindicated by parliament instead of pardoned. The main losers were the Hamiltons who were driven into such a hard bargain Châtelherault feared for his kindred. The violence of the Lennox–Hamilton feud returned to the West as the Lennox Stewarts reasserted themselves in Glasgow and upset the political stability of Renfrewshire, Lanarkshire and Dumbartonshire. Based in Edinburgh to woo the court, Lennox launched into a high-spending public relations exercise, entertaining lavishly and gathering support from those quick to latch onto his rising star. Having succeeded Atholl as leader of the Stewart group, Lennox's instant supporters' club challenged the triumvirate of Moray, Maitland and Argyll. They mistakenly assumed that, because of his English background, Lennox would support their own Anglophile policy. By rapidly adopting him as a chief adviser, the queen had gone far beyond welcoming Lennox back to the fold. The speed of the turnaround in royal favour drove the Hamiltons into the political wilderness and caused Mary's previously secure advisers to feel vulnerable.

In March 1565, negotiations over the marriage to Dudley, now earl of Leicester, foundered on the succession. When Elizabeth reiterated she would not name a successor, Mary realised Moray's and Maitland's Anglophile policy had hit the buffers. Having firmly linked the English succession and her second marriage, the queen jettisoned those advisers and turned to Lennox. Released from England to join his father, Darnley fell ill shortly after his arrival and Mary chose to nurse him back to health. The emotional bond this created reinforced her political decision to marry him. The queen's feelings, and intense pressure from the Lennox camp, made her rush into a position from which there was no retreat. Mary made the momentous decision concerning a marital alliance for herself and her kingdom at impulsive speed.

If his suit had been accompanied by Elizabeth's approval or acquiescence, combining the two strongest claims to the English throne was a sound strategy; marrying Darnley as a defiant gesture to the English queen and a blatant attempt to pressurise her was a different proposition. When James IV repudiated his English alliance, he had explicit French backing, was fully in command in his kingdom and had a carefully-prepared military and naval arsenal. Mary had none of those things, forging ahead regardless, like her grandmother. Embassies were dispatched seeking the backing of the French, the Spanish and the pope, but Mary did not wait until the arrival of the necessary papal dispensation. Her Lennox advisers did not remind her to take thought as to Darnley's exact role and status after the marriage. Under his father's coaching, Darnley behaved himself in the couple of months before Mary's decision became irrevocable, though, as soon as he knew of his success, his immature and impulsive behaviour re-surfaced. Rumours he was to be kidnapped and forcibly returned to England gave an incentive to celebrate the wedding and on 29 July in the Holyrood chapel the couple exchanged vows and Darnley placed three rings on Mary's right hand before retiring to his apartments to avoid the Roman Catholic nuptial Mass. The following day when Darnley was proclaimed king, a title normally bestowed by the Scottish parliament, there followed an awkward silence with only Lennox crying, 'God save his grace'. At his insistence, Darnley shared a dual monarchy whose official style ran, 'Henry and Marie King and Queen of Scotland'.

THE 'CHASE-ABOUT RAID'

Over the summer the king and queen of Scots acted in harmony following one objective: the defeat of the rebellion. Moray, Argyll and their supporters were handicapped by conflicting aims, based upon their twin achievements in 1560: to protect the Protestant settlement and to maintain the English alliance. Mary made substantial concessions to reassure the kirk, and Lennox and Darnley took pains to attend the Sunday service in St Giles', though Knox's barbed references to King Ahab and Queen Jezebel enraged Darnley. Trying to protect the English amity left Argyll and Moray wide open to Mary's patriotic appeal to defend Scotland against its old enemies. The promised English financial and military assistance never materialised, and the rebels would not oppose the reigning monarch on the battlefield. Dressed in a steel cap with pistols at her saddle and enjoying herself hugely, Mary personally led her troops, driving the rebels before her in the 'Chase-about Raid'. Moray and his supporters slipped into England and Argyll retreated to the Western Highlands. Mary was triumphant; she had successfully defied the English queen and quashed the rebellion.

The ease of that triumph disguised underlying problems. With the re-establishment of Lennox power far from complete, the earl made a poor military showing and his and Atholl's territories suffered badly from Argyll's raids. Mary rapidly turned to Bothwell, recalled because he was Moray's enemy, appointing him Lieutenant-General alongside Lennox, provoking a row with her husband. A more acrimonious dispute followed, when Mary made terms with Châtelherault and the Hamiltons in December 1565. Darnley became determined to break his other enemies; using the 1563 precedent for full forfeiture after the condemnation for treason. Nobody had forgotten the severity of the treatment of the Gordons, though the newly-recognised Huntly proved a loyal supporter in the Chase-about Raid.

MARY'S POLICY SWITCHES

Mary's willingness to settle with the Hamiltons suggested an inclusive policy maintaining the broad coalition achieved during her triumphant summer. A contrary signal was given in her religious policy by the dramatic swerve towards the Roman Catholics. The 'Catholic interlude' coincided with, and sought to benefit from, the efforts to bring France and Spain close enough to allow them to fight the Protestant heresy. In the minds of alarmed Protestants this became a grand Catholic conspiracy to eradicate their faith: the meeting at Bayonne between the French and Spanish rulers served to confirm their fears. The pro-Catholic steps Mary took, such as personally urging her nobility to attend the Mass, looked like the opening of a crusade to re-Catholicise Scotland. Having ridiculed Moray's and Argyll's cry of 'religion in danger' six months before, Mary's subsequent actions destroyed the trust she had built. Scottish Protestants believed their faith was under threat and the queen had duped them; they were not alone in being alarmed by these quick-fire policy reversals.

Whatever their religious beliefs, a broad section of the Scottish political community were alarmed and suspicious of the possible ramifications of Mary's dramatic re-alignment in foreign policy. Despite its strong patriotic appeal, open hostility with England, with backing from the Catholic powers of Europe, could turn into a forceful assertion of the Scottish monarchs' united claim to the English throne. When it was a more plausible goal during Mary of Guise's regency there had been scant support for the Franco-Scottish dream of Francis and Mary ruling the British mainland. There was even less enthusiasm for the imperial fantasies of Henry and Mary. The new policies and Darnley's behaviour rocked Scottish politics. The new king had inherited none of his parents' political skills: having been indulged as a child, he expected instant gratification and flew into a rage when denied. Even Lennox could no longer moderate his son's behaviour nor direct his political actions. While his heavy drinking, sexual promiscuity and petulant rudeness made him exceptionally unpleasant as a companion, his self-centredness and political ineptitude made him a disaster as Mary's consort. The queen frantically backtracked on her promise of the crown matrimonial, having realised her mistake in proclaiming her husband King Henry. The rift became glaringly public when the Privy Council ordered a new minting to replace the silver coin issued at the wedding. The 'Mary ryal' returned the queen's name to first place in the royal style and the coin's reverse showed a crowned palm tree (Mary) and tortoise (Darnley) creeping up the trunk: the unflattering depiction of his relative status exacerbated Darnley's monumental sense of grievance.

As swiftly as she had raised Lennox to favour, she dropped him, ruining the budding Stewart party. From the peerage's viewpoint, worse followed as members of Mary's household, especially Riccio, became important political advisers and the queen ignored the Privy Council, formerly a mainstay of her personal rule. However, Mary's personal position was considerably strengthened when she realised she was carrying Darnley's child. Seeing his dynastic hopes come a significant step closer, Lennox was delighted, though he could not persuade Darnley to rejoice; myopically, the king viewed the child as a threat to his own authority. In his obsessive pursuit of the crown matrimonial, he focused upon the forthcoming parliament where the complete forfeiture of the Chase-about rebels would be accomplished.

By the beginning of 1566, Mary's policy upheavals in domestic and foreign affairs, her new style of government and her husband had shattered the consensus within Scottish politics. Extreme policies provoked a correspondingly extreme response: a conspiracy to murder Mary's favourite, seize political control and stop the return of Catholicism. The brains and organisation behind the Riccio murder came from the Douglases, the countess of Lennox's kin. It was a measure of his desperation that Morton, a skilled political operator, as careful as he was ruthless, resorted to such crude methods. Darnley was persuaded his wife was having an affair with Riccio, providing a pretext to bring armed men into Holyrood and thus engineer the coup d'état. Concurrently, a grisly warning went to Roman Catholics through the murder of the Dominican, John Black, by leaders of Edinburgh's Protestants. On 9 March 1566 all initially went according to plan and the unfortunate Riccio was dragged from Mary's side and repeatedly stabbed. Fearing they might be the next victims, Huntly, Atholl and Bothwell escaped, with Bothwell climbing out of a window on a sheet. Darnley, reassuring the Edinburgh citizens, also prorogued the parliament. Having been waiting outside the burgh and on hearing the news, the Chase-about rebels rode into Edinburgh in safety. Recovering from the trauma of armed men bursting into her quiet supper, murdering her servant before her eyes and threatening her, with remarkable composure Mary talked Darnley round to her side. They escaped from Holyrood and made the five-hour ride, particularly gruelling for the pregnant queen, to the safety of Dunbar held by Bothwell. As his father immediately realised, by his volte-face, Darnley had publicly and irrevocably betrayed his Douglas kindred, who were banished in the full intensity of Mary's wrath, whilst the queen rehabilitated the returning rebels.

Mary's impulsive adopting and discarding of favourites and their policies had dramatically intensified political competition among the nobility, increasing its ruthlessness as the stakes climbed higher: to be in favour gave excessive power, to be in disgrace spelled disaster. In the aftermath of Riccio's murder, Mary's 1565 policy changes were reversed, the pro-Catholic stance was abandoned and an uneasy peace reached with England. These seismic tremors had severely shaken Scottish government and the queen's friends abroad were confused and wary, unsure whether it remained safe to support her.

THE BIRTH OF PRINCE JAMES

Almost as if the past year had not happened, Mary adopted an inclusive domestic policy for the remainder of 1566, which augured well for a gradual return to stability. The conciliar style of government returned including a broad cross-section of the peerage, after reconciliations between those previously at feud. Mary reluctantly allowed the Riccio murderers to return, though Morton had to wait until December. By far the most significant event of the year was the birth of the queen's son: by securing the Stewart succession she fulfilled her prime duty as a monarch. Being a woman her triumph was the greater, because she survived the dangerous and protracted labour to deliver a healthy child. When only five days old, her son was unwrapped for inspection by the English ambassador, so the news he was a 'goodly prince' could be broadcast round the European courts.[3] Mary's standing reached new heights in her own realm and in the English succession stakes. Edinburgh Castle's entire battery was fired in celebration and across the country the event passed into collective memory: as a child James Melville went to the 'head of the muir to sie the fyre of joy burning upon the stiple heid of Montrose'.[4] The queen started planning a baptismal celebration in the style she had known in France and her outgoings soared to £5,500 per month from July. To pay for this 'triumph', direct taxation was risked for the first time in the reign with £12,000 anticipated via a loan from Edinburgh merchants.

Stirling Castle made a magnificent setting for the tournament and fireworks display outside and the feasting inside. In December the baptism was performed according to Roman Catholic rites, with the countess of Argyll deputising for Queen Elizabeth as the baby's godmother and the French ambassador for his master as godfather. Although the Protestant nobility and English ambassador remained outside the chapel, all participated in the banquet where the pairing of Protestant and Catholic nobles to serve the ambassadors signalled the theme of internal reconciliation. Music and dancing followed with a hunt the next day, after which an Arthurian-style round table appeared on a moving stage, accompanied by nymphs and satyrs, and the obligatory laudatory verses were recited by an angel lowered from the ceiling. The party witnessed the chilly spectacle of a mock battle fought by Highlanders in their mythical role as 'wild Scots' and the firing of cannon and £190 worth of other fireworks provided a noisy and dramatic end.

[3] *Memorials of transactions in Scotland 1569–72 by Richard Bannatyne*, ed. R. Pitcairn (Bannatyne Club, 51, Edinburgh, 1836), 238.

[4] J. Melville, *The autobiography and diary of Mr James Melvill*, ed. R. Pitcairn (Wodrow Society, Edinburgh, 1842), 18.

DARNLEY'S MURDER

Prince James' father had not attended the baptism, thereby adding another count to the list of his failures to observe the basic requirements of his position. Precisely what that position was remained unresolved, since the royal couple had barely been on speaking terms after the breakdown of the fragile truce at James' birth. A loose cannon and danger to all, Darnley could neither control himself nor accept control from anyone else. Even he wondered if it might be wise to leave and wrote to his mother about a harebrained scheme to go to the Scilly Isles or Scarborough Castle.

The intractable problem of how to cope with the king made a mockery of the imperial symbolism of beneficent rule and internal harmony gloriously portrayed at Stirling. In the polished Latin verses of his 'Genethliacon', written to mark the prince's birth, Buchanan had described the virtues of a model king. His strong endorsement of the necessity of the virtues of moderation, chastity and loyalty to one's kin, attributes Darnley manifestly lacked, were both a Lennoxman advising his regional lord and a poet within the 'mirror-of-princes' tradition. There was also general criticism of the queen's imperial rhetoric, the anti-English foreign policy and rapid switches in domestic affairs.

Mary's increasingly unhappy marriage was also preoccupying the queen's chief advisers. Though muddied by subsequent controversy over what was discussed and who agreed to what, the 'Craigmillar conference' provides a fascinating insight into the process of decision-making at court. Mary was recuperating from her illness in the Edinburgh provost's residence, outside the burgh. With its guest accommodation linked by an unusually large number of interconnecting passages and stairs making it easier to slip undetected from one room to another, Craigmillar might have been designed for intrigue. One morning Maitland and Moray arrived in Argyll's chamber early enough to find him still in bed and started talking about what to do with Darnley and how to get a pardon for the Riccio murderers. They sent for Huntly and all four went to Bothwell's room and finally to see Mary. The queen was torn between wanting release from an intolerable personal situation and seeing no way to accomplish it. What she failed to do was make plain the limits of what she was prepared to tolerate.

The available options were limited by the overriding need to protect the prince's legitimacy. Since Darnley was unlikely to accept a compromise, a solution would have to be forced upon him. The exact nature of the force was probably left unexplored at this juncture but some or all of these men were later involved in specific planning at the start of 1567. Morton and the Douglases betrayed by Darnley were also part of the plot or plots that were hatched to accomplish the king's permanent removal.

On 9 February 1567, after Mary had visited the sick Darnley in his lodgings at Kirk o' Field, just outside Edinburgh's boundaries, an explosion wrecked the house. Shortly afterwards, the bodies of Darnley and a servant were found strangled or asphyxiated, half naked and without blast marks, in a neighbouring garden. The king's murder was a botched job which raised extremely difficult questions. Having become one of the most celebrated historical whodunits, the complexities of the plots and the events of Kirk o' Field have offered endless fascination, not least because the extensive cover up and subsequent accusations and counter-accusations have made it impossible to be sure exactly what happened and which people were involved.

Whatever Mary's personal knowledge or legal guilt, what really mattered for her future standing was the disastrous way she handled her husband's murder. She made a succession of catastrophic mistakes, behaving like a woman relieved of a terrible personal burden instead of a ruler conscious of her regal position. Almost inexplicably, she failed to utilise the framework offered by court protocol to recover and assess the situation. While not stricken by the personal grief experienced at the death of her first husband, she needed to go into mourning for forty days. Attending the wedding of her servant the day after the murder was extremely bad form as was her delay in putting the court into black and her visits to Seton during the next few weeks. An obvious opportunity was lost to express grief in public and impose the order of ritualised pomp through a state funeral for Darnley. He was buried in Holyrood chapel during the night with scant ceremony. Insult was compounded when Mary later gave Bothwell some of Darnley's clothes and horses. For a woman raised to appreciate the power of symbolism, pageantry or even the potency of small gestures, this was staggeringly inept. During these months, the queen seemed to forget how to reign, as well as how to rule.

News of the murder sped round the courts of Europe immediately altering Mary's standing abroad. Negotiations over the English succession were terminated and a horrified Elizabeth wrote directly to her Scottish cousin, probably the only occasion she did so without deviousness, and her message was simple: Mary had to be seen to administer justice to those responsible, whoever they were. An identical point was made by the French.

MARY'S DOWNFALL

Placards started appearing and rumours circulating within a few days of the murder that Bothwell had masterminded Darnley's death. Expecting the queen to take up his case, as would be normal, Lennox called for justice. Instead of arresting Bothwell or at the least banishing him from her presence, Mary showered him with favours. The rise of his old enemy persuaded Moray he required a continental vacation; one of his shrewdest political decisions. As in 1565 when she had rapidly switched her favour to Lennox and Darnley, Mary now bestowed her complete trust upon Bothwell. Taking their cue from the queen, the rest of the nobility acquitted Bothwell at his trial for Darnley's murder. Lennox departed for England, having been left to make his own case. Shortly afterwards, lands and offices were distributed in parliament looking suspiciously like rewards for acquiescing in the king's death. Gathering his fellow magnates in Edinburgh's Ainslie's tavern, Bothwell persuaded them to sign a bond declaring his innocence and seeking to persuade Mary to marry him. The proposal ignored his existing marriage to Jane, Huntly's sister. Bothwell secured his wife's and brother-in-law's agreement and in collusive proceedings before the Edinburgh commissary court, was granted a divorce on grounds of adultery, as well as getting an annulment in the St Andrews consistory court for lack of a dispensation which, though granted, was conveniently suppressed.

Always impatient and seeking direct action, Bothwell abducted Mary to ensure nothing would prevent his marriage to her and carried her off to Dunbar. Combining persuasion and violence, he got the queen to marry him in a Protestant ceremony on 15 May. Whatever the reasons, this decision was yet another political disaster instantly creating an opposition and within a month the two sides were facing each other on a battlefield. The political fate of the kingdom briefly narrowed down to a power struggle between rivals in East Lothian. Mary viewed Lord Seton's residence of the same name as a special place of comfort and retreat and Bothwell's territories around Crichton and Hailes made them close neighbours to Morton, one of the Confederate leaders, based at Dalkeith and Tantallon. Mary and Bothwell gathered their forces at Dunbar to return to Edinburgh in strength, but were met at Carberry, near Musselburgh, by the confederate lords who had assembled troops from across the kingdom.

At the end of a long day in the sun with the battle lines drawn up, Mary surrendered and Bothwell was allowed to escape. By a whisker, the traditional Scottish method of keeping talking, even when in armed array, prevented a battle: instead of coming to blows, the contest was decided by assessing the relative strength of each side's forces. Having proved stronger, the confederate lords rode the short distance to Edinburgh carrying in front of the queen their banner proclaiming, 'Judge and revenge my cause O Lord' (Psalm 43). On their arrival, the well-primed crowd hurled insults at Mary and instead of Holyrood Palace she was lodged in Henderson of Fordell's house. Despite assurances during the surrender negotiations, early the next morning Mary was rowed the half mile across Loch Leven to become a prisoner in its castle.

MARY'S PERSONAL REIGN

Due to her prominent dynastic position during the battle for Britain in the 1550s, Mary made the understandable mistake during her personal rule of overestimating the cards she had to play in the European diplomatic game. She was severely handicapped by France's preoccupation with internal troubles, since this removed the Scottish monarchy's natural ally. In her negotiations over the English succession, she did not realise the weaknesses, as well as the strengths, of her position and lacked the skill to play the long game, the way most dynastic prizes were won. By swallowing whole the English suggestion her second marriage was central to the succession negotiations, she further restricted the pool of suitors. The attempt to keep her options open for the English succession and the rapid oscillations in religious policy in 1565–6 eroded the trust of her Roman Catholic allies in the papacy and Spanish and French courts. Consequently, in the crisis following Darnley's murder, she found few friends abroad.

Having placed herself so completely under Bothwell's control, Mary found even fewer friends at home. Writing to the English queen about her third marriage, Mary explained she could find no other method of controlling the factions within her kingdom, saying,

> we wer destitute of ane husband, our Realme not throuchlie purgit of the factiounis and conspiraceis that of lang tyme hes continewit thairin, quhilk occuring sa frequentlie, had alreddie in a maner sa weryit and brokin ws, that be oure self we wer not abill of ony lang continewance to sustene the panis and travell in oure awin persoun, quhilkis were requisite for

repressing of the insolence and seditioun of our rebellious subjectis.[5]

An admission she was not up to the job of ruling was hardly calculated to engage Elizabeth's sympathy. Despite her special pleading, it was true Mary's task was extremely difficult. As Charles Utenhove had reminded her in a sonnet sent after his visit to Scotland, Mary was a king as well as a queen, ruling as well as reigning. With her presence, her charm and her courtly panache she made an excellent queen presiding over a cultured court. Mary performed her role with French flair, having been trained to do so in the Valois royal nursery, and she accomplished her fundamental task as a ruler by marrying and producing a legitimate male heir; unlike her English cousin's self-centred dereliction of this royal duty. Elizabeth jettisoned her role as queen in favour of being a king and her longevity mitigated the consequences. Ruling as a king required a different set of skills from being a queen, and Mary did not possess them. She had inherited little of the sense of timing her mother displayed in recognising when to withdraw gracefully or when painstakingly to construct a position of strength. Her judgement of men was as impulsive as her grandmother's, and on both occasions when she chose a husband she created insuperable problems. During the last six months of her personal reign, Mary was freed from her second and her third husband: it was a violent and messy business. By imprisoning their adult reigning queen, the confederate lords took a great risk. It was a desperate move, and seemed to prove Knox's contention that the 'empire of a woman' was indeed 'repugnant to nature' and was 'a subversion of good order, of all equitie and justice'.[6]

---

[5] Instructions to Robert Melville to deliver to Elizabeth, June 1567, R. Keith, *History of the Affairs of Church and State in Scotland, from the beginning of the Reformation to the year 1568*, eds J. P. Lawson and C. J. Lyon (3 vols, Spottiswoode Society, 1, Edinburgh, 1844–50), II, 601–6 (at 602).

[6] Knox, J., *The Works of John Knox*, ed. D. Laing (6 vols, Edinburgh, 1846–64), IV 373.

CHAPTER 12

Civil Wars (1567–73)

After the catastrophic months marking the end of Mary's personal reign, the Scottish political community was in an exceptionally fragile state. The precipitate abdication of Mary, Moray's regency and the crowning of James opened a major rift between the king's and queen's parties and Mary's escape from prison confirmed the two armed camps were prepared to fight it out. Following her defeat at Langside, the queen's disastrous flight to England devastated her party and condemned her to life in prison and death on a scaffold. It opened an already vulnerable kingdom to international exploitation, especially by the English, whose machinations helped prolong the domestic conflict. Moray's assassination brought the country to the brink of anarchy. Though Scotland's civil wars neither lasted as long nor spilt as much blood as those raging in France, they left wounds that took until the end of the century to heal. Between 1570 and 1573 the final assault upon Edinburgh Castle was the only major military confrontation, but there were endless skirmishes and some substantial local destruction. In a more intense manner than elsewhere, Edinburgh was subjected to the bitter divisions of civil war. The experience of being fought through and over indicated how far the burgh had already become the capital of Scotland and how far it still was from being the exclusive controlling centre of the kingdom. During previous minorities, having control over the monarch had proved crucial – during the civil wars James remained safe and unthreatened in Stirling and, since she was in England, Mary could not be 'rescued'. With attention moving to controlling the mechanisms of political power, the capital and the central institutions grew in importance. However, holding Edinburgh did not guarantee control over the realm and the capital was never the single decisive factor in the wars. Regional power remained of fundamental importance as was demonstrated by the Pacification of Perth that brought the wars to an end months before the fall of Edinburgh Castle.

Alongside the military activity, a major propaganda battle raged, making it far harder to end the conflict. With most of the kirk's leading preachers aligned with the king's men, that party adopted a high ideological and confessional profile. Despite labelling its opponents as backsliding, evil and in league with the Catholic powers, the split between king's and queen's men did not follow straightforward confessional lines: most Catholics fought on Mary's side, but Protestant conviction was found in good measure among both king's and queen's men. Scotland was not embroiled in a religious as well as a civil war.

Foreign intervention rather than domestic support decided the wars' outcome, with an English army preventing the military collapse of the king's party in 1570 and capturing Edinburgh Castle in 1573. The English queen sent just enough soldiers and money to aid the regents, whereas the French Queen Mother and her son, Charles IX, could not furnish adequate assistance to the queen's party. In contrast to the mid-century Battle for Britain, the Tudor state was the sole European power with a compelling interest in Scotland's fate: sharing the mainland and tied in the tangle of the English succession, it could not remain aloof. Consequently, Scotland became confined within the British context and moved into greater dependency upon its southern neighbour. In the diplomatic cosmos, Scotland was reduced to a moon circling England's sun.

MARY'S ABDICATION

The bubble of Bothwell's support was punctured at Carberry and he became a man on the run. Having found no help at Spynie Palace, he took ship for the Northern Isles hoping to use his new title of duke of Orkney. Rebuffed at Kirkwall, he sailed to Lerwick. The confederate lords only intended to give Bothwell a head start and once caught the earl would probably have died while 'resisting arrest'. Kirkcaldy of Grange tracked his man to Shetland, but was foiled by local knowledge when Bothwell's pilot sailed his ship over hidden rocks in Bressay Sound, wrecking the pursuers when they tried to follow. The fully-armoured bishop of Orkney executed an amazing leap from the ship's deck and lived to tell the tale of the Unicorn rock, named after his sunken ship. A laughing Bothwell sailed to Norway where his luck ran out; recognising him, a former lover sued for broken promise and had him arrested. Christian IV of Denmark was happy to tuck Bothwell away in comfortable confinement in case he might be of use in a future diplomatic game. Unlike most other noble exiles, there was no way back to Scotland and Bothwell drank himself to death in Dragsholm prison in 1578.

Having secured possession of the monarch's person at Carberry, the Confederate Lords faced the dilemma of what to do next. Maitland later described the situation as like leaping into the water from a burning ferry and trying not to drown. The lords' stated aim was to free Mary from Bothwell's clutches, but knowing she was carrying his child, the queen was not willing to ditch her third husband, the man she still viewed in some sense as her protector. Even if Bothwell were removed, a 'safe' marriage for a reigning queen was almost a contradiction in terms and trusting her to rule under the lords' guidance was equally problematic. Imprisoning the queen was an initial step, though it aroused unease. A nascent queen's party formed around the Hamilton interest and a week after Carberry, Argyll defected from the Confederate Lords. The situation was extremely confused; as a contemporary diarist put it, the position was as messy as a Welshman's hose.

With a directness born of desperation, the lords ceased trying to disentangle the Gordian knot and cut Mary out of the situation. In the type of radical move made by those with essentially conservative instincts, they abandoned any attempt to control how she ruled, returning to the familiar political territory of a royal minority. They decided the queen should abdicate in favour of her infant son, for whom Moray should act as regent; if he refused, a regency council of peers should act. While remaining true to the ideal of the Stewart monarchy, it started afresh by removing a female incumbent burdened by political mistakes. However, Mary's enforced abdication in 1567 was deposition by any other name and little thought had been given as to how to make this revolutionary step palatable to either a domestic or an international audience. Their radical decision sailed the king's party into uncharted waters, forcing them to adopt justifications for their action, which brought further unseen hazards. A motley group of Scottish nobles instigated a momentous constitutional revolution, in a fit of absence of mind.

The choice of Lord Lindsay confirmed this was probably an 'act-first-and-think-later' decision, since he was a 'sword and buckler' man who believed a straight fight was the best way to solve problems. The lords sent him to his brother-in-law's castle to get the queen's signature on three documents. Lodged in the claustrophobic cosiness of Lochleven's Glassin tower, weak from her recent miscarriage of twins and believing her life in danger, Mary signed on 24 July. The following day Lindsay, overriding the Clerk to the Privy Seal's protests, forced him to attach the seal to the documents. By treating the deposition as an abdication, a fig-leaf of legality covered the deed.

Douglas of Lochleven, the queen's gaoler, had deliberately absented himself from the room when Lindsay conducted his business. He then took a notarial instrument recording his ignorance of what had taken place and Mary's 'allowance' that she was not his captive and had declined his offer to convey her to Stirling for the coronation of her son. He then moved his royal charge from the modern tower, with its charming oriel window too conveniently overlooking the loch, placing her on the third floor of the more secure main tower house. Mary's detention represented the secular equivalent of confining a high-born woman in a nunnery: contained within a small noble household, it was not oppressively restrictive. The queen was able to exercise outside and take the occasional boat trip on the loch, though her favourite pastime of riding was not possible.

MORAY'S REGENCY

On 29 July in the large expanse of Stirling's Holy Rude church, a pathetic group gathered to witness the crowning of the 'cradle king', James VI. With most of the nobility absent and only five earls in attendance, it was the worst-attended coronation in Scottish history and one no foreign representative deigned to dignify. Since it was the first under a Protestant regime, there were changes to the ceremony, including a variation on the coronation oath, taken by Morton on James' behalf. By using the bishop of Orkney to anoint, and together with the superintendents of Angus and Lothian, to crown the king some vestige of sacral kingship remained. Knox preached a rousing sermon, likening the boy king to Joash, the young ruler of Israel who had led his people back to true religion. As a celebration, the coronation was a pathetic damp squib, despite the firing of the guns and the lighting of a thousand fires in Edinburgh.

The next hurdle to surmount was the regency. Moray's gamble of departing the day before Darnley's murder and travelling abroad had paid dividends, leaving him with 'clean hands'. Two other potential candidates for the regency, Châtelherault and Lennox, were in exile and neither rushed back to Scotland to contest the issue. In August Moray, having returned from his 'holiday', went to his mother's house in Lochleven to visit his half-sister. After a lengthy harangue concerning her failings followed by gentler persuasion, Mary agreed he must take the regency. Being neither the closest male relative to the young king nor the automatic choice, Moray clung to the polite fiction that the queen accepted his regency. His speedy assumption of the title indicated he was unwilling to negotiate and wanted full political authority for himself. His illegitimate birth and former clerical status had been major stumbling blocks and with his undoubted political ambition he probably considered the possibility of 'king hereafter'; in the meantime the regency offered the next best thing.

By the autumn of 1567, Moray had achieved a grudging acquiescence of his rule. He had both royal personages under his control, with Mary in safe custody at Lochleven and James being raised within Mar's household in Stirling Castle. It was a time for his opponents to wait and see. The regent had the support of Morton and his Douglas affinity and the kirk. Past feuds brought opposition from the Gordons and the Hamiltons and, while they were anti-Marian, the Lennox Stewarts were not natural allies. Both Châtelherault and Lennox remained in exile and Huntly stayed in the north-east. Further narrowing his support base, Moray's assumption of the regency and unbending stance concerning Argyll's divorce created a breach with his former friends and staunch allies, the Campbells. Internationally, the new regime was in an even weaker position, with England, its natural ally, hamstrung by Elizabeth's horror at the deposition of a fellow queen. Although shocked by Mary's behaviour over the preceding months, the rest of Europe was even less sympathetic towards Moray. Nevertheless, the regent consolidated his position and was strong enough to call a parliament in December 1567. He repaid the kirk for its support by re-enacting the 1560 Acts of the Reformation Parliament, rescuing that legislation from the legal limbo of never having been ratified by Mary. An attempt was made to come to grips with the kirk's other problems, notably financial ones.

Although the decision to force Mary's deposition was made on the hoof, arguments to justify such drastic action against the ruler had been circulating even before the deed was done. Accusations that the queen was involved in Darnley's murder and was an adulteress with Bothwell had been fuelled by Lennox supporters who ensured placards appeared on Edinburgh streets, such as the one depicting the mermaid (the symbol of a whore) and the hare (Bothwell's badge). Craig and Knox, the capital's preachers, were ready to sanction the removal of a ruler who had committed capital crimes and they assembled a range of precedents from Scottish history in addition to their central biblical arguments. The most sophisticated and intellectually-satisfying justification was written by Buchanan and many of his ideas were found in simplified form in the broadsides produced by the king's party.

The right of resistance

Immediately following Mary's deposition, Buchanan wrote his treatise *De iure regni apud Scotos Dialogus* though it was not published until 1579. In a lucid, humanist dialogue written in Latin and so reaching an international audience, he set out an unambiguous right of resistance to a ruling monarch drawing upon Greek and Roman authors to produce an argument based upon classical republican values. Noticeable by its absence was the use of the Bible as the overriding authority and neither the tone nor the argument was explicitly Protestant. In Buchanan's *History* (1582) he narrated the story of the Scottish kings where deposition of unsatisfactory rulers formed part of Scotland's ancient constitution. Buchanan offered the most radical exposition of a thread present within Scottish political thought from the fifteenth century assuming the centrality of the common weal and the need to set its welfare above that of individual kings. The moralising mirror-of-princes tradition exemplified by Ireland's tract of 1488, or the more direct explanation offered for resistance to James III by Livingstone, expressed the belief of the political nation that the mutual obligations between king and common weal might lead to forms of direct action. Mair's writings in the first decades of the sixteenth century discussed political authority in general, drawing upon concillarist theories. Into the mix of ideas came the humanist return to the wisdom of classical authors and Greek and Roman history. The Protestant rebellion of 1559–60 was justified by a mixture of arguments, calling for resistance to foreign tyranny and the removal of idolatry, whilst being careful not to espouse a revolutionary ideology. The presence of support for a right to resistance to the monarch surfaced explicitly in the debate in the General Assembly in 1564 between Maitland, Knox and Craig and in the repartee between Knox and the queen. Although in 1488, 1559–60 and 1567 there was resistance and revolution against Scottish regimes and radical ideas were important, there were equally strong arguments stressing obedience to the monarch. It was this strand James VI later elaborated in his own political thought which totally rejected that of his tutor, Buchanan.

Although most magnates proved willing to serve on the Privy Council, the fragility of Moray's support was revealed when Mary made her escape from prison on 2 May 1568. With about six thousand men rallying to her cause in the eleven days following her escape, fighting a battle appeared a reasonable risk. Outmanoeuvred by Kirkcaldy of Grange's military acumen, the battle of Langside, just outside Glasgow, was a crushing defeat for the queen's forces. It did not spell disaster for her party, which needed to withdraw to a safe retreat and raise further forces. However, Mary went into a panic-stricken flight, fearful she would be locked up again or, like James III, 'happen' to be slain, and she rode sixty miles non-stop into the south-west. Mary made the most damaging decision of her life when she crossed the Solway to seek the help of Queen Elizabeth to regain her throne. By removing the incalculable asset of her person from Scotland, Mary crippled her supporters: they could not restore an absent queen. Having thought solely about escape and nothing about her chosen refuge, Mary did not consider the implications of her arrival on English soil. For the following nineteen years she was to have a profoundly disruptive effect upon English domestic politics and her presence also created an international problem. Within the British mainland, the balance of power was shifted even further in England's favour, handing Queen Elizabeth the perfect excuse to interfere directly in Scottish affairs.

Having Mary outside the country was a mixed blessing for Regent Moray, since he could not be sure how Elizabeth would deal with her uninvited guest. The solution devised by Cecil involved a quasi-judicial commission to investigate the king's party's charges against Mary. It rested upon the exercise of England's imperial rights over the whole British mainland and neatly placed Moray in the role of supplicant and prosecutor, while Mary found she needed to defend herself. Using the notorious 'Casket Letters', the king's party sought to implicate Mary in Darnley's murder and show she had had an adulterous affair with Bothwell. The 'first trial' provided an ingenious course for the English government out of the Scylla and Charybdis of holding Mary captive. Having gone through long sessions in York and Westminster, the commission's inconclusive ending, the equivalent of a 'not proven' verdict, suited England well enough.

THE ASSASSINATION OF REGENT MORAY

Following the end of the trial in December 1568, Moray returned to Scotland with £5,000 and a form of recognition. His dependence upon English support opened the regent to the charge of being a quisling unpatriotically abandoning Scottish interests and pandering to the old enemy. Moray brought into Scotland the war of words started in front of the English commission. The ensuing pamphlet battles were the first major Scottish propaganda war aimed at swaying a wide spectrum of the political nation. With neither side capable of military victory, persuading influential Scots and making appeals to the literate and semi-literate reader and listener through ballads, poetry, tracts and proclamations gained a new significance. Despite mounting a show of strength in Aberdeen, in an attempt to bring Huntly and the north-east into line, during 1569 the regent's regime appeared increasingly shaky. Moray's talent for alienating former allies showed itself in his dealings with Maitland. Although he had played an important part in Mary's deposition, establishing Moray's regency and acting for the king's party at the first trial, the regent harboured suspicions about his loyalty. While in England, Maitland supported the project to marry Mary to the duke of Norfolk, which would have achieved his grand strategy of her restitution alongside a form of union between the two realms.

On Christmas Eve, Moray's unpopularity increased when he arrested the earl of Northumberland, one of the English northern earls who had slipped into exile after their rising had failed. Moray's action violated the long-standing acceptance by both realms of political asylum for fugitives and was portrayed as a sign of being an English lapdog. The regent was in an extremely weak position, needing much stronger financial and diplomatic backing from his English allies to prevent the haemorrhaging of domestic support. Ignoring warnings he was in danger, Moray rode through Linlithgow directly under the window of Archbishop Hamilton's house from which Hamilton of Bothwellhaugh shot him, achieving the first political assassination in Scotland using a firearm. For the king's party the murder was a political disaster that almost sunk their cause. Personal tragedy for the regent's pregnant widow was compounded by Mary, Queen of Scots' crowing letter of condolence and having to fend off creditors. Margaret Erskine neither forgave nor forgot her son's murder, ensuring her other sons, the Douglases of Lochleven, entered a bloodfeud with the Hamiltons.

Moray's death turned him into a martyr and Knox moved the congregation of 3,000 to tears with his funeral sermon on the text 'Blessed are those that die in the Lord'. In other eulogies, comparisons with Old Testament and classical worthies such as Abraham, Solomon, Samson, Jethro, Daniel and Scipio came easily to describe this stern man whose Protestant commitment and exemplary lifestyle had been obvious to all. The regent's dignified marble tomb in St Giles' suited the restraint characteristic of a classical republican hero and tributes to his service to his *patria* poured into Scotland. For the Scottish nation, the dead regent was a far more acceptable victim than Darnley, and the two murders were conflated over the next twenty years within a vengeance theme whose main target was the Hamiltons. His death left permanently unanswered the question of whether Moray would have turned into a 'wicked uncle', by seeking to become a different King James, or been content to remain the Good Regent.

THE YEAR 1570: ANNUS HORRIBILIS

Following Moray's assassination, Scottish politics imploded, with 1570 witnessing a bewildering series of fights and talks as groups pursued their feuds and tried to make alliances. With political life slipping into chaos the conflict generated a new level of bitterness as the emphasis switched from gaining power to hurting one's enemy. The general level of jumpiness was demonstrated by large armed retinues accompanying each lord on every journey, with some sleeping in their armour, which did nothing to sweeten the atmosphere of the negotiations.

With even Regent Moray's tenuous hold over the regions gone, there was a breakdown of national governance. When the burgh and cathedral of Dornoch was burned by the Sinclairs and their allies the Mackays, as part of their feud with the Gordons of Sutherland, it occasioned no action and virtually no comment in the south. In national politics the Sinclairs and Gordons supported the queen's men, but events in Sutherland were following their own regional pattern. Being also out of sight and out of mind, the feuding in Perthshire met the same reaction as that in Sutherland. The violence between Clan Gregor and the Campbells of Glenorchy was exacerbated by the judicial execution of the MacGregor chief. His distraught wife, herself a Campbell, cursed her kin in a Gaelic lament and lullaby, a poetic masterpiece of emotional force and literary skill. With no central oversight, noble violence went unchecked, as had happened during James V's minority. Those with overwhelming regional power, such as Cassillis, 'king of Carrick', used torture to obtain lands with his literal 'roasting' of the abbot of Crossraguel.

After the loss of Moray those left supporting the young James, a dwindling band leaking numbers through 1570, faced the tricky dilemmas of how to appoint a new regent and who should have the job. Mary had at least formally accepted Moray's regency, but there was no machinery for the election of a successor. The king's party needed to maintain English support and looked to the bi-national status of Lennox, the young king's grandfather, to secure it. In May 1570, after one of Elizabeth's characteristic procrastinations, Lennox returned to Scotland accompanied by 1,000 English troops. The king's party regarded the earl's implacable opposition to Mary and the Hamiltons as excellent credentials and a way to block Elizabeth's search for a compromise, without sacrificing her help. Distancing himself from his wife's Roman Catholicism, Lennox accepted the strong Protestant flavour of the king's party without demur and took the oath as regent that included defending the kirk. The leading ministers kept silent about the depth or otherwise of the new Regent's religious commitment. An unexpected hazard remained: most of Lennox's previous Scottish network had run through Roman Catholic lines of communication and he was embarrassed to discover his servant had been informing the Marians of his plans.

Hitting the Hamiltons, everyone's favourite enemy, was a policy on which the king's supporters could unite. The little-loved kindred were an easy target, especially since they had indulged in a wild party to celebrate Moray's assassination. With the duke sitting quietly in prison in Edinburgh Castle, the Hamiltons were led by his brother, the archbishop of St Andrews, and surviving sons Lords Claud and John, fighting for their place in the Scottish succession (see Table 2.1) and their regional powerbase. During the summer of 1570, the military campaign spearheaded by English troops and artillery concentrated upon the west, re-asserting Lennox Stewart dominance in Glasgow and along the Clyde. Targeting the Hamiltons ensured that the Douglas affinity, led by Morton and including Ruthven and Murray of Tullibardine, could join wholeheartedly in Lennox's campaign. The divisive question of vengeance for Darnley's death receded quietly into the background. Clydesdale was ravaged and Hamilton residences were taken, with one friend lamenting how the fine gallery at Cadzow (Hamilton) where he had used to walk had been completely destroyed in the fire, as had the nearby burgh. Having got their enemies on the run, the English soldiers were frustrated when their queen pulled them up short, refusing to let them finish the job. In the long run English intervention proved a decisive turning point in the wars by preventing the king's party from disintegrating.

Sussex, in overall command, received orders to seek a ceasefire and open negotiations for the carefully-restricted return of Mary to Scotland. Conflicting messages and policies added to the confusion and suspicion, with king's and queen's parties accusing each other of breaching the ceasefire. In military terms, the English troops and the ceasefire prevented the queen's party from defeating their rivals. Lennox was eager, as he phrased it, to pull the feathers from the wings of the other party, and spread his ruthless dealings to other queen's men. In a notorious case in August 1570 he gave no quarter after surrender, summarily executing a company of Huntly's troops who had fortified themselves in Brechin's steeple. Such harsh tactics did little to bring to Lennox's allegiance the growing number of war-weary Scots nobles and by the summer of 1570 a *politique* party who sought peace in their own regions was casting around for leadership.

All the negotiations were routed through the English government which produced assorted schemes to restore Mary to a limited position in Scotland or joint rule with her son. Lennox was adamant against compromise and most of the king's party were profoundly wary of allowing the queen they had deposed and whose character they had destroyed to regain any authority over them. Relying upon Maitland's diplomatic skills, the queen's party thought they could achieve a deal. The harsh truth for all Scots was that the key decisions were made in England and calculated in relation to the English succession crisis, not the Scottish situation. Two external events effectively ended any chance of compromise over Mary: the papal bull excommunicating Elizabeth in 1570 and the Ridolphi plot to put Mary on the English throne in September 1571. Though Cecil used these events to convince Elizabeth to discontinue her half-hearted and extremely limited support of Mary, they both wanted to maintain maximum leverage in Scotland with minimum cost and so procrastination and obfuscation continued.

AN ALTERNATIVE GOVERNMENT IN THE REGIONS

At the start of 1570, Mary had issued new commissions of lieutenancy to Huntly and Argyll and in the power vacuum following Moray's assassination, this gave authority to the string of proclamations they issued on the queen's behalf. In the north and north-east Huntly set up an alternative system to administer justice, using a royal signet to issue documents in the queen's name. Both Huntly and Argyll consulted with their separate councils, comprising the regional nobility, and Argyll continued to employ his office of Justice-General to authorise holding courts in areas under their control. The minting of coins in Edinburgh Castle and the holding of parliaments with the official regalia were additional indications the queen's men were conducting themselves as a legitimate government, though they never established a semi-independent state as the Huguenots did in south-western France. Since the queen's men did not possess a resident monarch nor control the capital until 1571, they failed to attract the administrators and lawyers to their cause. By the skin of their teeth, the king's men held on to sufficient of the administrative and patronage systems to sustain their regime.

The holding of six rival parliaments demonstrated the unresolved power struggle. Whereas in the previous century parliament had offered an arena away from the battlefield where major issues could be addressed or a dominant group could impose itself, the civil war parliaments settled little: instead they degenerated into a battle of forfeits. A question hung over the legality of every assembly, especially in May 1571 when the king's party's parliament in the Canongate required replicas of the Honours of Scotland because the originals were in use by the Marian parliament being held in Edinburgh's Tolbooth. To the amusement of onlookers, the king's men faced the indignity of ducking to avoid the cannon fire from the castle, earning themselves the sobriquet of the 'creeping parliament'. Although only managing a ten-minute session, there was time to forfeit the Maitlands. The king's men's next parliament, held more conveniently in Stirling, targeted the peers, becoming known as the Black parliament among the queen's men. To improve the aura of legitimacy, the young king was dressed in his royal robes to attend the session. As a contemporary painting showed, James was a serious enough child to play his ceremonial role, and had recited a polished little speech to the Estates, though he would have preferred hunting with the sparrow hawk he proudly held in his portrait. Bored by the proceedings, James spotted light coming through the roof and, with more accuracy than he realised, announced in the penetrating voice four-year-olds use, 'Thair is ane hole in this parliament'.[1]

THE FALL OF DUMBARTON CASTLE

The three royal castles on the rock in Scotland – Stirling, Edinburgh and Dumbarton – illustrated the division of forces and advantage between the two parties during the civil wars. Stirling was held throughout for the king's party by Mar, the Keeper, supplying the protected environment for the young James VI. Edinburgh, held by Kirkcaldy of Grange, was a law unto itself until its captain eventually declared for the queen and held it to the bitter end. Dumbarton provided an important base for French supplies to reach the queen's party and, as Fleming boasted, it gave him the fetters of the kingdom in his hand. Dumbarton's domination of the Clyde and the Lennox area was particularly galling for the regent who made its capture a high priority.

---

[1] *Memorials of transactions in Scotland 1569-72 by Richard Bannatyne*, ed. R. Pitcairn (Bannatyne Club, 51, Edinburgh, 1836), 185.

Its location meant storming and artillery bombardment were virtually impossible and a protracted siege impractical. In a daring feat Crawfurd of Jordanhill and a hundred men climbed the cliff in the dark and took the castle and Archbishop Hamilton prisoner. A delighted regent arrived the next day to sup triumphantly in the castle in which he had been born and magnanimously returned to Lady Fleming her clothes, silver plate and some of her husband's confiscated lands. There was never going to be mercy for the archbishop who was rushed to Stirling and tried for the murders of Darnley and Moray. Fearing English pressure to spare him, three days after his capture the archbishop was hanged as the bell struck 6 p.m. at the Stirling Mercat Cross gallows. The bitterness of his enemies was expressed in a Latin verse affixed to the gallows, 'Forever flourish, happy tree, and always bear lush foliage, that you may again produce such fruit for us'. A reply, in less proficient Latin, appeared the following day nailed to the church door.[2]

The cult of bloodfeud and personal vengeance was not confined to one side in the increasingly bitter struggle between the factions. The long-established feud between the Gordons and Forbes for control over Banffshire, Buchan and Aberdeenshire aligned the two families on opposite sides. The attempt in the autumn of 1571 by Forbes, as the king's lieutenant, to mobilise sufficient troops to challenge Gordon control, provoked a series of devastating attacks from Gordon of Auchindoun, most infamously on the towerhouse of Forbes of Towie at Corgarff, guarding the Cairngorm pass at the Lecht. Towie's wife locked the gates and shot at the Gordon troops who in retaliation burned the castle with its twenty-four inhabitants including the lady and her children inside. Such a massacre of the innocents was probably one source for the ballad Edom o'Gordon and had Bannatyne reaching for the biblical comparison, commenting Adam Gordon, 'plays King Herod in the north'.[3] Securing upper Strathdon and the strategic passes across the Grampians to Atholl, whose earl was a supporter of the queen, was important to the war effort. Nevertheless, such wanton violence left a sufficiently bitter local legacy for Adam Gordon to depart for France at the close of the wars.

In August 1571 Lennox met his own death during a skirmish in Stirling. In an ambitious raid to rival the taking of Dumbarton, the queen's men almost succeeded in capturing the king's men sleeping in

[2] D. Calderwood, *The History of the Kirk of Scotland*, ed. T. Thomson (8 vols, Wodrow Society, Edinburgh, 1842–9), III, 59; *Abbey of Paisley*, ed. J. C. Lees (Paisley, 1878), 204.
[3] *Memorials of transactions in Scotland 1569–72 by Richard Bannatyne*, ed. R. Pitcairn (Bannatyne Club, 51, Edinburgh, 1836), 187.

their town lodgings having assembled for parliament. By using the back way from the castle to his urban palace, 'Mar's Wark', the earl gained enough time for reinforcements to sally out from the castle and foil the raid. Shot before he was rescued, the regent made a fine dying speech commending his grandson the king to his party's care. In a considerable flap, the following day the shaken king's men elected Mar as the next regent. The replacement of the abrasive Lennox by the peace-loving Mar removed some of the acrimony of the conflict in the regions, but the bitter struggle over Edinburgh had already begun.

THE BATTLE FOR EDINBURGH

The two sides engaged in a serious struggle to control the capital city in 1571–2. A long as the castle was held for the king, the queen's men could not hold the burgh. News of Dumbarton's fall and Maitland's influence persuaded Kirkcaldy, its captain, unequivocally to declare for the queen's party and in April 1571 Hamilton troops arrived in Edinburgh. Since they had been the object of Knox's condemnations, his friends convinced the preacher to leave for St Andrews. Though the provost was taken prisoner and his wife killed in the scuffle, the rest of the burgh was left to get on with its business. That was not what the king's party wanted. They imposed a blockade and unsuccessfully besieged the burgh. From Dalkeith Castle, Morton took the leading role in the battle for Edinburgh, sometimes called the 'Douglas wars'. The Edinburgh burgesses were split down the middle, with half abandoning the burgh, settling in Leith and operating a rival council and kirk session. They formed the 'Edinburgh band' of militia led by Fullerton, a Protestant radical. During the exceptionally cold winter of 1571–2 some exiles' houses were torn down for fuel by the queen's party's 'Captain of the Chimneys'. The constant raiding and skirmishing produced a cycle of reprisal and counter-reprisal; however, trade did not stop and it remained possible to move between the two burghs. The tactics of attrition brought dislocation and hardship for Edinburgh with the food blockade and destruction of the mills increasing the price of commodities: ale doubled in cost and the price of wheat rose fivefold.

The capital was also the setting for a battle of the broadsheets, with the king's party dwelling upon the sufferings of Edinburgh's population at the hands of the Castilians. Though written by the educated, these broadsheet poems often purported to come from ordinary citizens in a 'Jack the Commonweal' genre. The use of reporting techniques with specific names and stories, such as the shooting of James Dalzell's wife

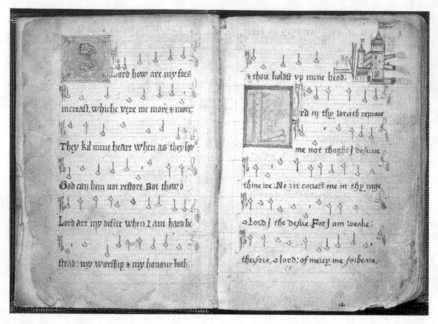

Figure 12.1 Drawing of cannons firing in the Bass Part Book of Wood's Psalter, started in the 1560s. [EUL La.III.483.3]

from Dean village, gave immediacy to the polemic. The female voice was chosen to express grievances, with Lady Scotland and the 'twa wyfeis' making their appearance and 'Maddie of the kail mercat' taking on a life of her own. This fictional wifey was a stock character relaying market gossip and Edinburgh events, whom Sempill employed in his vitriolic attacks upon 'the lords of the meal market', so called because the queen's party met in Maitland's town house in Edinburgh's market. Maddie lambasted those lords in her 'Lamentatioun' and her 'Proclamation' and she had walk-on parts in other pamphlets. The lively internal rhyming of her 'Proclamation', much more in character than the Lamentation's 'lofty' verse, lent itself to oral circulation either said or sung. With her frequent Old Testament allusions, Maddie appealed to Edinburgh's 'godly', who were vehement supporters of the king's cause. Reared on the Wedderburn ballads and singing psalms as battle hymns of the Lord, verse and song became the vehicle for their 'holy hatred' against their enemies. Psalm 43 in particular became a leitmotiv for the king's party, being sung, written and portrayed on banners. By adapting existing cultural forms and injecting them with a distinctly Protestant flavour, this helped establish a Protestant consciousness.

Maitland faced a propaganda barrage because he kept the queen's party moving, the axle driving the wheels, as opponents described him. The intensity of the attack was a tribute to his immense influence and ability to manage at least three tasks at once, satirised as being able to whistle and cluck like a hen while his mouth was full of meal. He was portrayed as switching allegiances as a chameleon changes colour, and being the schoolmaster who taught Michael Wylie's (the satirical version of Machiavelli's name) political principles to the 'glaikit' lords supporting Mary. 'Mitchell Wylie's sore feet' were also lampooned, for his infirmity brought the queen's men to his room or his bedside. Maitland was suffering from a debilitating sickness and increasing paralysis, though his brain remained as lively as ever. He had to be carried on a litter and in 1571 held discussions with Edinburgh's ministers whilst confined to a chair with a lapdog on his knee.

Following a truce in the summer of 1572, the Edinburgh exiles marched back into the burgh led by Brand, minister of Canongate, in his preaching gown with a Bible tucked beneath his oxter, and his clerical colleague, Durie, wearing armour, carrying a musket on his shoulder and two pistols in his belt. Prepared for peace or war, the exiles came determined to exert military, political and ecclesiastical pressure upon those who had remained within Edinburgh or co-operated with the Castilians. During the next year the burgh's kirk session enforced penitential submissions upon those on the losing side, leaving deep rifts within the urban elite. The civil wars had an even greater effect upon the city's poor who had to rebuild their homes and livelihoods and continue to pay high food prices. As a consequence the gap between the haves and the have-nots dramatically increased, pushing more people into an urban underclass.

THE ENDING OF THE CIVIL WARS

When Morton succeeded in detaching Argyll, his Campbells and magnates from the south-west from the queen's party, the circumspect Edinburgh moneylenders promptly refused further credit to the queen's men. Foreign assistance was urgently needed and the only sources were Scotland's traditional ally, France, or the major European power of Spain, particularly via the duke of Alva with his Spanish army in the Netherlands. Though the chimera of foreign aid was constantly before the eyes of the queen's men only limited funds and supplies were extracted from Charles IX. The St Bartholomew's Eve massacres of the French Huguenots in August 1572 sent shock waves around Europe, confirming the scare stories previously circulating among Protestants. Apart from making any Scottish association with the French regime problematic, their domestic situation ensured Scottish concerns slipped even further down the French diplomatic agenda.

Thanks to the growing pressure from the *politiques* and following protracted and delicate negotiations, by February 1573 most of the queen's party in the regions agreed to settle in the Pacification of Perth. It was finally completed under Morton who had succeeded as regent when Mar died unexpectedly at the end of October 1572. Mar's quiet constancy and ability to remain friends with all sides were widely appreciated, though these sterling qualities made his regency a difficult one, as the *Diurnal* remarked, 'The maist caus of his deid wes that he lufit peace, and culd nocht have the same.'[4]

To the puzzlement and annoyance of their former allies among the queen's party, the Castilians flatly refused to agree terms. Morton was able to utilise their intransigence to persuade Queen Elizabeth to send artillery and expertise. Assaulting Edinburgh Castle was one of the toughest military challenges in the British Isles and most of Scotland's heavy artillery lay inside its walls. In the end, Kirkcaldy's main problem was lack of water, with St Margaret's well below the crag having been poisoned and the main supply inside the castle blocked when part of David's Tower collapsed under the steady bombardment which demolished the spur, and left it open to assault. Instructions from the parsimonious Elizabeth encouraged the recovery of the 3,000 rounds fired at the castle, allowing the brave and enterprising among the population to earn a bawbee (small coin) for each shot returned. When the castle finally surrendered on 29 May most of its 164 inhabitants went free with many of the defending troops immediately signing up for mercenary duty in Sweden. An example was made of Kirkcaldy and his brother who were hanged alongside two Edinburgh goldsmiths, Mossman and Cockie, responsible for minting coin for the queen's cause and raising loans by pawning the royal jewels. Their executions appeased some of the lust for vengeance animating Edinburgh's former exiles.

Though it was rumoured he had chosen the 'Roman way' and committed suicide, Maitland escaped the rope by dying in Leith Tolbooth where he was a prisoner. Having appealed to Elizabeth, the redoubtable Mary Fleming ensured her husband's body was not posthumously tried

---

[4] *A diurnal of remarkable occurrents that have passed within the country of Scotland since the death of King James the Fourth till the year MDLXXV*, ed. T. Thomson (Bannatyne Club, 43, Edinburgh, 1833), 317.

for treason. The English queen delighted in adopting a high moral tone, telling the regent not to show cruelty to the corpse of an unconvicted man, though Morton managed his revenge by locking the body in a room until the vermin came creeping under the door. Whilst recognising its necessity, Elizabeth found the siege costly and annoying and she wanted rid of such Scottish headaches. A more military-minded Tudor might have been tempted to hold onto the castle or secure alternative Scottish strongholds, but the English commanders knew reducing costs by a swift withdrawal would best please their royal mistress. Finally, Regent Morton was left with a relatively free hand.

ANARCHY AVOIDED

Since Lennox's return in 1564, the Scottish ship of state had been steering an erratic course and, when it was deluged by the waves of Mary's deposition and Moray's assassination, it listed so badly it nearly sank. Scots had only to look to contemporary France to witness how easily a frightening spiral of bloodshed, destruction and national disintegration could grip a realm. In one sense 1567 completed some unfinished business of the 1559–60 revolutions and in his later years James VI bracketed together the two episodes, equally unfortunate in his opinion. The revolution of 1567 did not bring religious war, but it was a gigantic step to depose a reigning monarch, far beyond the 1559 removal of the regent. The radicalism of the action was hidden by the conservative cloak of a Stewart minority and with power held by regents rather than a new dynasty. Constitutional and institutional innovations were avoided, with the 1569 plan for completely conciliar government remaining on the drawing board. While the conflict was never short of ideology and propaganda, the Scottish political elite behaved as if it were a traditional struggle for power with the five main kin groups ranged against each other; the Douglases and Lennox Stewarts for the king's men opposing the Hamiltons, Gordons and Campbells of the queen's party (see Table 4.1). When the music stopped in 1573, the Douglases held the parcel with the power. The quiet pressure of a substantial group of *politiques* who wanted a return to order above all else brought the conflict within the regions to an end by the use of feud-settlement techniques. There was a military ending for the capital whose two-year battle hit Scotland's overseas trade hard, increased poverty and fractured the burgh's oligarchy. The rest of the country suffered disruption and some destruction but little compared to the mid-century

Battle for Britain. The intervention of English forces in 1570 and 1573, turning the military tide in favour of the king's party, ensured the diplomatic realignment of 1559–60 was virtually irreversible. A much weakened Scotland was dependent upon England, but the kingdom remained intact.

CHAPTER 13

The Last Douglas Ascendancy (1573–8)

When the dust settled after the surrender of Edinburgh Castle in 1573 and the rapid departure of the English troops, Regent Morton no longer faced armed opposition within the realm. Thanks to widespread *politique* support for a return to conventional politics and governance and long familiarity with the techniques of feud settlement, Scotland was able to build a peace following its civil wars. For many Scots, Morton's regency brought a reassuring sense of *déjà vu* with a minority regime run for the benefit of the magnate in charge and everyone else at least aware of the rules of the game. Kin and allies were rewarded with loyal king's men forming the core of the regime, though room was found for some prominent Marians, such as Boyd, whose political career blossomed. Aided by the profound war weariness that had hammered out the Pacification of Perth, this regency lasted long enough for a sense of stability and normality to return to Scotland: an achievement underplayed in the grudging description after his fall, that Morton

> be his providence and foirsicht be the help of God pacifeit the
> seditionis and civile weir by the quhilk the said realm was
> miserablie afflictit, quhairthrow oure said soveranis liegis enjoyit
> ane reassonabil quietnes and rest during the tyme of his regiment.[1]

It has been easy to dismiss Morton as the last in the line of Douglas villains, grasping power for its own sake, raking in the rewards of office with a fierce concentration and steering the gravy train for his kinsmen. The regent did not have the benefit of a good apologist and received a

---

[1] *The Register of the Privy Seal of Scotland 1575–80*, ed. G. Donaldson (Edinburgh, 1966), VII, 1528.

particularly bad press from the Presbyterian historians because of his clashes over the kirk's polity and his traditional 'help yourself and your kin' attitude to ecclesiastical revenues and posts. He has received little credit for being a committed Protestant from at least the mid-1550s, never wavering in his support of his faith. Following Douglas tradition, he had also remained a consistent Anglophile, and having spent part of his youth and a period of exile in England he retained contacts and friendships south of the border as well as traces of English diction: it would have taken a brave man to mock Morton about this 'southron' accent, as Ninian Winzet derided Knox. In common with many nobles, the regent's religious conviction contained a strong philosophical element with a marked Stoical flavour, and he was particularly fond of withdrawing to the Aberdour gardens he had designed. At the same time he was the ruthless, worldly-wise politician, quite prepared to kill and torture when he deemed it necessary.

MORTON'S TRADITIONAL STYLE OF GOVERNANCE

During Morton's regime, traditional attitudes and methods of ruling prevailed and they provided the key to his successes and failures. As regent, he undertook the kingly duties of administering justice and having a military presence, alongside the more peaceful arts of display and the distribution of patronage. Unlike his uncle Angus in 1525, Morton came to power with the approval or acquiescence of the political elite and received parliamentary confirmation for his regency. However, both Douglases believed their strong regional base in the Eastern Midlands of Scotland was essential to maintain their authority and that kinsmen and close supporters should form the administrative heart of their regimes. As with the mid-century regime of Regent Arran, the Douglas ascendancy automatically attracted criticism from those outside that charmed circle of favouritism for kin, friends and allies. Having ended the warfare, Morton assumed the realm should be ruled by the tried and tested methods of Stewart kingship, though he encountered major difficulties assembling the resources to make the system run smoothly. The distribution of patronage became a central and contentious issue and Morton's attempts to employ the old pool of patronage brought him into direct conflict with the kirk and fellow nobles, thereby undermining the regime's strength. By the 1570s the breeze that had sprung up in 1559 had developed into a whirlwind, blowing away the old system on which Stewart rule had rested. It was Morton's misfortune the traditional methods and style of governance he wanted to employ were no longer available because the church–crown hybrid was dying.

Though a man of action with a tough and autocratic manner, Morton worked extensively through the Privy Council. During Mary's personal reign the Council had been fully employed for the first time by an adult ruler and Morton had served on it. The Privy Council became a normal and permanent feature of governance during his regency, meeting at least three times a week and developing into the government's main executive arm, vital to its administrative health. In contrast, Morton ignored Parliament once the civil war had ended. His style was conciliar rather than broadly consultative; he could dominate the Privy Council but doubted he could manage parliament and thought it wiser not to give the extended political community a chance to air its grievances.

Morton found it easier to dominate the Council because of the quirky pattern of noble mortality during the 1570s. He unexpectedly found himself as the sole survivor among the magnates and politicians active since the mid-1550s and with experience of the turbulent years from 1558–73. Until his premature death in 1573, Argyll had been acting as Morton's right-hand man, and his successor proved a less effective politician. In 1575 following the exertions of a football game, Huntly collapsed and died; Châtelherault, having withdrawn from public life to Kinneil as a tired and broken man whose Hamilton dynasty was falling apart, had also died. Similarly, his regional rivals, the Lennox Stewarts, had not recovered from the death of Regent Lennox and Darnley's murder. The shake-up among the major kin groups left Morton possessing the authority of experience others lacked, but isolated as an older man having little in common with a younger generation trying to make their mark. Tending to be high-handed and disdainful of those he regarded as second rate or second rank, Morton had the bad habit of falling out with his supporters. He lacked the grace or inclination to win over enemies or the uncommitted and made scant effort to cover his directness with a coating of charm. Although there were instances of his generosity or care, he did not strive to overturn his reputation for avarice or ruthlessness which caused his Dalkeith castle to be known locally as the 'lion's den'.

Being a regional magnate, Morton gave a high priority to enforcing justice in the localities, especially through the well-grooved system of justice ayres. Border expeditions, that touchstone of regal activity, were employed to demonstrate his serious intent to enforce law and order in the realm and between 1573 and 1576 he led six expeditions. A central component of the regent's judicial visit to Aberdeen in 1574 was to impose authority in areas previously beyond the reach of the king's party. However, collecting judicial fines was a lucrative business, with Aberdeen's burgh council having to pay 4,000 merks, and such legal revenues made a significant dent in the crown's debts. This method of enforcing justice appeared to fall heaviest upon the lower levels of society, as Pitscottie wryly commented, 'thair was no thing at that tyme bot haulding of justice airis from schyre to schyre and the puir men war hereit'.[2] The more serious charge against Morton was that the justice he dispensed, as at Aberdeen, was partial, hitting former enemies and passing over friends and allies.

DEALING WITH 'MASTERLESS MEN'

Morton assumed the smooth operation of regional and local governance was the key to Scotland's stability. To preserve the integrity of the localities he was willing to innovate to counter the newly-perceived menace of 'masterless men'. On such an important national social issue he consulted parliament and in 1574 passed a Poor Law modelled on the 1572 English Act. The main thrust of this legislation was the attempt to control those designated as 'vagabonds' or 'sturdy beggars', the able-bodied unemployed or destitute who moved around the country. They were to be caught, branded on the ear and expelled from the parish unless they found a master willing to employ them. By banishing the 'vagabonds', poor relief could be distributed to those local people unable to support themselves, such as the very young or old and those crippled or handicapped. The 'virtuous poor' had been the object of praise in the verses penned in 1569 by Lauder, minister at Forgandenny in Strathearn, though more as a foil for rich and greedy hypocrites. There was little understanding of the underlying demographic and economic pressures from the rise in population, gathering momentum from the mid-century, and the depressed urban economies facing loss of markets and the rural dislocation after the fighting, combining to create the pool of rootless unemployed. Contemporaries' sharp division into deserving or undeserving poor remained blurred in practice, especially in the burghs where it was recognised that economic downturns meant fellow craftsmen and citizens might fall on hard times. Piecemeal provision had been made, as in Edinburgh when in 1568 the wine duties collected from the vintners, that had previously been destined

---

[2] *The Historie and Cronicles of Scotland . . . by Robert Lindesay of Pitscottie*, ed. A. J. G. Mackay (3 vols, STS, Old Ser. 42–3, 60, Edinburgh, 1899–1911), II, 312.

Backpacking in Poland and the Scandinavian timber trade

One socially-acceptable way of remaining a 'masterless man' was to take up 'backpacking', the life of a travelling pedlar. These individual traders played a vital role moving goods around Scotland, especially into the Highlands, and also worked extensively abroad, particularly in Poland where Scots were so prevalent that 'Scot' became the name for every travelling pedlar. During the sixteenth century Scotland's trade through the Sound into the Baltic increased, building upon its existing medieval links with ports such as Lübeck, Danzig and Königsberg where Scottish merchants had settled. Scottish ships brought consignments of small goods, *Krämerwaren*, such as skins, hides, cheap cloth and salt which were then sold by the Scottish pedlars who spread throughout Poland–Lithuania and the eastern Baltic provinces. On the return leg Scottish vessels carried processed timber for building materials, with pine boards and beams, barrel hoops and even birch firewood. On the North Sea, Norwegian ports such as Stavanger had a thriving timber trade with Dundee and the other east-coast burghs. The scarcity of good, sizeable oak had caused James IV to import timber for his naval construction and oak boards for his Great Hall at Edinburgh Castle, and James V's work at Stirling Castle also utilised Baltic wood. Pine boards were brought in for less high-quality building, especially in urban areas, and Scotland became increasingly dependent upon timber imports for its construction materials.

for St Anthony's altar, their patron saint, were auctioned; if consulted, the poor might have opted to receive their dole in kind.

In contrast to English experience, the Scottish Poor Law did not become the vehicle for a local government administrative structure. Although theoretically a national system envisaging a local stent or tax throughout the realm, only burghs had the existing administrative machinery to collect it, and in landward areas any provision was likely to be organised through kirk sessions. Under the kirk, the office of deacon and regular collections for the parish's poor replaced the welfare previously provided by pre-Reformation guilds and almsgiving. At best, Reformation changes had brought organisational confusion and at worst, resources had been lost to charitable use. Kirk sessions frequently linked poor relief to religious conformity and integrated it within the parish system of social control. Although in post-Reformation Scotland its theological justification had altered, an emphasis on personal philanthropy remained strong and social custom dictated alms should be distributed on special occasions, particularly baptisms, marriages and funerals. Despite making the legislation permanent in 1579, the state did not move decisively into this area of social welfare, leaving it to the church to act as the main conduit of poor relief.

The fate of the poor, especially the urban underclass in Edinburgh, was made worse by the wartime inflation in food prices which remained high when the fighting ended. Price increases were the ostensible reason for the debasements of the coinage, from which Morton appeared to profit or, on the kindest interpretation, recoup his governmental expenses. Although it had not happened since the black money of James III's reign, the lure of debasement was too great for Morton's regime and in 1575 the poor faced a devastating blow when the 'hardheads', worth one and half pennies, and the 'placks', worth four pennies, were cried down to one penny and two pennies respectively. The members of the Convention of Estates authorising the debasement had to walk to Holyrood through a gauntlet of abuse from angry townsfolk. As Calderwood commented, it 'procured great invy and hatred of the commouns against the Erle of Morton, for the people's hands wer full of that money'.[3] As a result the economy slowed just when it needed to rebuild after the dislocation of the civil wars.

REGENCY DISPLAY

Morton faced the catch-22 that no regency avoided: splendour was welcomed by the political nation or regarded as a necessary attribute of the monarchy, while display focused upon the regent was stigmatised as personal aggrandisement. During times of financial hardship, simple equations were made between wealth expended in conspicuous consumption and the level of taxation. Such calculations were made to his detriment when Morton was observed riding in a coach, a particularly costly luxury item. The rebuilding of Edinburgh Castle with its fine half-moon battery on top of the ruins of David's Tower was a more justified expense since it contributed to the nation's security. However, the new entrance gate displaying the arms of Morton, in addition to those of the monarch, showed no reticence about where the credit should lie. As happened in Arran's regency, Morton proclaimed his status through building and

[3] D. Calderwood, *A History of the Kirk of Scotland*, ed. T. Thomson (Wodrow Society, 8 vols, Edinburgh, 1842–9), III, 302.

Figure 13.1 Seton family portrait by Frans Pourbus the elder, 1572. [SNPG]

cultural patronage. Drochil was his major architectural project and work was also undertaken at Tantallon and Dalkeith. Gardening was one of Morton's greatest loves and he laid down the beautiful south-facing terraces and orchards at Aberdour and designed further projects when staying at Lochleven following his first fall from power. Morton's pride in the magnificent towers and outline of Tantallon ensured they featured in the background of his portrait by Van Bronckhorst.

With his distinctive big black hat and authoritarian pose, Morton's portrait presented an image of a powerful regent, though without any overtly Protestant symbols. By contrast, when the exiled Seton had his family painted by Frans Pourbus the scene contained an ostentatious display of the badges of Roman Catholic identity, sending a plain message to his fellow Scots concerning his allegiance to queen and faith (see Figure 13.1).

Although few Scots emulated Morton and Seton and commissioned their portraits, they rushed to have the interior of their houses painted. With the re-establishment of peace, a willingness to invest in display and a more general cultural confidence rapidly returned to Scotland.

Decorative painting

Found across the country in royal palaces, noble residences and burgess houses, Renaissance decorative painting was a distinctive feature of Scotland's artistic culture. The figures and designs were derived from continental prints and emblem books, indicating an extensive trade in printed ephemera that has scarcely survived in its original form. In a similar manner to embroidery and jewellery, a complex set of symbols and emblems were employed which assumed viewers possessed a reasonable level of visual and verbal literacy. Within a broadly humanist context, the subject matter would sometimes follow an identifiable theme, such as the cycle of the Good Samaritan with its life-size figures in the earliest surviving Renaissance paintings at the Hamilton palace of Kinneil, West Lothian, decorated in the 1550s by Regent Arran. The depiction of the Muses and the Virtues, found in full at Crathes and Culross, painted in the last decades of the century, were accompanied by inscriptions. Their presence demonstrated how proverbs, aphorisms and biblical quotations were part of both literary and oral culture, and that the Geneva Bible, although written in English, was pronounced in Scots, the version appearing on the ceilings at Traquair and Crathes. Other designs had a less serious purpose, such as grotesques often with a scatalogical emphasis, found especially at Prestongrange, East Lothian. These were painted for Mark Ker, the commendator of Newbattle, in 1581, the earliest dated decoration, and made extensive use of the pattern book of Hans Vredeman de Vries being placed against a 'Pompeian red' background to give the impression of a Roman room.

Morton also strove to create a culturally sophisticated domestic setting, particularly through music. He patronised musicians, such as his harper, Robert Galbraith, probably from the Mac s'Bhreatnaich harping family, whose artistic rivalry with a fiddler produced the musical equivalent of literary 'flyting' in the composition of the 'port' called 'The Fiddler's Comtempt'. The regent was equally fortunate to retain the services of the talented composer, Andro Blackhall, minister in parishes close to Dalkeith, who wrote secular as well as sacred music. Blackhall was particularly known for his musical settings of the psalms, and Morton commissioned a complex, polyphonic version of Psalm 128 for his nephew's wedding in June 1573 at Dalkeith that blossomed into a celebration of the recent ending of the wars. Ten years later, with the darker purpose of his anti-Hamilton campaign in mind, Blackhall's special setting of the revenge psalm 43 was presented to James VI. Also in 1579 there was a belated effort to prevent Scotland's musical skills base from disappearing with a Parliamentary Act to re-establish the 'sang schules', thereby providing for the continuation of professional musical training, previously supplied by the pre-Reformation church.

FINANCIAL PRESSURES

During Mary's personal reign Morton had served as chancellor, though his experience mainly related to the office's status and ceremonial role. During his regency, the treasurer and comptroller faced the sharper end of financial policy and the need to control expenditure. In 1574 the treasurer's account deficit was £37,000, in part an accumulation from the civil war period, though by the end of Morton's rule Treasurer Tullibardine still had a shortfall of £5,377. With the re-assertion of authority throughout the realm, collecting revenues from crown lands was regularised, bringing a modest increase in income, supplemented by fines from justice ayres contributing about £28,000. As previous rulers had found, these income sources were never enough to sustain the royal household and cover other expenses. For a man with such a tough reputation, Morton was lax about collecting crown compositions for feudal casualties, though some remissions constituted a specific political favour to a fellow noble. There were aggrieved squawks from Edinburgh merchants that half the fines collected from the burgh's Marians disappeared into Morton's pocket instead of being employed to rebuild the buildings torn down in the siege. Persistent mutterings about the regent's greed indicated he was believed to be profiting unduly from his position. Demanding 'loans' with menaces from Edinburgh merchants and pressurising other burghs did nothing to endear the regent to the mercantile community.

With direct taxation difficult to justify in times of peace, and the regent unwilling to call parliament, he relied upon any expedient that presented itself, such as selling licences to export salt. With a Scottish scarcity due to a continent-wide shortage, it was more lucrative to sell this vital commodity in the European market than at home. To satisfy domestic consumers, particularly the vociferous herring-fishing industry, salt export was forbidden. However, those involved in the growing salt-panning industry on the Forth were willing to buy export licences and Morton was prepared to sell them. Culross benefited from George Bruce's utilisation of the abundant local coal to dry salt, making its production lucrative and the foundation of the burgh's prosperity. He extracted the coal from the first effective mine to run beneath the Forth by using new machinery, such as his ingenious 'Egyptian wheel' which became something of a tourist attraction.

THE DEMISE OF THE CHURCH–CROWN HYBRID AND CLASHES WITH THE KIRK

The regency's financial difficulties were compounded by problems within the old patronage system resulting from the demise of the church–crown hybrid. Using clerical personnel to staff the royal administration was no longer possible since the kirk enforced a strictly ministerial role upon its clergy. By now the old guard had either died out or shed their clerical skin to become laymen. A sign of the change from clerical personnel and expectations was the transfer of the treasurer's accounts from parchment to paper and from Latin into Scots. Whilst on the surface the hybrid appeared to function as before, that appearance was deceptive. The secretary's office was held by the conscientious civil servant, Robert Pitcairn, commendator of Dunfermline Abbey. Having been educated for a church career, he succeeded his uncle, also a royal servant, at Dunfermline. At the Reformation, Pitcairn had undergone a metamorphosis from a quasi-cleric to a married layman. Having no children, in 1570 Dunfermline passed to Henry, his nephew. He also granted abbey lands to his brother-in-law James, who also entered the royal administration. In this manner, though dynasties of government servants were still being rewarded from Dunfermline Abbey revenues, there was less direct royal involvement. Overall the change was almost imperceptible, but, crucially, the crown had lost control over the succession to the abbey: the formal erection of the commendatorships into secular lordships in James' adult reign recognised a *fait accompli*.

Since the spiritual role of monasteries had been abolished, it was a comparatively simple matter for commendators, three quarters of the way there already, to move completely into the secular world: the bishops, with their cure of souls, were in a different position. With their position as lords spiritual, bishops had been an essential component within regional and national governance in addition to their place within the royal patronage pool. From the perspective of patronage, the handful of bishops who had retained their pastoral involvement by actively working within the kirk had merely complicated the situation. Being a convinced Protestant, the regent was content to advance as bishops only those with sound Protestant credentials. However, Morton also wanted to continue their dual role of public functionary alongside ecclesiastical official: he did not want to unpick the strand of episcopacy from the cloth of the traditional body politic.

A dual role was what the kirk feared; it did not want the old ways to continue, even in Protestant colours. On the one hand, it regarded bishops exclusively as clergy, judged by their usefulness or not as parts of the ecclesiastical organisation, without regard for their wider political or social position. On the other hand, the kirk did not want diocesan revenues going the way of monastic property and fought to retain this section of the pre-Reformation church's resources. This generated a series of clashes between the regent and kirk leaders and the dispute over financial provision sucked a range of other issues into the argument. The subconscious pressure upon Morton was his desire to rule the kingdom along old-fashioned lines that included drawing heavily upon the personnel, wealth and authority of the pre-Reformation church.

BEYOND DOUGLAS CONTROL

With their powerbase in the eastern and southern part of the country, the Douglases had not been involved in the regional politics of the Highlands or northern Scotland. No major effort was made by Morton's regime to quell the serious internecine troubles of the MacLeods, causing a succession of murders and unsettling the entire Northern Hebrides and adjacent mainland, as neighbouring clans found themselves sucked into the struggle. A different internal inheritance dispute in Cromarty among the family of Munro of Foulis led to a black comedy of bungled witchcraft. Lady Foulis had been attempting to poison and kill by sorcery her stepson and sister-in-law Lady Balnagown. First the 'pig' of poison killed her nurse, who unwisely drank the liquid, the rat poison inserted in deer kidneys proved insufficient to kill, though causing sufficient 'vomit and vexation' to leave Lady Balnagown permanently ill. With elf bolts missing their targets, butter and wax images also failed. At the 1577 trial, Lady Foulis extricated herself on oath though her flight to Caithness confirmed her involvement and in 1590 she faced a more serious trial. Her escape was aided by her father's fearsome reputation. Ross of Balnagown's activities were sufficiently notorious for his own kinsmen to reprimand him in 1577 for jeopardising the proud family record of 'immaculate' behaviour in favour of 'the prince and autorities'.[4] Clan Ross's concerns about its national reputation and involvement in court affairs was not met by a reciprocal interest. Edinburgh's attitude to the north was encapsulated in Douglas of Lochleven's sentence after Morton's fall defining internal exile as residing beyond 'the wattir of Cromatie'.

A traditional *laissez-faire* attitude to Scotland's farther reaches paid little attention to the expansion of two Highland kindreds. The Privy Council did not impose its authority in Ross-shire where, as elsewhere, church lands were causing contention. Symptomatic of their gradual push from Kintail to the east coast, the Mackenzies were embroiled in a dispute on the Black Isle, involving Mackenzie of Kintail's brother, who had occupied the cathedral steeple at Fortrose and used it to terrorise the neighbourhood. The rise of the Mackenzies was only beginning to have significance outside their immediate region, not reaching national importance until the next century. Though Clan Campbell had been closely involved in national politics since the fifteenth century, it was possibly its penetration into Angus, a Douglas area, as well as Campbell support for the queen's party that alerted Morton to its all-pervasive spread and helped provoke his serious spat with Argyll. The 1570s saw the consolidation of Campbell families in Angus based around the ecclesiastical lands granted by Donald, Abbot of Coupar Angus, to his illegitimate sons and kinsmen and assisted by the influence of the 'noble and potent lady' Katherine, countess of Crawford.[5] By settling in Angus, Clan Campbell completed a corridor of territory stretching from the western seaboard of Scotland to the eastern shires. Much of that corridor, including many main routes through the Central Highlands, were held by the most successful and ruthless Campbell cadet branch, named after their original Argyll territory of Glenorchy but based at Balloch, at the east end of Loch Tay in Perthshire. In Nairn, following marriage to an heiress, another branch had taken over Cawdor Castle, neighbourhood and name. This outpost on the Moray coast acquired renewed importance in 1572 when Annas, countess of Moray, married Argyll. The clan's most detached section had been settled for several centuries in Ayrshire, across the Clyde from the Argyll heartland, though as a kin group the Campbells were unusual in their cohesion and willingness to support their chief. As a Lowland magnate, in addition to being a Highland chief Argyll had clan interests in many Scottish regions, giving him extra power in national politics, though since his own extensive lands were mostly in the Western Highlands he was richer in men than in money. Having largely taken over the role of 'King of the Gael' from the Lord of the Isles, Argyll ruled unchallenged by Lowland politicians and, as Morton discovered, putting Argyll to the horn had little effect. Throughout the period no Stewart ruler successfully managed to forfeit the chief of Clan Campbell – an effective immunity placing him in a different category to his northern equivalent, Huntly, the chief of the Gordons.

THE REFORM OF THE UNIVERSITIES

Persuaded to leave Geneva to return to Scotland, in 1574 Andrew Melville brought with him decided views on university education in addition to his glittering scholarly reputation, especially in the 'new' studies of Greek and Hebrew. After some debate over returning to his *alma mater* St Andrews, he went instead to be Glasgow's Principal, and during the next six years transformed the ailing university into a flourishing centre of progressive humanist learning. His clear vision, steely determination and genius for organisation introduced a new curriculum with a strong emphasis upon liberal arts and biblical languages. In addition to Greek and Hebrew, he lectured on Syriac and Chaldaic, bringing greater precision to the understanding of biblical philology. Having personally attended Peter Ramus' lectures in Paris and Lausanne, Melville was an enthusiast for the new method, introducing Ramist texts into the Glasgow curriculum. In line with such methods the regenting style of teaching, whereby a regent took his students through their entire Arts studies, was abandoned in favour of specialist teaching by different professors lecturing upon their own expertise. Smeaton, Melville's successor, having followed the unusual path of entering the kirk's ministry via the Jesuit order, consolidated the reforms in a new constitution. At King's College, Aberdeen, Arbuthnot, Melville's enthusiastic ally, brought the Glasgow model of university education north and the foundation of Marischal College in 1593 helped consolidate its hold within Aberdeen. The new 'tounis college' at Edinburgh, opening in October 1583 with Rollock as Principal, also offered a modern humanist curriculum, which a growing segment of Scottish society was seeking, and these broad educational needs were reflected in the provision of a class in human anatomy. Among the elite, the tradition of attendance at European universities and continental travel for educational purposes continued, though the confessional divide was beginning to influence destinations, with more Scottish students studying in the Netherlands and a shift to southern France where the Huguenots were strong.

Melville moved to St Andrews where he took charge of St Mary's College. There he created one of the leading European schools of Protestant theology, providing the rigorous academic training for the ministry that by the end of the century had become a hallmark of the Scottish clergy. It was a bracing regime, with the Psalms in Hebrew taught by Melville from 5 to 6 a.m. followed by grammar and the Prophets from 7 to 8 a.m. He had less success with the other two Colleges of St Salvator and St Leonard and his direct attacks upon Aristotelianism provoked such acrimonious disputes that his nephew summed up Melville's time in the university as 'meikle feghting and fascherie'.[6]

MORTON'S REGIONAL POWERBASES

Much of Morton's authority and prestige rested upon his regional power which was strongest in an arc from the East March of the Borders through East Lothian, with Tantallon and Dalkeith, across the Forth to Aberdour in Fife and into the shire of Angus, with his nephew's base. This swathe of influence incorporating the Eastern Midlands of Scotland had formed the geographical heartland of the king's party. While it was substantial enough to give Morton the power to rule, its regional coverage was too limited to secure control over the whole realm. With the relative eclipse of the other four magnate families, Morton did not face political pressure to make further alliances to give him a more balanced support and he relied primarily upon the Douglas affinity and localities.

[6] J. Melville, *The autobiography and diary* . . . ed. R. Pitcairn (Wodrow Society, Edinburgh, 1842), 123–4.

A top priority was the consolidation of the Douglas hold upon its areas of strength. The building of Morton's innovatively-designed elaborate hunting lodge at Drochil near Peebles indicated Morton was maintaining the Douglas presence in upper Tweeddale. It was the regent's good fortune that, with Bothwell languishing in a Danish prison, Hepburn power in East Lothian and the East March was in abeyance. Similarly, as a former Castilian, Lord Hume remained in prison and, hastened by his bad treatment, he died in 1575, whilst the Marian Ker of Ferniehurst was in exile. Border lairds, such as Home of Manderston, having benefited from the turmoil of the civil wars, sought to retain their gains, and Morton, after initial success by distributing patronage, had to pick his way through these local rivalries. The regent's policy of advancing his kin alienated other supporters: Manderston was annoyed when the marriage of his heiress niece was granted to Morton's illegitimate son. There was a similar outcome in the western Borders. Maxwell's existing Douglas ties were reinforced by marriage to Angus' sister, hosted by Morton at Dalkeith. However, when the regent replaced Maxwell as Warden of the West March and Lieutenant of the Borders by Angus, marital kinship did not prevent the two men from falling out and Maxwell joined Morton's opponents the following year. Beginning as a small local problem, such issues escalated into regional tensions and had a direct effect upon the national political balance.

With Ruthven as treasurer and Murray as comptroller, Morton's regime, rested securely in Perthshire and the Lothians. A close collaboration between the Ruthvens and Murrays of Tullibardine, and Morton, their distant Douglas kinsman, had been forged in the 1560s. At Dirleton in East Lothian where he built a fine palace within the medieval castle, Ruthven was close to the Douglas stronghold of Tantallon. Through his Perthshire base, Ruthven was linked by marriage to the Murrays. Close to Perth was the newly-constructed Balmanno tower house, home of Auchinleck, Morton's relative and man of business, who displayed some of his kinsman's arrogance in his handling of Perthshire affairs. The long-standing Angus affinity of the Douglases made it easier to reconnect with Glamis, another distant kinsman and loyal king's man who became chancellor in 1573. The solid base of support in Lowland Perthshire and Angus helped Morton face Atholl's hostility, but Ruthven's own kinship with Atholl separated him from Morton in 1578. During that crisis the regent found those he had alienated by his national policies and attempts at regional control formed a more powerful coalition than his own Douglas affinity. In particular, his methods had upset Atholl and Argyll, who formed the core of the coalition.

THE FEUD WITH ARGYLL

Morton's first clash with Argyll came through his drive to recover crown property and resources distributed during the civil wars. Tracking down Queen Mary's jewels became an obsession for the incoming government

Jewellery

In addition to being an adornment to the wearer, jewellery had a variety of other functions. Late medieval cloak brooches and rings often named or portrayed saints, thus having a protective as well as a decorative purpose. A more mundane service was performed by the heavy gold chains commonly worn by the social elite that acted like credit cards: when necessary a link or two could be taken from the chain to provide payment in gold, the universal currency. Displaying quantities of precious metal was an ostentatious sign of wealth in itself, turning everyday items into precious objects, such as the gold pomander belonging to Mary, Queen of Scots. Jewellery was also employed to convey more subtle messages through designs and inscriptions. The Renaissance passion for complex emblematics and symbolism used jewellery to encode communications for public and private consumption. The famous Darnley or Lennox Jewel (Royal Collection) made for the countess of Lennox was an intriguing example. It was shaped as a golden heart set with jewels with three sections, front, reverse and interior, which had twenty-eight emblems and six verses or mottoes. It encapsulated the hopes of the Lennox Stewarts with regard to the English and Scottish thrones made either as part of Lennox's return to Scotland in 1564 or after his death in 1572. The jewellery of Mary, Queen of Scots was particularly fine, much given by the French royal family, such as the magnificent rope of pearls gifted by Catherine de Medici and described by the poet Brantôme as the best in the world. They were sold in April 1568 to Queen Elizabeth and probably appear in some of her later portraits. The treatment of the queen's jewels as a financial asset underlay the row between Regent Morton and the countess of Moray and Argyll. Gems, and the goldsmiths who handled them, formed part of an emerging loan industry, with jewellery frequently pawned or taken as security for debt. The international contacts required to obtain gems and their use as gifts between monarchs involved these merchants in diplomatic missions, such as George Heriot, father and son, the latter the founder of the Edinburgh school with his name.

and the parliament of January 1573 authorised the pursuit of any who had dealt with them. The Castilians were an obvious target since Mary Fleming, one of the famous four Maries and Maitland's widow, and Lady Hume had received jewels. Far graver consequences ensued when Morton pursued those on the king's side, especially Regent Moray's widow, for jewels in her possession. When first lady in the land, the countess of Moray had probably been delighted to wear the large royal diamonds or rubies or even the great 'H' set with diamonds, probably Henry II's gift to Queen Mary. However, Moray had appropriated them as an alternative form of cash and Annas and her second husband, Argyll, vehemently asserted the jewels were the means of settling Moray's debts and now constituted his daughters' inheritance. Morton, intent upon proving a point about crown property, possibly also wanted to cut the Campbells down to size. The row escalated when the Argylls were outlawed and appealed directly to Queen Elizabeth.

Although a settlement on the jewels was finally reached in 1575, Argyll believed Morton was vindictively blocking him at every opportunity, especially in his legal cases before the Court of Session and he did not take kindly to the regent's intervention in his feud with Atholl over their neighbouring jurisdictions and Clan Cameron's treatment. Argyll found himself outlawed once more, with a major campaign planned against him. Atholl, who also felt badly served by Morton, decided it was preferable to reconcile himself with Argyll, and their partnership forged in October 1577 formed the basis for the opposition that toppled Morton.

LOYAL FRIEND TO ENGLAND

For his entire political career Morton had supported an Anglophile policy and had been one of the most consistent and loyal of England's friends. The southern kingdom had furnished a place of refuge for him, as well as for his uncle and his father, and he had made personal friendships with English politicians, such as Cecil, Leicester, Walsingham and Huntingdon as well as English Border officials. As a committed king's man, he knew only too well how much his cause had relied upon English support, and without the troops and artillery sent north during the civil wars, victory would not have been won. Morton had no qualms about borrowing English models, whether for a new poor law or the official formulae for episcopal appointments. The regent wanted more than friendship and close alignment of practice; he sought an alliance based on common Protestantism and mutual security within the British mainland.

Queen Elizabeth, counting upon Scotland's dependent status and knowing Morton was the last person to lift a finger to assist Mary, Queen of Scots, knew she had the whip hand. She refused to make a treaty and disdained to offer the regent a pension. Her exaggerated reaction in 1576 to the Redeswyre incident demonstrated how little she valued Scotland as an ally. Despite Morton's efforts to bolster Anglo-Scottish co-operation and amity he had little to show for it. Almost imperceptibly the Border came to enjoy a more settled, if not entirely peaceful, atmosphere, attested by the building of town houses, such as the fashionable MacLellan's lodging constructed in 1577 in Kirkcudbright. In 1578 and in 1581 Elizabeth, being so intent upon international affairs, acted too little and too late to save Morton or prevent his death. As in a classic moral tale, once he had gone, she realised what a friend she and England had lost. Watching from the sidelines, James VI saw all these things and pondered them; as an adult, he did not make the same mistake in his dealings with the English queen.

MORTON'S FALL FROM POWER

In their opposition to Morton the regional strength of Argyll and Atholl and their extensive Campbell and Stewart kindreds acquired the crucial extra component of access to the young king through his guardian, Sir Alexander Erskine. Concentrating upon the Privy Council instead of the court, Morton's relative neglect of the royal household proved a costly political miscalculation. When Erskine persuaded James VI to call a Convention of Estates, the regent realised he had been outmanoeuvred and meekly resigned. Philosophical contemplation in his garden seemed to beckon, but Morton discovered he was not ready for retirement after all and started rebuilding his political power. Through enlisting the young earl of Mar within the royal household, by the summer of 1578 Morton had recovered much of his authority though armed confrontation between the 'Falkland Fellowship' of opponents and the Douglas affinity had been narrowly averted by the English ambassador's intervention. Morton's comeback might have been driven by a sense of unfinished business. In 1579 he launched an anti-Hamilton campaign, a shrewd ploy allowing the rest of the nobility to unite behind him. The legal excuse for this vendetta against the Hamiltons was failure to keep the terms of the Pacification of Perth and while Lords John and Claud managed to escape to France, their bewildered and insane elder brother Arran was left to face the destruction of his House. Morton rapidly lost the temporary unity of the anti-Hamilton campaign when his adversary Atholl died suddenly. Following an early form of autopsy with the report confirming poison as the likely cause of death, the finger was pointed at Morton.

At the end of 1579, the arrival of Esmé Stewart, the king's relative, transformed the court and the king and marked the definitive end of Morton's rule. Not permitted a quiet retirement, Morton was arrested and tried for his part in Darnley's murder. As regent he had made many enemies, and amongst the jury were those with scores to settle, such as friends of Kirkcaldy of Grange whom the regent had sent to the gallows in 1573. Morton's Stoic philosophy and his religious convictions afforded him considerable dignity in his last days and he made a 'good Protestant death', going to the embrace of the 'Maiden', a form of guillotine he had probably introduced to Scotland. It was the end of a generation as much as of a man.

Morton's conservative approach founded upon his regional authority and his affinity based within the eastern midlands of Scotland had kept him in power while also making him vulnerable. The traditional methods of governance were being undermined by the demise of the church–crown hybrid and its pool of patronage and personnel. By trying to keep the old system functioning in a Protestant guise, Morton hit serious opposition from the kirk and was unable to distribute patronage freely or broaden his support. Though his Anglophile policy enabled him to cope with Scotland's satellite status, it did not add to his strength or popularity. Despite these fundamental weaknesses, Morton's regime had managed with some skill to bring stability to the country following the civil wars and allowed the young king to grow up within a relatively secure environment and without being treated as a political pawn.

CHAPTER 14

James' Long Apprenticeship: (1578–87)

Three months before his twelfth birthday, James VI was declared of age. Having had three monarchs in a row each of whom had started their reigns as infants, few Scots were aware of any other pattern. In common with the experience of his grandfather and mother, James' official coming of age did not mark his assumption of power. Like his great-grandfather, James IV, he moved slowly through a political apprenticeship, accumulating authority gradually, making incremental moves from reigning to ruling until he became the sole ruler of Scotland. By 1587 the king was ready to cope by himself with one of the greatest challenges he encountered during his long reign. For the entire period of his apprenticeship, James faced an unprecedented awkwardness: the previous monarch of Scotland was alive and, by a strictly legitimist interpretation, his reign should not begin until his mother's death. Fortunately for him, by the late 1570s there was no serious Marian party left in Scotland and the issue had almost slipped from view within Scottish politics, though it retained a shadowy presence in European diplomacy and would re-emerge with a vengeance at Mary's trial and execution. In contrast to the fevered English worries about the succession, James and his advisers saw no necessity to rush headlong into a royal marriage. Taking his time, the king was prepared to wait until 1589 before making an advantageous match with Anna, the king of Denmark's daughter.

LEAVING THE SCHOOLROOM

Whilst growing up the young king had been afforded the luxury of a safe and secure environment ensconced in the Mar household at Stirling Castle. Regent Morton had taken to heart the mistake his uncle had made with James V and had left the Erskines in charge of the king's person. Far from dominating the young boy with his personality, as Angus had sought to do half a century before, Morton had distanced himself too far from the royal household, failing to appreciate how it might be used against him. In the prelude to Morton's brief comeback, Alexander Erskine's son was killed in front of James in a sword fight and the young king experienced for the first, but not the last, time a direct and frightening threat to his life.

As with the rest of his lessons, James also learned from this unpleasant one. He thrived in the schoolroom despite the beatings administered by Buchanan, his tutor, emerging as a major scholar in his own right and the most intellectual king to grace the Scottish or British throne. James' later wry comment, that he learnt Latin before he could speak Scots, indicated the massively classical thrust of his learning, inevitable given Buchanan's standing as the greatest living humanist scholar in the British Isles. Fortunately for the king, James' other tutor, Peter Young, was humane in the conventional as well as the learned sense, and did not terrify his royal pupil. In addition to studying with the 600 books Young had collected in the royal library, James was given time to use the small bow and arrows and develop his great passion for riding and hunting. Since James displayed little interest in the traditional role of warrior king, the aristocratic pursuits of the chase and running the ring provided convenient substitutes. The young king was temperamentally suited to leading his courtiers in the peaceful arts of court culture and through his own literary works setting an example and a high standard of performance. Unlike other Stewart monarchs, throughout his long reign James viewed work in his study as an integral part of the business of kingship.

Given his precocious literary talents, James began to assert his political authority by making his mark upon the court's cultural and social life. His enjoyment of poetry acted like a magnet drawing those with literary and political ambitions to his side. Once freed from the maternal supervision of his 'Lady Minny', the awe-inspiring countess of Mar, and the confines of his schoolroom, James' household adopted more of the attributes of a young men's club full of drinking and banter, literary and otherwise. Since his intellectual gifts allowed him to outshine his fellows, James had the advantage over his French cousin, Henry III, who had adopted a similar mixture of intellectual patronage and ostentatious display in his Academy. By stages James emerged into the limelight and when in June 1579 the prince rode out from Stirling Castle, it 'was the first tyme the king come furthe to the feildis accumpanied only with his owin domestickis'.[1] The reference to the 'fields' suggested either hunting in the countryside or a more warlike purpose, since this was shortly after the anti-Hamiltons campaign. There was a double resonance for the young king personally leading his immediate followers to the chase or battle and the gesture's significance was underlined by Hume of Polwarth's poem celebrating the occasion printed the following year. The 'Promine' dripped with hyperbole and flattery of the most imperial king who was compared to Solomon and Job. Martial themes found their way easily into James' verse with his bombastic poem on the Christian victory over the Turks at Lepanto and the earlier battle of Pavia forming the chivalric setting for William Kinloch's keyboard composition with its sparkling virtuosity. The musical continuity from Mary's reign had been preserved by families such as the Hudsons, noted for their playing and composing for the viols. Despite his £100 fee, William Hudson was unable to discover a way to teach James to dance as his mother had done, fluently and with grace. The king's intellectual and courtly muscles stretched more easily than his physical ones, and his delight in literary exercise ushered in the golden age of Jacobean culture within Scotland where his adolescent drive propelled forward the poetical enterprise: a momentum lost as the adult king turned to other pursuits and the rich vein of poetry that surrounded him ran dry.

In the autumn following the riding out from Stirling, James made his royal entry into the capital, the established device for raising the monarchy's profile, especially emerging from a minority. On 19 October with the capital packed with the political community assembled to attend parliament, James entered the West Port of Edinburgh and rode through the burgh beneath a canopy of purple velvet held aloft by thirty-two prominent burgesses. Along his route were tableaux, with portraits of former Scottish kings and assorted orations, in addition to a full sermon in St Giles', all rendering advice on how to be a good king copiously illustrated by biblical and classical models and allusions. At the mercat cross Bacchus sat distributing wine from a hogshead, enabling all to join in the song *Nou let us sing*. The party, which had begun at the start of the month, continued in the newly-refurbished palace of Holyrood.

The atmosphere at court underwent a gradual change as it shed its last associations with nursery and schoolroom, and the household became a political as much as a domestic space. Such a hothouse arena was the essential meeting ground for personalities and policies and James had to master the royal craft of creating personal and political alliances with

---

[1] D. Moysie, *Memoirs of the affairs of Scotland*, ed. J. Dennistoun (Bannatyne Club, 39, Edinburgh, 1830), 22.

IACOBVS · 6 · DEI · GRA · REX · SCOTOR.

IN VTRVNQVE
PARATVS.

Figure 14.1 Engraving of James VI, arrayed for peace or war, from Theodore Beza's *Icones*, 1580.

nobles and courtiers and, where necessary, separating the two relationships. Although James did not turn him into a political favourite, he enjoyed the teasing familiarity of addressing the Earl Marischal as 'my little fat pork', and he developed a more mature friendship with Mar, his boyhood companion, 'Jock o' the slates'.[2]

---

[2] James VI to Earl Marischal, 28 September 1589, in *Letters of James VI and I*, ed. G. P. V. Ackrigg (Berkeley, CA, 1984), 95.

THE RISE OF THE CHAMBER

The arrival from France of his relative Esmé Stuart in September 1579 added greater impetus to James' creation of his own circle and gave it sharper definition. By surrounding himself with favourites or *mignons*, nobly born though not from the top rank, the Scottish king followed a similar path to Henry III. Because he had been born and educated in France, Stuart had remained outside the Scottish aristocratic elite and his meteoric rise in favour was charted by his titles, being created earl, then duke, of Lennox in 1580 and 1581. Lennox was the first of a line of favourites whose close friendship with James gave them political power. For the remainder of James' apprenticeship, the royal household, especially the Chamber, acquired a heightened political importance and became the battleground for an intense struggle for patronage and rewards. It started the trend lasting the rest of his reign of James running a costly household whose expenditure ran out of control.

During the next decade obtaining the king's ear brought major political prizes as well as lavish patronage consequently there was great competition to become a gentleman of the Privy Chamber or at least one of the king's companions. Since the men who ruled the kingdom were also those with whom the king wanted to spend his leisure, this created intense political rivalry between Chamber and Privy Council. With different factions struggling at court for the upper hand, securing the person of the king became ever more vital. The 1580s and early 1590s witnessed a succession of coups d'état and attempted seizures of the king, some violent or apparently threatening James' life. Such volatility within court politics was largely the function of James' age and relative inexperience. In an unfortunate correlation, the more James personally decided where to bestow his favour, the more likely he was to be kidnapped. Those who seized the king assumed he was still young enough to be forced to abandon a favourite or switch policies. When he put his leg across the doorway preventing the king from leaving following the Ruthven Raid, the Master of Glamis callously explained to a weeping James, 'Better bairns greet then bearded men', a remark the king never forgave.[3] The institution of the Royal Guard failed to solve the problem, though even the parsimonious Elizabeth thought its expense worthwhile. As James gained control, the fiction of replacing bad advisors wore so thin that the attempted coups and kidnaps transmogrified into failed rebellions.

---

[3] D. Calderwood, *The History of the Kirk of Scotland* (Wodrow Society, 8 vols, Edinburgh, 1842–9), III, 643.

An additional destabilising factor was the arrival of a new political generation, producing a similar effect to the turbulence of the post-Flodden years. Both Esmé Stuart (Lennox) and James Stewart (Arran) had burst as unknowns upon the Scottish political scene from the continent. Huntly and Bothwell were merely five years older than James, and of the other major kindreds, the Hamiltons had been banished and Angus was suffering from Morton's fall, whilst Argyll died in 1584 leaving a minor. More significant than age was the high level of hot temper, violent tendencies and ruthlessness found among the king's companions, an unusual counterpart to James' physical timidity. Arran's mercenary past made him notorious for a readiness to execute opponents, such as Morton or Gowrie. He also employed casual violence to those who crossed his path, such as knocking Lady Gowrie to the ground so forcibly that she fainted and was left lying in the Edinburgh street where she had come to beg the king for assistance. The brawling of local feuds found their way into court, sometimes perilously close to the king's person, as in 1583 when adjacent to the king's room, Bothwell launched an attack upon David Hume and the Captain of the Royal Guard had to break up the fracas. The following year, Bothwell ambushed Hume and cut him to pieces. When the poet William Fuller characterised James as a bringer of peace, this seemed a good distance from reality and his metaphor of spears being turned into pens a fond hope. These experiences and his intellectual assessment made James determined to end feuding among his nobility and his declaration in 1583 that he was a 'universal king' was intended to convey the message that the crown was above faction. He made strenuous efforts to separate court rivalries from local feuding and having tried particular and general reconciliations of feuding kindreds, moved to a general ban in the next decade, though he had a long struggle to make it fully effective.

CLASHES WITH THE KIRK

In addition to the struggle over the king's person and favour, the factions gathered around broad policy issues, though not always with great consistency. Friendship with England had been the automatic line of the king's party and the regents, though the satellite relationship brought frequent rubs and there was a continuing debate as to how it should be handled. Returning to a closer link with France or seeking Spanish help seemed a possibility, especially for Roman Catholics and those traditionally associated with the queen's men. With England acutely conscious of its own precarious position, any suggestion of influence in Scotland by the Catholic powers of France or Spain produced panic in London. The fate of the Dutch rebels and the Huguenot cause in France were hanging in the balance during the 1580s and the division of Europe along confessional lines was almost impossible to avoid. Although in retrospect the Catholic missions to Scotland had little political impact, the suggestion that James VI and the Scottish nobility might convert was seriously mooted.

Jesuit missions

As the Scottish Reformation had arrived on the back of a revolution leaving the former ecclesiastical structure intact, it was difficult for the Roman Catholic church to know how to recover its position, so in 1562 the Jesuit Father Nicholas de Gouda was sent to Scotland to assess the situation. Though an open secret, his mission was not officially countenanced by Mary, Queen of Scots and he filed a depressed report about the state of Catholicism in the kingdom. The collapse of Mary's cause at the end of the civil wars helped the Roman Catholic hierarchy treat Scotland as a mission field and it turned to the regular orders to undertake the task of reconversion. Though the dynamic, recently-founded order of the Jesuits was in the forefront of the European Counter-Reformation drive, Scotland was never one of its high priorities, and in the final decades of the century neither the pope nor the Jesuit General was entirely convinced a Jesuit presence in the country was helpful. Rivalry at Rome and in the field between the different orders also generated problems. One influential group of Scots who joined the Jesuits spearheaded the missions to their homeland. Linked with the diocese of Dunkeld and the Crichton family who had supplied its bishops, they comprised William Crichton, Edmund Hay, James Tyrie, Robert Abercrombie, James Gordon, John Hay and William Murdoch. Their main strategy was to target the king and courtiers for conversion and this inevitably drew them into a tangled web of political intrigue involving the Spanish and French monarchies. Preferring high-profile converts, they paid much less attention to supporting Catholicism in the regions. Tense relations between Seton, from the most steadfast of the Roman Catholic noble families, and William Crichton also upset the smooth running of the Jesuit mission during the 1580s. Along with the secular clergy and the other regulars, the Jesuits contributed to the preservation of Roman Catholicism in Scotland, though with hindsight their court conversion strategy seemed misplaced.

Preserving Scotland's alignment with the international Protestant cause was of overriding concern to the kirk and its political supporters. On the domestic front, the role of the kirk in the political process and its organisation and finances had become major areas of contention and direct confrontation. Opposing policies formed one element in the power struggles, though no faction became a single-issue party and individuals sometimes paid scant concern to the broader matters of policy.

Since Lennox was to all intents and purposes a Frenchman, his presence at the heart of Scottish affairs appeared to threaten the English amity. His previous association with the duc of Guise convinced the kirk it would only be a matter of time before he showed his true colours and turned into a persecuting Catholic. Levels of fear about Guisian influence reminiscent of Knox caused Durie, the current minister of St Giles', to inveigh against Lennox, even criticising the king for accepting horses from his French relative, as if they were the Trojan variety stuffed with papists. Lennox's conversion to Protestantism failed to ally such fears and a new Confession was drawn up containing a detailed attack upon specific Roman Catholic doctrines which was solemnly adopted by king and parliament in January 1581. The parading of its Protestant credentials in the King's (or Negative) Confession did not defuse the clash six months later between Lennox's regime and the General Assembly. The appointment of Robert Montgomerie to the archbishopric of Glasgow was a gift to the presbyterian opposition because the battle was fought where they had particular strengths, in the newly reorganised university of Glasgow and within the Edinburgh presbytery. By combining a glaring abuse of practice with the general principle of episcopacy, Montgomerie's appointment united moderates and hard-liners in opposition to the blatant use of royal authority to override due process in the kirk.

When advising the king to nominate Montgomerie, Lennox was following the well-worn path of treating episcopal revenues as a source of wealth to be exploited. In return for a yearly income of £1,000, Montgomerie, later characterised as 'a stolid asse and arrogant', had agreed to lease all the archdiocesan lands to Lennox. When the Glasgow chapter refused to elect him, royal provision was used. Although the General Assembly was forbidden to meddle, it was able to dig up a mixture of charges against Montgomerie arising from his previous ministry at Stirling, including the prosaic accusation of drunkenness and holding the eccentric view that women were circumcised 'in the foreskinne of their forehead'.[4]

---

[4] Cited in D. G. Mullan, *Scottish Puritanism, 1590–1638* (Oxford, 2000), 163–4.

In March 1582 the presbytery of Stirling followed by the General Assembly suspended Montgomerie from his ministry, though the accompanying sentence of excommunication was blocked by royal command. Despite submitting to the Assembly, Montgomerie was pressurised to proceed by Lennox and Arran. On a communion Sunday with the entire congregation assembled in Glasgow Cathedral, the royal guard evicted the burgh's minister from the pulpit in favour of Montgomerie. The students, who had initially rioted on news of Montgomerie's appointment as archbishop and *ex officio* chancellor of the university, repeated the performance. In Edinburgh, Durie thundered from the pulpit about apostates, the presbytery excommunicated Montgomerie and the capital's streets were lined with people waiting with rotten eggs, sticks and stones to catch him as he left the burgh. With the provost's help, the harried archbishop escaped this gauntlet, though he faced similar condemnation in his diocese during his visit to Ayr. Highly amused by the tale of Montgomerie's capital farewell, the king still declared the excommunication null. For those plotting the Ruthven Raid, this episode provided a convenient polarising issue and a platform for keeping the anti-Catholic and anti-French debate alive. Gowrie was probably seeking a way to undermine Lennox and Arran when he received the excommunicated Montgomerie into his Edinburgh house, though in the end he chose the more forceful route of capturing the king: the standard ploy of royal minorities.

THE RUTHVEN RAID

A pro-English stance coupled with virulent anti-Catholicism were key unifying factors gathering the faction opposing the Lennox–Arran regime. They seized power when many of the nobility were away at justice ayres and the king was returning from a hunting trip in Atholl. The Raiders comprised nobles from Perthshire, Angus, Forfarshire and Fife, regions with long Protestant pedigrees, headed by Gowrie who, as treasurer, was bearing the brunt of the excessive household expenditure run up by Lennox and Arran. He was joined by Angus and Mar, the Master of Glamis, and continuity with the previous Morton regime was further emphasised by the involvement of Douglas of Lochleven, Glencairn and the Master of Oliphant. Concerns about the Francophile policies of Lennox and Arran had been vividly expressed the previous year by its veteran member, Lindsay of the Byres, who remarked on his departure from court, 'this sworde and buckler hath helped to dryve the Frenche men furthe of Scotland, and I fear yt muste be imployed to that use agayne'.[5] Having extracted Mary's abdication documents, he was no stranger to direct action against the ruler. Whilst being the pro-English faction helped broaden their appeal within Scotland, it failed to bring the expected assistance from the Elizabethan government.

Seizure of power by such an anti-Catholic regime was fulsomely and imprudently welcomed by the General Assembly as 'the lait actione of the Reformatione'.[6] In the event the Raiders proved better at grand gestures than passing presbyterian measures. In a piece of carefully stage-managed Protestant theatre, Durie made a triumphalist return to Edinburgh, starting from the Netherbow and coming up instead of down the High Street, deliberately reversing the route for a royal entry. Two thousand people with heads uncovered accompanied the minister around the burgh and processed to St Giles' singing Psalm 124, using the Peebles four-part setting (see the box on psalms and Protestant singing, p. 227). Though in this instance they celebrated divine deliverance, their consciousness of being a persecuted group remained dominant, having become an enduring feature of the radical Protestant mentality.

Continuing to hold James against his will coupled with the Master of Glamis' stinging observation that the teenager should return to playing with his hobbyhorse increased royal resentment. During the ten months they held the king, the Raiders failed to persuade him of their point of view or reconcile him to their control. Not even the delights of the fair town of Perth, the comfort of the newly-constructed Gowrie House with its picture-lined walking gallery, or exercise in the parks among the earl's favourite chestnut and walnut trees at Ruthven (Huntingtower) could compensate James for being a prisoner. The king continued to transact routine business, for example ordering Douglas of Lochleven to show consideration to a tenant, adding a revealing postscript, 'mak me quite (quit) of this sillie auld manis cummer (bother)'.[7] The death of Lennox in France in 1583, after he had been forced to leave the country, deeply upset James who blamed the Raiders for the loss of his closest friend and, turning to poetry, poured out his grief in 'The Phoenix'. Lacking the charm or arguments to woo the king, the Raiders and their policies were overthrown as soon as James escaped their clutches in June 1583. Having learnt enough of kingly craft not to make victims, James did not immediately pursue Gowrie and his associates.

[5] Cited in S. Adams, 'Patrick Lindsay, 6th Lord Lindsay of the Byres, 1521?–1589', *Oxford Dictionary of National Biography*.
[6] *Acts and Proceedings of the General Assemblies of the Kirk of Scotland* (3 vols, Edinburgh, 1839–45), II, 594.
[7] Cited in M. Sanderson, *Mary Stewart's People* (Edinburgh, 1987), 60.

THE ARRAN REGIME

They lost their power to Arran who rapidly became the dominant force in Scottish politics, bringing his particular brand of ruthless determination to the assertion of royal authority. His cruelty and naked pursuit of power were combined with learning, wit and one of the most persuasive tongues of his generation. With many of the policies he pursued being continued after his fall, it is not clear how far James was originating them or being convinced by Arran. However, the confrontational style of implementation bore Arran's mark as did the violent language of the threat to the Edinburgh ministers in 1584, 'though their craig wer als great as hay stacks, ther head suld ly at their heeles'.[8] For all his bullying talk, Arran acted in the name of the king, used legal process to execute his enemies and employed the parliament of May 1584 to implement his programme. In the drafting of its legislation and the efficient running of government he was assisted by John Maitland of Thirlstane who had been appointed secretary and proved to be his successor.

The first of the Acts labelled 'black' in presbyterian historiography was a sweeping assertion of 'the royall power and auctoritie over all statis alsweill spirituall as temporall within this realme' and declaring the king was judge over every subject. Criticism of the crown or writing books undermining regal power were made offences and, with his tutor safely dead, James named Buchanan's *De iure* and his *History* as containing 'offensive materis'. Forbidding any assembly that did not possess the king's licence caught the newly-established presbyteries, and all other unauthorised religious gatherings, within its copious net. Another heavy blow to the kirk's presbyterian wing was the jurisdiction granted to Patrick Adamson, archbishop of St Andrews. At the same time the moderates could take comfort from the re-affirmation that, 'the word of God salbe prechit and sacramentis administrat in puritie and synceritie' and that something would be done for ministerial stipends.[9] A tough line was taken with the clergy, requiring them to subscribe to the Parliamentary Acts. Though mitigated by Maitland's negotiations that permitted a conditional subscription, the high profile of the twenty-two ministers and university professors who went into exile rather than subscribe turned it into a significant revolt. The exiles congregated in London where they were the toast of their English puritan brethren and could conduct a propaganda campaign against Adamson. In an important extension of protest to include lay

---

[8] Calderwood, *The History of the Kirk of Scotland* IV,143.
[9] *The Acts of the Parliaments of Scotland* (12 vols, Edinburgh, 1844–75), III, 292–303.

women, Janet Guthrie and Margaret Marjoribanks, daughters of prominent burgesses and wives of the two Edinburgh ministers, seized the
opportunity to move into print against the archbishop showing the 'godly
sisters' were more than willing to enter the fray. Those clergy trying to find
a *modus vivendi* with the Arran regime, such as Rollock, counselled moderation and the avoidance of bitter attacks upon royal policies. Such compromise was later dismissed by Calderwood in his description of Rollock
as 'a godly man but simple on the matters of church government'.[10]

Arran's target was the independence of the burghs as well as that of the
kirk. He made a concerted effort to draw them directly under royal control
by placing royal appointees in seven of the dozen leading burghs, with
Dundee, Perth, Glasgow, Stirling, Dumfries and Cupar suffering alongside the capital. Most noble placemen were inserted to boost their regional
influence at the expense of a member of the Ruthven Raiders: Rothes was
put into Cupar to counter Lindsay of the Byres whose main residence at
Struthers lay close to the burgh, and in Stirling an Erskine client was no
longer acceptable. In Dundee the arrival of Crawford as Provost threatened to embroil the burgh in his long-standing feud with Glamis. Getting
Montrose in and Gowrie out of Perth had to wait until the disgrace and
execution of the Raiders' leader in 1584, and the attempt to unseat
Maxwell from Dumfries was flatly refused. Arran made himself Provost
in the capital, nominating the other burgh officers and, in an unprecedented move, the burgh council elected the kirk session. The year-long
struggle for dominance in Edinburgh marked the changing of the generations and the withering of the radicalism among the leading merchants
so noticeable during the civil wars. It was the last point involving the political generation active during the Reformation: most, like 'King Guthrie',
had died or retired, like Alexander Clerk. With them the strong
Anglophile sentiments disappeared that had connected the capital so
closely to the English ambassador. Arran's rough handling of the burghs
did not outlast his hold on power and proved an extreme example of how
electing noble provosts embroiled burghs in political faction fighting.

Grabbing Hamilton estates in addition to their earldom, Arran
set himself up at Kinneil, the stylish residence on the upper Forth, and
collected further rewards, such as the keepership of Stirling, wrested
from the Raider, Mar. After the Raiders' unsuccessful attempt to regain
control over the king, Arran secured Gowrie's execution and took the
Ruthven lands in East Lothian and Dirleton Castle. Thanks to Argyll's
death, he was also able to act as chancellor. Arran's accumulation of

[10] Calderwood, *The History of the Kirk of Scotland*, VIII, 47.

offices, control of the royal signature and near monopoly of influence upon the king 'maid the haill subiectis trimble under him, and every man dependit upon him'.[11] According to his opponents his power was used for corrupt and greedy ends. Arran's 'divelish wife', Elizabeth, who was Atholl's daughter, brought her forceful personality into the political arena. Having earlier divorced her second husband to marry her lover, Arran, she relished being the principal lady in the land. The kirk's ministers named her 'Lady Jezebel' and other enemies claimed she sat with the judges in the Court of Session to guarantee her financial gain; there was even a rumour she was to be made comptroller. Contemporaries' mutterings about the countess' consultation of witches have suggested she might be the model for Shakespeare's Lady Macbeth.

Based upon their control at court and capitalising upon their Stewart names, Arran and his countess created a new Stewart kin network. Bothwell, the king's cousin, was initially drawn into that circle, but being a magnate with his own Borders powerbase, he was more a rival than a client. In the long run the consolidation of a Stewart group benefited the king, who was able to draw those of his surname to him. Although appearing all powerful, Arran did not have the time to construct a regional base and relied entirely upon the king's favour for his position. Once toppled in 1585 and stripped of his title, he was forced to depart for his wife's jointure lands in Inverness-shire. Though he plotted busily, 'Lord Quondam', as his enemies nicknamed him, found no way back to court. His past ruthlessness in executing Cunningham of Drumquhassill prevented a full reconciliation with the kirk and in 1596 he was hacked to death by Douglas of Torthowald and his retinue in revenge for the execution of Morton, Douglas' uncle.

ANOTHER STEP TOWARDS INDEPENDENT RULE

When Arran was expelled from Stirling Castle on 1 November 1585 by the unlikely combination of the Protestant Raiders returned from English exile and the Roman Catholic Maxwell, he was not replaced by a single favourite. The secretary, Maitland of Thirlstane, who along with the Master of Gray had masterminded the plot, became James' most important adviser and the king decided to spread his favour across a broader range of the nobility. Misjudging the strength of his new position,

[11]   Sir James Melville, *Memoirs of his own life 1549–93*, ed. T. Thomson (Bannatyne Club, 18, Edinburgh, 1827), 324.

Maxwell's overt attendance at Mass in his Dumfries lodgings and then more publicly in nearby Lincluden college landed him in trouble. His conversion the previous year and the high profile of the king's friend Huntly caused alarm in the kirk. Huntly led a regionally-based alliance of Crawford, Montrose and Errol, all of Catholic persuasion and local opponents of the Ruthven Raiders. It was possible their religious stance might furnish the makings of a Catholic party in Scotland willing to ally with France and Spain. James, though personally firmly convinced of Protestant doctrines, refused to accept individual Catholics should be excluded from his court or from his friendship. By such an attitude, he remained in tune with most Scottish peers who held fast to birth and kindred and avoided rigid divisions among themselves along confessional lines. Nevertheless, while 'church papists' were acceptable, a minimal outward conformity to Protestant religious practice was expected. The militant Counter-Reformation Catholicism of recent converts, such as Maxwell, introduced a confessional dimension into magnate politics.

James took relations with his fellow European monarchs extremely seriously and it was the area in which his personal stamp was most visible. As soon as he reached adolescence the matter of his marriage was raised and significantly the king took his time over the decision; in the end, he chose a bride from Denmark and not England. Despite the lack of a direct heir and controversy over who might be the heir presumptive, the Scots never suffered the succession twitchiness afflicting the English. That Tudor succession tangle formed part of the other major issue James had to face: his relations with England in the light of his mother's imprisonment and his own claims to the throne. If anything had been learned from Mary, Queen of Scots' diplomacy, it was that the English succession should not become the sole objective of foreign relations. Keeping his options open and not alienating fellow rulers formed the central components of James' approach. What he was unable to countenance in public he was willing to discuss in secret with representatives of the French and Spanish monarchies and even the pope. Dangling the possibility of his co-operation or even conversion to the Roman Catholic faith enabled James to keep negotiating channels open and not irrevocably alienate any continental power. At the minimum this ensured he was not completely bypassed during discussions concerning the restoration of Mary, Queen of Scots, or the conversion of Scotland and the British mainland. The fanciful portrait of Mary and James was probably painted as visual propaganda for their joint rule, one of the options under consideration.

Such a foreign policy stance did not constitute the clear-cut and heroic espousal of the Protestant cause the militant clergy were constantly urging upon him. The mid-1580s were a particularly dangerous time for Protestantism with a resurgent Tridentine Catholicism regaining ground within Europe and mounting a fierce polemical campaign, with the veteran Catholic theologian James Laing weighing into the fray with his Latin treatises attacking the Reformers. The death of Anjou provoked the rise of the Catholic League to block the Huguenot heir to the French crown, and the assassination of William of Orange in June 1584 gave Spain hope that Parma could end the Dutch Revolt. Elizabeth finally made a treaty with the Dutch, sending an expeditionary force to the Netherlands that created almost as many problems as it solved. With outright war between England and Spain around the corner, there was a new English willingness to talk about an alliance with Scotland. Aware a formal treaty had not hitherto been on offer, James was anxious to conclude one and secure a regular subsidy from Elizabeth. A sign of James' personal confidence was his decision to agree the terms of the Treaty of Berwick, though Secretary Maitland thought a better deal might have been extracted. The Scottish king had sought, but not received, a firm gesture of recognition of his legitimate place in the succession, with an English title, such as duke of Cornwall, giving him lands and a position to counter the charge that, as a foreigner, he could not inherit the throne. The subsidy did materialise, referred to as an 'annuity' by the Scots and 'gratuity' by the English, which spoke volumes about the different views of the same sum. Being a pensioner of the English queen did not sit easily with Scottish pride, but the irregular and varying payments worth on average £30,000 (Scots) a year made a significant difference to the Scottish king's income, running at approximately £150,000 a year, though, thanks to inflation, not stretching very far.

THE GREAT TEST: MARY, QUEEN OF SCOTS' EXECUTION

The greatest test James faced in Anglo-Scottish relations was his handling of the trial and execution of his mother. By November 1586 he had become more adept at the diplomatic game, and his letter following the verdict at Mary's trial to William Keith, his ambassador in London, was composed with great care. Knowing his exact words would reach the English queen, he wrote of the dishonour of subjects condemning a sovereign prince and pointedly remarked how Henry VIII's reputation was not impaired by 'anything but in the beheading of his bedfellow. But yet that tragedy were far inferior to this'. It was a shrewd dig, predictably provoking Elizabeth's anger, and the second part of the letter reported how James could hardly move within his realm 'for crying out of the whole people' against the English queen which, as James explained, he could not criticise 'except I would dethrone myself, so is whole Scotland incensed with this matter'.[12] The rest of Europe was gripped by the unprecedented spectacle of the public trial of a queen followed by her formal condemnation. Within English domestic politics, obsessed by the succession and the Roman Catholic threat, the removal of Mary had acquired a compelling logic, though few outside that fevered atmosphere believed execution would follow.

When the execution came, the queen of Scots played her final and triumphant scene to perfection, successfully portraying her adopted role as

---

Mary, Queen of Scots' last letter

Nothing so became Mary as her death, when she achieved great regal dignity as she went to her execution, convinced in her own mind she was dying for her faith. Her last letter was written at 2 a.m. on the morning of 8 February to her brother-in-law, Henry III of France, asking him to pay her servants and organise prayers for her soul and sending as a remembrance two gems as talismans against illness to keep him in good health. In a calm manner, Mary related her view of how she had come to this position:

Royal brother, having by God's will, for my sins I think, thrown myself into the power of the Queen my cousin, at whose hands I have suffered much for almost twenty years, I have finally been condemned to death by her and her Estates . . . Tonight, after dinner, I have been advised of my sentence: I am to be executed like a criminal at eight in the morning. I have not had time to give you a full account of everything that has happened . . . you will learn the truth, and how, thanks be to God, I scorn death and vow that I meet it innocent of any crime, even if I were their subject. The Catholic faith and the assertion of my God-given right to the English crown are the two issues on which I am condemned, and yet I am not allowed to say that it is for the Catholic religion that I die, but for fear of interference with theirs . . .[13]

---

[12] James VI to William Keith, ?27 November 1586, in *Letters of James VI and I*, ed. G. P. V. Ackrigg, 74–5.
[13] Mary, Queen of Scots' last letter is held by the National Library of Scotland; images, a transcription and translation from the French are on the NLS website, http://www.nls.uk/.

a Roman Catholic martyr, complete with rosary, crucifix and the startling red underskirt revealed as she disrobed for her execution. Rather than religious sacrifice, it was the blood's cry for vengeance that was uppermost in the minds of outraged Scots. There was a prolonged and deep-felt outcry in Scotland, demonstrated at the end of the meeting of the Scottish Parliament in August when the assembled company dropped to their knees and swore to avenge Mary's death. James, as the aggrieved monarch and son, very much in that order, wrote to Elizabeth after the execution, in one of the most important letters he ever composed. It was a short missive full of bitter irony, especially concerning the tortuous plea of innocence the English queen had produced when she protested that the execution warrant was served without her knowledge. As James dryly commented, 'I wish that your honourable behaviour in all times hereafter may fully persuade the whole world of the same'; meanwhile he would expect 'a full satisfaction'.[14]

One intractable problem for James was that if he satisfied his honour by attacking England, as Maxwell was straining on the West March to do, he might well find himself tucked up with the powerful bedfellows of France and Spain, unable to resist their Catholic embrace. The French had conveniently remembered Mary was a Queen Dowager, with a reputation for beauty now rounded off with religious martyrdom. Their outcry at her execution was deafening and overnight Mary became a popular saint in France. It was fortunate for James and Scotland that Henry III was so far embroiled in the religious wars he was unable to exploit this wave of emotion. For Philip II, by contrast, Mary the safely dead martyr offered an extremely useful additional justification for launching the Armada against heretical England.

Despite the extreme strain placed upon it, the Anglo-Scottish alignment held in 1587 and, of equal or greater importance, in 1588 in face of the Armada; the Scottish king and his kingdom had become sufficiently Protestant for a full Roman Catholic alliance to be unacceptable. There was also the matter of the English succession. Though no-one dared breathe it, the death of Mary removed any lingering doubt about James' right to rule in Scotland. There was little sign within the kingdom of the legitimism that was to surface as part of the royalist and Jacobite credo during the next two centuries. What was of greater concern to James, and something he wanted publicly removed, was any threat to his own succession rights in England that might follow from Mary's condemnation as an English traitor.

In the trial and execution of his mother James skilfully handled an unprecedented situation that would have taxed the most experienced

---

[14] James VI to Queen Elizabeth, late February 1587, in *Letters of James VI and I*, 84–5.

monarch. It provided an exceptionally hard first test for a king still finding his feet in the treacherous mires of foreign relations. He absorbed the sharp lesson that it was a lonely and thankless duty taking the final decision where every option was unpalatable. In the end, he chose to keep the alliance with Elizabeth and the hopes of succeeding to the English crown on her death. He avoided the grand, but futile, gesture of marching across the border in a revenge raid with the risk of unwelcome foreign entanglements. While not the most honourable of stances and disappointing many of his subjects, James' policy ensured the crisis was weathered, a catastrophe avoided and his long-term goals preserved intact. The dilemma facing James VI in 1587 had curious echoes of the situation confronting James IV after Sauchieburn. In each case a crowned ruler of Scotland met a violent death bringing some taint of regicide and a faint whiff of patricide or matricide. The similarity ended there because the psychological dimension was entirely different for the two successors. With no personal recollection and only a formal relationship by correspondence with his mother, there was no equivalent of the iron belt for James VI. In his old age the nightmare character haunting the king's dreams was neither his executed mother nor his murdered father; it was Buchanan, his harsh tutor.

A FRESH START

The brand new robes sported by its members gave the parliament of 1587 the air of a fresh start and several of its acts provided pointers as to how James VI's reign would develop in the future. The inclusion of the lairds regularised their position as an estate of the realm and added their consent to the constitutional mechanisms expected to fund the crown through regular taxation. Marking the symbolic end to the church–crown hybrid, episcopal revenues were annexed to the crown by an act that finally unravelled the different roles played by medieval bishops. The act imposing a General Band upon the Highlands tried to deal with disorder there by applying a method previously employed in the Borders. It also signalled that Lowland perceptions of justice and civilisation had become the standard for all Scottish regions: uniformity was now a goal of the sovereign state of Scotland and its monarch, James VI.

Belatedly by European standards, in the 1580s taxation and some elements of state-building became a permanent feature of life for Scots. One group who could afford to pay were the merchant elite of Edinburgh with their stranglehold over international trade and their financial dominance within their own burgh (see Table 14.1). By the 1580s the burgh had

Table 14.1 Edinburgh and taxation

Taxation within Edinburgh

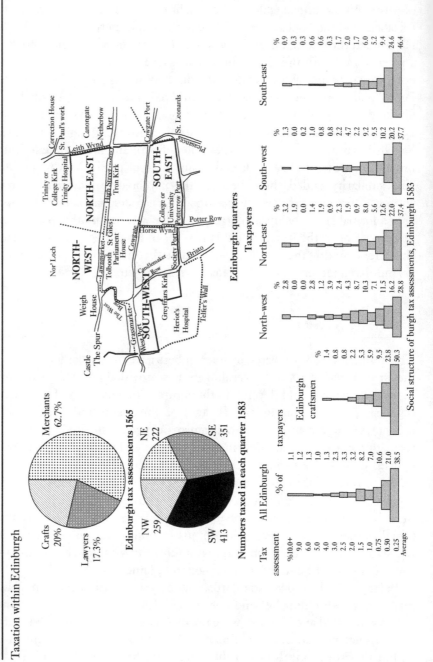

Social structure of burgh tax assessments, Edinburgh 1583

Edinburgh's share of burgh assessments 1587

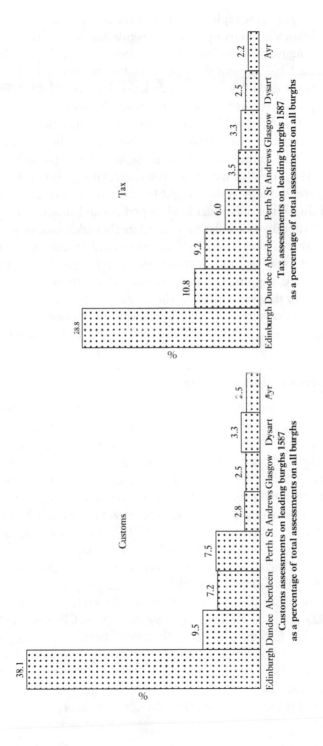

Customs

38.1 9.5 7.2 7.5 2.8 2.5 3.3 2.5

%

Edinburgh Dundee Aberdeen Perth St Andrews Glasgow Dysart Ayr
Customs assessments on leading burghs 1587
as a percentage of total assessments on all burghs

Tax

28.8 10.8 9.2 6.0 3.5 3.3 2.5 2.2

%

Edinburgh Dundee Aberdeen Perth St Andrews Glasgow Dysart Ayr
Tax assessments on leading burghs 1587
as a percentage of total assessments on all burghs

clearly emerged as the capital of the country in the political and economic spheres. From a low starting point, Glasgow had begun its rise to prominence, having reached the level of St Andrews by this decade, though the west and the Clyde remained the poor relation compared to the east-coast burghs. By the end of the 1570s trade levels had picked up sufficiently to create a proper recovery. However, some burghs remained in decline and others faced painful re-adjustments as they switched products and Scottish merchants had to find ways to compensate for the reduction in their traditional French and Spanish markets. Unfortunately, there was little sign they were learning from the enterprising Dutch how to establish an entrepot trade, as they might have organised in the Baltic, instead of remaining at the individual level of pedlars and single ships' cargoes.

The European-wide inflation was belatedly making major inroads into the Scottish economy and its effects were exacerbated by the currency debasements that saw the Scottish pound plummet in relation to the pound sterling, slipping from approximately a fifth to a twelfth of sterling's value in the second half of the century. The currency crash coincided with a particularly bad shift in climatic conditions during the 1580s when temperatures dropped and sea ice between Iceland and Greenland

---

Wadwives and moneylending

In 1579 when Esmé Stuart first came to Scotland he stayed with Janet Fockhart, an Edinburgh merchant and 'wad-wyfe' or moneylender. Janet had recently faced the trauma of her third husband's suicide, giving the crown rights to his goods and leaving her to bring up her seven children and run the business. Her shrewd business sense allowed her to accumulate sufficient capital from her trading ventures to move into straight moneylending with her clients drawn from the nobility, professions and the government. The earl of Orkney was a long-term customer and at one time borrowed 1,200 merks, whilst Glamis owed over £1,000. Valuables were pledged as security or pawned, possibly accounting for Janet's large collection, including a jewel portraying Noah's Ark. On her death her moveable estate was worth over £22,000 and her house in Fowler's (now Anchor) Close was extremely comfortably furnished. Elspeth Nair, who lived in Edinburgh's High Street, dealt in smaller amounts, loaning to the local baxter's wife and neighbours who might pledge a gold ring or a silver belt or clothes. The great demand for credit and cash, previously supplied by foreign merchants and goldsmiths, allowed wadwives to flourish.

continued throughout the summer with storms generating great sand-blows, changing the coastline as at Udall in Harris. Crops failed, bringing a serious subsistence crisis in the middle of the decade accompanied by plague, producing great hardship and slowing the economy. With the growing dominance of a cash economy in the Lowlands, the value of money became important to increasing numbers of Scots, forcing some into vagrancy or extreme poverty. Since the wealth of many nobles could not easily be liquidised, the urge to borrow cash to pay for luxury items proved overwhelming and this was fed by a rapidly emerging credit system with the accompanying problems of debt.

The more enterprising nobles found sources of income by marketing their agricultural produce and fish or exploiting resources such as coal and salt. Alongside these new industries was the more traditional and lucrative export trade in Scottish soldiers, with mercenaries going in increasing numbers to Ireland, the Netherlands and France, and to Denmark and the Baltic.

THE LESSONS OF APPRENTICESHIP

The minority and apprenticeship of James VI had not lasted as long as that of James V, though the civil strife had been more intense. As before, foreign interference increased the kingdom's instability but, with France no longer a serious player, Scotland had become a satellite state of England. As James was ending his apprenticeship, the realm experienced a return to some notice in European affairs, in part due to the conspiracies of Mary, Queen of Scots in England and Philip II's growing interest in launching his Armada to invade the British Isles. Firmly located on the Protestant side of the confessional fence, Scotland possessed none of the bargaining counters in international relations enjoyed by James V in the 1530s.

Having been carefully educated as a 'Rex Stoicus', James developed a conscious strategy of kingship, though reacting against the Buchanan mould he sought to re-establish the status and authority of the Stewart monarchy at home and abroad. The political volatility during his apprenticeship and early adult rule taught him painful lessons about the need to react and adapt his tactics to the current situation. He learned to hold his political cards tightly to his chest, leaving his subjects, and later historians, guessing as to his precise intentions. The personal element within ruling, and the person of the monarch, remained central to Scottish national politics, ensuring that James' character was of critical importance. Over the sixteenth century, the context of governance had altered and that great prop of the monarchy, the church–crown hybrid, had died. When James IV had considered exercising his imperial kingship throughout his realm, he travelled to the different regions. His great-grandson's sense of being a 'universal king' rested upon a more abstract conception of royal authority, assuming his writ should be obeyed across the kingdom. Rather than a reaction to residing in London following the 1603 union of the crowns, 'government by pen' was an attitude of mind already present in Scotland in the 1580s.

In retrospect, Mary's personal rule appeared a brief interruption to the succession of regents and the power struggles provoked by royal minorities. By the 1580s there was a tangible feel of the changing of the guard within magnate politics since the main protagonists, the Hamiltons, the Douglases and the Lennox Stewarts had either suffered an eclipse or been superseded and the other major Houses of Argyll and Huntly were led by young heirs. That decade witnessed one of the cyclical adjustments periodically experienced by the nobility when the personnel shifted while the social group retained its political pre-eminence. In addition to a reconfiguration of the peerage, there was a strengthening of the bottom of the noble pyramid with the addition of the 'bonnet lairds' as a consequence of the feuing movement. This alteration in land-holding slowly introduced a new breadth and depth to local and regional politics. To preserve their social and political position at national, regional and local level, existing noble families were also adapting their attitudes and learning new skills. A new twist to an old theme was to acquire legal training and the second half of the sixteenth century saw the emergence of the 'men of law' as a distinct professional group, having entirely shed their clerical past. They were joined by the professionalised ministers, a different breed of clergy from their late medieval predecessors, and by the medical practitioners. By the 1580s the lawyers, ministers and doctors, who would do so much to shape Scottish society in the future, had arrived.

The kingdom's international standing had declined as France's and the rest of Europe's interest moved elsewhere in the second half of the century and Scotland was reduced to being a minor counter on the Protestant side of the confessional board. Its diplomatic and religious position and its weakness after 1567 had turned the realm into an English client and this British context, especially in the guise of the English succession, had dominated Scottish foreign policy-making. Ironically, his mother's execution gave James VI considerably more freedom to manoeuvre, which he employed to excellent effect in his foreign policy. The revival of the Danish alliance was a reinvigoration of the fifteenth-century alignment with Scotland facing east again across the North Sea and through the Sound into the Baltic. What had been lost for good was the North Atlantic community linking the Northern Isles to Norway and Iceland. The most obvious consequence of the constitutional revolution of 1567 and the queen's deposition was the determination it engendered in her son and a significant section of the political nation to bury its memory. These efforts only served to bring the issue of sovereignty to the forefront of political debate and that inevitably became associated with the equally vigorous discussion about the role and place of the kirk within the Scottish polity.

Amidst the considerable heat and less light generated by these quarrels, it was easy to overlook the broad consensus in favour of 'civil values'. Drawing its inspiration from late Renaissance humanism, this vision of a 'civilised' society could be found across the artistic range in the construction of country houses and their carefully planned gardens to the philosophical sentiments of Neo-Stoicism and the composition of elegant Latin poetry. At a more mundane level, it informed the drive for social control among the urban oligarchies and the *politique* stance in political life that eschewed ideological categorisation. To a limited extent, the search for this 'civility' helped fill with lay patronage part of the immense gap left by the disappearance of the commissions and personnel sustained by the late medieval church.

The double character of the death of the medieval Scottish church, being both instant and protracted, disguised its long-term effects upon the nature of governance in Scotland. Since the institutional organisation of the church was left intact in 1560, the church–crown hybrid took another twenty years to wither and die. Its death finally removed one ladder of social mobility, making it more, rather than less, difficult for a bright commoner to rise through crown service to the top of the tree. The monarchy was left without a rival, fully sovereign and imperial in theory, but in practice having to adapt to the loss of ecclesiastical finance and personnel.

The mid-1580s filled Scots with fear and foreboding as three years of bad harvests starting in 1585 were followed, as so often before, by the plague. In 1588 the sense of apocalyptic tension was heightened by the launching of the Spanish Armada, ostensibly to avenge the Roman Catholic martyr, Mary, Queen of Scots. Scottish Protestants, including James VI, rejoiced as 'God's wind blew' and scattered the fleet. They looked forward with hope, but no sure expectation, to a presaged new age when God's providential mercies would transform Scotland into a holy people, the new Israel ruled by its godly king.

Conclusion: Scotland Re-formed

TIMOTHY PONT'S SCOTLAND

Much of everyday life in the 1580s would have been deeply familiar to those living a hundred years earlier. The remarkable set of maps sketched by Timothy Pont during the final twenty years of the sixteenth century offer a unique window into the fascinating mixture of continuity and change he encountered when, as a young graduate, he put on his boots, took his travelling satchel and began to walk through Scotland. For about ten years between the 1580s and 1590s, Pont walked and sketched and looked and listened as he made his way across most of the kingdom, creating a series of sketch maps and recording the names and details of twenty thousand places he visited or noted. His work became the basis for the magnificent set of maps of Scotland published the following century by Bleau, and many of his sketches and descriptions survive. The son and brother of clerics, Pont later became minister in Dunnet, Caithness. Like Archdeacon Monro' *Description of the Western Isles*, Pont's project was associated with the territorial structure of the church in Scotland: it was planned to replace the diocesan framework underlying Monro's description by a complete system of district presbyteries and Pont was charged with discovering suitable locations. Significantly, Pont's remit was the whole of Scotland rather than a single region, symptomatic of the subtle shift of emphasis from region to kingdom. It reflected a sense of public or civil spirit which had been incorporated into a form of nationalism that had developed alongside the appreciation of 'place' in one's region and locality.

Pont employed a qualitative approach to geographical data, called chorography, that showed the political and social contours of each region, in addition to its geographical features. He had recently left St Andrews

University where he had been a member of the Melvillian circle of radical, Presbyterian intellectuals. Taught by Welwood, the lawyer and mathematician, chorography formed a vital methodology allowing the development of a dynamic vision that institutional change and adaptation were possible and desirable. This was a profoundly important conceptual shift away from the standard distrust of innovation encapsulated by George Hay in 1569, 'the very name of innovation is rightly detested by all men of wisdom'.[1] Thanks to chorography, Pont and his fellow radicals believed they could work out practical solutions to the problems the kingdom faced in the closing decades of the century.

On the surface, Pont's maps, with their spidery writing and little pictograms, appear to present a static picture of the realm moulded by the contours of the land, its coasts, rivers, hills and glens and the difficulties of travelling by land through its different regions. His careful recording of the patterns of communication was the result of having walked most of the routes himself. Pont had an excellent eye for the shape of mountains and their place in the landscape, such as his sketch of Ben Lawers dominating Loch Tay (see Figure C.1). He drew the distinctive outlines of mountains such as Ben Vorlich, Suilven (named Skormynag in Pont) or Fuar Tholl (Benn Leckderg) and included mountain profiles such as Mount Keen, to signal the pass and the direction of the route to Glen Tanar. Scotland's river system dominated Pont's maps and the water courses provided the central features and orientation points for his sketches. With its indications of where rivers could be crossed and bridges or ferries existed, the maps illustrated how the pattern of Scottish settlement was moulded by the river system. They demonstrated the importance for all Scots of location and communications; here was a rural kingdom whose basic agricultural patterns had not altered. The land remained the kingdom's fundamental resource and the source of most political power. Resting within that rural landscape, feudal relationships had ordered place and people and, though still recognisable on Pont's sketches, that feudal world was in the process of transition. In particular, the loss of the great monastic estates can be glimpsed: the Valliscaulian priory at Ardchattan on Loch Etive retained its ecclesiastical symbol on the map, though by the time Pont passed, it had already become a comfortable family home for the last commendator, who successfully established his lineage there.

The sketches cleverly revealed the changing social contours of Scotland since one of the chief characteristics of Pont's choreographical

---

[1] George Hay's oration to King's College Aberdeen in 1569, cited in D. Stevenson, *King's College, Aberdeen, 1560–1641* (Aberdeen, 1990), 20.

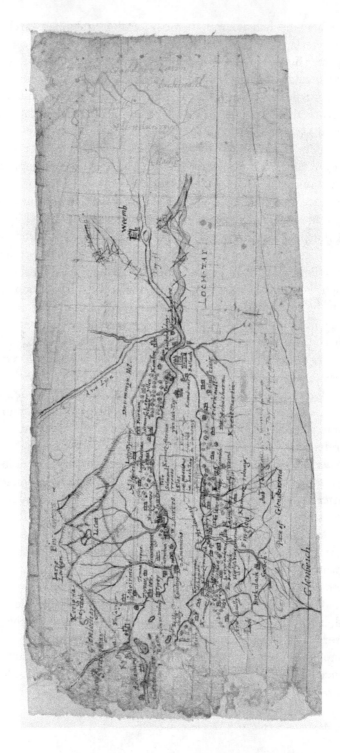

Figure C.1 Pont's sketch of Loch Tay and Ben Lawers, c. 1590s. [NLS Pont 18]

approach was his attention to the visible manifestations of noble power within the regional landscape. Whilst many settlements were indicated by a simple sign, noble houses received special attention with accurate elevations of the buildings. The wave of new building in the countryside and within the burghs appearing on the sketches demonstrated how the higher levels of Scottish society were especially concerned to leave their architectural mark upon the landscape. In the written descriptions accompanying the maps, comment was made upon noble lineages and their deeds, expressing the chivalric milieu of late medieval and early modern Scotland where the feudal nobility continued to function as the powerful hub of each region. A close look at the details on the maps revealed the sixteenth-century changes: instead of castles with moats or other defences, many noble residences were newly-constructed country houses surrounded by parks and gardens. The economic potential of estates was carefully noted on the sketches and in the descriptions, such as Pont's comments on Loch Maree surrounded by beautiful hills and woods of holly and Scots pine up to 80 feet in height 'of good and serviceable timmer for masts and raes (sailyards), in other places ar great plentie of excellent great oakes, whair may be sawin out planks of 4 sumtyms 5 foot broad'.[2] Changed days from the late fifteenth century, when the MacLeods of Gairloch and the incoming Mackenzies who settled around Loch Maree counted their wealth in men, without a thought to the trees. By noting the existence of minerals, coal, salmon or herring, and other resources, Pont reflected the growing concern with exploitation and profit that was rivalling lordship over men.

When drawing Scottish burghs and urban landscapes, the map-maker paid careful attention and used capital letters. The long-standing jurisdictional mentality that emphasised burgh privileges was visibly portrayed by the distinctive trons and mercat crosses, shown at Forfar, or a new tolbooth at Nairn or the drawing of burgh boundaries and proper stone walls encircling Stirling or Perth. Future expansion and prosperity can be seen in Glasgow's cruciform layout, already spreading beyond a basic street pattern, or the wealth displayed by the arcades on the houses in Linlithgow High Street. By contrast, the relative stagnation and lack of pressure on urban land can be viewed in the lines of burgage plots in Dumfries which, unusually, have no building on the backlands.

Since the territorial pattern of parish churches remained intact, the visual impact of the Reformation upon a map of Scotland's localities was

---

[2] *Macfarlane's Geographical Collections*, ed. A. Mitchell (3 vols, Scottish History Society, 1st ser. 51–3, Edinburgh, 1906–8), II, 540.

muted rather than startling. In both town and countryside, churches continued to dominate the landscape, with drawings of St Mary's in Dundee, the broadest church (174 feet) in Scotland, or Pont's fine depictions of Elgin Cathedral or the Kirk of Farr in Strathnaver. In a wider context, the entire mapping project was linked to the creation of accurate information for siting Scotland's presbyteries. The apparent fixity of the sketches hid the underlying framework of a radical rethink about the ecclesiastical and civil administrative structures of the kingdom. Janus-like, Pont's maps look both backwards, showing the great continuities, and forwards, marking the changes. They give a visual representation of the imprint of the previous hundred years as well as signalling some forthcoming developments.

RE-FORMING THE KINGDOM

In the century following the accession of James IV, the kingdom of Scotland had been re-formed by a series of dramatic events combined with slower transformations of cultural, social and political life. The country had been shaken by personal tragedy and national humiliation after the battle of Flodden in 1513, though its long-term consequences pale into insignificance beside the trauma of the mid-century Battle for Britain, which marked a turning point in Scotland's economic, military and diplomatic fortunes. The Reformation crisis of 1559–60 generated two revolutions, confessional and diplomatic, that proved permanent whilst the constitutional revolution of 1567 had a more ambiguous legacy.

Alongside these eye-catching events were the deeper transformations which re-formed the world known to James IV and his contemporaries. What no Scot could fail to notice, when comparing the state of his or her country in 1587 with the kingdom's position in 1488, was the disappearance of the pre-Reformation church. So much more than a religious revolution, its demise had massive consequences for the political, cultural, social and economic life of Scots. It lay at the centre of the kingdom's re-formation within four broad areas: the nature of its governance and political structure; its religious life; the integration of the kingdom; and its place in Europe.

In one way or another, the consequences of the disappearance of the pre-Reformation church were immense and affected the life of everyone in Scotland. The cultural consequences were at their most dramatic when the skills and patronage deficit following the Reformation proved nearly fatal, particularly for the continued existence of a musical culture in

Scotland and for the survival of the tradition of monumental sculpture in the West Highlands. The legislation of the 1560 Parliament removed the *raison d'être* of the song schools, the collegiate choristers and singing clergy and many other musicians in Scotland: the existing corpus of church music could not be performed and no further commissions would be forthcoming. Within a relatively short time the skill base started to disappear and only the Act of 1579 re-establishing musical education stopped the rot. There was no such intervention to assist the decline in carving skills among West Highland sculptors. The loss of their secure ecclesiastical base and the dearth of commissions following the iconoclasm and the Protestant rejection of purgatory brought uncertainty over the future of funerary monuments. The hereditary families of sculptors either moved into another branch of the Gaelic learned orders or took up other occupations. Since their carving skills were not properly transmitted, there was a noticeable decline in quality when gravestones were next commissioned at the start of the seventeenth century. Although other branches of the arts fared better, all were affected by the loss of patronage and the institutional structure which had previously supported them.

The church-crown hybrid had accelerated the use of monastic commendatorships and put pressure upon all branches of the church to raise cash to sustain the crown. From a trickle at the start of the sixteenth century, feuing of church lands became a flood in the 1530s and the practice was also adopted on crown and noble estates. The great reservoir of monastic lands passed from the hands-on control of the abbey to the second-hand direction of the commendator and finally into the new hands of the feuars. The feuing movement created a much broader group of occupiers holding heritable possession of the land they farmed; the beginnings of the heritors who had such a long run in subsequent Scottish history. Those tenants unable to gain possession of their lands tended to be pushed down the social ladder and sometimes lost both lands and livelihood. The feuing movement altered the social, economic and political mix of the regions and helped establish a new market in land. The existence of a variety of types of landholder assisted the drift away from social rank and towards possession as a marker of social status alongside the recognition of a property qualification as proof of social reliability. The multiplication of feus helped dissolve the medieval association of landholding with manpower and with jurisdiction, and increased the importance of amassing wealth from the land, instead of merely drawing income from it. One consequence of looking for wealth creation was to encourage the systematic economic exploitation of the land's additional resources, such as Highland timber, or the coal and salt available for extraction along the Forth. Since the major products of the land were agricultural, there was a gradual growth in the marketing of foodstuffs over wider areas and distances. Even in the Highlands where supporting fighting men remained a high priority, the cattle trade was gathering momentum during the second half of the sixteenth century and 'frontier' burghs, such as Perth and Inverness, were supplying more goods to their hinterlands, usually in the packs of pedlars. The gradual change from holding land and jurisdiction towards running estates had a profound effect upon Scotland's economy and landward society.

The disappearance of the late medieval church caused a serious dislocation in the former methods of charitable provision and new channels were only slowly being created by the 1580s. With the population increase predictably placing greatest pressure upon the poor, more Scots found themselves in the precarious position of labouring for a wage and without any work during an economic downturn. Forming an underclass of the urban poor was a growing group of semi-employed or completely unemployed people, heavily dependent upon charitable assistance, especially when times were hard. The burgh oligarchies viewed these 'vagrant poor' with growing fear and distrust and made major efforts to rid themselves of this social problem, through the Poor Law legislation and using the kirk sessions as a means of social control.

THE NATURE OF GOVERNANCE

The 1580s witnessed the ending of the governmental world known by James IV and James V, as the church–crown hybrid they created disappeared. Its demise brought changes to the nature, aims and style of governance, but with a general distrust of innovation there was no proliferation of new institutions to take its place. Whilst in 1560 the medieval church institution had survived intact, it subsequently deflated like a slow puncture, leaving the crown without its main rival as a source of authority. The monarchy gradually absorbed most of the jurisdiction and political authority of the pre-Reformation church. As the single surviving pillar of society by the 1580s, the monarchy had little option but to reinvent itself and James VI, having the wit to realise the job needed doing, set about the task of asserting his sovereignty with a will. The legislative programme of 1584 and 1587 embodied the view that the crown's temporal authority had become the sole foundation underpinning society and all non-royal jurisdictions and authorities should be subordinated to the king. While authority might be delegated, it could not permanently be transferred or alienated. Hot debates flared over the precise location of sovereignty and the plenitude of power flowing from it, some asserting they lay with the crown in parliament, rather than with the king himself. During his adult reign, James VI vehemently contested this point, asserting that his authority originated directly from God and was not mediated via the people. Though a Presbyterian voice continued to uphold a distinct spiritual jurisdiction, the loss of the medieval church as a pillar of society had fundamentally redefined the understanding of political authority within Scotland. This concept of national sovereignty had replaced the imperial power proclaimed by James IV and James V.

The loss of ecclesiastical resources and clerical personnel entailed a fundamental reconfiguration of Scottish government. The greatest impact was felt in royal finance when church revenues and taxation were no longer available and ecclesiastical benefices, posts and pensions did not automatically refill the pool of patronage. Since it was imperative to find other sources of revenue to sustain government, regular taxation first became a feature of Scottish life in the 1580s. Equally profound consequences followed the shift from ecclesiastical to civilian personnel in royal government and administration. The disappearance of the spiritual lords left one type of nobility on which the crown could rely in the regions, removing the option of employing the substantial landed powerbases of the bishops or abbots as an alternative or counterweight to a magnate's regional authority. The structure and balance of national and regional political power was altered as the majority of ecclesiastical lands found their way into lay hands. The effects were most noticeable in parliament with the loss of power by the first estate. As commendators completed their metamorphosis into laymen, monastic representation ceased and the rump of the clerical estate, the bishops, became government yes-men with no political weight of their own. Since the clergy no longer constituted a proper estate, there was room for an 'extra' one, with the arrival of the lairds. This development brought the lower nobility into closer and more direct contact with the crown, although the lairds' links to, and through, the peers remained significant. The less welcome aspect of the increased consultation with the entire nobility was the regular taxation to which they found themselves agreeing in parliament.

At the more intimate level of counsel, the crown found its options restricted as climbing the clerical ladder to become a statesman, like Bishop Elphinstone or Cardinal Beaton, was no longer possible and all close royal advisers and members of the Privy Council were laymen. Though they had been king's men through and through, these prelates possessed the independent ballast and high status of their ecclesiastical positions to lend them political weight at the council table. In the 1580s Arran's authority rested entirely and precariously upon the king's favour and he was rendered powerless by his fall from grace.

A quick glance at the men who laboured in the royal administration suggested little had altered since the late fifteenth century. The clothes royal advisers wore were different, with courtly fashions replacing clerical attire, but legal expertise and training were proving as important in 1587 as they had been in 1488. Whilst the framework of legal expertise and even the curriculum in Roman and canon law remained constant, the context was new. The 'men of law' had broken free from their ecclesiastical chrysalis to form an independent legal profession. They had transformed the College of Justice into a body of professional judges, with the clerical requirement for the Presidency finally being dropped in 1579. When sitting in the Court of Session, the judges heard cases presented by advocates, who had established their own corporate identity in the Faculty of Advocates. The foundation of the College of Surgeons indicated the medical profession was following a similar path towards professional status and the kirk's ministers exhibited many characteristics of a professional body. Together these professional groups increased the diversity and formed a new element within Scottish society.

The growing emphasis upon legal expertise and formal training in the law gradually altered the prerequisites for holding an important office, such as the chancellor's post. While there had been plenty of legally-trained specialists in the past and their expert knowledge had been sought whenever needed by those making the decisions, a level of expertise was coming to be regarded as necessary for the decision-maker himself. Carrying the highest status, the chancellorship had been fought over by peers and coveted by spiritual lords anxious for the political authority and prestige it brought. Despite his university education, Angus deemed the office beyond his grasp in 1585 because 'it required skill in the lawes and more learning than hee had'. His friends retorted, 'learning does not alwayes [serve] the turne, knowledge of the customes of the Countrey is more requisite, and is onely required in Counsell'.[3] This exchange encapsulated the clash between the divergent views of the chancellor, as either a royal counsellor of the highest rank or a royal official discharging a specific set of duties. The legally-trained administrator *par excellence*, Maitland of Thirlstane, who received the vacant chancellorship not long afterwards, utilised the political power it brought to full effect. His elder

---

[3] Cited and discussed in K. Brown, *Bloodfeud in Scotland 1573–1625* (Edinburgh, 1986), 196.

brother, Maitland of Lethington, had been one of the closest of Mary, Queen of Scots' advisers, though holding the less prestigious office of secretary, because great magnates such as Huntly or Morton had been chancellor. In the interval between the two brothers' careers, assumptions concerning the chancellor's office had altered. Having carried into their new incarnation characteristics from their ecclesiastical past, the lawyers strove to redesign the style and purpose of civil governance. The need for uniformity, together with due and formal process, so beloved of the legal and administrative mind, were applied to the workings of national and regional governance, replacing the less formalised pattern where decisions based upon experience and tradition were taken by non-specialists.

FROM JUSTICE TO LAW

Such a formal and legal approach to governing brought an increased stress upon the 'rule of law', turning it into a defining attribute of government. The concept of a 'crime' was developing and becoming distinct from a wrong that needed to be righted, leading to the acceptance of a role for 'public prosecution'. A significant milestone was passed in 1579 when the Lord Advocate became able to prosecute a case on behalf of the crown and his role was to represent the 'common good', rather than a specific royal interest or grievance. Such developments downgraded traditional methods of private justice and feud settlement, emphasising instead disputes should be settled exclusively within the law courts. In addition, lower courts were treated as part of an integrated system whereby they were answerable to the central courts and the crown and run by those trained in law.

A legalistic approach to governing also brought greater stress upon legislation as a method of tackling problems. By giving priority to the most recent statute law, this reversed the previous assumption that the older the law or custom, the better it was. Statute law was assumed to have universal application, comprehending the entire kingdom and potentially omnicompetent. Parliament's willingness to encroach upon what had unequivocally lain within ecclesiastical jurisdiction was demonstrated in the anti-heresy legislation begun in 1525. Whatever its other reservations, there seemed few jurisdictional qualms in 1560 when parliament passed statutes abolishing the pope's authority in Scotland and forbidding the celebration of the sacraments according to the Roman Catholic rite. Major changes to the kirk continued to be made by statute, although the General Assembly was extremely active in passing its own legislation. In a less spectacular, but equally important, extension of its competence, parliament enacted statutes to solve social problems, such as the Poor Law passed in 1579.

Supplementing the formality and comprehensive reach of statute, the central courts generated a more legalised style to governance. The most significant institutional development in central government during the period was James V's establishment of the College of Justice, closely followed by the arrival of the Commissary Courts in 1564. By rapidly establishing the Court of Session as the highest court of appeal in civil cases and the court of first instance in key areas, its judges were literally able to lay down the law to lesser courts. The imposition of a clear hierarchy and structure within the court system cut across the self-enclosed existence of separate jurisdictions and undermined the 'jurisdiction mentality' of late medieval Scotland. The attention to making new law was matched by a desire to codify existing laws. This had a long pedigree with Scotland's first printers being granted a licence in 1507 to publish previous statutes, though they failed to exploit it and the first publication of the Acts of Parliament appeared in 1566. From at least the middle of the sixteenth century, collections of court decisions were circulating in manuscript in the *Practicks* compiled by Sinclair, Balfour and Maitland. The end of the century saw Skene's *Lawes and Actes* and his *Dictionary* of legal words and terms and Craig's major discussion of Scottish law in the *Ius Feudale*. Formal, written records became common in more branches of the administration and greater concern was demonstrated about their preservation with an act passed in 1587 directing the protocol books of deceased notaries to be lodged with the Lord Clerk. By the start of the next century this initiative had produced a central land register, the Register of Sasines: a stroke of bureaucratic genius that continues to serve Scots.

These early efforts to systematise the legal principles and practices of Scotland laid bare considerable variations in local practice and as legal uniformity became an increasingly important target, they ceased to be a matter of indifference. While at the start of the sixteenth century, Bishop Elphinstone had appreciated the variety of laws and customs operating within the realm, his successors made the equation that one kingdom should mean one law. With scarcely a whimper in 1560, the legal privileges enjoyed by churchmen disappeared and the courts spiritual were transferred and transformed into the Commissary Courts operating within the secular court system. A similar fate awaited in the seventeenth century for the differing legal practices found in the Northern Isles, the Highlands and Islands and the Borders.

Although utilising a similar vocabulary, the rule of law was different from the cry for 'justice' heard in fifteenth-century political struggles and reverberating through the royal minorities of the early sixteenth century. When demanding 'justice', many Scots had previously expected to receive the recompense and pacification achieved by feud settlement, and looked to the king to impose that type of peace and equity within their region. The rule of law enforced through the legal system was something different and, whilst the language of justice might be converted from one meaning to the other, the practice did not move as smoothly. James VI's long subsequent struggle to suppress feuding indicated that in the 1580s attachment to the ways of private justice remained remarkably strong and Scots were willing to fight to retain their right to feud. As was indicated by the bloodfeud in St Andrews in the closing decades of the century involving Welwood, the professor of civil law, the legal and urban elite were not immune from such kin pressure. Ironically, the feud completely disrupted the teaching of civil law in the university, from which the subject never recovered. The assumption that the government and the courts should monopolise the means of force, the right to employ coercion and legitimate violence, was very slow to take root in early modern Scotland.

The new ecclesiastical courts, which had inherited part of the jurisdiction of the former courts spiritual, lay outside the drive for legal uniformity found in the secular court system. The kirk session's astonishing success as the most effective institutional innovation of the period was due to the classic combination of mixing something old with something new. In a curious reversal, the legalised and procedure-bound methods of the courts spiritual and the canon lawyers who had staffed them moved into the civil courts and the royal administration. Conversely, in their procedure the kirk sessions adopted the less formalised style and methods associated with local courts and with private justice, under increasing pressure within that civil sphere. Since the higher nobility showed little desire during this period to become entangled at such a low level, the elders who sat on the session were those holding immediate local power and influence. For those on the middle rungs of the social ladder, the kirk session offered a forum for exercising power and an arena where social rank did not automatically count. The experience of exercising local control gained by a broad social group was to prove important in the next century. The kirk session also formed part of a comprehensive national administrative system, which complemented, though could also offer an alternative to, the traditional links of kinship, lordship and locality. The call for ideological solidarity to fight God's cause alongside spiritual kindred had the potential to cut across loyalties towards blood-kin and political and social leaders. As the Covenanting Wars of the following century demonstrated, when that call was heeded the comprehensive national organisation provided by the kirk's courts could furnish the basis for civil and military government.

The pattern of moral behaviour enforced by the kirk sessions suited the needs of the local oligarchies that ran them, especially in urban areas where session and burgh council frequently operated hand in glove. One noticeable effect of the emphasis upon policing sexual behaviour was to bring women into legal 'sight' in a way not experienced before, thereby making it easier to prosecute witches. Both the parish sessions and the district presbyteries were influenced by the pronounced urban perspective characteristic of Reformed Protestantism throughout Europe. The model of a strong burgh providing a catalyst for reform within its rural hinterland lay behind the experiments in the kirk with both regional superintendents and district presbyteries. Such a framework did not fit well within the Highlands, where kirk sessions and the style of ecclesiastical discipline they brought were not easily established. Since the methods employed to evangelise the Highlands deviated from the new 'norm' of Lowland practice, this created a further source of division between the two parts of the kingdom.

RELIGIOUS LIFE

Between 1488 and 1587 the greatest upheaval faced by most Scots occurred within their religious lives. Instead of being part of the sprawling multinational corporation of the medieval church, they found themselves within the tightly-focused national kirk. The Protestants who went into rebellion in 1559 wanted a doctrinally-driven root-and-branch reformation of the medieval church: they achieved a religious revolution. Putting the theology in place proved straightforward, with the positive adoption in 1560 of the Protestant Scots Confession of Faith and the negative abolition of papal authority and celebration of the Roman Catholic sacraments. Overnight this altered Scotland's official religious allegiance, rejecting the shared faith of medieval Christendom and replacing it by Reformed Protestant doctrine. For some, the removal of the rule of Antichrist was a cause for rejoicing, while others watched with sorrow as merriment and medieval piety departed, and a third group remained indifferent. Despite Protestant fears and forebodings, the religious revolution endured and proved a permanent change. The far harder tasks were establishing the new ecclesiastical organisation of the kirk and transforming the kingdom into a Protestant country and they proved to be long, difficult processes rather than speedy events. In seeking to create the new Israel on Scottish soil, the kirk became the driving force towards a new uniformity of belief and practice.

By the second half of the sixteenth century and having experienced two generations of reforming turmoil, most European states, including Scotland, found themselves propelled towards one or other confessional camp. The labels 'Protestant' and 'Catholic' were becoming indispensable badges of international alignment and elements within national identity. This European-wide process of confessionalisation emphasised the theological positions that divided the two camps, producing an 'ink divinity' among both Protestants and Roman Catholics.[4] In Scotland 'true doctrine' was especially glorified as the rock on which the kirk had been built, making doctrinal uniformity throughout the land an essential goal. Subscription to a written document with doctrinal statements, previously part of medieval heresy trials, had become the approved method of affirming religious orthodoxy and national identity. Between 1488 and 1587 the definition of being a Christian in Scotland had changed dramatically: it had started as a willingness to participate in the community of Christendom and had become an ability to affirm Protestant formulae.

For Scottish Roman Catholics as well as their Protestant neighbours, the world of late medieval Catholicism had vanished. By the 1580s the Catholics who had lived through the 1560 revolution were dying out, taking to the grave the assumption that they were still the church in Scotland. The Roman Catholic hierarchy had finally switched to a mission mentality, employing the religious orders to spearhead the attempt to bring the country back to Mother Church. Efforts were concentrated more upon the re-conversion of Scots, especially the king and nobility, than sustaining those communities where Catholic practice had been protected and survived. A new Counter-Reformation Catholic programme and identity were beginning to emerge in the 1580s which were as much a response to confessionalisation as the Protestantism they opposed.

The drive for Protestant conformity and uniformity banished the diversity of religious provision characteristic of the Scottish medieval church as the varieties of regular orders and secular clergy and the wide range of buildings and locations available for worship vanished. By choice

---

[4] The phrase was coined by John Bossy in his *Christianity in the West 1400–1700* (Oxford, 1985).

and by necessity, the kirk was a more compact organisation than its predecessor, with a single system and one main location and focus, the parish
church. Following the Reformation, a Scot was taught there was only one
model of religious practice and behaviour and a single style of holiness to
which one should aspire. With the individualistic Protestant emphasis
upon faith as the door to salvation, different forms of devotional expression developed. For the majority of Scots the attack upon previous pious
practices would have been most keenly felt. The boundaries between the
sacred and profane had been redrawn as a result of the major religious
changes in Scotland with a substantial contraction of those aspects of life
deemed 'sacred'. Compared to the sprawling 'spiritual domain' associated
with the medieval church, the kirk occupied a tightly-defined area
and policed it effectively. Altering the deeply-rooted underlying beliefs
proved a harder task, and the strong sense of place found throughout
Scottish life continued to assert the sacredness of particular locations.

During the second half of the sixteenth century a new Protestant culture
was establishing itself in Scotland based upon pride in the Reformation
achievement. The assumption that Scotland as a new Israel was in a
covenant relationship with God gave a sense of collective assurance and
reinforced the Protestant identity of the kingdom, breeding a particular
toughness to face the battle with those archenemies, Antichrist and the
Devil. It encouraged a self-consciously 'godly' wing whose affective piety
was coupled with a firm adherence to the rigorous tenets of neo-scholastic
Protestant theology. In common with their fifteenth-century predecessors,
these religious enthusiasts suffered spiritual anguish. While their ancestors
had turned to pictures and holy objects associated with divine and saintly
intercessors, they were offered words of scriptural comfort: the verbal was
supplanting the visual. The centrality of the Word placed a new premium
upon being able to read the Scriptures, encouraging the printing of other
religious literature, the mainstay of the emerging market in books. Since
the majority of Scots remained non-literate, Protestant culture could not,
and did not, rely exclusively upon printed texts. Much was committed to
memory, often through the aid of singing, and the Psalter in particular
offered a familiar repository of biblical imagery sustaining many Scottish
Protestants. New communal rituals became part of the experience of
Scottish worship and, by the 1580s, had acquired the patina of perman-
ence. In defence of such practices during the next century many Scots were
prepared to defy or even fight their king.

The Protestant stress upon order and morality owed much to the
Christian humanist ideals circulating since the fifteenth century.
Humanism, offering a way of life as much as an educational programme,

had become the dominant ethos in Scottish schools and universities by the 1580s and its civil values sat easily alongside the emerging Protestant culture. Apart from a few spats in academic disputations, there was no dramatic rejection of the scholastic and medieval past and the strong attachment to chivalry and the concept of honour were absorbed rather than contested by the humanist assertion of civic virtue. Within the comparatively small compass of the Scottish elite, sharp intellectual or social divides among the landed, urban or emerging service nobility were avoided, though there were plenty of disputes over the key political and religious issues of the day. The oral world remained strong though with the increasing influence and importance of printing there were signs of a greater division between literate and non-literate. An oral culture flourished within the communities provided by place and people, where locality, region and kinship continued to provide the key points of reference for Scots.

INTEGRATION

Scotland's geographical consolidation was completed by the end of the fifteenth century. The acquisition of the Northern Isles gave the kingdom its final territorial extent and the forfeiture of the Lordship of the Isles removed the remote possibility the Western Isles might form part of a separate Gaelic polity spanning the North Channel. The last piece of the jigsaw of the realm's boundaries was put in place when the Debateable Land between England and Scotland was formally divided in 1551–2 and the Scots Dike was constructed, with its stand of trees running in a nearly straight line still visible in today's landscape. The sea boundary was more problematical and there was still uncertainty in the early seventeenth century as to whether Rathlin Island, off the Antrim coast, formed part of the kingdom of Scotland or of Ireland.

It was a short step from drawing lines on the ground or on a map to treating Scotland as a territorially-defined national polity. Such a viewpoint stretched the conceptual distance between crown and kingdom and placed a greater emphasis upon the territory of Scotland and the polity as an entity in its own right, a common weal or *respublica*. This altered the perceived relationship between the king and his people, with the monarch regarded as a king of Scotland whose subjects lived within the boundaries of the realm, rather than a king of Scots whose subjects were defined by their allegiance to him. To prevent any diminution of the bond of personal loyalty owed to them, Stewart kings tenaciously clung to their

traditional title King of Scots. During the sixteenth century, geographical consolidation assisted the development of political consolidation and
the integration of the kingdom, setting the scene for the adoption of an
ideal of national uniformity, embodied by one king, one law and one faith.
In a poem, probably written in his youth in the 1580s, Alexander Hume
summed up this sentiment, 'How mekill mair sall love and lautie stand,
Amang the pepill native of a land, Quhilk dois imbrace, obey and onely
knaw, A kirk, a King, a language and a law'.[5] Paradoxically, the drive
towards uniformity and integration succeeded in dividing the realm in
two, with the Highlands and Lowlands increasingly viewed as mutually
antagonistic societies and cultures. By submerging the diversity of the
Scottish regions beneath these simplistic labels, a conceptual boundary
was manufactured that changed the future history of Scotland. As they
became barriers, linguistic frontiers increased in significance, preventing
the monoglots among the Gaelic or Norn-speakers from participating
fully in the predominantly Scots-speaking world of politics. The long-
term linguistic pressure upon the Norn language in Shetland pushed it
out of usage during the seventeenth century and increased the introver-
sion within the much larger Gaelic-speaking areas of Scotland.

   The concentration upon the kingdom at the expense of the region
altered the relationship between crown and regions. The traditional
medieval style of governance had allowed the temporal and spiritual lords
to rule the regions, while the king ruled the lords. Provided the king's will
had been implemented, it had mattered less how and by whom it was
done. This flexibility permitted regional communities to remain relatively autonomous and subject only to sporadic interference from the
royal administration. The attempt to spread an identical pattern of government across the realm ran counter to this *laissez-faire* approach. As the
century progressed, there was an increasing tendency to assume that
doing the king's will necessitated doing it the king's way. Diversity was
regarded as divisive and a source of weakness, rather than strength. Initial
steps were taken which slowly turned the government of the localities
into local government. The emergence of a capital city also modified the
experience of governance for the regions. As was demonstrated by the
independent administration in the north-east run in the Civil Wars, such
a centre was not indispensable, though both sides in the conflict expended
much effort to capture or hold the capital. The rise of Edinburgh to political dominance, matching its economic weight within the country, was

[5] Alexander Hume, *Poems*, ed. A. Lawson (Scottish Text Society, 48, Edinburgh,
1902), 70.

gradual and inexorable, with no appreciable rival, since Glasgow was still well down the burgh league table. From the mid-century, there was a noticeable decline in the political significance of Stirling, whose strategically crucial location and magnificent castle diminished in importance as fear of an English invasion decreased, though it continued to be the safest environment in which to rear a child monarch.

By the end of the period, the executive arm of the crown, the increasingly Edinburgh-based Privy Council, was reaching directly into the localities on a daily basis with its specific orders and instructions. The summoning of individuals from the regions into the Council's presence at court marked a significant change from the previous method and location of dealing with intractable local problems, such as persistent feuding. At the start of his reign, James IV had arrived in person accompanied by a military contingent to quash the trouble in Ayrshire between the Cunninghams and the Montgomeries. In the 1580s the same families were locked in a different feud and the Privy Council summoned Glencairn and Eglinton to court where they ordered a permanent settlement to be found.

As the sixteenth century progressed, it became more difficult for the regions to remain semi-detached from the court and the centres of power clustered in or around Edinburgh. As a consequence, minimal political participation became an obligation and a necessity for each region. An entirely different set of problems was created for those communities at a political, social or geographical distance from the corridors of power at court. With the emergence of a 'centre', and its accompanying mentality relegating parts of the kingdom to the 'periphery', some regions found themselves marginalised, rather than ignored. The structures of regional politics were disrupted and destabilised by this unwelcome new status. During the next century, the Gaelic bards recognised the consequences of this 'curse of the capital' for Hebridean chiefs, compelled to make an annual appearance in Edinburgh. Long periods of absence leaving their 'country' without effective leadership were bad enough, but worse was the acquisition of Lowland habits, especially the gambling and purchase of luxury items running the chiefs into crippling debt. Once in the capital, Islanders came under the spell of its inhabitants who believed Edinburgh was the centre of the kingdom, and possibly the world as well.

Whilst the Western Isles were to experience the harshest and most disruptive effects of the rise of the capital, other regions developed different coping strategies. A greater consciousness of regional identity was emerging in the 'conservative' north-east, with sufficient confidence in its locality for new universities to be founded at Marischal College,

Aberdeen's second foundation, and a short-lived attempt at Fraserburgh. Deliberately avoiding involvement in national politics, though having a solid local and regional standing, Forbes of Tolquhon fashioned himself into a typical late Renaissance man, all the while staying on his Aberdeenshire estate. At the opposite end of the country, the south-west developed a strongly radical flavour in its ecclesiastical stance and its regional politics and was equally divergent from the centre.

SCOTLAND AND EUROPE

Nothing dampened the Scots' immense enthusiasm for all things European which remained remarkably constant throughout the period. In the cultural and artistic fields they were keen followers of fashion, adopting current trends and cheerfully adapting them for Scottish conditions, ensuring, for example, that the effect of an Italian facade and loggia could be created in a Scottish country house like Crichton. With population pressure increasing at home, more Scots sought their fortune abroad with Scottish soldiers and pedlars plying their trades from the River Shannon in Ireland to the Vistula River in Poland–Lithuania and all stops between. The well-trodden route to French and other European universities continued to be travelled by Scottish intellectuals and it remained for many a one-way journey. By the closing decades of the century confessional considerations were beginning to be felt, making the Protestant universities in the Netherlands and the Huguenot academies in France more attractive destinations. However, the kingdom's international weakness had little or no effect upon the involvement of Scots within Europe.

In the economic sphere, involvement was not enough, as old markets contracted and new products and destinations needed to be found. National confidence had not been translated into commercial enterprise, as was achieved in later periods. Whilst the volume of overseas trade had recovered by the 1580s to its earlier medieval levels, the Scottish mercantile community remained comparatively conservative in its outlook and methods. There was no rush to join in European exploration of the wider world. The exotic discoveries of the New World, Africa and the Far East reached the emblem books and embroideries of Scotland, but this was not an age when Scots were found in every corner of the globe. Most migration was much closer to home, with a substantial flow of colonists and soldiers crossing the North Channel to Ireland, destined with the Ulster Plantation at the start of the seventeenth century to become one of the most significant links within the British Isles. Scottish pedlars and soldiers showed how individuals of low rank were not short of the enterprising spirit and had no fear of finding their fortune overseas. The Scots abroad continued to be a significant element within the Scottish common weal.

Between the reigns of James IV and James VI Scotland's diplomatic standing in Europe had dropped. The mid-century Battle for Britain marked a watershed, when Scotland quietly slipped out of the European military league tables. James IV had lived and died a warrior king and his navy had given him an internationally-significant military asset. By contrast, James VI was by temperament and deeply-held conviction a 'Rex Pacificus', though this succeeded in making a virtue out of necessity for his kingdom. During the campaigns of the 1540s, France had taken over Scotland's military machine and had paid for the campaigns. As a consequence of France shouldering these military and financial burdens, subsidising the regime of Mary of Guise and providing the dower income for Mary, Queen of Scots, Scotland was protected from many of the pressures towards government transformation and state formation that war had brought to continental Europe. It was only during the 1580s that the Scottish crown felt the necessity of taxing, administering and organising its subjects on a regular basis and of striving to monopolise military activity and legitimate violence: tasks leading European powers had undertaken for decades.

The world of Flodden had disappeared by 1550 and with a sturdy realism the Scots made no serious attempt to resurrect it. The English military interventions in 1560, 1570 and 1573 served to underline the dismal truth that by the second half of the sixteenth century the Scottish kingdom no longer possessed the capability to engage in full-scale war. This contributed to, and reflected, Scotland's slide into satellite status. The price of the country's survival during the Rough Wooings was an ever closer French alliance, creating in the 1550s a Franco-Scotland culminating in a dynastic union and leading to inclusion within the Valois empire. That path was rejected in the diplomatic revolution of 1560, when dependency upon English assistance was the price of success for the Lords of the Congregation. Internal conflict during the Civil Wars following Mary's deposition in 1567 substantially weakened the kingdom's position. The queen's flight a year later locked Mary and the realm into an English embrace, as Scotland became a satellite of the Tudor state. It served to confirm the European view that relations with Scotland were merely part of the struggle for control over the British Isles and one aspect of the English succession question. As a consequence, the Scots found themselves marginalised in international diplomacy and further enclosed within a British dimension. At the close of the century, the future for Scotland's king and his kingdom lay within the British Isles. In 1603 James VI did what none of his Stewart ancestors had managed and through the union of the crowns became king of England. From that time, Europe had to cope with a new diplomatic partner: the king of Greater Britain.

Table of Events

		Scotland	England/Europe

James IV's reign

		Scotland	England/Europe
1473	Mar	Birth of Prince James	
1486	July	Death of Queen Margaret	
1488	June	Battle of Sauchieburn. James IV crowned	
1488	Oct	Parliament explained James III's death	Anglo-Scottish truce
1489	Apr	Rebellion by Lennox	
1489	Dec	End of siege of Dumbarton	
1490	summer	Council reshuffled. Burning of Monzievaird church	
1491	Nov		Angus agreement with Henry VII
1492	Jan	Archbishopric of Glasgow created	
1492	Feb		Anglo-French treaty of Etaples
1492	Mar		Auld Alliance renewed
1492	June		Treaty with Denmark
1492	Aug		Columbus set sail
1493	May	Lordship of Isles forfeited	
1493	June		Anglo-Scottish truce
1493	June	Act of Revocation	
1493	Aug	James at Dunstaffnage	
1494	spring	Heresy trial of Lollards of Kyle	
1494	July	Royal force sailed to Isles	
1494	autumn		French invasion of Italy
1495	Feb	Foundation of University of Aberdeen	Charles VIII of France entered Naples
1495	Mar	King assumed personal rule	
1495	May	Start of expedition to the Isles	
1495	Nov	Perkin Warbeck received	

1496	June	Education Act	
1496	Nov		England declared war on Scotland
1497	Jan	Death of Archbishop Scheves	
1497	July		Warbeck sent to Ireland
1497	Sept	Fall of Angus	Anglo-Scottish truce
1498	Mar	Act of General Revocation	
1498	summer	James in Kintyre	
1499	July	MacIain of Ardnamurchan sacked Finlaggan	
1500	Apr	Argyll made Lieutenant of Isles	
1501	Aug	Huntly made Lieutenant	
1502	Feb		Anglo-Scottish Peace Treaty
1502	May		Scottish force to Denmark
1503	Aug	Wedding of James and Margaret	
1504	Jan	Death of archbishop of St Andrews	
1504	May	Arran sent to Isles	
1504	Aug	James' expedition to Eskdale	
1506	summer	Huntly attacked Lewis	
1507	Feb	Birth of Prince James	
1507	Apr		Papal gifts of sword and hat
1507	Sept	James' completed record-breaking ride to Tain. Chepman & Millar printing press licensed	
1508	Feb	Death of Prince James	
1508	May	Royal tournament started	
1508	July	Death of Archbishop Blackadder	
1509	Apr		Accession of Henry VIII of England
1509	May	Last Parliament before 1524	
1509	Oct	Birth of Prince Arthur. Aberdeen Breviary printed	
1510	June	Death of Prince Arthur	
1511	June		Andrew Barton killed in sea fight
1511	Oct	Launch of *Great Michael*	
1512	April	Birth of Prince James	
1512	July		Renewal of French Treaty
1513	June		Treaty with O'Donnell
1513	July	Scots fleet sailed to France	
1513	Sept	Death of James IV	Battle of Flodden

James V's minority

| 1513 | Sept | Coronation of James V | |
| 1514 | Aug | Marriage of Margaret and Angus | Anglo-French Treaty |

1514	Oct	Death of Bishop Elphinstone	
1515	Jan		Accession of Francis I of France
1515	May	Albany lands at Dumbarton	Anglo-French treaty
1515	July	Albany acknowledged as Governor	
1515	Aug	Margaret surrendered custody of her sons	
1515	Sept		French victory at Marignano (Italy)
1516	Jan	Battle of Kittycrosshill	Peace between Charles V and Francis I
1516	Mar	Arran and Angus return to Council	
1516	Oct	Execution of Lord Hume	
1516	Nov	Albany recognised as second person in realm	
1517	June	Albany left. Margaret returned	
1517	Aug		Franco-Scottish Treaty of Rouen
1517	Sept	De la Bastie murdered by Humes	
1517	Oct		Luther posted his ninety-five theses
1518	Nov	Agreement between Margaret and Angus	
1519	Jan		Death HRE Maximilian. Charles V succeeded
1519	Feb	Angus returned to Council	
1520	Apr	'Cleanse the Causeway' in Edinburgh	
1521	Mar	Death of Archbishop Forman	
1521	Nov	Albany returned	
1522	Oct	Albany left for France	Angus in exile in France
1522	winter	Scots army refused to attack England	English raid Borders
1523	Oct	Albany campaign in Borders with French troops	
1524	May	Albany returned to France for last time	
1524	July	Margaret's second Regency	
1525	Feb	Angus readmitted to Council	French defeat at Pavia. Francis I captured
1525	May		Peasants' Revolt in HRE
1525	July	Rota for keeping James	
1525	Nov	Angus refused to hand over King	
1526	Mar	Marriage of Margaret to Henry Stewart	
1526	June	Bond between James and Lennox	
1526	July	Darnick raid by Scott of Buccleuch	

1526	Sept	Lennox killed	
1527	May		Charles V's troops sack Rome
1527	Aug	Angus Chancellor. Cassillis murdered	
1528	Apr	Margaret's divorce decree arrived	
1528	May	James escaped from Douglases	

James V's adult reign

1528	July	Angus ordered into ward	
1528	Nov	Failure to capture Tantallon	
1528	Dec		Anglo-Scottish truce
1529	May		Angus arrived in England
1529	Nov	Justice ayres in Dumfries, Galloway and Ayrshire	Start of English Reformation Parliament
1530	Apr	Campaign against rebels in Isles	
1530	July	Execution of Johnnie Armstrong	
1531	Sept		Pope agreed clerical taxation
1531	Nov	MacLean and Macdonald submitted; Argyll lost Kintyre	
1532	Apr		Order of Golden Fleece for James
1532	May	College of Justice erected	
1532	Oct	Moray made Lieutenant-General of army. Western chiefs to attack in Ireland	English raids
1533	Sept		Formal truce with England
1534	May		Anglo-Scottish Peace
1534	Nov		Henry VIII became Head of Church of England
1535	June	Act against Lutheran opinions	
1536	Sept	James sailed for France	Start of 'French holiday' (see Map 5.1)
1537	Jan		Marriage in Paris of James and Madeleine
1537	May	Return of James and Madeleine	
1537	July	Death of Madeleine. Trial of Lady Glamis	
1538	June	Wedding of James and Mary of Guise	
1540	Feb	Coronation of Mary of Guise	
1540	May	Birth of Prince James	
1540	July	James completed his circumnavigation of Scotland	
1540	Aug	Execution of Hamilton of Finnart	
1541	Aug		Henry VIII waited for James V in York

1541	Nov	Death of Queen Margaret	
1542	Aug	Hadden Rig, skirmish with English	
1542	Oct		English raids
1542	Nov		Battle of Solway Moss
1542	Dec	Birth of Princess Mary. Death of James	

Mary's minority

1543	Jan	Arran proclaimed Governor	
1543	Mar	Act allowing Scripture in the vernacular	
1543	July		Anglo-Scottish Treaties of Greenwich
1543	Sept	Beaton released	
1543	Oct	Lennox returned	
1543	Dec	Parliament re-affirmed French alliance	
1544	Jan	Perth iconoclasts hanged	
1544	July	Frasers killed by Clanranald	Lennox married Margaret Douglas
1544	summer	Rough Wooings start	English invaded Scotland
1544	Sept		English captured Boulogne
1545	Feb	Scottish victory at Ancrum Moor	
1545	Apr	Castle Urquhart sacked	
1545	Sept	English attacked Kelso	English invaded Scotland
1545	Oct	Last rebellion of Isles	
1545	Dec		First session of Council of Trent
1546	Mar	Execution of Wishart	
1546	May	Murder of Cardinal Beaton	
1546	June		Anglo-French Treaty of Camp
1547	Jan		Death of Henry VIII
1547	Mar		Death of Francis I
1547	July	French captured St Andrews castle	
1547	Sept	Battle of Pinkie	
1548	July	Treaty of Haddington with French	Mary, Queen of Scots arrived in France
1549	Aug	Scottish Provincial Council	
1550	Feb	Recapture of Broughty Ferry	
1550	Mar		Anglo-French Treaty of Boulogne
1550	summer	Execution of Wallace	
1550	Sept	Mary of Guise sailed to France	'Triumph' at Rouen
1550	Dec		Peace between Charles V and Scots

1551	June		Anglo–Scottish Treaty of Norham
1552	Aug	Scottish Provincial Council, Hamilton's Catechism	
1553	July		Mary Tudor seized English throne
1553	Dec		*Parlement* declared Mary, Queen of Scots 'of age'
1554	Apr	Mary of Guise installed as Regent	
1554	July		Mary Tudor married Philip of Spain
1555	Jan	Tax of £20,000	
1555	Feb	Refoundation of St Mary's College, St Andrews	
1555	Oct		Peace of Augsburg in HRE
1556	Jan		Charles V abdicated
1556	May	Rejection of new tax system	
1556	summer	Regent's northern progress	
1556	autumn	Knox started preaching tour	
1557	May	Knox left for Geneva	
1557	July		England joined war against France
1557	Oct	Scots army disbanded without crossing Border	
1557	Dec	First Band signed by Protestant nobles	
1558	Jan		Calais recaptured by French
1558	Apr		Marriage of Mary to Dauphin
1558	Nov	Crown matrimonial granted to Dauphin	Accession of Elizabeth I
1559	Jan	Beggars' Summons	
1559	Mar	Provincial church Council	
1559	Apr		Treaty of Câteau–Cambrésis
1559	May	Knox's Perth sermon started Wars of Congregation	
1559	June	Congregation took Edinburgh	
1559	July		Death of Henry II of France
1559	Aug	Congregation re-organised	Arran escaped from France
1559	Oct	Regent deposed	
1559	Nov	Regent regained Edinburgh	
1560	Jan		English fleet sent to Scotland
1560	Feb		Treaty of Berwick
1560	Apr	English army besieged Leith	
1560	June	Death of Mary of Guise	
1560	July	'Concessions' to Scots	Anglo–French treaty of Edinburgh
1560	Aug	Reformation Parliament	French and English troops withdrawn

| 1560 | Dec | First General Assembly | Death of Francis II |
| 1561 | Jan | First Book of Discipline not fully accepted | |

Mary's personal reign

1561	Aug	Mary returned	
1561	Sept	Protestant Lords confirmed in power	
1562	Jan		Final session of Council of Trent
1562	Mar		Massacre of Huguenots at Vassy, France
1562	June		Meeting of Queens in York cancelled
1562	July		French religious wars started
1562	Aug	Mary's northern progress	
1562	Oct	Huntly defeat at Corrichie	
1563	Feb		Duke of Guise assassinated
1563	May	Gordons forfeited	
1564	Mar		Leicester marriage proposal
1564	Apr		Anglo-French Peace Treaty of Troyes
1564	Sept	Lennox returned	
1564	Dec	Parliament restored Lennox	
1565	Feb	Darnley returned	
1565	Mar	Mary's decision to marry Darnley	
1565	May	MacDonalds heavily defeated in Antrim	
1565	June		Bayonne meeting, France and Spain
1565	July	Mary married Darnley	
1565	Aug	Chase-about Raid	
1566	Mar	Murder of Riccio	
1566	June	Birth of Prince James	
1566	Aug		Iconoclastic fury and start of Dutch Revolt
1566	Dec	Craigmillar conference	
1567	Feb	Darnley murder	
1567	Apr	Bothwell acquitted of murder	
1567	May	Mary married Bothwell	
1567	June	Carberry Field. Mary imprisoned at Lochleven	
1567	July	Mary abdicated	

James VI's minority

| 1567 | July | Coronation of James VI | |
| 1567 | Aug | Moray became Regent | |

1567	Aug		Spanish army in Netherlands
1567	Dec	'Second Reformation' Parliament	
1568	May	Mary escaped. Battle of Langside	Mary fled to England
1568	Sept	Truce between King's and Queen's Men	
1568	Oct		Mary's trial opened at York
1568	Dec		Trial moved to Westminster and ended
1569	Feb	Moray returned	
1569	June	Regent's northern progress	
1569	Oct		Scheme of Mary/Norfolk marriage
1569	Nov		Rebellion of Northern earls
1569	Dec	English earls arrived	
1570	Jan	Moray assassinated	
1570	May	English army arrived	
1570	July	Lennox proclaimed regent	
1570	Aug	Executions at Brechin	
1571	Apr	Capture of Dumbarton, Archbishop Hamilton hanged	Dutch Sea Beggars captured Brill
1571	Sept	Regent Lennox killed. Mar appointed Regent	
1571	Oct		Victory over Turks at Lepanto
1572	Aug		Massacre of St Bartholomew's Eve
1572	Oct	Death of Regent Mar	
1572	Nov	Morton became Regent	
1573	Feb	Pacification of Perth	
1573	May	Fall of Edinburgh Castle	Accession of Henry III of France
1574	July	Andrew Melville returned	
1575	Feb	Debasement of coinage	
1575	Mar	Settlement with Argylls over royal jewels	
1576	July	Redeswyre incident, last Border 'battle'	
1578	Mar	Morton's first fall. James declared 'of age'	
1578	Apr	Second Book of Discipline	
1578	June	Morton recovered power	
1579	Oct	James' formal entry into Edinburgh	
1579	Nov	Forfeiture of Hamiltons	
1580	Mar	Ascendancy of Lennox	
1580	Dec	Morton's second fall. General Assembly condemned episcopacy	
1581	June	Execution of Morton	
1581	Jan	King's or Negative Confession	

1581	Aug	Lennox created a duke	
1581	Oct	Montgomerie appointed archbishop of Glasgow	
1582	Aug	Ruthven Raid captured James	
1583	June	James escaped. Arran regime	
1583	Oct	Edinburgh's 'Tounis college' opened	
1584	May	'Black' Acts. Gowrie executed	
1585	Nov	Arran overthrown	
1586	June		Anglo-Scottish Treaty of Berwick
1586	Oct		Mary's trial
1587	Feb		Mary's execution
1588	summer		Defeat of the Spanish Armada

Guide to Further Reading

SOURCES AND REFERENCE WORKS

Documentary sources are discussed in Donaldson's *James V–James VII* and Webster's *Scotland from the eleventh century to 1603* with the Stevensons' *Scottish Texts* being a guide to the Scottish historical clubs. Non-documentary sources are equally important and Scotland has a wealth of historical sites with Historic Scotland supplying guides to individual buildings and further information on the Royal Commission of Ancient and Historic Monuments' database (http://www.rcahms.gov.uk/). Scottish material culture and paintings can be viewed at the National Museum of Scotland, the Scottish National and Portrait Galleries, the Glasgow Museums and many others throughout Scotland. The Scottish Cultural Resources Access Network offers a central gateway to most internet resources (http://www.scran.ac.uk/), with archives on the Scottish Archive Network (http://www.scan.org.uk/). Early modern Scottish music can be heard on many recordings, especially on the Gaudeamus label.

Standard published bibliographies are being overtaken by electronic databases, and bibliographies produced by the Royal Historical Society (http://www.rhs.ac.uk/bibl/bibwel.asp) offer the best starting point. Annual updates of journal articles and essays are found in *Scottish Historical Review*. The *Oxford Dictionary of National Biography* (printed and online http://www.oxforddnb.com/) and *Biographical Dictionary of Scottish Women* are invaluable. The Dictionary of the Older Scottish Tongue, now part of the *Dictionary of the Scots Language* (http://www.dsl.ac.uk/dsl/index.html) opens up the language of early modern Scotland. The early maps of Scotland, including Pont's, are on the National Library of Scotland site (http://www.nls.uk/) and British maps can be seen on the British Library and Collect Britain (http://www.bl.uk/collections/maps. html; http://www.collectbritain. co.uk/). Far more than an atlas, the *Atlas of Scottish History to 1707* remains essential. *The Oxford Companion to Scottish History* and *The Companion to Gaelic Scotland* provide brief summaries on most important topics. From the general histories, Lynch's *Scotland* is particularly strong for this period with the *New Penguin History* and Wormald's *Scotland: A History* providing recent overviews, and *A Companion to Tudor Britain* has good Scottish coverage.

The following books provide a starting point or overview of their subject and most offer a route into the dense undergrowth of articles and essays dealing with specific subjects.

POLITICS AND GOVERNANCE

Monarchs: James IV Macdougall's *James IV* dominates the reign and has an excellent discussion of the sources. **James V** *Princelie Majestie* by Thomas with its emphasis upon the court complements Cameron's study of the adult reign, but the minority is only adequately covered in Emond's unpublished thesis. **Mary** The Battle for Britain is encompassed in Merriman's exhilarating *Rough Wooings* and Ritchie's *Mary of Guise* covers the Regency and Franco-Scotland. Different treatments of Mary's personal reign are found in Wormald's *Mary, Queen of Scots*, Lynch's *Queen in Three Kingdoms* and Guy's *My Heart is my Own*. **Minority of James VI** Goodare and Lynch's *Reign of James VI* contains the closest thing to a study of the minority. There is no proper treatment of the civil war, though Potter's *Edinburgh Under Siege* discusses the capital. Lee's *Moray* and Hewitt's *Scotland under Morton* deal with those Regencies. Marshall's *Scottish Queens* and *Queen Mary's Women* reveal much about the women at court.

Governance: Goodare's analytical *Government of Scotland* and *State and Society* discuss governance in the later part of the period and Brown et al.'s *Scottish Parliament I & II* heralds the Scottish Parliament Project's forthcoming edition of the *Acts*. Murray's articles on the royal administration are invaluable. Wormald's groundbreaking *Lords and Men* reveals the political world of lordship and Donaldson analyses political allegiance in *All the Queen's Men*.

THE CHURCH AND THE KIRK

Despite its age, McRobert's *Essays on the Scottish Reformation* contains some of the best discussions of the pre-Reformation church, supplemented by economic analysis in Kirk's Introduction to *The Book of Assumption*. Sanderson's *Cardinal of Scotland* and Macfarlane's *Elphinstone* illuminate two prelates' lives. Dilworth's admirable survey *Scottish Monasteries* covers the regular orders with the Domincans treated by Foggie. Ryrie's *Origins of the Scottish Reformation* provides the most recent survey while Cowan's *Scottish Reformation* remains eminently readable and Lynch's essay in *The Renaissance in Scotland* has introduced some qualifications to the positive picture found in studies such as Kirk's *Patterns of Reform*. Macdonald has studied the *Jacobean Kirk* and the comparative perspective is revealed in Heal's *Reformation in Britain and Ireland* and Hazlett's *The Reformation in Britain and Ireland*. Todd's *The Culture of Protestantism in Early Modern Scotland* broke new ground and discipline is discussed in Graham's *Uses of Reform* and Dunbar's *Winram*. The post-Reformation Catholic church lacks an overview, though the Jesuits have been studied by Yellowlees and McCoog. Goodare's database and book provide a detailed picture of witch trials and fairy culture is treated in Henderson and Cowan.

CULTURE AND THE ARTS

The first volume of the *History of Scottish Literature* edited by Brown et al., though too late for this book, provides an excellent guide as does Jones' *History of Scots Language*. John Durkan and his festschrift, *The Renaissance in Scotland* (ed. Macdonald et al.), open many cultural byways. Thomson introduces Gaelic poetry and Macgregor and Meek explain Gaelic culture in Kirk's *Church in the Highlands*. Ballads are discussed in Cowan's edited volume and Preece and Ross bring alive the world of sixteenth-century music. The Architectural History of Scotland volumes by Fawcett and Howard, Dunbar's *Scottish Royal Palaces* and McKean's persuasive *Scottish Chateau* give rich coverage for architecture. Macmillan's *Scottish Art* is a starting point and decorative painting is covered by Bath. Embroidery is explained by Swain and Glenn provides a fascinating guide to metalwork, with Burnett et al.'s *Scotland's Heraldic Heritage* encouraging further exploration into the heraldic world.

INTELLECTUAL LIFE

Individual universities are covered by Durkan and Kirk, Cant, Horn and Anderson et al., and Stevenson while schools await the publication of Durkan's research. Broadie has studied late medieval philosophy and Mann describes the *Scottish Book Trade* with Simpson's *Scottish Handwriting* being indispensable. MacQueen's volume treats humanism and new aspects of intellectual life have been explored by Williamson's *Scottish National Consciousness*, articles and editions and Allen's *Philosophy and Politics*. Scottish identity has been discussed in Broun et al.'s *Image and Identity* and Fergusson's *Identity of the Scottish Nation*. Burns' *Trew Law* lucidly explains Scottish political thought and Mason has provided text and introductions on Knox and Buchanan and insights in his edited collections.

LAW AND MEDICINE

Meston et al.'s *Scottish Legal Tradition* helps the non-specialist move onto the Stair Society introductions and miscellanies. Finlay's *Men of Law* charts the development of the legal profession and in *Stair Miscellany Five* (ed. MacQueen) the foundation of the College of Justice is explained by Cairns whose history of Scots law is eagerly awaited. Wormald's seminal article 'Bloodfeud, kindred and government' and Brown's *Bloodfeud* discuss a different aspect of justice. No overall sociological study of crime exists, though women are discussed in Brown's *Twisted Sisters*. Dingwall's *History of Scottish Medicine* and Bannerman's *Beatons* show how the medical profession operated.

ECONOMY AND SOCIETY

Whyte's *Scotland before the Industrial Revolution* and *Scottish Society* offer an overall introduction, with Gibson and Smout dealing with *Prices, Food and Wages*, Gemill and Mayhew with *Changing Values in Medieval Scotland* and Houston with *Literacy*. Dennison [Torrie] has studied particular burghs and Lynch's wide-ranging *Edinburgh and the Reformation* is a model of its kind with the *History of Urban Britain* giving a comparative setting. Fascinating insights into Scottish rural life and the lives of ordinary people are found in Sanderson's *Mary Stewart's People; A Kindly Place?* and *Scottish Rural Society*. Dodgshon's *From Chiefs to*

Landlords illuminates Highland economic and social history. The essays and biographical dictionary edited by Ewan et al. make Scottish women more visible. Brown's *Noble Society in Scotland* shows the world inhabited by nobles and Mitchison discusses the poor. Mackay introduces *Early Scottish Gardens* and Smout's *People and Woods* opens up environmental history.

SCOTLAND AND EUROPE

Ditchburn's *Scotland and Europe* has deepened the understanding of Scotland's place in Europe with the auld alliance explained in Macdougall's *An Antidote to the English*. Riis has described Scottish–Danish relations in *Should Auld Acquaintance* and Kellar's *Scotland England and the Reformation* covers Anglo-Scottish relations while Phillip's *Anglo-Scots Wars* discusses the military aspects. The British dimension has been explored in the volumes edited by Bradshaw, Ellis, Grant et al. and Dawson's *Politics of Religion in the age of Mary, Queen of Scots* places Argyll's career in its British context.

SCOTTISH REGIONS

Each region has its local history with collections edited by Baldwin, Omand, Oram, and Sellar providing guides. Rae's *Administration of the Scottish frontier* and Meikle's *British Frontier?* illuminate the Borders. The Gaelic regions of Scotland and their relationship with Ireland are discussed in McLeod's *Divided Gaels*. Though concentrating upon religion, Sanderson's *Ayrshire and the Reformation* is a model of how a shire history should be written.

Select Bibliography

PRIMARY AND REFERENCE SOURCES (MANUSCRIPT SOURCES HAVE NOT BEEN INCLUDED)

Websites

BL MAPS http://www.bl.uk/collections/maps.html
COLLECT BRITAIN http://www.collectbritain.co.uk/
DOST http://www.dsl.ac.uk/dsl/index.html
NLS http://www.nls.uk
OXFORD DNB http://www.oxforddnb.com/
RCAHMS http://www.rcahms.gov.uk/
RHS http://www.rhs.ac.uk/bibl/bibwel.asp
SCAN http://www.scan.org.uk/
SCRAN http://www.scran.ac.uk

Abbey of Paisley, ed. J. C. Lees (Paisley, 1878).
Accounts of the Collectors of Thirds of Benefices, 1561–1572, ed. G. Donaldson (SHS, 3rd ser. 42, Edinburgh, 1949).
Accounts of the Lord High Treasurer of Scotland, eds T. Dickson et al. (12 vols, Edinburgh, 1877–1970).
Acts of the Admiral's Court of Scotland, ed. T. C. Wade (Stair Society, 2, Edinburgh, 1937).
Acts of the Lords of Council in Public Affairs, ed. R. K. Hannay (Edinburgh, 1932).
Acts of the Lords of the Isles, 1336–1493, eds J. and R. W. Munro (SHS, 4th ser. 22, 1986).
Acts of the Parliaments of Scotland, eds T. Thomson and C. Innes (12 vols, Edinburgh, 1814–42).
Ancient Criminal Trials in Scotland, ed. R. Pitcairn (3 vols, Bannatyne Club, 42, Edinburgh, 1833).
Argyll, An Inventory of the Ancient Monuments (7 vols, RCAHMS, Edinburgh, 1971–92).
Atlas of Scottish History to 1707, eds P. McNeill and H. L. MacQueen (Scottish Medievalists, Edinburgh, 1996).

Ayr Burgh Accounts, 1534–1624, ed. G. S. Pryde (SHS, 3rd ser. 28, 1937).

Balfour's Practicks, ed. P. G. B. McNeill (Stair Society, 21 & 22, Edinburgh, 1962–3).

Bàrdachd Albannach: Scottish Verse from the Book of the Dean of Lismore, ed. J. W. Watson (SGTS, I, Edinburgh, 1937).

Biographical Dictionary of Scottish Women, eds E. Ewan, S. Innes, S. Reynolds and R. Pipes (Edinburgh, 2006).

'*The Booke of the Universall Kirk of Scotland': Acts and proceedings of the General Assemblies of the Kirk of Scotland*, ed. T. Thomson (3 vols, Bannatyne Club, 81, Edinburgh, 1839–45).

The Books of Assumption of the Thirds of Benefices: Scottish Ecclesiastical Rentals at the Reformation, ed. J. Kirk (Records of Social and Economic History, N.S. 21, Oxford, 1995).

Buchanan, G., *A Dialogue on the Law of Kingship among the Scots*, eds R. A. Mason and M. S. Smith (Aldershot, 2004).

Buchanan, G., *The History of Scotland*, ed. J. Aikman (4 vols, Edinburgh, 1827).

Buchanan, G., *Political Poetry*, eds P. J. McGinnis and A. H. Williamson (SHS 5th ser. 8, Edinburgh, 1995).

Calderwood, D., *The History of the Kirk of Scotland*, ed. T. Thomson (8 vols, Wodrow Society, Edinburgh, 1842–9).

Calendar of State Papers relating to Scotland and Mary, Queen of Scots, 1547–1603, eds J. Bain et al. (13 vols, Edinburgh, 1898–1969).

Campbell Letters, 1559–1583, ed. J. E. A. Dawson (SHS, 5th ser. 10, Edinburgh, 2000).

Catechism of John Hamilton, ed. T. G. Law (Oxford, 1884).

Collectanea de rebus Albanicis (Iona Club, Edinburgh, 1847).

Companion to Gaelic Scotland, ed. D. S. Thomson (Oxford, 1987 ed.).

Correspondence of Sir Patrick Waus of Barnbarroch, ed. R. V. Agnew (2 vols, Ayrshire and Wigtonshire Archaeological Association, 14, Edinburgh, 1887).

Court of the Barony of Carnwath, 1533–42, ed. W. C. Dickinson (SHS, 3rd ser. 29, Edinburgh, 1937).

Dictionary of Scottish Church History and Theology, ed. N. M. de S. Cameron (Edinburgh, 1993).

A diurnal of remarkable occurrents that have passed within the country of Scotland since the death of King James the Fourth till the year MDLXXV, ed. T. Thomson (Bannatyne Club, 43, Edinburgh, 1833).

Early Records of the University of St Andrews, ed. J. Anderson (SHS, 3rd ser. 9, Edinburgh, 1926).

Estimate of the Scottish Nobility, ed. C. Rogers (Grampian Club, 6, London, 1873).

Exchequer Rolls of Scotland, ed. J. Stuart et al. (Edinburgh, 1878–1988).

Extracts from the records of the burgh of Edinburgh, 1403–1589, ed. J. D. Marwick (4 vols, SBRS, 2–6, Edinburgh, 1869–92).

Fasti Ecclesiasae Scotiae, ed. H. Scott (8 vols, Edinburgh, 1915–50).

The First Book of Discipline, ed. J. K. Cameron (Edinburgh, 1972).

Foirm Na N-Urrnuidheadh: John Carswell's Gaelic translation of the Book of Common Order, ed. R. L. Thomson (SGTS, Edinburgh, 1970).

Fraser, W., *The Lennox* (2 vols, Edinburgh, 1874).

Hamilton Papers, ed. J. Bain (2 vols, Edinburgh, 1890).

The Heads of Religious Houses in Scotland from Twelfth to Sixteenth Centuries, eds D. E. R. Watt and N. F. Shead (SRS, N.S. 24, Edinburgh, 2001).

Highland Papers, ed. J. Macphail (4 vols, SHS, 2nd ser. 5, 12, 20; 3rd ser. 22, Edinburgh, 1914–34).

Historical Memoirs of the reign of Mary, Queen of Scots by Lord Herries, ed. R. Pitcairn (Abbotsford Club, 6, Edinburgh, 1836).

The Historie and Cronicles of Scotland . . . by Robert Lindesay of Pitscottie, ed. A. J. G. Mackay (3 vols, STS, Old Ser. 42–3, 60, Edinburgh, 1899–1911).

The Historie of Scotland . . . by Jhone Leslie, ed. E. G. Cody (2 vols, STS, 4 and 5, Edinburgh, 1888–95).

The History of the House of Seytoun to the year MDLIX by Sir Richard Maitland of Lethington Kt, ed. J. Fullarton (Maitland Club, 1, Glasgow, 1829).

Keith, R., *History of the Affairs of Church and State in Scotland, from the beginning of the Reformation to the year 1568*, eds J. P. Lawson and C. J. Lyon (3 vols, Spottiswoode Society, 1, Edinburgh, 1844–50).

King James's Secret: Negotiations between Elizabeth and James VI relating to the execution of Mary, Queen of Scots, from the Warrender Papers, eds R. S. Rait and A. I. Cameron (London, 1927).

Knox, J., *The Works of John Knox*, ed. D. Laing (6 vols, Bannatyne Club, Edinburgh, 1846–64).

Knox, J., *History of the Reformation in Scotland*, ed. W. C. Dickinson (2 vols, London, 1949).

Knox, J., *On Rebellion*, ed. R. Mason (Cambridge, 1994).

Letters of James VI and I, ed. G. P. V. Ackrigg (Berkeley, CA, 1984).

Lettres et Mémoires de Marie, Reine d'Escosse, ed. A. Labanoff (7 vols, Paris, 1859).

Liber Officialis Sancti Andree, ed. J. H. Forbes, Lord Medwyn (Abbotsford Club, 25, Edinburgh, 1845).

Longer Scottish Poems Volume One, 1375–1650, eds P. Bawcutt and F. Riddy (Edinburgh, 1987).

MacFarlane's geographical collections, eds A. Mitchell and J. Clark (3 vols, SHS, 1st ser. 51, 52 and 55, Edinburgh, 1906–8).

Maitland Folio, ed. W. A. Craigie (STS, N.S. 7 and 20, Edinburgh, 1919 and 1927).

Maitland Quarto, ed. W. A. Craigie (STS, N.S. 9, Edinburgh, 1920).

Melville, J., *The autobiography and diary of Mr James Melvill*, ed. R. Pitcairn (Wodrow Society, Edinburgh, 1842).

Memoirs of the affairs of Scotland by David Moysie, ed. J. Dennistoun (Bannatyne Club, 39, Edinburgh, 1830).

The Memoirs of Sir James Melville of Halhill, ed. T. Thomson (Bannatyne Club, 18, Edinburgh, 1827).

Memorials of transactions in Scotland 1569–72 by Richard Bannatyne, ed. R. Pitcairn (Bannatyne Club, 51, Edinburgh, 1836).

Miscellany of Wodrow Society I, ed. D. Laing (Wodrow Society, 11, Edinburgh, 1844).

Muniments of the Royal Burgh of Irvine (2 vols, Ayrshire and Wigtonshire Archaeological Association, 15, Edinburgh, 1890–91).

Munro's Western Isles of Scotland and Genealogies of the Clans, 1549, ed. R. W. Munro (London, 1961).

Musica Britannica, Vol XV: Music of Scotland, 1500–1700, ed. Kenneth Elliott (London, 1975).

The Oxford Companion to Scottish History, ed. M. Lynch (Oxford, 2001).

Oxford Dictionary of National Biography (Oxford, 2004).

Papal negotiations with Mary, Queen of Scots during her reign in Scotland 1561–7, ed.
    J. H. Pollen (SHS 1st ser. 37, Edinburgh, 1901).
Poems of Alexander Hume, ed. A. Lawson (STS, 48, Edinburgh, 1902).
Poems of Alexander Scott, ed. J. Cranstoun (STS, 36, Edinburgh, 1896).
*Register of the minister, elders and deacons of the christian congregation of St Andrews,
    1559–1600*, ed. D. Hay Fleming (2 vols, SHS, 1st ser. 4 and 7, Edinburgh, 1889–90).
Register of the Privy Council of Scotland, eds J. Burton et al. (1st ser., 14 vols,
    Edinburgh, 1877–98).
Registrum honoris de Morton, eds T. Thomson et al. (2 vols, Bannatyne Club, 94,
    Edinburgh, 1853).
Registrum Magni Sigilii Regum Scotorum, Register of the Great Seal of Scotland, eds
    J. Thomson et al. (11 vols, Edinburgh, 1882–1914).
Registrum Secreti Sigilli Regum Scotorum, Register of the Privy Seal of Scotland, eds
    M. Livingstone et al. (8 vols, Edinburgh, 1908–82).
'Report by de la Brosse and d'Oysel on conditions in Scotland, 1559–60', ed. G.
    Dickinson, in *Miscellany of the Scottish History Society*, IX (SHS, 3rd ser. 50,
    Edinburgh, 1958).
River Clyde and the Clyde Burghs, ed. J. D. Marwick (SBRS, 20, Edinburgh, 1909).
Satirical Poems of the time of the Reformation, ed. J. Cranston (2 vols, STS, Old ser. 20
    and 24, Edinburgh, 1891–3).
Scotland before 1700 from Contemporary Documents, ed. P. Hume Brown (Edinburgh,
    1893).
The Scots Peerage, ed. J. B. Paul (8 vols, Edinburgh, 1904–14).
The Scottish Correspondence of Mary of Lorraine, 1542/3–60, ed. A. I. Cameron (SHS,
    3rd ser. 10, 1927).
Second Book of Discipline, ed. J. Kirk (Edinburgh, 1980).
Selections from unpublished manuscripts . . . illustrating the reign of Queen Mary, ed.
    J. Stevenson (Maitland Club, 41, Edinburgh, 1837).
St Andrews Formulare, ed. G. Donaldson and G. Macrae (Stair Society, 7 and 9
    Edinburgh, 1942–4).
Statutes of the Scottish Church, ed. D. Patrick (SHS, 1st ser. 54, 1907).
Stevenson, D. and W. B., *Scottish Texts and Calendars: An analytical guide to serial
    publications* (Edinburgh, 1987).
Steer, K. and J. Bannerman, *Late Medieval Monumental Sculpture in the West Highlands*
    (RCAHMS, Edinburgh, 1977).
Three Scottish Reformers, ed. C. Rogers (Grampian Club, 9, London, 1986).
Two Missions of Jacques de la Brosse, ed. G. Dickinson (SHS, 3rd ser. 36, Edinburgh,
    1942).
The Warrender Papers, ed. A. I. Cameron (2 vols, SHS, 3rd ser. 18–19, Edinburgh,
    1931–2).

SECONDARY SOURCES

NB Collective volumes rather than the individual essays within them have been listed.
Separate entries in the *Oxford Dictionary of National Biography* have not been
included.

Allan, D., 'Manners and Mustard: Ideas of Political Decline in 16c Scotland', *Comparative Studies in Society and History* 37 (1995), 242–63.

Allan, D., *Philosophy and Politics in Later Stuart Scotland: Neo-Stoicism, culture and ideology in an age of crisis, 1540–1690* (East Linton, 2000).

Amos, N. S., A. Pettegree and H. van Nierop, eds, *The Education of a Christian Society* (Aldershot, 1999).

Anderson, P., *Robert Stewart earl of Orkney, 1533–93* (Edinburgh, 1982).

Anderson, R. D., M. Lynch and N. Phillipson, *The University of Edinburgh: An illustrated history* (Edinburgh, 2003).

Anson, P. F., *A monastery in Moray: the story of Pluscarden Priory, 1230–1948* (London, 1959).

Ash, M., *This noble harbour: A History of the Cromarty Firth* (Edinburgh, 1991).

Baldwin, J. R., ed., *The Province of Strathnaver* (Scottish Society for Northern Studies, 2000).

Bannerman, J. W., *The Beatons: a medical kindred in the classical Gaelic tradition* (Edinburgh, 1986).

Bardgett, F. D., *Scotland Reformed: The Reformation in Angus and the Mearns* (Edinburgh, 1989).

Barr, N., *Flodden, 1513: The Scottish Invasion of Henry VIII's England* (Stroud, 2001).

Barrell, A. D. M., *Medieval Scotland* (Cambridge, 2000).

Barrell, A. D. M., 'Royal presentations to ecclesiastical benefices in late medieval Scotland', *Innes Review* 55 (2004), 181–204.

Bath, M., *Renaissance Decorative Painting in Scotland* (Edinburgh, 2003).

Bawcutt, P., *Gavin Douglas: A Critical Study* (Edinburgh, 1976).

Bawcutt, P., *Dunbar the Makar* (Oxford, 1992).

Bawcutt, P., 'English books and Scottish readers in the fifteenth and sixteenth centuries.', *Review of Scottish Culture* 14 (2001), 1–12.

Bawcutt, P. 'James VI's Castalian Band: A modern myth.', *Scottish Historical Review* 80 (2001), 251–9.

Bjorn, C., A. Grant and K. J. Stringer, eds, *Social and Political Identities in Western History* (Copenhagen, 1994).

Boardman, S. and A. Ross, eds, *The Exercise of Power in Medieval Scotland, c. 1200–1500* (Dublin, 2003).

Bonner, E., *The French reactions, to the Rough Wooings of Mary, Queen of Scots* (Journal of the Sydney Society for Scottish History, 6, 1998).

Bonner, E., *The politique of Henri II: De facto French rule in Scotland, 1550–1554* (Journal of the Sydney Society for Scottish History, 7, 1999).

Bonner, E., 'The earl of Huntly and the King of France, 1548: Man for Rent', *English Historical Review* 120 (2005), 80–103.

Bossy, J., *Christianity in the West, 1400–1700* (Oxford, 1985).

Bowdith, L., *The Thistle and the Rose (Exhibition at Stirling Castle 2002)* (2002).

Bradshaw, B. and J. Morrill, eds, *The British Problem, c. 1534–1707: State Formation in the Atlantic Archipelago* (London, 1996).

Bradshaw, B. and P. Roberts, eds, *British Consciousness and Identity: The Making of Britain, 1533–1707* (Cambridge, 1998).

Broadie, A., *George Lokert: Late Scholastic Theologian* (Edinburgh, 1983).

Broadie, A., *The Circle of John Mair: Logic and Logicians in Pre-Reformation Scotland* (Oxford, 1985).

Broadie, A., *The shadow of Scotus: philosophy and faith in pre-Reformation Scotland* (Edinburgh, 1995).

Brooke, C. J., *Safe Sanctuaries: Security and Defence in the Anglo-Scottish Border Churches, 1290–1690* (Edinburgh, 2000).

Brotherstone, T. and D. Ditchburn, *Freedom and Authority: Historical and Historiographical Essays presented to Grant G Simpson* (East Linton, 2000).

Broun, D., R. J. Finlay and M. Lynch, *Image and Identity: The Making and Re-making of Scotland through the ages* (Edinburgh, 1998).

Brown, I., T. O. Clancy, S. Manning and M. Pittock, eds, *The Edinburgh History of Scottish Literature Volume 1* (Edinburgh, 2006).

Brown, J., ed., *Scottish Society in the Fifteenth Century* (London, 1977), 209–40.

Brown, K. M., *Bloodfeud in Scotland, 1573–1625* (Edinburgh, 1986).

Brown, K. M., *Noble Society in Scotland: Wealth, Family and Culture from Reformation to Revolution* (Edinburgh, 2000).

Brown, K. M. and R. J. Tanner, *The Scottish Parliament Volume 1: Parliament and Politics, 1235–1560* (Edinburgh, 2004).

Brown, K. M. and A. Mann, *The Scottish Parliament Volume 2: Parliament and Politics, 1567–1707* (Edinburgh, 2005).

Brown, Y. Galloway and R. Ferguson, *Twisted sisters: Women, crime and deviance in Scotland since 1400* (East Linton, 2002).

Buchanan, P. H., *Margaret Tudor Queen of Scots* (Edinburgh, 1985).

Burnett, C. J. and C. J. Tabraham, *The Honours of Scotland* (Edinburgh, 2001 ed.).

Burns, J. H., *The True Law of Kingship: Concepts of monarchy in early modern Scotland* (Oxford, 1996).

Cairns, J., 'Academic feud, bloodfeud and WilliamWelwood: Legal education in St Andrews, 1560–1611', *Edinburgh Law Review* 2 (1998), 158–79; 255–87.

Cameron, J., *James V* (East Linton, 1998).

Campbell of Airds, A., *The History of Clan Campbell* Vols 1 and 2 (Edinburgh, 2000 and 2002).

Cant, R. G., *The University of St Andrews* (St Andrews University Library, 1992 ed.).

Cathcart, A., *Kinship and Clientage: Highland Clanship, 1451–1609* (Leiden, 2006).

Cherry, T. A. F., 'The library of Henry Sinclair, Bishop of Ross 1560–65', *The Bibliotheck* 4 (1963), 13–24.

Cowan, E. J., 'The Angus Campbells and the origin of the Campbell-Ogilvie feud', *Scottish Studies* 25 (1981), 25–38.

Cowan, E. J. and D. Gifford, eds, *The Polar Twins: studies in the relationship between Scottish history and Scottish literature* (Edinburgh, 1999).

Cowan, E. J. and R. A. McDonald, eds, *Alba: Celtic Scotland in the Medieval Era* (East Linton, 2000).

Cowan, E. J., ed., *The Ballad in Scottish History* (East Linton, 2000).

Cowan, E. J. and R. J. Finlay, eds, *Scottish History: The Power of the Past* (Edinburgh, 2002).

Cowan, I. B. and D. Shaw, eds, *The Renaissance and Reformation in Scotland* (Edinburgh, 1982).

Cowan, I. B., *The Scottish Reformation: Church and society in sixteenth-century Scotland* (London, 1982).

Crawford, B., ed., *Church Chronicle and Learning in Medieval and Renaissance Scotland* (Edinburgh, 1999).

Cunningham, I. C., *The Nation Survey'd: Timothy Pont's Maps of Scotland* (East Linton, 2001).

Dawson, J. E. A., 'William Cecil and the British Dimension of early Elizabethan foreign policy', *History* 74 (1989), 196–216.

Dawson, J. E. A., 'Argyll: The Enduring Heartland', *Scottish Historical Review* 74 (1995), 75–98.

Dawson, J. E. A., *The Politics of Religion in the age of Mary, Queen of Scots: The Earl of Argyll and the struggle for Britain and Ireland* (Cambridge, 2002).

Dennison, E. P., D. Ditchburn and M. Lynch, *Aberdeen before 1800: A New History* (East Linton, 2002).

Dilworth, M., *Scottish Monasteries in the late middle ages* (Edinburgh, 1995).

Dilworth, M., 'Dunfermline, the Duries and the Reformation', *Records of the Scottish Church History Society* 31 (2002), 37–67.

Dingwall, H., *History of Scottish Medicine* (Edinburgh, 2003).

Dingwall, H., *'A famous and flourishing society': The History of the Royal College of Surgeons of Edinburgh, 1505–2005* (Edinburgh, 2005).

Ditchburn, D., *Scotland and Europe: the medieval kingdom and its contacts with Christendom, 1214–1560* (East Linton, 2000).

Dodghson, R. A., *From Chiefs to Landlords: Social and economic change in the Western Highlands and Islands c.1493–1830* (Edinburgh, 1998).

Donaldson, G., *Shetland Life under Earl Patrick* (Edinburgh, 1958).

Donaldson, G., *The Scottish Reformation* (Cambridge, 1960).

Donaldson, G., *The First Trial of Mary, Queen of Scots* (London, 1969).

Donaldson, G., *Scotland: James V – James VII* (Edinburgh, 1978 ed.).

Donaldson, G., *All the Queen's Men: Power and politics in Mary Stewart's Scotland* (London, 1983).

Donaldson, G., *Reformed by Bishops* (Edinburgh, 1987).

Dunbar, J., *Scottish Royal Palaces: The Architecture of the Royal Residences during the late medieval and early Renaissance periods* (East Linton, 1999).

Dunbar, L., *Reforming the Scottish Church: John Winram (c. 1492–1582)* (Aldershot, 2002).

Durkan, J. and J. Kirk, *The University of Glasgow, 1451–1577* (Glasgow, 1977).

Durkan, J., 'Heresy in Scotland, the second phase 1546–58', *Records of the Scottish Church History Society* 24 (1992), 320–65.

Dyer, J., R. A. Mason and A. Murdoch, *New Perspectives on the politics and culture of early modern Scotland* (Edinburgh, 1982).

Edington, C., *Court and Culture in Renaissance Scotland. Sir David Lindsay of the Mount* (East Linton, 1994).

Ellis, S. and S. Barber, eds, *Conquest and Union: Fashioning a British State, 1485–1725* (London, 1995).

Ellis, S. G., *Tudor Frontiers and Noble Power: The Making of the British State* (Oxford, 1995).

Evans-Jones, R., ed., *The Civil Law Tradition in Scotland* (Stair Society, Supp. 2, Edinburgh, 1995).

Ewan, E. and M. Meikle, eds, *Women in Scotland c. 1100–c1750* (East Linton, 1999).

Farrow, K. D., *John Knox: Reformation Rhetoric and the Traditions of Scots Prose, 1490–1570* (Bern, 2004).

Fawcett, R., *The Architectural History of Scotland: Scottish Architecture from the Accession of the Stewarts to the Reformation, 1371–1560* (Edinburgh, 1994).

Fergusson, W., *The Identity of the Scottish Nation: An Historic Quest* (Edinburgh, 1998).

Finlay, J., *Men of Law in Pre-Reformation Scotland* (East Linton, 2000).

Finnie, E., 'The House of Hamilton: patronage, politics and the church in the Reformation period', *Innes Review* 36 (1985), 3–28.

Foggie, J., *Renaissance Religion in Urban Scotland: The Dominican Order, 1450–1560*, Studies in Medieval and Reformation Thought, XCV (Leiden, 2003).

Forte, A. D. M., 'Kenning be Kenning and Course be Course': Maritime Jurimetrics in Scotland and Northern Europe, 1400–1600' *Edinburgh Law Review* 2 1998, 56–89.

Foster, S., A. Macinnes and R. MacInnes, eds, *Scottish Power Centres from the early middle ages to the twentieth century* (Glasgow, 1998).

Fox, A. and D. Woolf, *The spoken word: Oral culture in Britain 1500–1850* (Manchester, 2002).

Fradenburg, L. O., *City, Marriage, Tournament* (Madison, WI, 1991).

Fraser, A., *Mary, Queen of Scots* (London, 1970 ed.).

Furgol, E., 'The Scottish Itinerary of Mary, Queen of Scots, 1542–8, 1561–8', *Proceedings of the Society of Antiquaries of Scotland* 117 (1987), 219–31.

Gemill, E. and N. Mayhew, *Changing Values in Medieval Scotland: A study of prices, money, and weights and measures* (Cambridge, 1995).

Gibson, A. J. S. and T. C. Smout, *Prices, food and wages in Scotland, 1550–1780* (Cambridge, 1995).

Gifford, D. and D. McMillan, *A History of Scottish Women's Writing* (Edinburgh, 1997).

Glenn, V., *Romanesque and Gothic: Decorative Metalwork and Ivory Carvings in the Museum of Scotland* (NMS Edinburgh, 2003).

Godfrey, M. 'The assumption of jurisdiction: Parliament, the King's Council and the College of Justice in sixteenth-century Scotland', *Journal of Legal History* 22 (2001), 21–36.

Goodare, J. and M. Lynch, eds, *The Reign of James VI* (East Linton, 2000).

Goodare, J., *State and society in early modern Scotland* (Oxford, 2000).

Goodare, J., 'The admission of lairds to the Scottish parliament', *English Historical Review* 116 (2001), 1103–33.

Goodare, J. et al., *The survey of Scottish witchcraft* (http://www.arts.ed.ac.uk/witches/).

Goodare, J., *The Scottish witch-hunt in context* (Manchester, 2002).

Goodare, J., *The Government of Scotland, 1560–1625* (Oxford, 2004).

Graham, M., *The Uses of Reform: Godly Discipline and Popular Behaviour in Scotland and Beyond, 1560–1610* (Leiden, 1996).

Grant, A. and K. J. Stringer, eds, *Uniting the Kingdom? The making of British history* (London, 1995).

Grant, I. F., *The Social and Economic Developments of Scotland before 1603* (London, 1930).

Grant, I. F., *The MacLeods: The history of a clan 1200–1956* (London, 1959).

Grant, I. F. and H. Cheape, *Periods in Highland History* (London, 1997 ed.).

Guy, J., *My heart is my own: The Life of Mary, Queen of Scots* (London, 2004).

Haldane, A. R. B., *The Drove Roads of Scotland* (Colonsay, 1995 ed.).

Hannay, R. K., *The College of Justice*, ed. H. L. MacQueen (Stair Society, Supp. 1, Edinburgh, 1990).

Hazlett, W. I. P., *The Reformation in Britain and Ireland* (London, 2003).

Heal, F., *Reformation in Britain and Ireland* (Oxford, 2003).

Henderson, L. and E. J. Cowan, *Scottish Fairy Belief* (East Linton, 2001).

Hewitt, G. R., *Scotland under Morton, 1572–80* (Edinburgh, 1982).

Hill, J. Michael, *Fire and Sword: Sorley Boy MacDonnell and the Rise of Clan Ian Mor 1538–90* (London, 1993).

Horn, D. B., *A History of the University of Edinburgh, 1556–1889* (Edinburgh, 1987).

Houston, R. A., *Scottish literacy and Scottish identity* (Cambridge, 1985).

Houston, R. A., *Literacy in early modern Europe* (Harlow, 1989).

Houston, R. A. and I. D. Whyte, eds, *Scottish Society 1500–1800* (Cambridge, 1989).

Houston, R. A., *The Population History of Britain and Ireland, 1500–1750* (Basingstoke, 1995).

Houston, R. A. and W. W. J. Knox, eds, *The New Penguin History of Scotland: From the earliest times to the present day* (London, 2001).

Howard, D., *The Architectural History of Scotland: Scottish Architecture from the Reformation to the Restoration, 1560–1660* (Edinburgh, 1995).

Inverness Field Club, *The Hub of the Highlands: The Book of Inverness and District* (Edinburgh, 1975).

Jack, R. D. S., ed., *History of Scottish Literature* Vol. 1 (Aberdeen, 1988).

Jones, C., ed., *The Edinburgh History of the Scots Language* (Edinburgh, 1997).

Kay, C. J. and M. A. Mackay, eds, *Perspectives on the older Scottish tongue* (Edinburgh, 2005).

Kellar, C., *Scotland, England and the Reformation, 1534–1561* (Oxford, 2003).

Kirk, J., *Patterns of Reform* (Edinburgh, 1989).

Kirk, J., ed., *Humanism and Reform: The Church in Europe, England and Scotland, 1400–1642* (Studies in Church History, Subsidia 8, Oxford, 1991).

Kirk, J., ed., *The Church in the Highlands* (Edinburgh, 1998).

Lavery, B., *Maritime Scotland* (London, 2001).

Lee, M., *James Stewart, Earl of Moray* (Westport, CT, 1953).

Lee, M., *John Maitland of Thirlstane and the foundation of the Stewart Despotism in Scotland* (Princeton, NJ, 1959).

Lee, M., *The 'Inevitable Union' and other essays on early modern Scotland* (East Linton, 2003).

Longley, E., E. Hughes and D. O'Rawe, eds, *Ireland (Ulster) Scotland: Concepts, Contexts and Comparisons* (Belfast, 2003).

Lyall, R. J., *Alexander Montgomerie: Poetry, politics and cultural change in Jacobean Scotland* (Tempe, AZ, 2005).

Lynch, M., *Edinburgh and the Reformation* (Edinburgh, 1981).

Lynch, M., *The early modern town in Scotland* (London, 1987).

Lynch, M., M. Spearman and G. Stell, *The Scottish medieval town* (Edinburgh, 1988).

Lynch, M., 'Queen Mary's Triumph: the Baptismal Celebrations at Stirling in December 1566', *Scottish Historical Review* LXIX (1990), 1–21.

Lynch, M., *Scotland: A New History* (London, 1991).

Lynch, M., ed., *Mary Stewart: Queen in Three Kingdoms* (Oxford, 1998).

Lythe, S. G. E., *The Economy of Scotland in its European setting, 1550–1625* (Edinburgh, 1960).

McClure, J. D., *Scotland and the Lowland Tongue* (Aberdeen, 1983).

McClure, J. D. and M. R. G. Spiller, eds, *Bryght Lanternis. Essays on the Language and Literature of Medieval and Renaissance Scotland* (Aberdeen, 1989).

McCoog SJ, T. M., *The Society of Jesus in Ireland, Scotland and England, 1541–1588* (Leiden, 1995).

Macdonald, A. A., M. Lynch and I. B. Cowan, eds, *The Renaissance in Scotland: Studies in Literature, Religion, History and Culture* (Leiden, 1994).

Macdonald, A. A., H. T. Wilcox and R. Todd, eds, *Sacred and Profane: Secular and devotional interplay in early modern British Literature* (Amsterdam, 1996).

Macdonald, A. R., *The Jacobean Kirk, 1567–1625: Sovereignty, Polity and Liturgy* (Aldershot, 1998).

Macdonald, F. A., *Missions to the Gaels: Reformation and Counter Reformation in Ulster and the Highlands and Islands of Scotland, 1560–1760* (Edinburgh, 2006).

Macdougall, N., *James III: A Political Study* (Edinburgh, 1982).

Macdougall, N., ed., *Church, Politics and Society: Scotland 1408–1929* (Edinburgh, 1983).

Macdougall, N., *James IV* (Edinburgh, 1989).

Macdougall, N., ed., *Scotland and War AD 79–1918* (Edinburgh, 1991).

Macdougall, N., *An antidote to the English: the auld alliance, 1295–1560* (East Linton, 2001).

Macfarlane, I., *Buchanan* (London, 1981).

Macfarlane, L. J., *William Elphinstone and the Kingdom of Scotland 1431–1514* (Aberdeen, 1985).

Macinnes, A. I., T. Riis and F. G. Pedersen, *Ships, guns and bibles in the North Sea and the Baltic states, c. 1350–c1700* (East Linton, 2000).

MacInnes, J., 'The Panegyric Code in Gaelic Poetry and its historical background', *Transactions of the Gaelic Society of Inverness* 50 (1976–8), 435–98.

MacIvor, I., *Edinburgh Castle* (London, 1993).

Mackay, S., *Early Scottish Gardens: A Writer's Odyssey* (Edinburgh, 2001).

McKean, C., *The Scottish Chateau: The Country House of Renaissance Scotland* (Stroud, 2004 ed.).

McKechnie, H., ed., *Introductory Survey of the Sources and Literature of Scots Law* (Stair Society, 1, Edinburgh, 1936).

MacLean-Bristol, N., *Warriors and Priests: The History of Clan MacLean, 1300–1570* (East Linton, 1995).

Maclean, L., ed., *The Middle Ages in the Highlands* (Inverness, 1981).

MacLeod, F., ed., *Togail Tir: Marking Time, The Map of the Western Isles* (Stornoway, 1989).

McLeod, W., *Divided Gaels: Gaelic Cultural Identities in Scotland and Ireland, c. 1200–c. 1650* (Oxford, 2004).

Macmillan, D., *Scottish Art, 1460–2000* (Edinburgh, 1990).

Macphail, I. M. M., *Dumbarton Castle* (Edinburgh, 1979).

MacQueen, H. L., ed., *Miscellany Four* (Stair Society, 49, Edinburgh, 2004).

MacQueen, H.L., ed., *Miscellany Five* (Stair Society, 52, Edinburgh, 2006).

MacQueen, J., ed., *Humanism in Renaissance Scotland* (Edinburgh, 1990).

McRoberts, D., 'The Scottish church and nationalism in the fifteenth century', *Innes Review* 19 (1968), 3–14.

MacRoberts, D., *Essays on the Scottish Reformation 1513–1625* (Glasgow, 1962).

MacRoberts, D., ed., *The Medieval Church of St Andrews* (Glasgow, 1976).

McWhannell, D., 'Ship service and indigenous sea power in the west of Scotland', *West Highland Notes and Queries*, ser. 3, I (2000), 3–18.

Mann, A. J., *The Scottish Book Trade, 1500–1720: Print Commerce and Print Control in early modern Scotland* (East Linton, 2000).

Mapstone, S. and J. Wood, eds, *The Rose and the Thistle. Essays on the culture of late medieval and Renaissance Scotland* (East Linton, 1998).

Mapstone, S., ed., *William Dunbar, 'The Nobill Poet': Essays in honour of Priscilla Bawcutt* (East Linton, 2001).

Marshall, R. K., *Mary of Guise* (London, 1977).

Marshall, R. K., *Costume in Scottish Portraits, 1560–1830* (SNPG, Edinburgh, 1986).

Marshall, R. K., *Scottish Queens, 1034–1714* (East Linton, 2003).

Marshall, R. K., *Queen Mary's Women: Female relatives, servants, friends and enemies of Mary, Queen of Scots* (Edinburgh, 2006).

Mason, R., ed., *Scotland and England 1286–1815* (Edinburgh, 1987).

Mason, R. A. and N. Macdougall, eds, *People and Power in Scotland: Essays in honour of T. C. Smout* (Edinburgh, 1992).

Mason, R., ed., *Scots and Britons: Scottish Political Thought and the Union of 1603* (Cambridge, 1994).

Mason, R. A., ed., *John Knox and the British Reformations* (Aldershot, 1998).

Mason, R. A., *Kingship and the Commonweal: Political Thought in Renaissance and Reformation Scotland* (East Linton, 1998).

Mayhew, N., 'The Brewsters of Aberdeen', *Northern Studies* 32 (1997), 71–81.

Meikle, M., *A British Frontier?: Lairds and Gentlemen in the Eastern Borders, 1540–1603* (East Linton, 2004).

Merriman, M., *The Rough Wooings: Mary Queen of Scots, 1542–1551* (East Linton, 2000).

Meston, M. C., W. D. H. Sellar and Lord Cooper, *The Scottish Legal Tradition* (Edinburgh, 1991).

Mitchison, R. and P. Roebuck, eds, *Scotland and Ireland* (Edinburgh, 1988).

Mitchison, R., *The Old Poor Law in Scotland: The Experience of Poverty, 1574–1845* (Edinburgh, 2000).

Mullan, D. G., *Episcopacy in Scotland: The History of an idea, 1560–1638* (Edinburgh, 1986).

Mullan, D. G., *Scottish Puritanism, 1590–1630* (Oxford, 2000).

Munro, R. and J. Munro, *Tain through the centuries* (Tain, 1966).

Murray, A., 'The Procedure of the Scottish Exchequer in the early sixteenth century', *Scottish Historical Review* 11 (1961), 89–117.

Murray, A., 'The Comptroller, 1425–1488', *Scottish Historical Review* 52 (1973), 1–29.

Murray, A., 'Huntly's rebellion and the administration of justice in north-east Scotland, 1570–73', *Northern Scotland* (1981), 1–6.

Newton, M., *A Handbook of the Scottish Gaelic World* (Dublin, 2000).

Nicholson, R., 'Feudal developments in late medieval Scotland', *Juridical Review* 1 (1973), 1–19.

Nicholson, R., *Scotland: The Later Middle Ages* (Edinburgh, 1974).

Normand, Lord, ed., *An Introduction to Scottish Legal History* (Stair Society, 20, Edinburgh, 1958).

Ollivant, S. D., *The Court of the Official in Pre-Reformation Scotland* (Stair Society, 34, Edinburgh, 1982).

Omand, D., *The Perthshire Book* (Edinburgh, 1999).

Omand, D., *The Fife Book* (Edinburgh, 2000).

Omand, D., *The Argyll Book* (Edinburgh, 2004).

Oram, R., *Galloway: Land and Lordship* (Scottish Society for Northern Studies, 1991).

Oram, R. and G. Stell, *Lordship and Architecture in Medieval and Renaissance Scotland* (East Linton, 2005).

Osborough, W. M. ed., *Explorations in Law and History: Irish Legal History Society Discourses, 1988–1994* (Dublin, 1995),

Paton, G. C. H., ed., *An Introduction to Scottish legal history* (Stair Society, 20, Edinburgh, 1958).

Pettegree, A. Duke and G. Lewis, eds, *Calvinism in Europe, 1540–1620* (Cambridge, 1994).

Phillips, G., *The Anglo-Scots War, 1513–50* (Woodbridge, Suffolk, 1999).

Potter, D., 'French Intrigue in Ireland during the reign of Henri II, 1547–1559', *International History Review* 5 (1983), 159–80.

Potter, H., *Edinburgh under siege 1571–1573* (Stroud, 2003).

Preece, I. Woods, *Our awin Scottis use: Music in the Scottish Church up to 1603* (Glasgow, 2000).

Rae, T. I., *The Administration of the Scottish Frontier, 1513–1603* (Edinburgh, 1966).

Riis, T., *Should Auld Acquaintance Be Forgot: Scottish-Danish Relations, c. 1450–1707* (2 vols, Odense, 1988).

Ritchie, P. E., *Mary of Guise in Scotland, 1548–1560: A Political Career* (East Linton, 2002).

Rixson, D., *The West Highland Galley* (East Linton, 1998).

Ross, D. J., *Musick Fyne: Robert Carver and the Art of Music in Sixteenth-Century Scotland* (Edinburgh, 1993).

Ryrie, A., *The Origins of the Scottish Reformation* (Manchester, 2006).

Sanderson, M. H. B., *Scottish Rural Society in the sixteenth century* (Edinburgh, 1982).

Sanderson, M. H. B., *Mary Stewart's People: Life in Mary Stewart's Scotland* (Edinburgh, 1987).

Sanderson, M. H. B., *Ayrshire and the Reformation: People and Change, 1490–1600* (East Linton, 1997).

Sanderson, M. H. B., *Cardinal of Scotland: David Beaton c.1494–1546* (Edinburgh, 2001 ed.).

Sanderson, M. H. B., *A kindly place?: living in sixteenth-century Scotland* (East Linton, 2002).

Sanger, K. and A. Kinnaird, *Tree of strings, crann nan teud: a history of the harp in Scotland* (Temple, Midlothian, 1992).

Sellar, W. H. D., 'Marriage, Divorce and Concubinage in Gaelic Scotland', *Transactions of the Gaelic Society of Inverness* 51 (1978–80), 464–93.

Sellar, W. H. D., ed., *Miscellany II* (Stair Society, 35, Edinburgh, 1984).

Sellar, W. H. D., ed., *Moray: Province and People* (Scottish Society for Northern Studies, 1993).

Sellar, W. H. D. and A. Maclean, *The Highland Clan MacNeacail (MacNicol): A History of the Nicolsons of Scorrybreac* (Waternish, 1999).

Shaw, D. W. D., ed., *In Divers Manners: A St Mary's Miscellany* (St Andrews, 1990).

Simpson, G. G., *Scotland and Scandinavia, 800–1800* (Edinburgh, 1990).

Simpson, G. G., *Scottish Handwriting, 1150–1650* (East Linton, 1998 ed.).

Smith, A., *The Nine Trades of Dundee* (Abertay Historical Society, 1995).

Smith, A., *The Guildry of Dundee* (Abertay Historical Society, 2005).

Smith, B., 'In the tracks of Bishop Andrew Pictoris of Orkney and Henry Phankouth, Archdeacon of Shetland', *Innes Review* 40 (1989), 91–105.

Smith, D., 'The Spiritual Jurisdiction, 1560–64', *Records of the Scottish Church History Society* 25 (1993), 1–18.

Smout, T. C., *A History of the Scottish People, 1560–1830* (London, 1972 ed.).

Smout, T. C., ed., *Scotland and Europe, 1200–1850* (Edinburgh, 1986).

Smout, T. C., ed., *People and Woods in Scotland: A History* (Edinburgh, 2003).

Stevenson, D., *King's College, Aberdeen, 1560–1641: From Protestant Reformation to Covenanting Revolution* (Aberdeen, 1990).

Stevenson, K., 'The Unicorn, St Andrew and the Thistle: Was there an Order of Chivalry in Late Medieval Scotland?', *Scottish Historical Review* 83 (2004), 3–22.

Stone, J. C., *The Pont Manuscript Maps of Scotland: Sixteenth century origins of the Blaeu atlas* (Tring, 1989).

Swain, M., *The Needlework of Mary, Queen of Scots* (New York, 1986 ed.).

Tanner, R., *The Late Medieval Scottish Parliament: Politics and the three estates, 1424–1488* (East Linton, 2001).

Thomas, A., *Princelie Majestie: The court of James V of Scotland, 1528–1542* (Edinburgh, 2005).

Thomson, D., *Painting in Scotland* (Edinburgh, 1975).

Thomson, D., *An Introduction to Gaelic Poetry* (Edinburgh, 1990 ed.).

Tittler, R. and N. Jones, eds, *A Companion to Tudor Britain* (Oxford, 2004).

Todd, M., *The Culture of Protestantism in early modern Scotland* (New Haven, CT, 2002).

Torrie, E. P. D., *Medieval Dundee* (Abertay Historical Society, 1990).

Tranter, N., *The Fortified House in Scotland* (5 vol., Edinburgh, 1962–70).

Van Heijnsbergen, T. and N. Royan, eds, *Literature, letters and the canonical in early modern Scotland* (East Linton, 2002).

Verschuur, M. B., 'The Outbreak of the Scottish Reformation at Perth, 11 May 1559', *Scotia* (1987), 41–53.

Verschuur, M. B., *A Noble and Potent Lady: Katherine Campbell, Countess of Crawford* (Abertay Historical Society, 2006).

Walker, D. M., *A Legal History of Scotland: The Sixteenth Century* (Edinburgh, 1995).

Watt, D. E. R., *Medieval Church Councils in Scotland* (Edinburgh, 2000).

Waugh, D. J., ed., *Shetland's Northern Links: Language and History* (Scottish Society for Northern Studies, 1996).

Webster, B., *The Sources of History: Scotland from the Eleventh Century to 1603* (London, 1975).

Whyte, I. D., *Scotland before the Industrial Revolution: An Economic and Social History, c. 1050–c1750* (Harlow, 1995).

Whyte, I. D., *Scottish Society and Economy in Transition c.1500–c1760* (Basingstoke, 1997).

Williams, J. H., ed., *Stewart style, 1513–1542: essays on the Court of James V* (East Linton, 1996).

Williamson, A. H., *Scottish national consciousness in the age of James VI* (Edinburgh, 1979).

Withers, C., *Gaelic Scotland: The Transformation of a culture region* (London, 1988).

Withers, C., *Geography, Society and National Identity in Scotland since 1520* (Cambridge, 2001).

Wood, D., ed., *Life and Thought in the Northern Church, c. 1100 – c. 1700: Essays in Honour of Claire Cross* (Studies in Church History, Subsidia 12, 1999).

Wormald, J., 'Bloodfeud, kindred and government in early modern Scotland', *Past and Present* 87 (1980), 54–97.

Wormald, J., *Lords and Men in Scotland: Bonds of Manrent, 1442–1603* (Edinburgh, 1985).

Wormald, J., *Mary Queen of Scots: A study in failure* (London, 1988).

Wormald, J., *Scotland Revisited* (London, 1991).

Wormald, J., ed., *Scotland: A History* (Oxford, 2005).

Wright, D. F., ed., *The Bible in Scottish Life and Literature* (Edinburgh, 1988).

Yellowlees, M., *'So strange a monster as a Jesuiste': The Society of Jesus in Sixteenth-Century Scotland* (Colonsay, 2003).

Unpublished theses

Boardman, S., 'Politics and the feud in late medieval Scotland' (University of St Andrews Ph.D. thesis, 1990).

Dotterweich, M., 'The emergence of evangelical theology in Scotland to 1550' (University of Edinburgh Ph.D. thesis, 2002).

Emond, W. K., 'The minority of King James V 1513–28' (University of St Andrews Ph.D. thesis, 1988).

Loughlin, M., 'The career of Maitland of Lethington c. 1526–1573' (University of Edinburgh Ph.D. thesis, 1991).

Macauley, S., 'Matthew Stewart, Fourth Earl of Lennox and the Politics of Britain, c. 1543–1571' (University of Cambridge Ph.D. thesis, 2005).

MacGregor, M., 'A political history of the MacGregors before 1571' (University of Edinburgh Ph.D. thesis, 1989).

Index